THE Amazing 1000

Puzzle Challenge

Text and puzzle content © British Mensa 2003

Design and artwork © Carlton Books Limited 2003

First edition published in 2003
by Carlton Books Limited
20 Mortimer Street
London W1T 3JW

Reprinted 2005

A CIP catalogue record for this book is available from
the British Library

ISBN 1 84442 907 5 (hardback)
ISBN 1 84442 979 2 (paperback)

Material in this book has previously appeared in:
Mensa Crossword Puzzles (Phil Carter & Ken Russell)
Mensa Puzzle Challenge (Robert Allen)
Mensa Puzzle Challenge 2 (Robert Allen, John Bremner)
Mensa Puzzle Challenge 3 (Robert Allen, John Bremner)
Mensa Brainwaves (Dave Chatten & Carolyn Skitt)
Mensa Biggest Puzzle Book Ever! (Harold Gale,
   John Bremner, Dave Chatten & Carolyn Skitt)
Mensa Mega Mazes (Robert Allen)
Mensa Riddles and Conundrums (Robert Allen)

Printed in Dubai

THE Amazing 1000 Puzzle Challenge

CARLTON
BOOKS

HOW TO SOLVE PUZZLES

If you're new to all this there are a few things you need to know before you get started. First, stay alert at all times! Puzzle setters are a tricky breed and prey on the unwary. Second, in puzzles numbers can be letters and letters can be numbers. Write down the alphabet and number it A = 1, B = 2, C = 3, etc. Then number it backwards (Z = 1 ... A = 26). Keep this list beside you at all times and it will save you a lot of trouble.

The simplest formula becomes difficult to solve if you don't know what to look for. For example, place three numbers under 10 at the points of a triangle, then add them together and put the sum in the middle. Simple. Any child could do it. But if you don't explain what you've done it is surprisingly hard for others to follow your reasoning.

As a general rule there is very little in this book that children under 10 could not work out if they had the secret formula. Think simple. Good puzzles are not complicated, merely tricky. Good luck! You'll probably need it.

There is a theory that being good at puzzles proves you are a being of superior intelligence. This is pure piffle. Some of the biggest lummoxes you could come across are puzzle fanatics. On the other hand, puzzles are loads of fun if you have a certain amount of patience, ingenuity and sheer low-down cunning. If you don't take them too seriously they can help while away many a pleasant hour or make tedious journeys pass quickly.

The aim in putting this book together was quite simply to give you, the puzzler, some good old-fashioned fun. This book *won't* improve your IQ, it *won't* qualify you for entry to anything and

INTRODUCTION

it *won't* tell the world anything it doesn't already know about your intelligence. So relax and let your mind slowly come to grips with the work of some of the world's most creative and successful puzzle compilers, who have been published in just about every corner of the globe.

You are cordially invited to join that happy band of brothers and sisters who have nothing better to do with their time than wrestle with puzzles. OK, you may never save the world but, on the other hand, you will do it very little damage and, in these strange days, there is much to be said for that.

1 DODGY DICE

Which of the following cubes cannot be made from this layout?

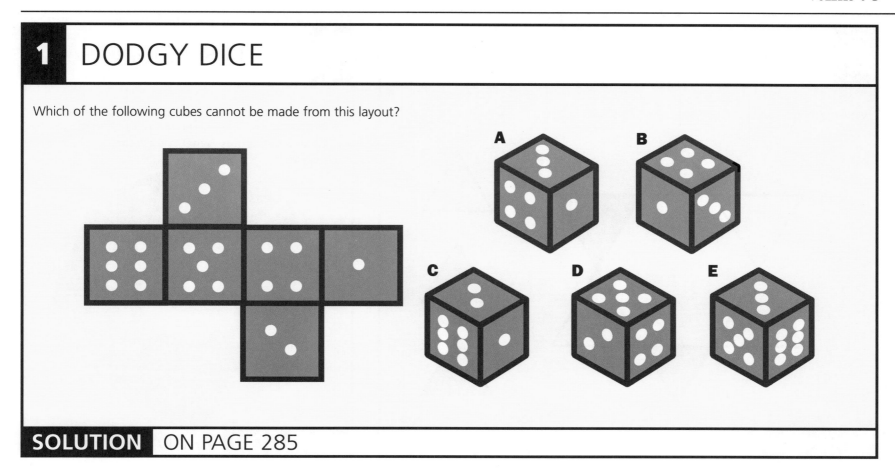

SOLUTION | ON PAGE 285

2 HERO HUE

These colours should remind you of a fictional hero

SOLUTION | ON PAGE 285

3 CIRCLE COUNT

Can you replace the question mark with a number to meet the conditions of the wheel?

SOLUTION | ON PAGE 285

4 STAR SEQUENCE

Which triangle should replace the question mark?

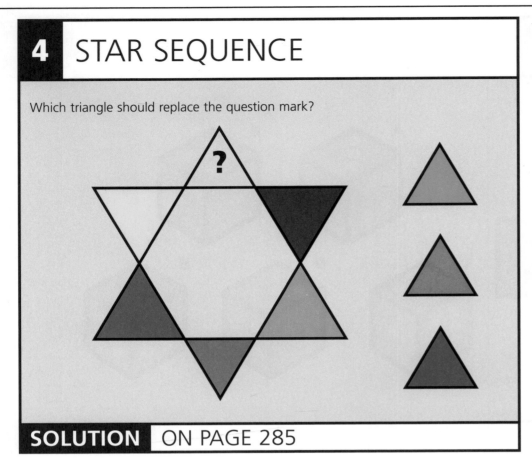

SOLUTION   ON PAGE 285

5 LETTER LOGIC

Place one letter in the middle of this diagram. Four five-letter words can now be rearranged from each straight line of letters. What is the letter and what is the word?

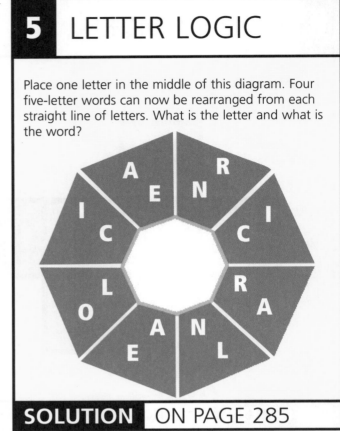

SOLUTION   ON PAGE 285

6 TILES IN TURMOIL

Arrange the tiles in this diagram so that they form a square. When this is done correctly four words can be read down and across. What are the words?

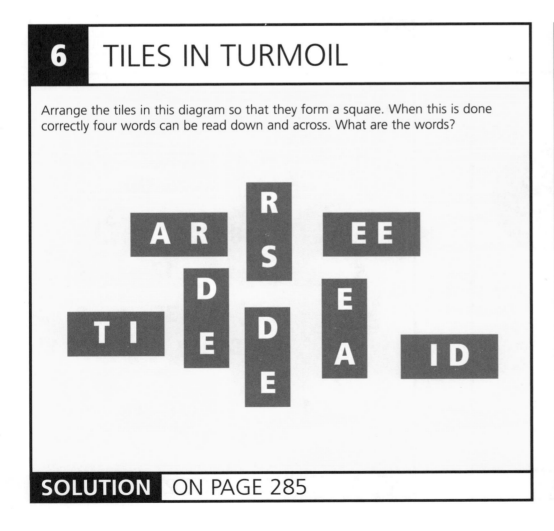

SOLUTION   ON PAGE 285

7 WEDGE WORDS

Make a circle out of these shapes. When the correct circle has been found a word can be read clockwise. What is the word?

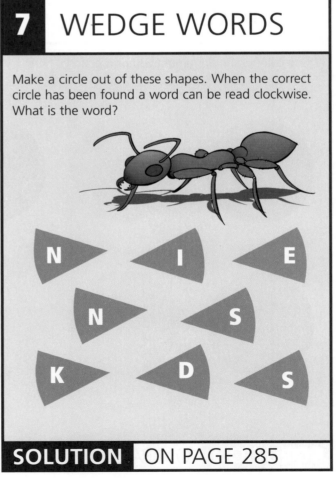

SOLUTION   ON PAGE 285

8 ODD ONE OUT

Which of these groups of triangles is the odd one out?

A

B

C

D

E

SOLUTION ON PAGE 285

10 SEEDY SOLUTION

Complete the word ladder by changing one letter of each word per step. The newly created word must be found in the dictionary. What are the words to turn SEEDS to GRASS?

S E E D S

G R A S S

SOLUTION ON PAGE 285

9 SHELL SHOCKER

Six of the words in the diagram are associated for some reason. Find the words and then work out whether SHELL belongs to the group?

B E A S T	A D D E R
D E C O R	P I L A F
H E R O N	P Y G M Y
B A T O N	T A X I S
H U M A N	R O U N D

SOLUTION ON PAGE 285

11 WORD LADDER

Change the second letter of each word to the left and the right. Two other words must be formed. Place the letter used in the empty section. When this has been completed for all the words another word can be read down. What is the word?

STAR		ANTS
PLAY		BLOW
SACK		WANE
ACID		SHUT
TEAR		ARKS
RIPE		VALE
GOAT		IONS

SOLUTION ON PAGE 285

12 BERMUDA TRIANGLES

Can you find the number to replace the question mark?

9
34
3   5

4
24
7   1

2
36
10   6

2
32
7   ?

SOLUTION ON PAGE 285

13 MOUNTAIN CLIMBERS

A family of four were going on a mountaineering holiday. The second morning they were all found dead in their cabin. The coroner declared that they had all died from drowning. The faucets in the cabin had not been left on and the boiler and water storage units were undamaged. There was no sign of any foul play. What caused them to drown?

1. They were a mile from the nearest lake.
2. It had not rained for five days. This wasn't a flash flood.
3. It was not caused by problems with a dam.

SOLUTION ON PAGE 285

14 DEVIOUS DIAGRAM

This diagram was constructed according to a certain logic. Can you work out which number should replace the question mark?

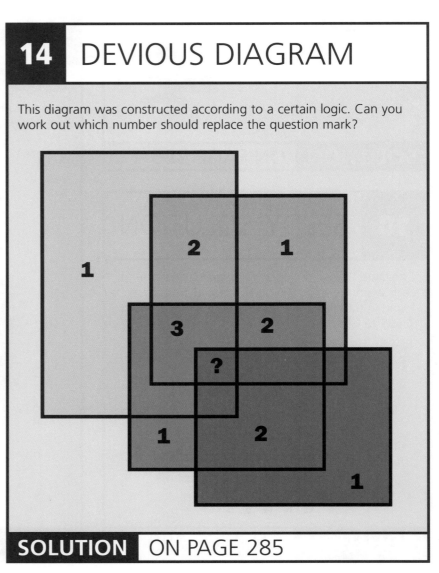

SOLUTION ON PAGE 285

15 WORD SNAKE

The names of three countries are to be found in the diagram. The letters of the names are in the order they normally appear. What are the countries?

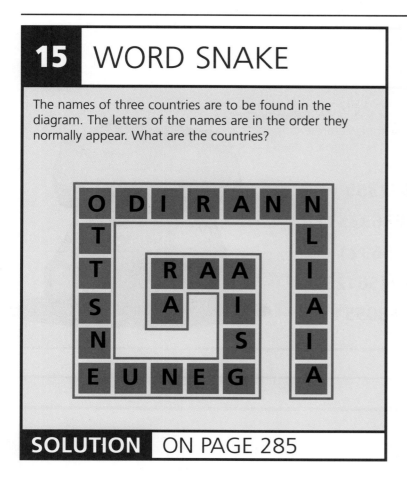

SOLUTION ON PAGE 285

16 LETTER SQUARE

Can you find out the relationship of the letters and numbers in this square and find out which number should replace the question mark?

SOLUTION ON PAGE 285

17 CLOCK CASE

Can you work out the time on the blank clock face?

SOLUTION ON PAGE 285

18 FINAL FIVE

Which word of five letters can be attached to the back of the words shown in the diagram to create six other words?

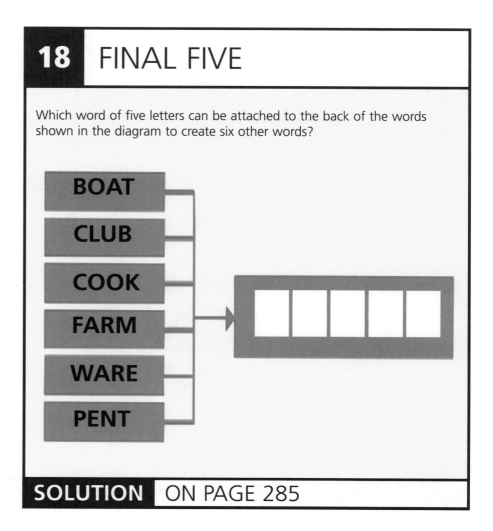

SOLUTION ON PAGE 285

19 PHONE FRENZY

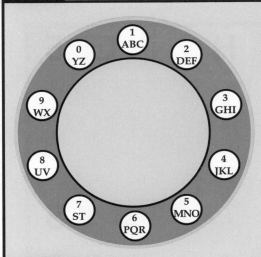

The diagram represents an old-fashioned telephone dial with letters as well as numbers. Below is a list of numbers representing 10 American States. Can you use the diagram to decode them?

A. 1143256531

B. 72917

C. 52161741

D. 141741

E. 32135

F. 562355

G. 83633531

H. 456321

I. 15456125

J. 1630551

SOLUTION | ON PAGE 285

20 STAR SOLUTION

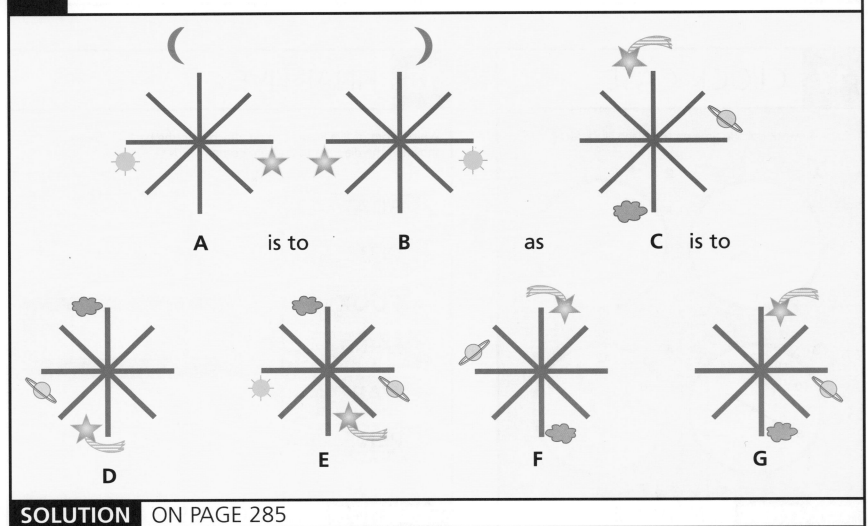

A   is to   **B**   as   **C**   is to

D   **E**   **F**   **G**

SOLUTION | ON PAGE 285

21 STARTING POINT

Find the starting point and move from square to adjoining square, horizontally or vertically, but not diagonally, to spell a 12–letter word, using each letter only once. What are the missing letters?

E		I
R	B	A
A		T
	O	I

SOLUTION ON PAGE 285

22 FUNNY FACES

Can you find the odd face out?

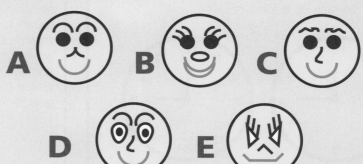

SOLUTION ON PAGE 285

23 MISSING NUMBER

What number should replace the question mark?

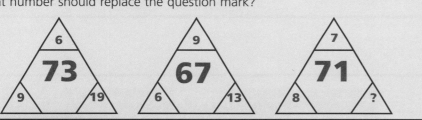

Triangle 1: top 6, centre 73, bottom-left 9, bottom-right 19
Triangle 2: top 9, centre 67, bottom-left 6, bottom-right 13
Triangle 3: top 7, centre 71, bottom-left 8, bottom-right ?

SOLUTION ON PAGE 285

24 ODD RELATIONS

Which two numbers below have the same relationship as the first pair?

482: 34

A. 218: 24
B. 946: 42
C. 687: 62
D. 299: 26
E. 749: 67

SOLUTION ON PAGE 285

25 QUOTE UNQUOTE

A quotation has been written in this diagram. Find the start letter and move from square to touching square until you have found it. It is permissible to move diagonally. What is the quotation and to whom is it attributed?

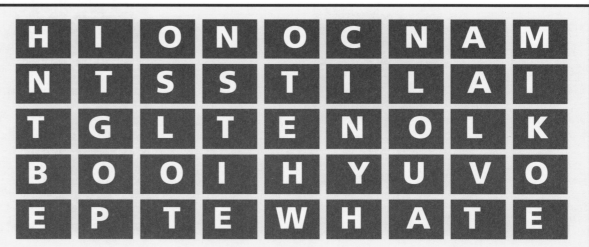

H	I	O	N	O	C	N	A	M
N	T	S	S	T	I	L	A	I
T	G	L	T	E	N	O	L	K
B	O	O	I	H	Y	U	V	O
E	P	T	E	W	H	A	T	E

SOLUTION ON PAGE 285

26 CLOCK CLUE

The alarm clocks move in a certain pattern. Can you work out the time on the last clock?

SOLUTION ON PAGE 285

27 LETTER LUNACY

The letters and numbers in this square follow a pattern. Can you work out which number is represented by the question mark?

SOLUTION ON PAGE 285

28 SYMBOL INSANITY

The symbols in the above grid follow a pattern. Can you work it out and find the missing section so that the logic of the grid is restored?

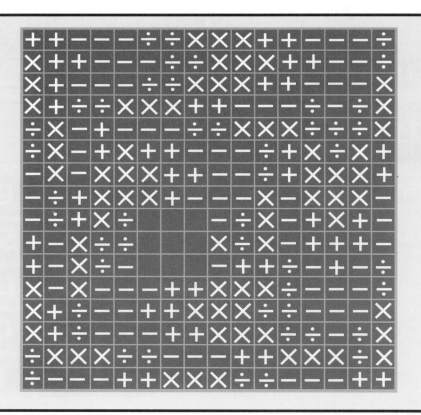

SOLUTION ON PAGE 285

29 STAR COLOURS

Which two colours are the odd ones out?

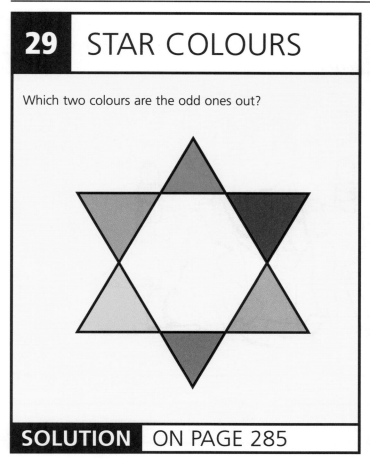

SOLUTION ON PAGE 285

30 SQUARE SEQUENCE

Unravel the logic behind these squares to find the missing letter.

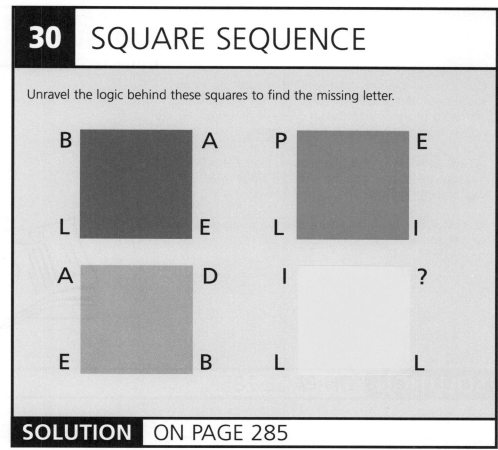

SOLUTION ON PAGE 285

31 BROWN UP OR DOWN?

Does brown go above or below the line?

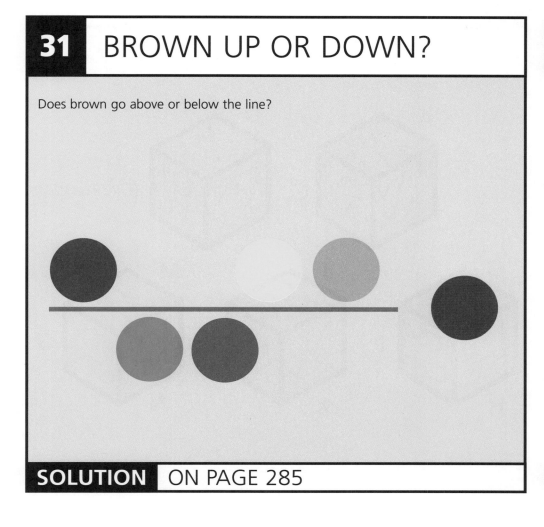

SOLUTION ON PAGE 285

32 PINK POSITION

Does pink belong with the other colours?

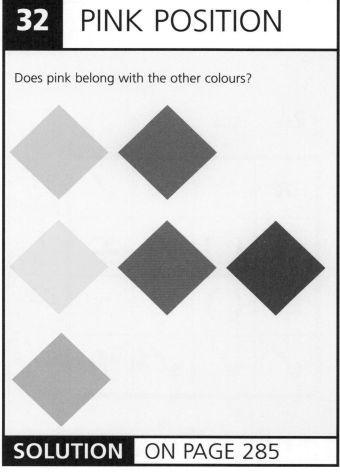

SOLUTION ON PAGE 285

33 BOB THE MISER'S LAST WILL

Old Bob was a miserly man who never spent his money. His last will and testament stated that he wished to be cremated together with the proceeds of his estate. He did not wish to give his money to his relatives.

When the will was read, the relatives stated that Bob was not sane when he made the will. The judge ruled that he was and Bob's wishes should be followed.

The judge did, however, find a way to comply with Bob's wishes and at the same time please the relatives. How was this done?

SOLUTION ON PAGE 285

34 SQUARE ADDER

Each symbol in this square represents a value. Can you work out how much the question mark is worth?

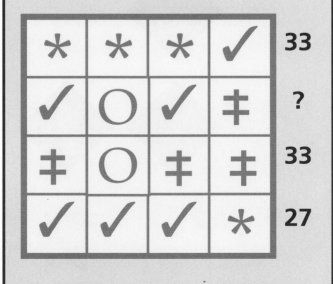

SOLUTION ON PAGE 285

35 LIKE LETTERS

Two sides of these cubes contain the same letters. Can you spot them?

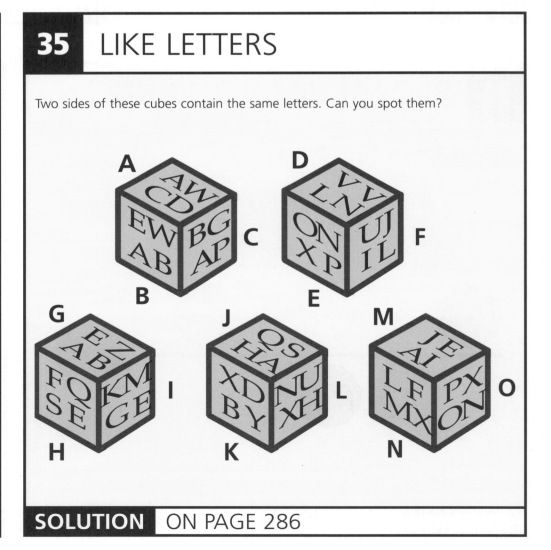

SOLUTION ON PAGE 286

36 LETTER MYSTERY

Can you find the letter which replaces the question mark?

Wheel 1 (positions 1–8): A, C, F, J, L, O, S, U

Wheel 2 (positions 1–8): X, B, D, G, K, M, P, T

Wheel 3 (positions 1–8): V, Y, C, E, H, L, N, ?

37 WHEEL WORDS

Select one letter from each of the segments. When the correct letters have been found a word of eight letters can be read clockwise. What is the word?

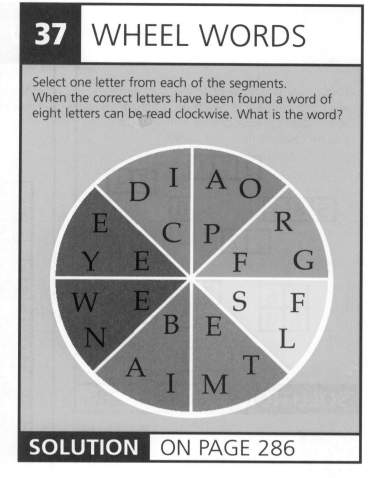

38 A-HAUNTING WE WILL GO

An ancient castle had been converted into a hotel. After a few months, many ghostly sightings had been reported. The manager was under pressure as many bookings were being lost, but he was getting some business from ghost hunters. The problem was that he could not guarantee to match the appearances with the right guests, until one day he noticed a pattern in the sightings and their timings. If he could predict where and when the ghost would appear, he would keep all of his guests happy.

He found that from January to March, room number 3 was haunted every other night. From April to June, room number 4 was haunted every third night. Then from July to September, room number 9 was visited by a ghost every fourth night. He then needed to plan which room would be visited in the last quarter of the year and the frequency. How did he work this out and what was his answer?

SOLUTION ON PAGE 286

SOLUTION ON PAGE 286

SOLUTION ON PAGE 286

39 TILE TROUBLE

These tiles, when placed in the right order, will form a square in which each horizontal line is identical with one vertical line. Can you successfully form the square?

SOLUTION ON PAGE 286

41 SQUARES

Find the missing number.

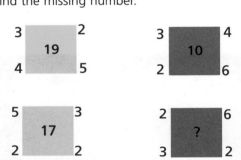

SOLUTION ON PAGE 286

42 STARSTRUCK

Which letter replaces the question mark in the star?

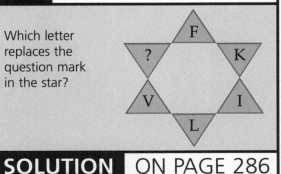

SOLUTION ON PAGE 286

40 WORDSEARCH

In this grid are hidden the names of 18 famous authors. Can you detect them? You can go forward or in reverse, in horizontal, vertical and diagonal lines.

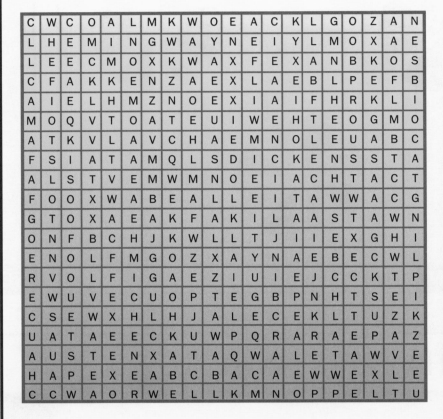

Austen
Chaucer
Chekhov
Dickens
Flaubert
Goethe
Hemingway
Huxley
Ibsen
Kafka
Kipling
Lawrence
Michener
Orwell
Proust
Tolstoi
Twain
Zola

SOLUTION ON PAGE 286

43 CLOCK CONUNDRUM

Can you work out what the time on the blank clock face should be?

SOLUTION ON PAGE 286

44 PATTERN PUZZLE

There is a logic to the patterns in these squares but one does not fit. Can you find the odd one out?

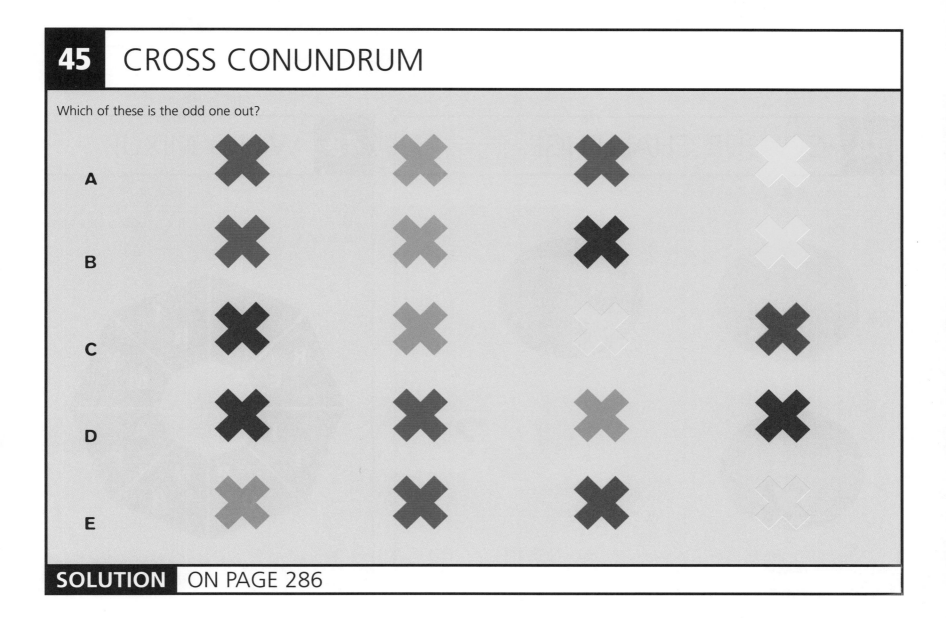

A   **B**   **C**   **D**

SOLUTION ON PAGE 286

45 CROSS CONUNDRUM

Which of these is the odd one out?

A

B

C

D

E

SOLUTION ON PAGE 286

46 FLOWER POWER

Find a flower hiding in this bunch.

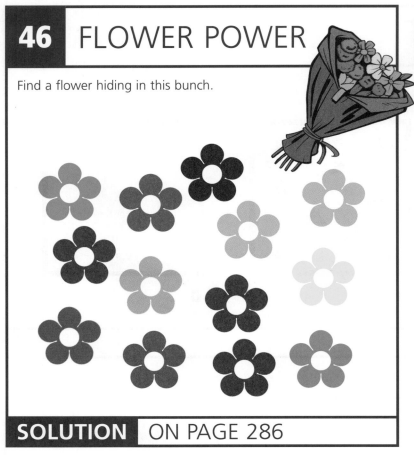

SOLUTION ON PAGE 286

47 OCCASIONAL LETTERS

Select one of the two letters from the grid, in accordance with the reference shown, and place it in the wordframe. When the correct letters have been chosen an occasion can be read. What is the occasion?

	A	B	C	D	E
1	T	I E	T	S	
2	G O	A	N	D	
3	A	V	H	N	H
4	S	M	G	I	K
5	G	I N	N	L	Y

A1 B2 A3 D2 D1 E1 A2 D3 C4 D4 C5 E4   E2 B2 D3

A4 C3 B3 C1 E4 E3 B5 B1 B3 D5 E3 A5   A4 C2 E5

SOLUTION ON PAGE 286

48 COLOUR CHALLENGE

Which colour of the spectrum could continue this series?

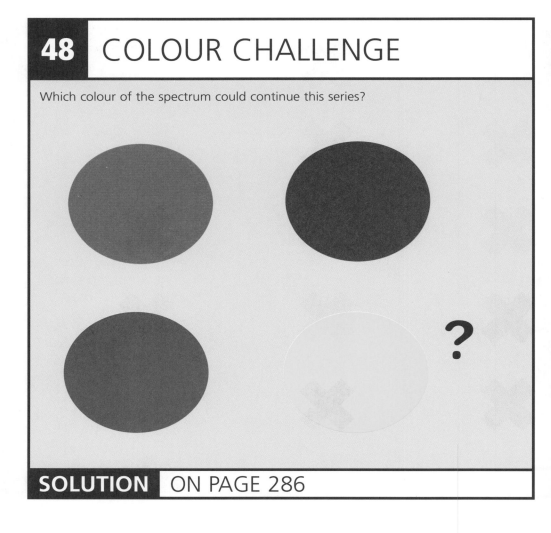

?

SOLUTION ON PAGE 286

49 WORD MIXUP

Place one letter in the middle of this diagram. Four five-letter words can now be rearranged from each straight line of letters. What is the letter and what are the words?

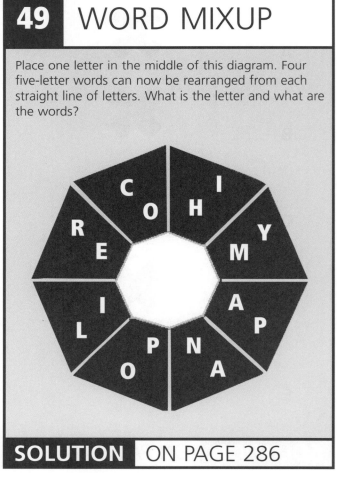

SOLUTION ON PAGE 286

50 | CUBE CHALLENGE

Which of these cubes cannot be made from this layout?

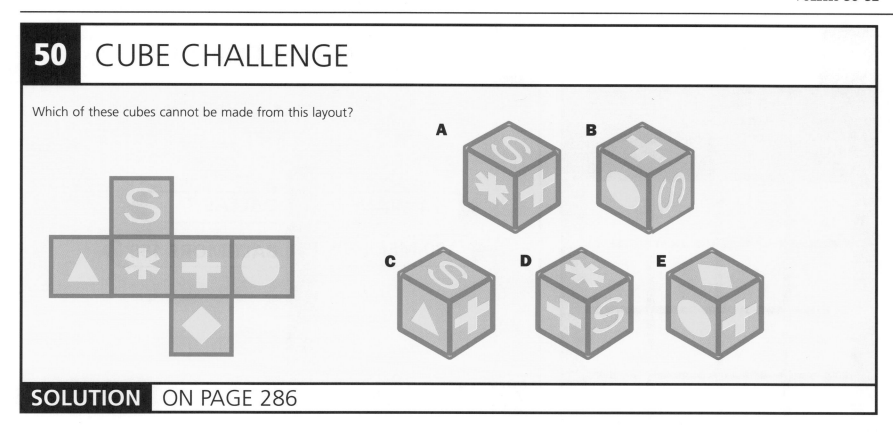

SOLUTION | ON PAGE 286

51 | NUMBER WHEELS

Can you find the missing number that fits into the sector of the last wheel?

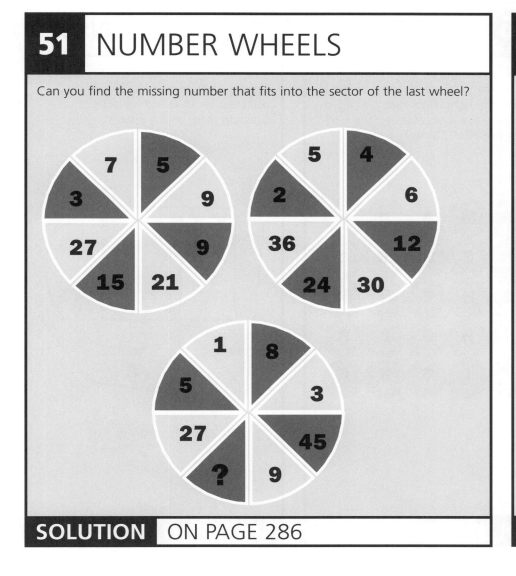

SOLUTION | ON PAGE 286

52 | PAINTER PROBLEM

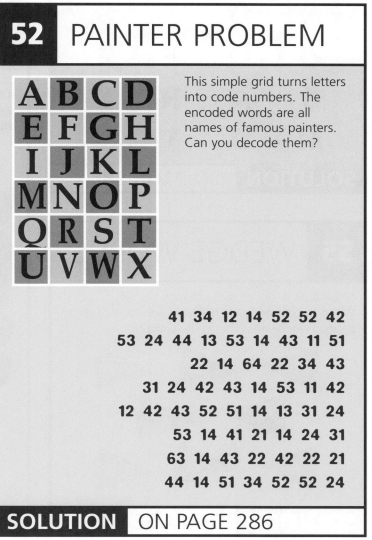

This simple grid turns letters into code numbers. The encoded words are all names of famous painters. Can you decode them?

A	B	C	D
E	F	G	H
I	J	K	L
M	N	O	P
Q	R	S	T
U	V	W	X

41 34 12 14 52 52 42

53 24 44 13 53 14 43 11 51

22 14 64 22 34 43

31 24 42 43 14 53 11 42

12 42 43 52 51 14 13 31 24

53 14 41 21 14 24 31

63 14 43 22 42 22 21

44 14 51 34 52 52 24

SOLUTION | ON PAGE 286

53 DEAD LETTERS

Take the letters and arrange them correctly in the column under which they appear. Once this has been done an historical character will appear. Who is the person?

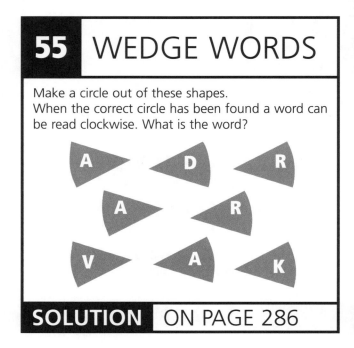

N	O	F	S
Q	O	E	E
C	A	R	Y
M	U	T	S

SOLUTION ON PAGE 286

54 DIRECTION DILEMMA

This is a meaningless signpost but there is a twisted form of logic behind the figures. Discover the logic and find the distance to Dallas. How far is it?

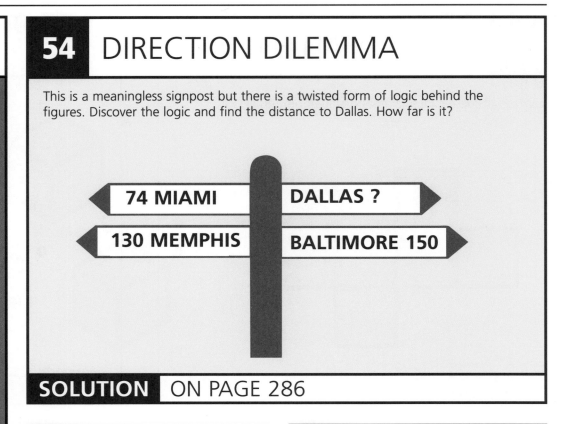

74 MIAMI   DALLAS ?

130 MEMPHIS   BALTIMORE 150

SOLUTION ON PAGE 286

55 WEDGE WORDS

Make a circle out of these shapes.
When the correct circle has been found a word can be read clockwise. What is the word?

A   D   R

A   R

V   A   K

SOLUTION ON PAGE 286

56 FISHING

Start at the bottom letter F and move from circle to touching circle to the N at the top right. How many different ways are there of collecting the nine letters of FISHERMAN?

R	M	A	N	N
H	E	R	M	A
S	H	E	R	M
I	H	S	E	R
F	I	S	H	E

SOLUTION PAGE 286

57 SEGMENTS

A certain logic has been used in making this diagram. Can you work out what the secret is and replace the question mark with a letter?

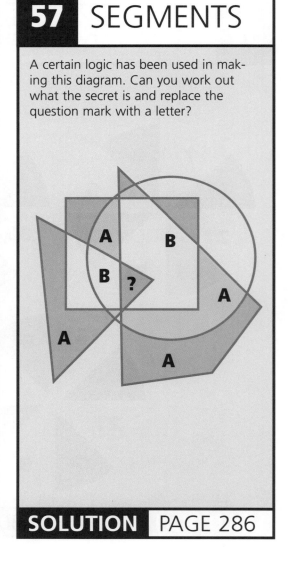

SOLUTION PAGE 286

58 CUBE FIGURES

Two sides on these cubes contain the same numbers. Can you spot them?

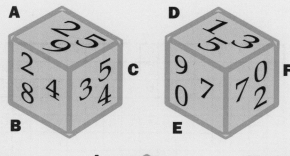
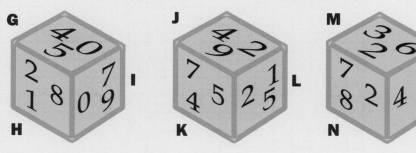

SOLUTION ON PAGE 286

59 MISSING WORD

Place a word of THREE letters in the empty space. This word, when added to the end of the three words to the left and to the beginning of the three words to the right, will form six other words. What is the word?

RED   **OUNCE**

BID   **TIN**

HID   **TIL**

SOLUTION ON PAGE 286

60 IT ALL ADDS UP

Can you find the missing symbol in the last triangle?

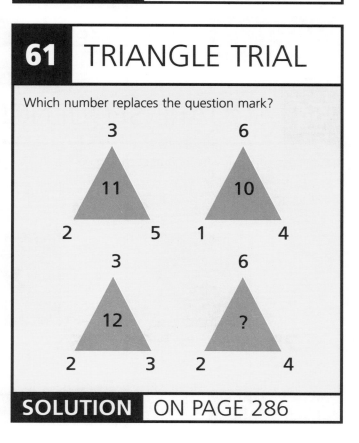

SOLUTION ON PAGE 286

61 TRIANGLE TRIAL

Which number replaces the question mark?

3
11
2   5

6
10
1   4

3
12
2   3

6
?
2   4

SOLUTION ON PAGE 286

62 SYMBOL SORT

Which of the faces A, B or C would carry on the sequence below?

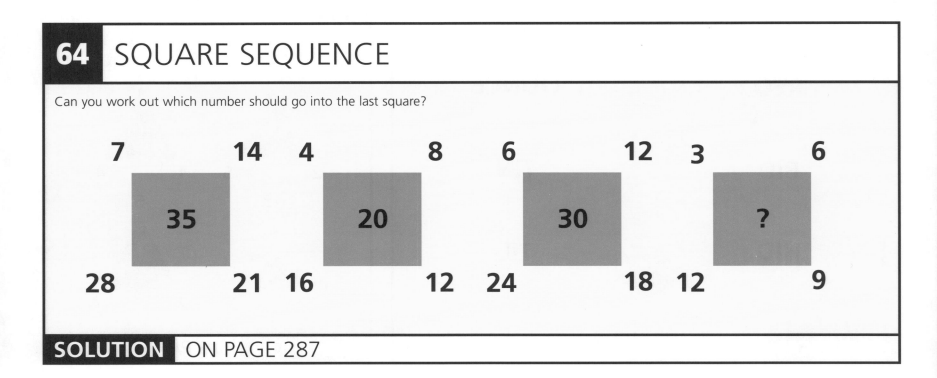

A   **B**   **C**

SOLUTION ON PAGE 286

63 WORDSEARCH

Hidden in this grid are the names of 16 well-known thespians. Can you spot them? You can move in horizontal, vertical and diagonal lines in a forward or backward direction.

Jane Asher

Mel Gibson

Julie Christie

Meryl Streep

Paul Newman

Jane Fonda

Gene Wilder

Richard Gere

Julia Roberts

Jodie Foster

Michael Caine

Brooke Shields

Dustin Hoffman

Tom Cruise

Emma Thompson

Robert Redford

P	B	A	W	N	W	O	C	H	K	T	V	E	N	T	A	C	Y	X	O
A	A	D	E	F	W	O	Y	J	U	L	I	A	R	O	B	E	R	T	S
C	D	U	S	T	I	N	H	O	F	F	M	A	N	B	R	M	O	N	L
K	A	O	L	W	O	L	N	N	Y	G	O	R	E	S	O	T	U	V	D
K	M	G	E	N	E	W	I	L	D	E	R	W	O	L	O	Z	B	R	R
C	A	S	K	L	E	M	U	O	T	L	B	W	J	L	K	K	E	G	O
P	C	M	W	V	U	W	E	A	I	J	L	G	A	H	E	T	E	B	F
E	L	K	E	F	O	Z	M	A	A	T	H	E	N	A	S	E	R	O	D
E	S	O	A	L	L	A	M	A	A	O	I	E	E	O	H	I	L	L	E
R	T	A	S	E	G	F	A	A	N	T	O	E	F	L	I	S	T	R	R
T	O	M	C	R	U	I	S	E	S	R	S	E	O	T	E	E	E	P	T
S	A	O	E	E	B	W	B	I	M	Q	I	A	N	E	L	G	N	O	R
L	A	A	O	H	E	H	R	S	T	D	A	B	D	C	D	O	A	T	E
Y	A	F	G	S	V	H	T	E	O	I	B	K	A	R	S	C	E	J	L
R	B	P	O	A	C	F	A	J	Z	N	A	Y	A	A	Y	I	X	Q	O
E	N	O	Z	E	A	L	M	A	O	C	Y	H	F	O	G	H	E	L	R
M	A	E	I	N	A	Z	E	N	I	A	C	L	E	A	H	C	I	M	B
C	P	L	M	A	N	N	V	W	X	I	E	R	S	F	L	A	Z	O	N
N	U	W	M	J	F	G	Q	S	R	A	E	L	L	A	E	S	S	O	E
J	O	N	Y	F	G	I	N	O	S	P	M	O	H	T	A	M	M	E	F

SOLUTION ON PAGE 287

64 SQUARE SEQUENCE

Can you work out which number should go into the last square?

7   14   4   8   6   12   3   6

35   20   30   ?

28   21   16   12   24   18   12   9

SOLUTION ON PAGE 287

65 HEARTY CHEER

Each symbol in the grid has a numerical value. Work out what those values are and replace the question mark with a number.

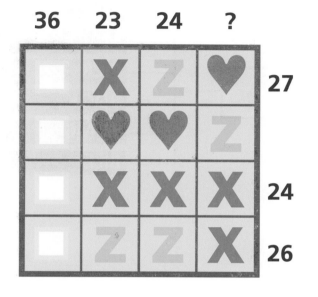

36	23	24	?	
	X	Z	♥	27
	♥	♥	Z	
	X	X	X	24
	Z	Z	X	26

66 SAME SYMBOLS

Can you find the two sides on these cubes which contain the same symbols?

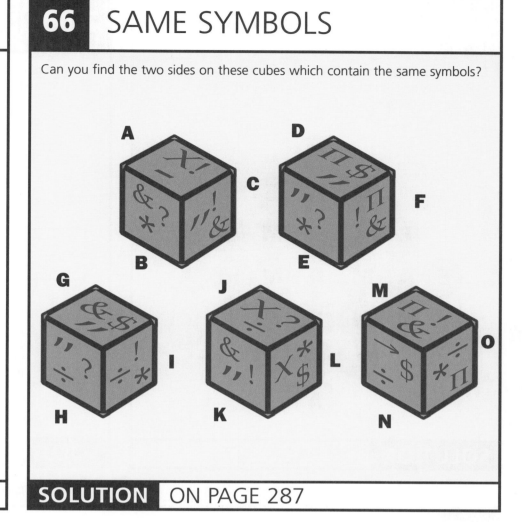

SOLUTION ON PAGE 287

67 PLANT PROBLEM

Five of the words in the diagram are associated for some reason. Find the words and then work out whether PLANT belongs to the group.

BURNT	EVENT
COUNT	CADET
MERIT	FAULT
FLINT	CARAT
ABBOT	GIANT

SOLUTION ON PAGE 287

68 CHANGING WORDS

Change the second letter of each word to the left and the right. Two other words must be formed. Place the letter used in the empty section. When this has been completed for all the words another word can be read down. What is the word?

AVID		EXIT
CORD		BORE
ACES		APED
BALL		MIND
OPUS		SLAP
SWAY		SHUN
TOIL		MUTE

SOLUTION ON PAGE 287

69 STRANGE GAME

Move from circle to touching circle collecting the letters of GAME. Always start at the G. How many different ways are there to do this?

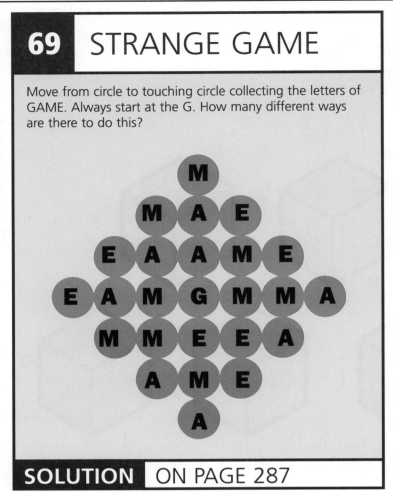

SOLUTION ON PAGE 287

70 PREFIX PUZZLE

Which word of four letters can be attached to the front of the words shown in the diagram to create six other words?

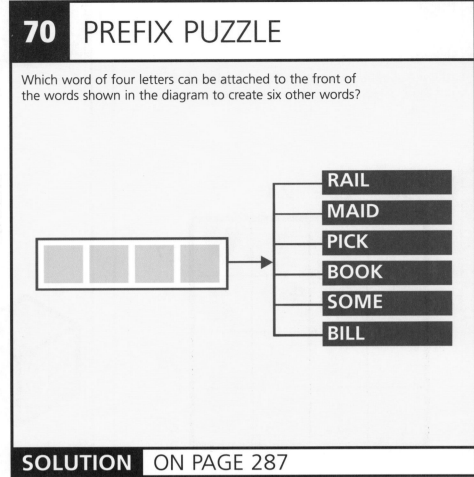

RAIL
MAID
PICK
BOOK
SOME
BILL

SOLUTION ON PAGE 287

71 ANALOGY GAME

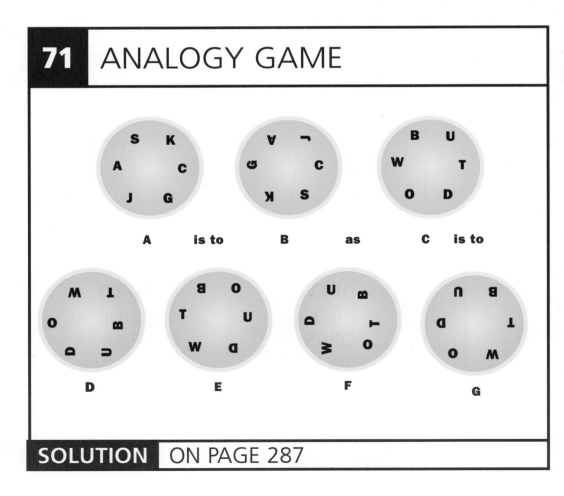

SOLUTION ON PAGE 287

72 WHEELIE

The letters and numbers in this wheel are related in some way, Can you find which letter should replace the question mark?

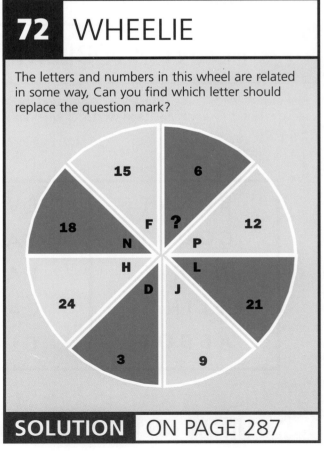

SOLUTION ON PAGE 287

73 SAME SYMBOLS

There are two sides on these cubes that contain exactly the same symbols. Can you spot them?

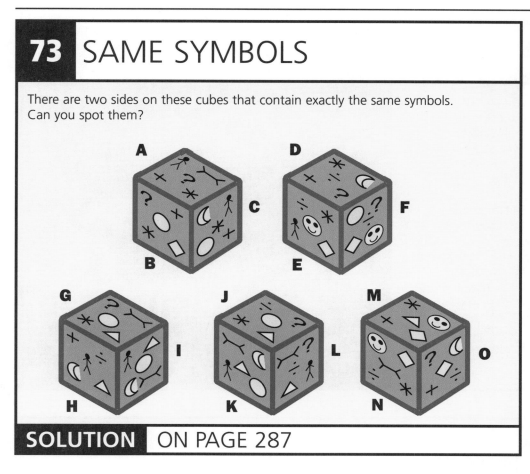

SOLUTION ON PAGE 287

74 STAR SOLUTION

Can you find the letter to complete the sequence starting at A?

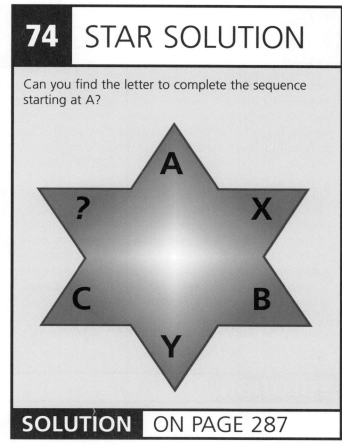

SOLUTION ON PAGE 287

75 FACE FACTS

Can you work out which number the question mark in the triangle stands for?

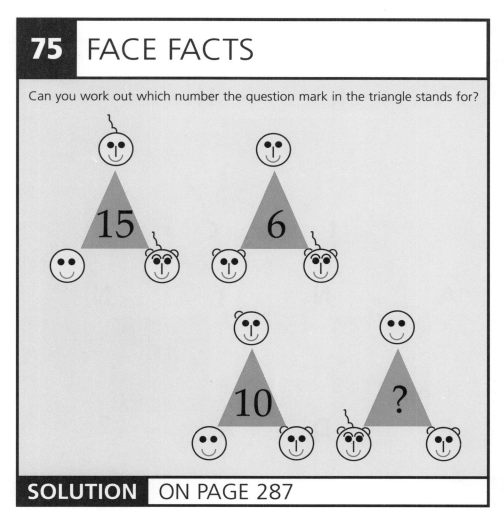

SOLUTION ON PAGE 287

76 TABLE TOTALS

Each symbol in this square represents a number. Can you work out which number should replace the question mark?

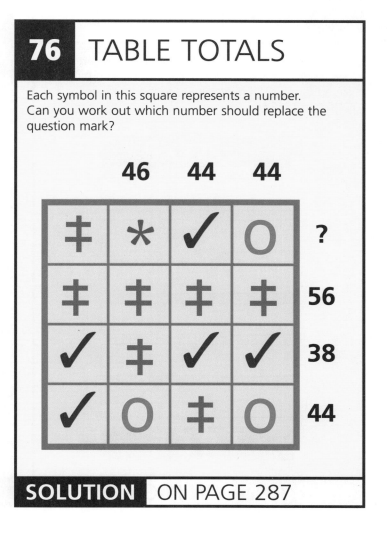

SOLUTION ON PAGE 287

77 UNEASY PEACE

The warring clans of the Campbells and the McPhersons were brought together by a marriage between the son and daughter of the opposing leading factions. The clan members, however, were still very loyal to their own clan and were very suspicious of the opposing clan. For the first few years all activities between the clans had an equal number from each clan in the teams of workers. This covered building homes, hunting, fishing, cooking etc.

On one fateful day the fishing boat, which had a crew of 30 (15 from each clan, and headed by the Campbell leader), ran into a very bad storm and the boat began to sink. The head of the expedition agreed with the crew that half of them would have to take a risk and swim for shore in order to save the boat and the remaining crew. The head man said that he would be fair in the selection of those to leave, and that he would line everyone up in a single line formed in a circle and every ninth person would have to go. The crew agreed, and each was allotted a position numbered from 1 to 30.

How did he line them up so that only the McPhersons were left?

SOLUTION ON PAGE 287

78 CHOP TO TREE

Complete the word ladder by changing one letter of each word per step. The newly created word must be found in the dictionary. What are the words to turn CHOP to TREE?

CHOP

TREE

SOLUTION ON PAGE 287

79 TRICKY PUZZLE!

Which letter replaces the question mark?

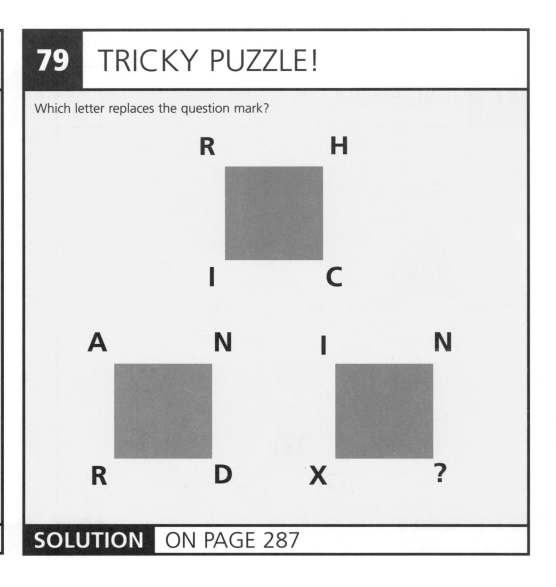

SOLUTION ON PAGE 287

80 NECTARINE

Start at the bottom letter N and move from circle to touching circle to the E at the top right. How many different ways are there of collecting the nine letters of NECTARINE?

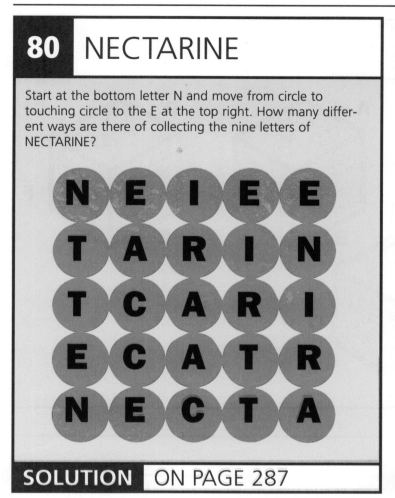

SOLUTION ON PAGE 287

81 HAPPY ENDING

Which word of four letters can be attached to the back of the words shown in the diagram to create six other words?

DOOR
FOOT
OVER
SIDE
QUICK
IN

SOLUTION ON PAGE 287

82 WHEEL WORD

Select one letter from each of the segments.
When the correct letters have been found a word of eight letters can be read clockwise. What is the word?

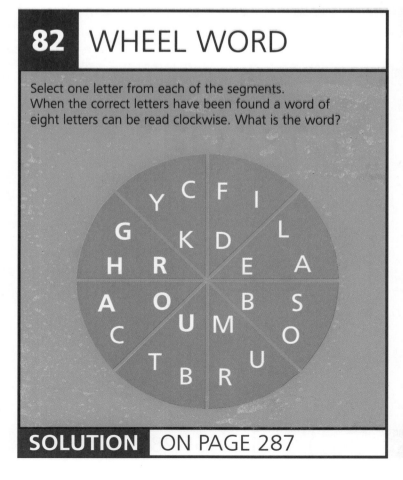

SOLUTION ON PAGE 287

83 PIGGIES IN THE MIDDLE

Place two letters in the empty space which, when added to the end of the words to the left and to the beginning of the right, form other words. When this is completed another word can be read down. What is the word?

WHO		ERA
BIT		GOT
BEG		ONE
DON		BIT

SOLUTION ON PAGE 287

84 SAME SYMBOLS

Can you work out which two sides on these cubes contain the same symbols?

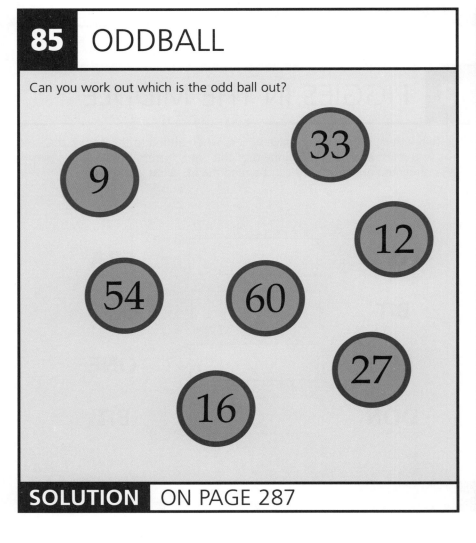

SOLUTION ON PAGE 287

85 ODDBALL

Can you work out which is the odd ball out?

33

9

12

54   60

27

16

SOLUTION ON PAGE 287

86 SYMBOL SIMILARITY

Can you find the two sides on these cubes that contain exactly the same symbols?

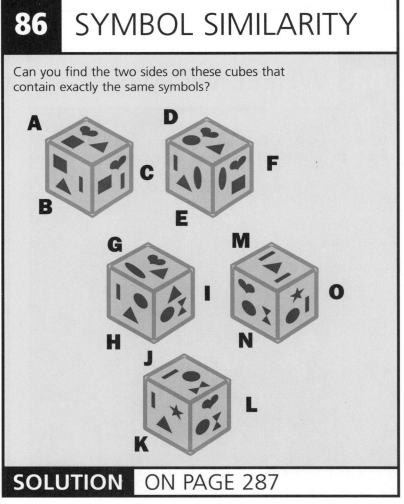

SOLUTION ON PAGE 287

87 SENTENCE SOLUTION

Two words using the same letters in their construction can be used to replace the dots in this sentence. The sentence will then make sense. Each dot is one letter. What are the words?

> AFTER THE DOUBLE WEDDING, THE TWO
> • • • • • • WALKED THROUGH THE
> HALL, WHICH WAS LITTERED WITH
> THE • • • • • FROM THE PARTY
> HELD THE PREVIOUS NIGHT.

SOLUTION ON PAGE 287

88 FRUITY PUZZLE

Here are some fruits. The number of each is set alongside the name of the fruits below. There is a relationship between the number and the letters of the names. How many peaches are there?

APPLES	69
PEARS	59
PEACHES	?
MELONS	78

SOLUTION ON PAGE 287

89 FOUR-LETTER WORD

Place a word of FOUR letters in the empty space. This word, when added to the end of the three words to the left and to the beginning of the three words to the right, will form six other words. What is the word?

LADY		WISE
APE		ABLE
GOD		NESS

SOLUTION ON PAGE 287

90 WORD WIGGLE

Place one letter in the middle of this diagram. Four five-letter words can now be rearranged from each straight line of letters. What is the letter and what are the words?

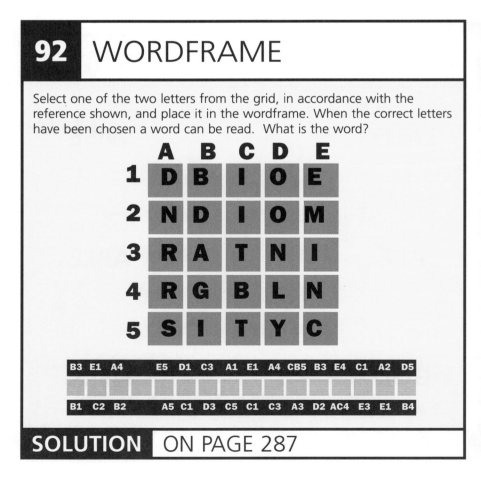

SOLUTION ON PAGE 287

91 TILE TROUBLE

Arrange the tiles in this diagram so that they form a square. When this is done correctly four words can be read down and across. What are the words?

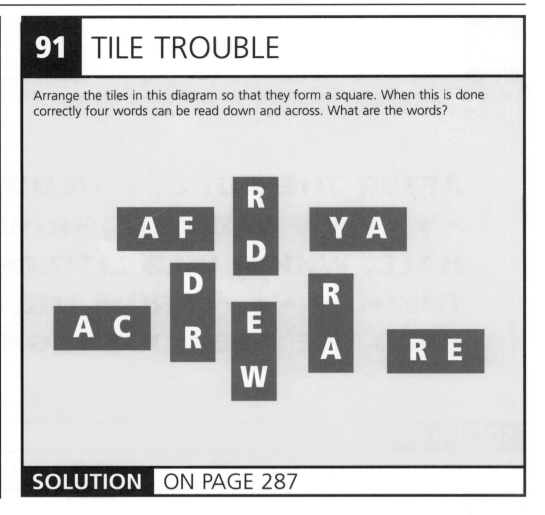

SOLUTION ON PAGE 287

92 WORDFRAME

Select one of the two letters from the grid, in accordance with the reference shown, and place it in the wordframe. When the correct letters have been chosen a word can be read. What is the word?

	A	B	C	D	E
1	D	B	I	O	E
2	N	D	I	O	M
3	R	A	T	N	I
4	R	G	B	L	N
5	S	I	T	Y	C

B3 E1 A4   E5 D1 C3 A1 E1 A4 CB5 B3 E4 C1 A2 D5

B1 C2 B2   A5 C1 D3 C5 C1 C3 A3 D2 AC4 E3 E1 B4

SOLUTION ON PAGE 287

93 WEDGE WORD

Make a circle out of these shapes. When the correct circle has been found a word can be read clockwise. What is the word?

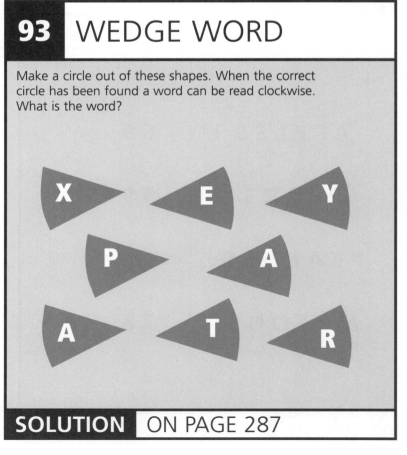

SOLUTION ON PAGE 287

94 LOTTERY WINNERS

This week's lottery was won by a syndicate of 10 people. Between them they won $2,775,000. They all contributed different amounts into the syndicate and their winnings were calculated against their contributions. If the amounts were all different but the cash differences between each step remained uniform, what amount did the second-highest winner get given that the sum of the lowest three amounts was equal to the sum of the top two amounts?

SOLUTION ON PAGE 287

95 DIAGRAM LOGIC

This diagram was constructed according to a certain logic. Can you work out which number should replace the question mark?

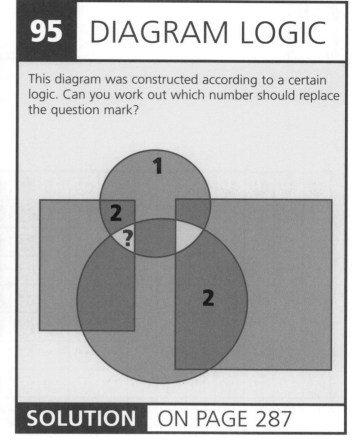

SOLUTION ON PAGE 287

96 DIAGRAM LOGIC

In this diagram the mathematical signs (+ and – only) between each letter (which has a value equal to its position in the alphabet) have gone missing.
Can you restore them in a way that you arrive at the letter in the middle of the diamond?

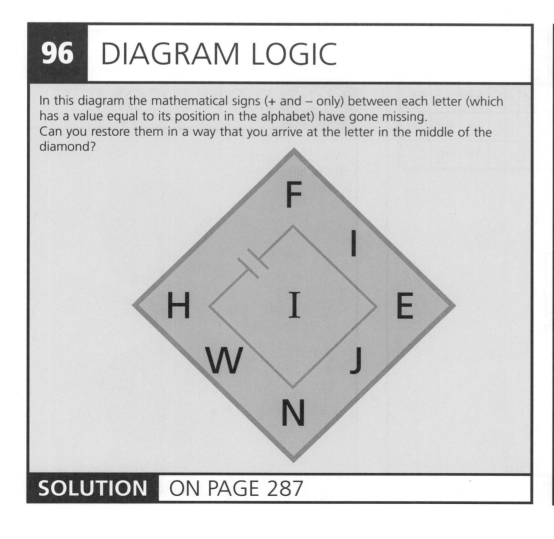

SOLUTION ON PAGE 287

97 SYMBOLIC

Can you work out whether + or – should replace the question mark to arrive at the letter in the middle of the circle?

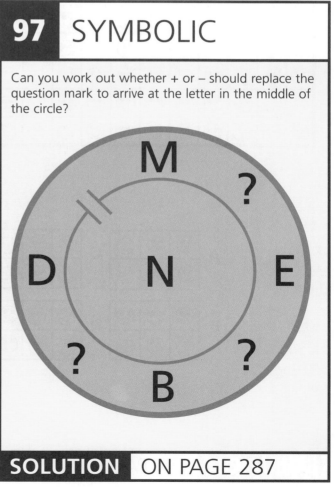

SOLUTION ON PAGE 287

98 FACE FRAME

The symbols in the grid follow a pattern. Can you work it out and find the missing section?

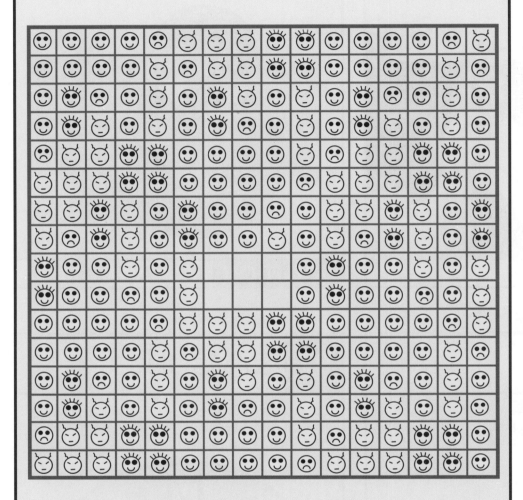

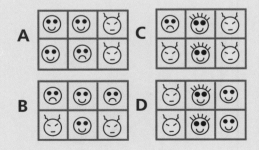

SOLUTION   ON PAGE 287

99 WORD LADDER

Complete the word ladder by changing one letter of each word per step. The newly created word must be found in the dictionary. What are the words to turn RIVER to BANKS?

R I V E R

B A N K S

SOLUTION   ON PAGE 287

100 DIDN'T COME?

Who is the person in this hidden code?

SOLUTION   ON PAGE 287

101 DRINK DILEMMA

The names of three drinks are to be found in the diagram.
The letters of the names are in the order they normally appear. What are the drinks?

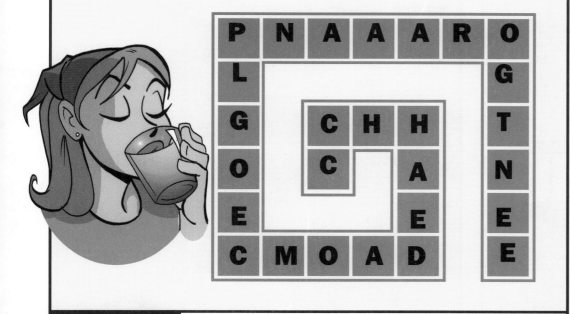

SOLUTION ON PAGE 287

102 TRIANGLES

What letter should replace the question mark?

SOLUTION ON PAGE 287

103 DOWNER?

Would the letter N go above or below the line?

SOLUTION ON PAGE 287

104 MOVIE MAGIC

Take the letters and arrange them correctly in the column under which they appear. Once this has been done a movie will appear. What is the movie?

P	H	M	V
O	Y	O	E
T	L	W	S
E	D	E	H

SOLUTION ON PAGE 288

105 FOUR-LETTER WORD

Which word of four letters can be attached to the back of the words shown in the diagram to create six other words?

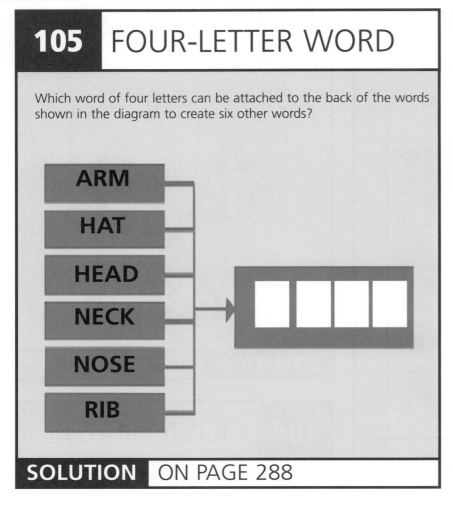

ARM
HAT
HEAD
NECK
NOSE
RIB

SOLUTION ON PAGE 288

106 MIDDLE MUDDLE

Place two letters in the empty space which, when added to the end of the words to the left and to the beginning of the right, form other words. When this is completed another word can be read downwards. What is the word?

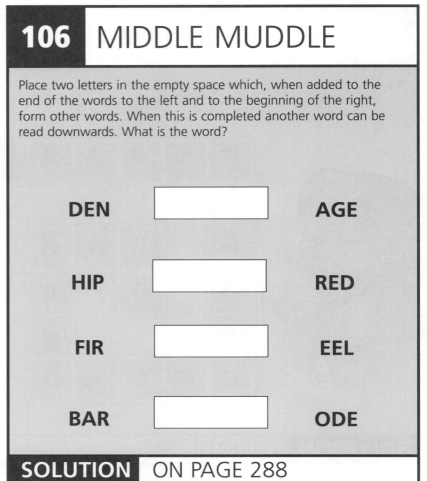

DEN		AGE
HIP		RED
FIR		EEL
BAR		ODE

SOLUTION ON PAGE 288

107 DEPARTURE DILEMMA

The distances on this departure board are fictitious. They bear a relationship to the letters in the names. What should replace the question mark?

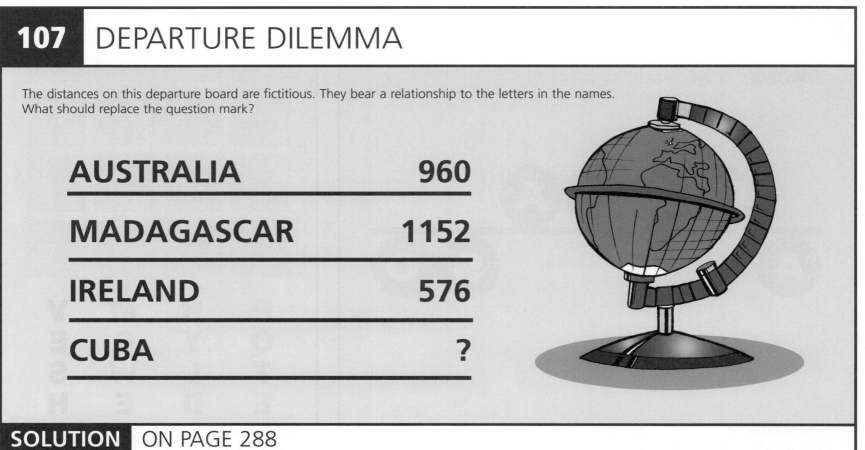

AUSTRALIA	960
MADAGASCAR	1152
IRELAND	576
CUBA	?

SOLUTION ON PAGE 288

108 FRAME WORDS

Select one of the two letters from the grid, in accordance with the reference shown, and place it in the wordframe. When the correct letters have been chosen two linked words can be read. What are the words?

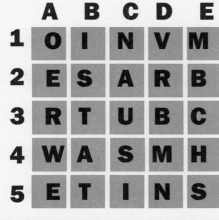

	A	B	C	D	E
1	O	I	N	V	M
2	E	S	A	R	B
3	R	T	U	B	C
4	W	A	S	M	H
5	E	T	I	N	S

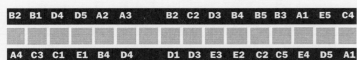

B2	B1	D4	D5	A2	A3		B2	C2	D3	B4	B5	B3	A1	E5	C4

A4	C3	C1	E1	B4	D4		D1	D3	E3	E2	C2	C5	E4	D5	A1

SOLUTION ON PAGE 288

110 LETTER LOGIC

Can you work out which of these letters is the odd one out?

SOLUTION ON PAGE 288

109 TRIANGLES

Can you work out which number fits into the first triangle?

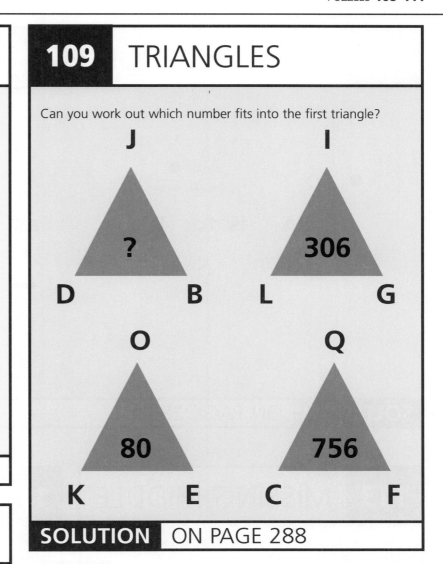

J
?
D   B

I
306
L   G

O
80
K   E

Q
756
C   F

SOLUTION ON PAGE 288

111 MISSING SYMBOLS

Can you replace the question marks with + or − so that both sections in this diagram add up to the same value?

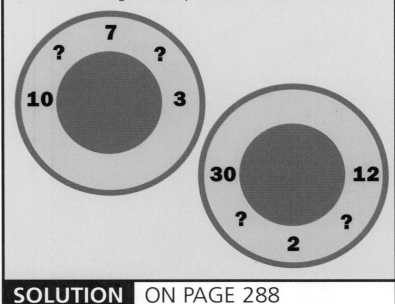

7
? ?
10   3

30   12
? ?
2

SOLUTION ON PAGE 288

112 ANALOGY PROBLEM

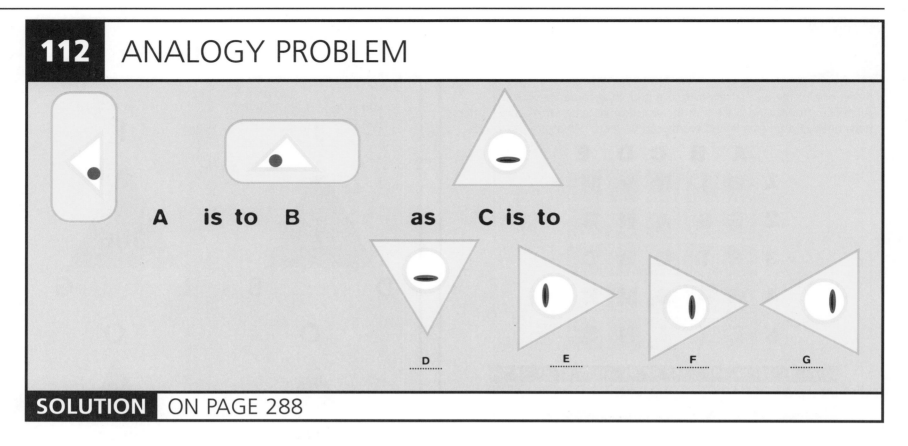

A   is to   B   as   C is to

D   E   F   G

SOLUTION | ON PAGE 288

113 MISSING MIDDLE

Place a word of FOUR letters in the empty space. This word, when added to the end of the three words to the left and to the beginning of the three words to the right, will form six other words. What is the word?

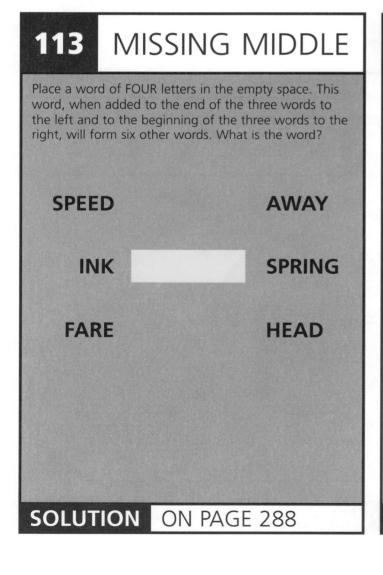

SPEED   AWAY

INK   SPRING

FARE   HEAD

SOLUTION | ON PAGE 288

114 GRID ENIGMA

Select one of the two letters from the grid, in accordance with the reference shown, and place it in the wordframe. When the correct letters have been chosen a 16-letter word can be read. What is the word?

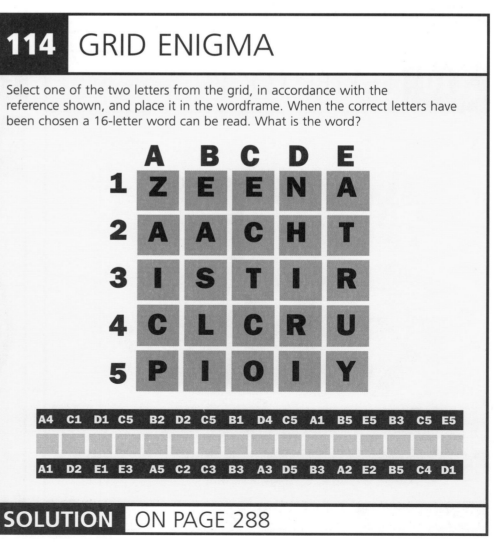

	A	B	C	D	E
1	Z	E	E	N	A
2	A	A	C	H	T
3	I	S	T	I	R
4	C	L	C	R	U
5	P	I	O	I	Y

A4	C1	D1	C5	B2	D2	C5	B1	D4	C5	A1	B5	E5	B3	C5	E5
A1	D2	E1	E3	A5	C2	C3	B3	A3	D5	B3	A2	E2	B5	C4	D1

SOLUTION | ON PAGE 288

115 TILE TROUBLE

Arrange the tiles in this diagram so that they form a square. When this is done correctly four words can be read down and across. What are the words?

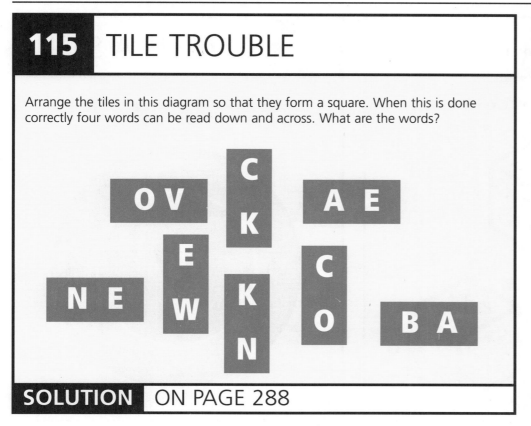

SOLUTION ON PAGE 288

116 WORD WHEEL

Place one letter in the middle of this diagram. Four five-letter words can now be rearranged from each straight line of letters. What is the letter and what are the words?

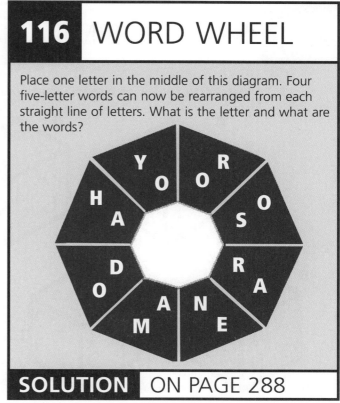

SOLUTION ON PAGE 288

117 WEDGE WORD

Make a circle out of these shapes.
When the correct circle has been found a word can be read clockwise. What is the word?

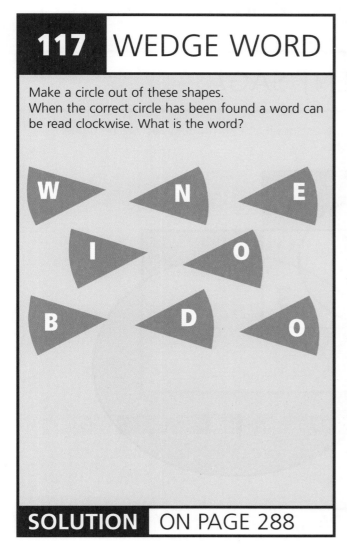

SOLUTION ON PAGE 288

118 COMPLETE THE GRID

The symbols in this grid follow a pattern. Can you work it out and complete the missing section?

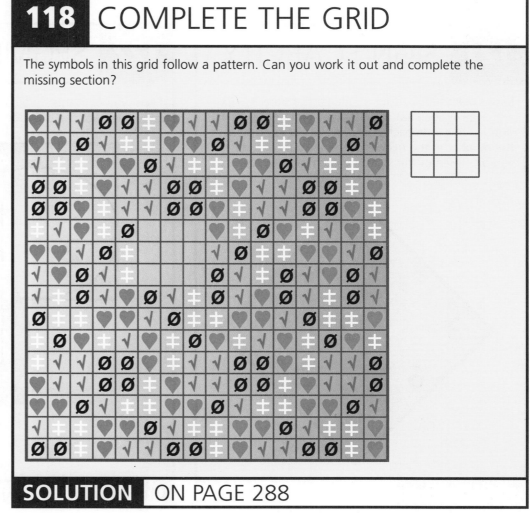

SOLUTION ON PAGE 288

119 SYMBOL SIMILARITY

Two sides of these cubes contain exactly the same numbers. Can you spot them?

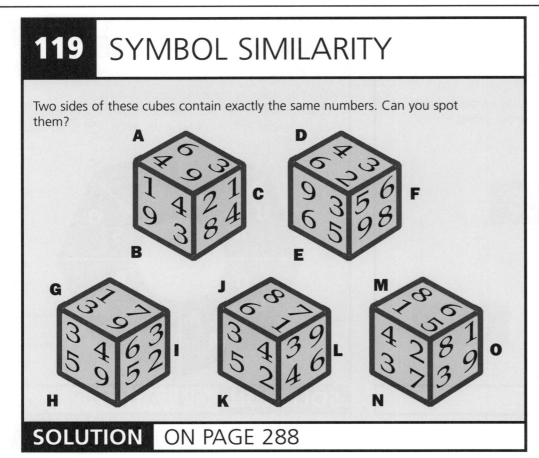

SOLUTION   ON PAGE 288

120 GIVE US A SIGN

Can you find the mathematical signs which should replace the question marks in the diagram?

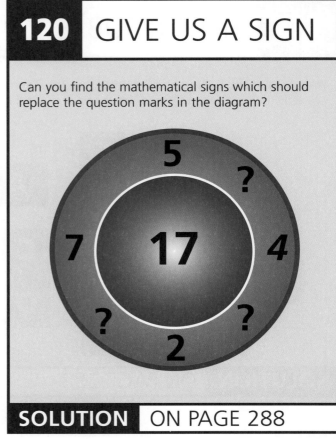

SOLUTION   ON PAGE 288

121 SIGN SCARCITY

In this diamond the four mathematical signs +, −, x and ÷ have been left out. Can you work out which sign fits between each pair of numbers to arrive at the number in the middle of the diagram? To start you off, three of the signs are each used twice.

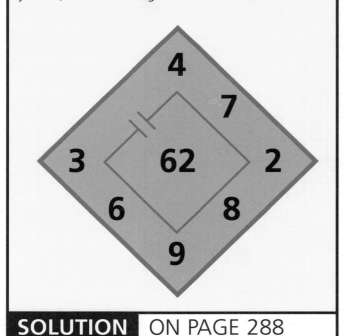

SOLUTION   ON PAGE 288

122 SEGMENT SAGA

Each symbol in this square represents a value. Can you find out which number should replace the question mark?

SOLUTION   ON PAGE 288

123 CUBE LAYOUT

Which of these cubes cannot be made from this layout?

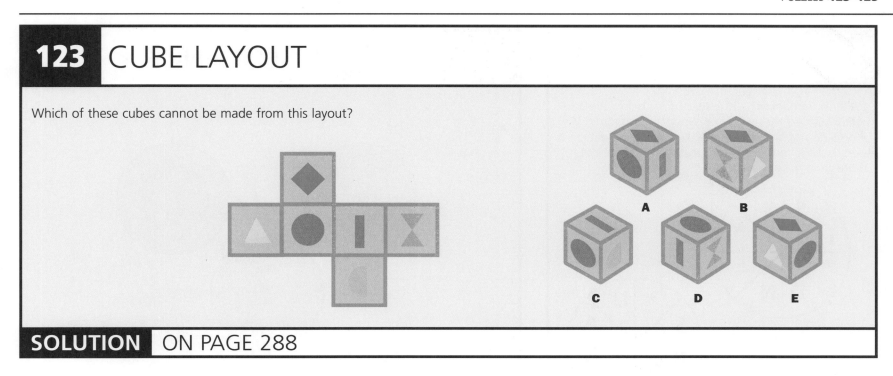

SOLUTION ON PAGE 288

124 SQUARE SEQUENCE

Can you work out the number needed to complete the square?

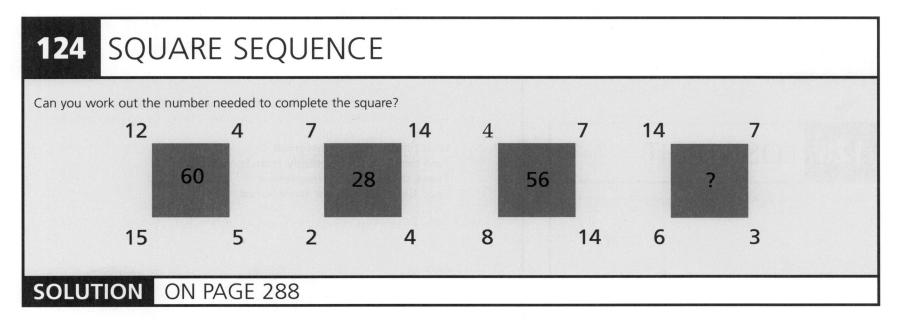

SOLUTION ON PAGE 288

125 TRIANGLE TURMOIL

The four triangles are linked by a simple mathematical formula. Can you discover what it is and then find the odd one out?

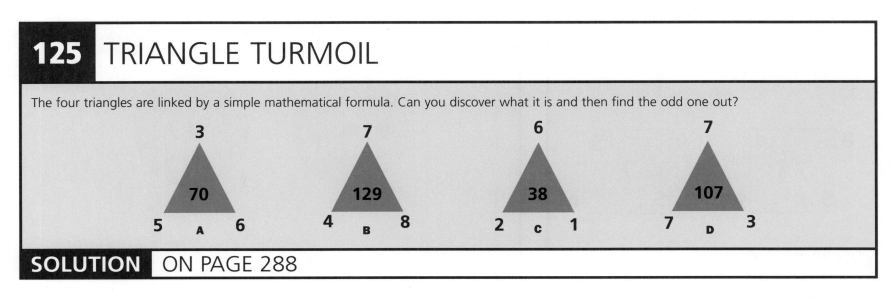

SOLUTION ON PAGE 288

126 MISSING LETTERS

If the missing letters in the two circles below are correctly inserted they will form synonymous words. The words do not have to be read in a clockwise direction, but the letters are consecutive. What are the words and missing letters?

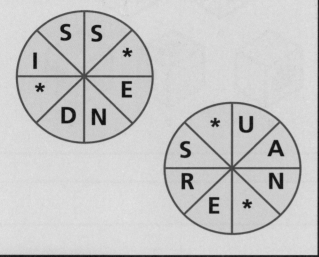

SOLUTION ON PAGE 288

128 LOST DIGIT

What number should replace the question mark?

A. 30
B. 32
C. 34
D. 36
E. 38

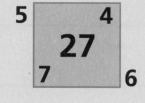

5		4
	27	
7		6

6		7
	40	
9		7

8		4
	71	
5		9

9		3
	?	
5		4

SOLUTION ON PAGE 288

127 SYMBOL SEQUENCE

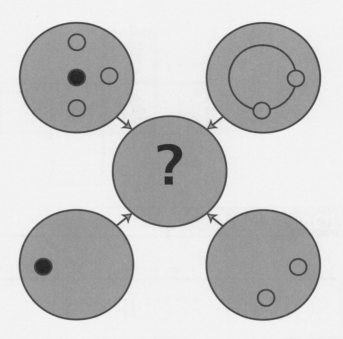

Each line and symbol that appears in the four outer circles, above, is transferred to the middle circle according to how many times it appears, as follows:

One time — it is transferred
Two times — it is possibly transferred
Three times — it is transferred
Four times — it is not transferred

Which of the circles below should appear as the middle circle?

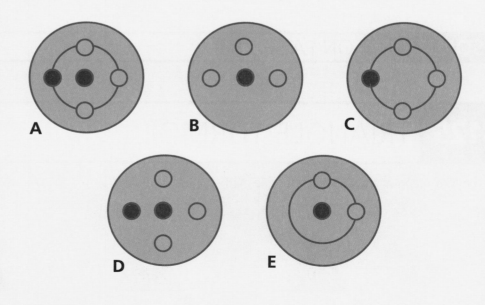

SOLUTION ON PAGE 288

129 WILD WEDGES

Which of the segments below is missing from the diagram above?

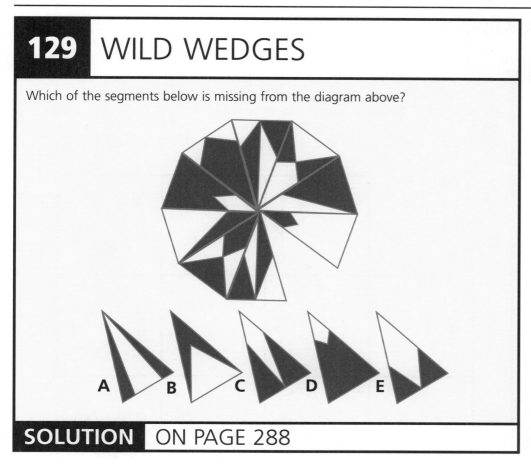

130 ODD ONE OUT

Which of the following is the odd one out?

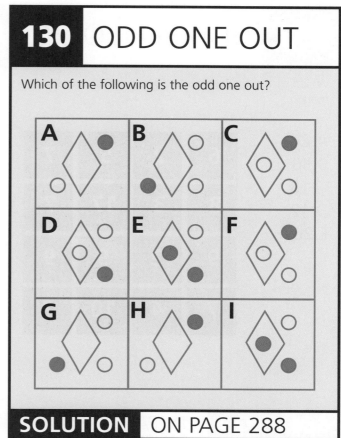

131 MISSING NUMBER

What number will replace the question mark?

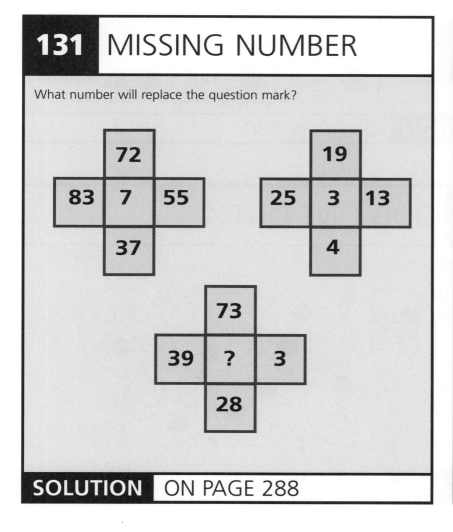

132 UNFOLDED CUBE

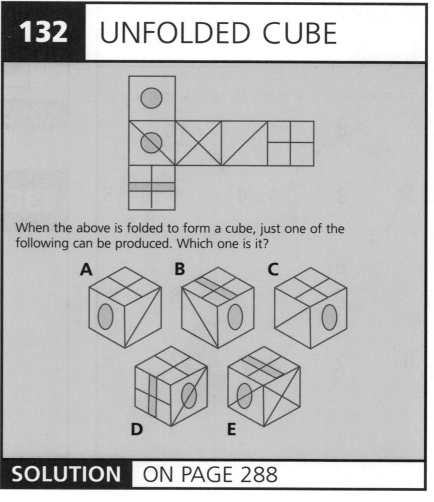

When the above is folded to form a cube, just one of the following can be produced. Which one is it?

133 NUMBER LOGIC

Which of the following should replace the question mark?

A. 24
B. 30
C. 18
D. 12
E. 26

6	2	5	7
8	3	17	7
9	2	9	9
7	4	10	?

SOLUTION ON PAGE 288

135 LOST NUMBER

What number should replace the question mark?

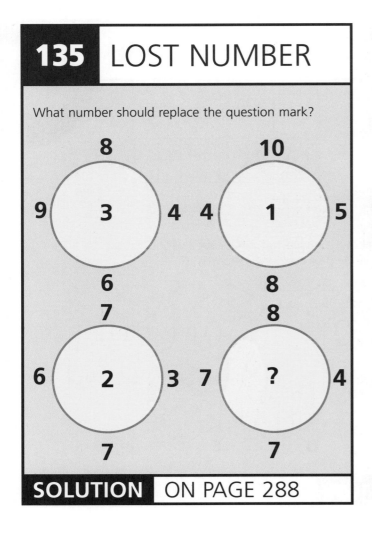

SOLUTION ON PAGE 288

134 SYMBOL SEQUENCE

Each of the nine squares in the grid marked 1A to 3C should incorporate all of the items which are shown in the squares of the same letter and number, at the left and top, respectively. For example, 2B should incorporate all of the symbols that are in squares 2 and B. One square, however, is incorrect. Which one is it?

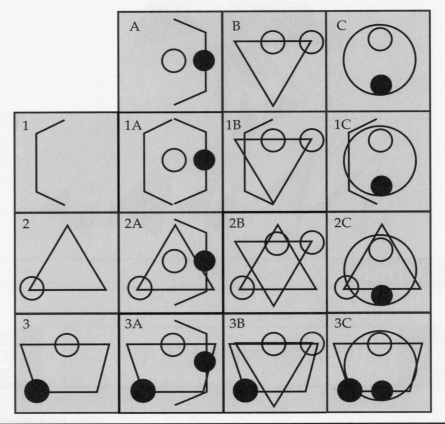

SOLUTION ON PAGE 288

136 ODD ONE OUT

Which of the following is the odd one out?

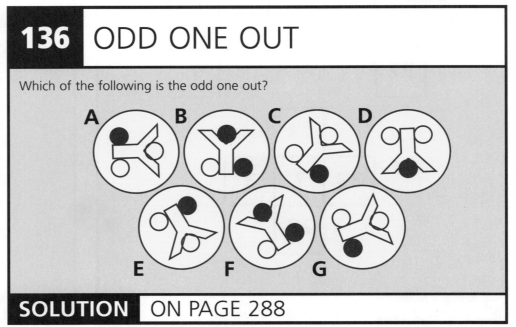

SOLUTION ON PAGE 288

137 SYMBOL ANALOGY

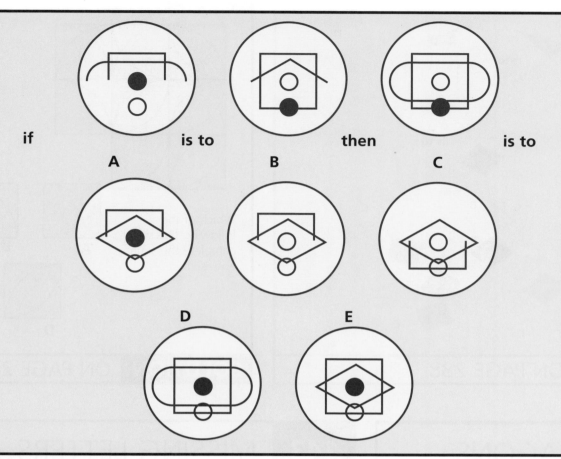

if ⬤ is to **A** then ⬤ is to

B   **C**

D   **E**

SOLUTION ON PAGE 288

138 MISSING LETTERS

If the missing letters in the two circles below are correctly inserted they will form synonymous words. The words do not have to be read in a clockwise direction, but the letters are consecutive. What are the words and missing letters?

T A
* D
E *
R E

E *
L R
I E
* V

SOLUTION ON PAGE 288

139 TAKE A BOW

Which is the odd one out?

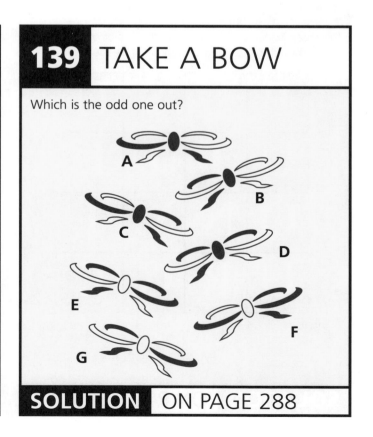

SOLUTION ON PAGE 288

140 ANALOGY PROBLEM

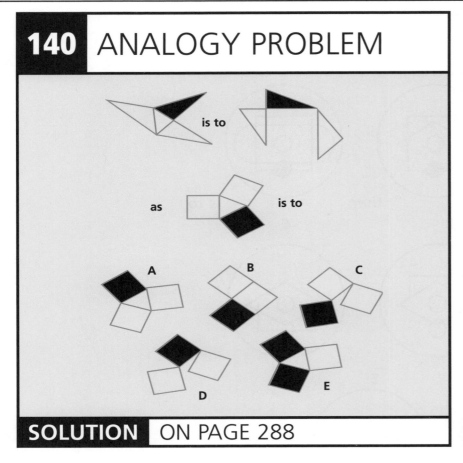

is to

as   is to

A   B   C

D   E

SOLUTION   ON PAGE 288

141 MISSING SEGMENT

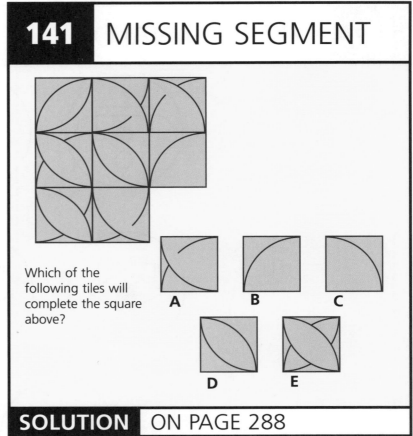

Which of the following tiles will complete the square above?

A   B   C

D   E

SOLUTION   ON PAGE 288

142 HEXAGONS

Three unrelated words are hidden in this grid. They are all of different lengths but all 16 letters are used once only to form them. The words are a game, timespan and an animal (three letters).

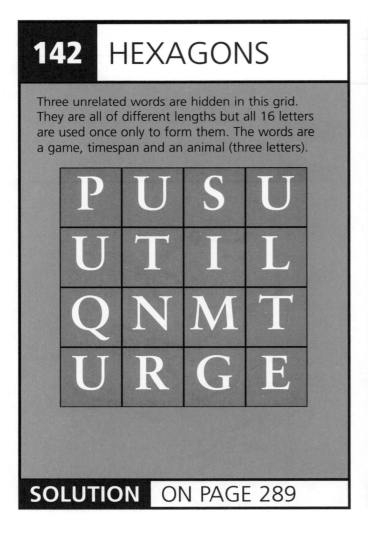

P	U	S	U
U	T	I	L
Q	N	M	T
U	R	G	E

SOLUTION   ON PAGE 289

143 MISSING LETTERS

If the missing letters in the two circles below are correctly inserted they will form synonymous words. The words do not have to be read in a clockwise direction, but the letters are consecutive. What are the words and missing letters?

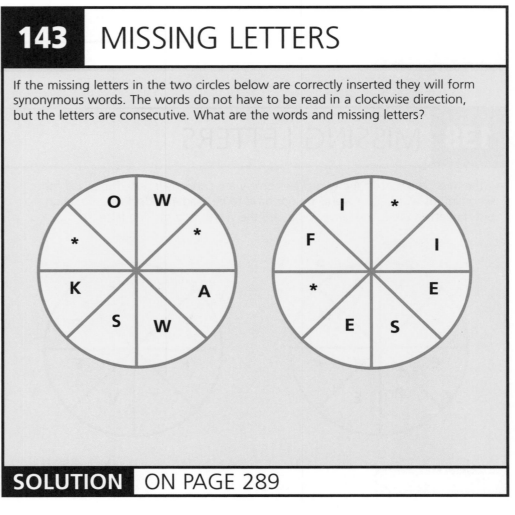

SOLUTION   ON PAGE 289

144 NUMBER WHEEL

What number should replace the question mark?

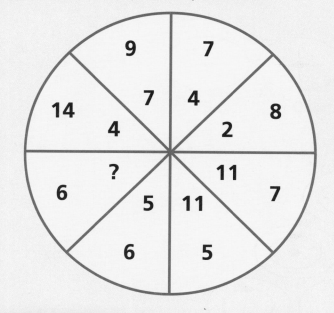

SOLUTION ON PAGE 289

145 SEQUENCE SENSE

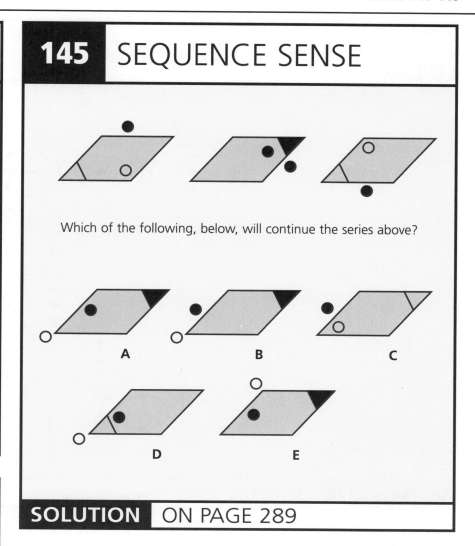

Which of the following, below, will continue the series above?

A   B   C

D   E

SOLUTION ON PAGE 289

146 MISSING LETTERS

Start at a corner square and move in a clockwise spiral to the middle to spell out a nine-letter word. What are the missing letters?

A	T	E
		M
A	N	E

SOLUTION ON PAGE 289

147 NUMBER LOGIC

Which number should replace the question mark?

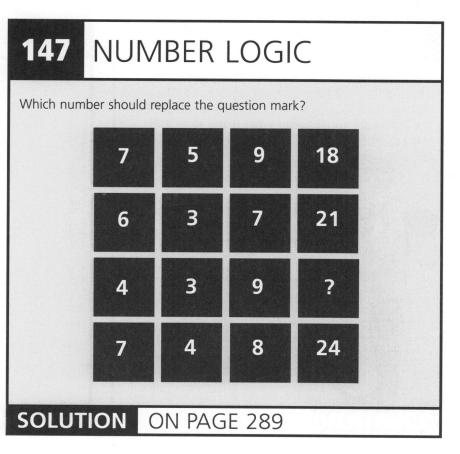

7	5	9	18
6	3	7	21
4	3	9	?
7	4	8	24

SOLUTION ON PAGE 289

148 ANTONYMS

What words are antonymous?

A. ABSTRUSE
B. DEFICIENT
C. PROFLIGATE
D. SECURE
E. CHASTE
F. EXOTIC

SOLUTION ON PAGE 289

149 SYMBOL SEQUENCE

Which of the following will replace the question mark and complete the series?

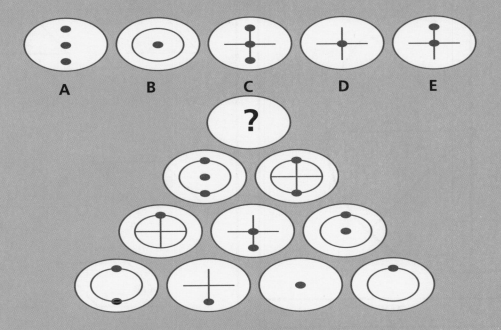

SOLUTION ON PAGE 289

150 MISSING LETTERS

If the missing letters in the circle below are correctly inserted they will form an eight-letter word. The word will not have to be read in a clockwise direction, but the letters are consecutive. What is the word and missing letters?

SOLUTION ON PAGE 289

151 NUMBER LOGIC

Each symbol in this square represents a value. Can you find out which number should replace the question mark?

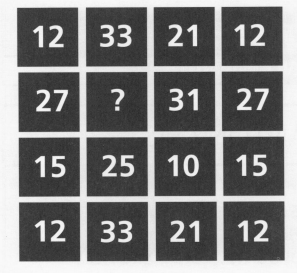

12	33	21	12
27	?	31	27
15	25	10	15
12	33	21	12

SOLUTION ON PAGE 289

152 NUMBER ENIGMA

What number should replace the question mark?

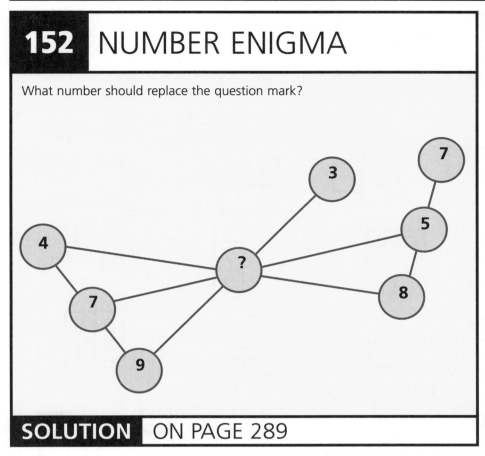

SOLUTION ON PAGE 289

153 ANALOGY PROBLEM

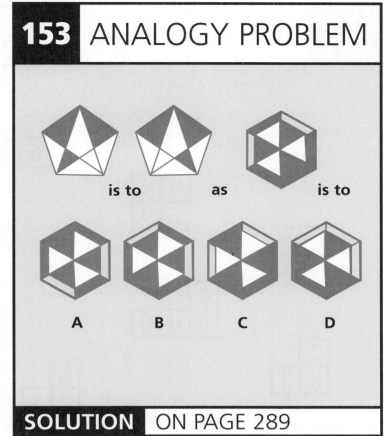

is to   as   is to

A   B   C   D

SOLUTION ON PAGE 289

154 LETTER LOST

Which letter replaces the question mark?

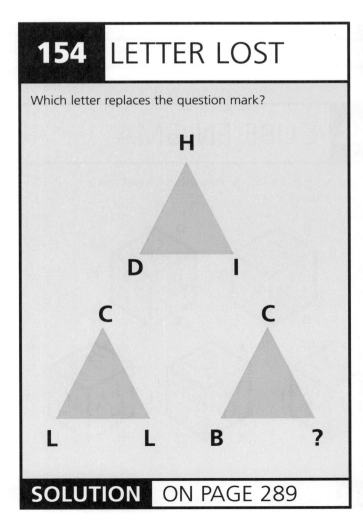

SOLUTION ON PAGE 289

155 CUBE CONUNDRUM

When the above is folded into a cube, only one of the following can be produced. Which one is it?

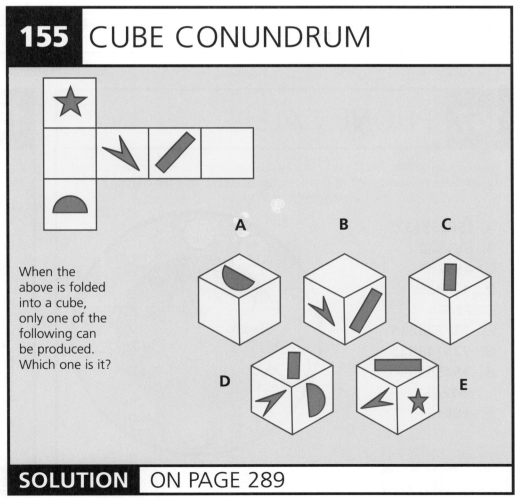

SOLUTION ON PAGE 289

156 TILE TERROR

These tiles when placed in the right order will form a square in which each horizontal line is identical with one vertical line. Can you successfully form the square?

SOLUTION   ON PAGE 289

157 PHONE CALL

The diagram represents an old-fashioned telephone dial with letters as well as numbers. Below is a list of numbers representing 10 international capital cities. Can you use the diagram to decode them?

A. 1562531325
B. 661382
C. 455255
D. 126435
E. 75405
F. 157726215
G. 775143545
H. 1545515
I. 512632
J. 154161

SOLUTION   ON PAGE 289

158 CUBE ENIGMA

Can you work out which sides on these cubes contain the same letters?

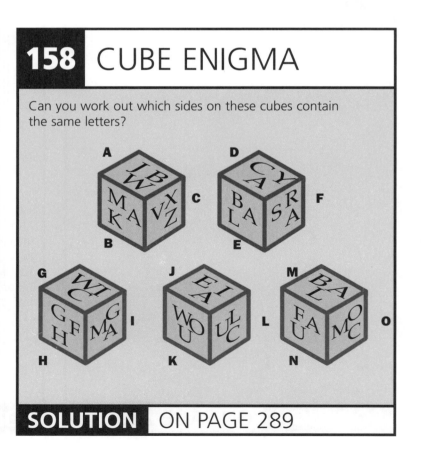

SOLUTION   ON PAGE 289

159 COLOUR CONUNDRUM

The words can be put in front of the colours to form well-known names or expressions.

BLOOD DEEP CODE TOBACCO SEA EMERALD

SOLUTION ON PAGE 289

160 WORD WHEEL

Can you find out which letter completes the wheel?

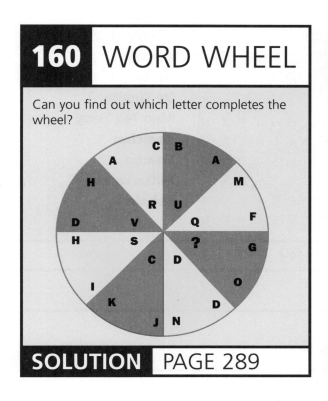

SOLUTION PAGE 289

161 LETTER SEQUENCE

Find the missing letter.

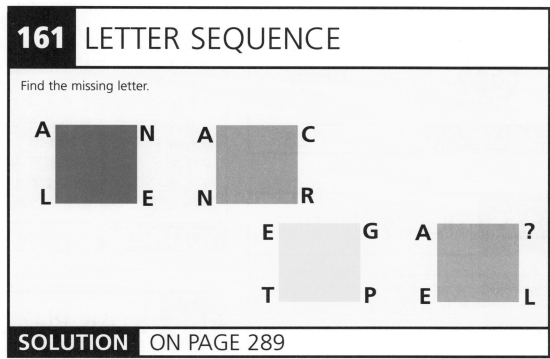

SOLUTION ON PAGE 289

162 COLOUR SERIES

How would you continue this series?

SOLUTION ON PAGE 289

163 ODDBALLS

Can you work out which of these balls is the odd one out?

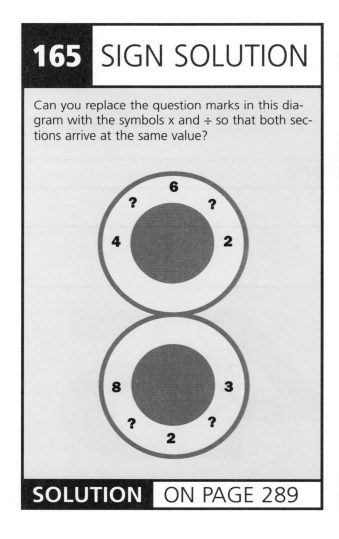

91   55   82
37   19   46
64   26

SOLUTION ON PAGE 289

164 WORDSEARCH

There are 18 politicians (love 'em or hate 'em) hidden below. Can you find them?

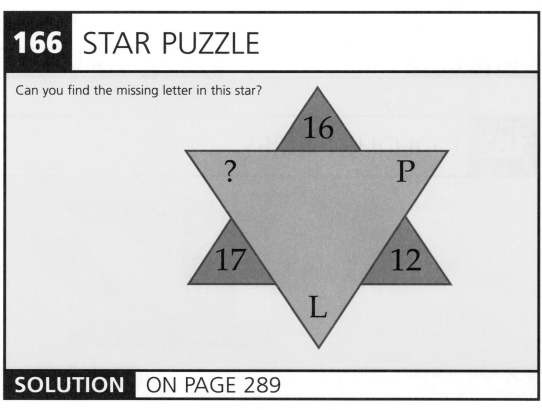

```
M O X A L T E F E I C H A L P X N O N S
F A L E F T I E X W K C R A M S I B P X
A L L L I H C R U H C E T P W O L I J L
M O N E D A L O X E G H N X E F A L A E
A X O N A E C E A L E I S P E E T F A E
G I A A O N E A B C A F I A A W S U P V
N G T E A A I Y D E N N E K O U S L E E
U S A R G H A N F A O S E L T A I X O H
T P F E Q R A A E C S E F A L N T A U C
E F A H S R A E H E A E N A C H I A E A
S A E C E A F E A E O N S O A T N A F B
T L O T A O T E A D F A L P E R I T O R
O L T A A S A A F E G N A E R L L O M O
A I N H O F S A F G P Q R N A E O M E G
M E A T B C E A D A D A U I F O S P X M
L M O X M N O P Q U R S T S A U S X A O
W V A E X F O H J L A A T T U B U C W N
O Z X A E F A O Z L A E H L U F M R A Z
A E N O I R U G N E B F A E E A K L M N
O Z A D A C A H P T S R S Y T R A E L M
```

Arafat
Gandhi
Mussolini
Ben Gurion
Gorbachev
Napoleon
Bismarck
Kennedy
Pinochet
Churchill
Lincoln
Stalin
De Gaulle
Mao Tse Tung
Thatcher
Franco
Mitterrand
Yeltsin

SOLUTION ON PAGE 289

165 SIGN SOLUTION

Can you replace the question marks in this diagram with the symbols x and ÷ so that both sections arrive at the same value?

6
? ?
4   2

8   3
? ?
2

SOLUTION ON PAGE 289

166 STAR PUZZLE

Can you find the missing letter in this star?

16
?   P
17   12
L

SOLUTION ON PAGE 289

167 NUMBER NONSENSE

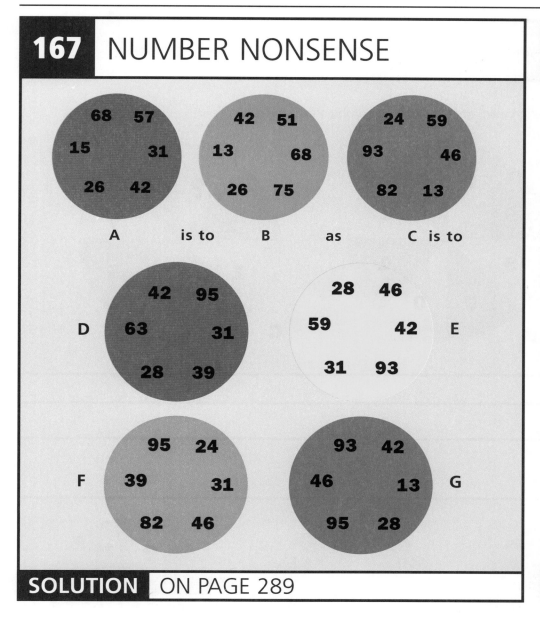

A	68 57 15 31 26 42
B	42 51 13 68 26 75
C	24 59 93 46 82 13

A is to B as C is to

| D | 42 95 63 31 28 39 |
| E | 28 46 59 42 31 93 |

| F | 95 24 39 31 82 46 |
| G | 93 42 46 13 95 28 |

SOLUTION ON PAGE 289

168 TRIANGLE TOTAL

Can you work out the rule these triangles follow and find the missing number?

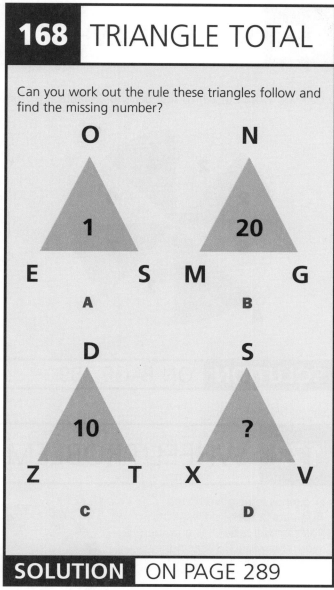

O
1
E   S
A

N
20
M   G
B

D
10
Z   T
C

S
?
X   V
D

SOLUTION ON PAGE 289

169 CUBE ENIGMA

Can you work out which three sides of these cubes contain the same symbols?

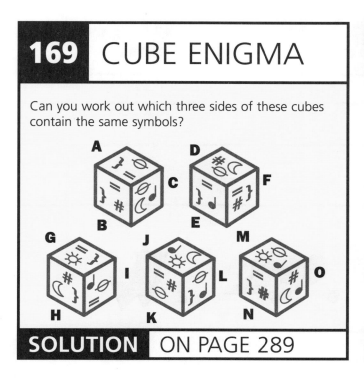

SOLUTION ON PAGE 289

170 SQUARE SEQUENCE

Can you work out which number should replace the question mark in the square?

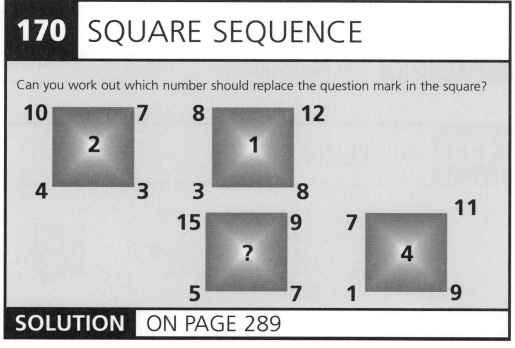

| 10 | 2 | 7 |
| 4 | | 3 |

| 8 | 1 | 12 |
| 3 | | 8 |

| 15 | ? | 9 |
| 5 | | 7 |

| 7 | 4 | 11 |
| 1 | | 9 |

SOLUTION ON PAGE 289

171 NUMBER WHEELS

Can you work out which number should replace the question mark to follow the rules of the other wheels?

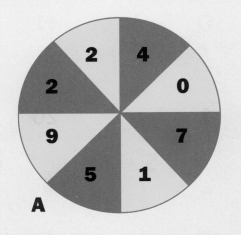

A

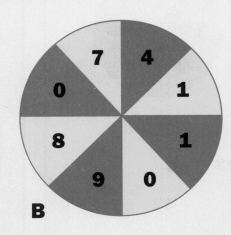

B

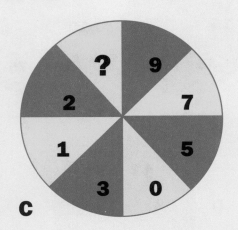

C

SOLUTION ON PAGE 289

172 WHEEL PROBLEM

A curious logic governs the numbers in these circles. Can you discover what it is and then work out what the missing number should be?

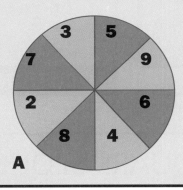

A

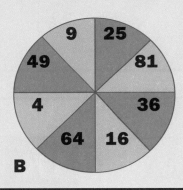

B

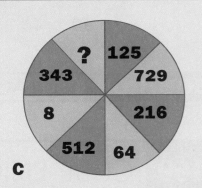

C

SOLUTION ON PAGE 290

173 PATTERN POSER

Can you work out which of these diagrams is different from the others?

 A

 B

 C

 D

 E

SOLUTION ON PAGE 290

174 ODD ONE OUT?

Can you find the odd one out of these symbols?

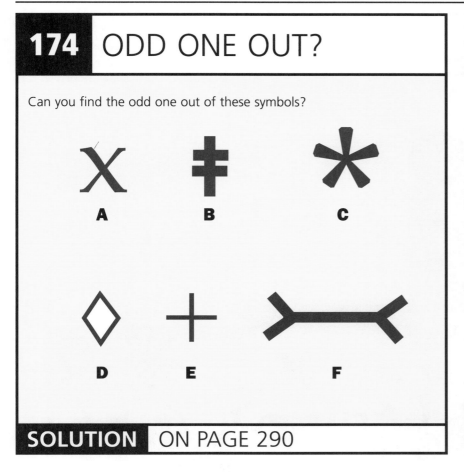

175 STAR TURN

Can you find the letter that would complete the star?

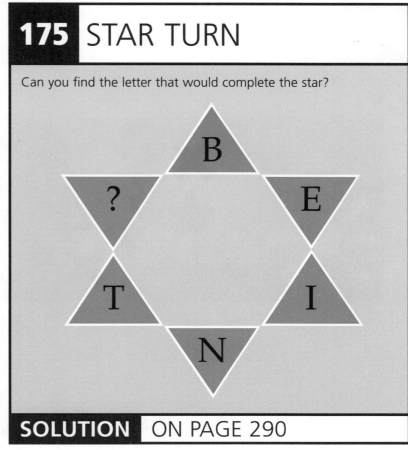

176 MISSING SYMBOLS

In this diagram, starting from the top of the diamond and working in a clockwise direction, the four basic mathematical signs (+, −, x, ÷) have been omitted. Your task is to restore them so that the calculation, with answer in the middle, is correct.

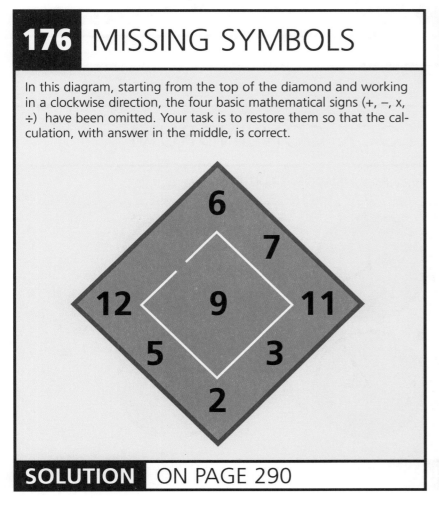

SOLUTION ON PAGE 290

177 SYMBOL HUNT

Can you work out which mathematical signs should replace the question marks in this diagram? You have a choice between − or +.

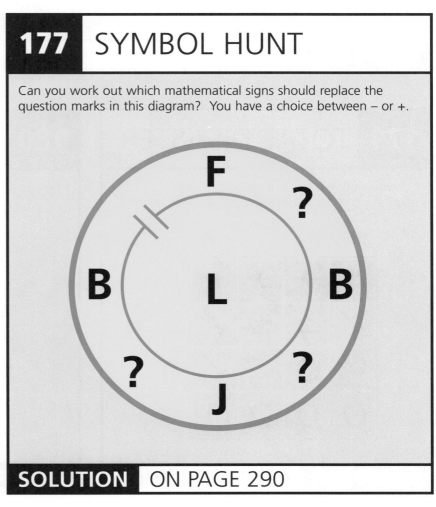

SOLUTION ON PAGE 290

SOLUTION ON PAGE 290

SOLUTION ON PAGE 290

178 PATTERN POSER

The two pictures are very similar but not quite identical. Find 10 ways in which they differ.

SOLUTION ON PAGE 290

179 TOTAL DISASTER

Can you work out what number each symbol represents and find the value of the question mark?

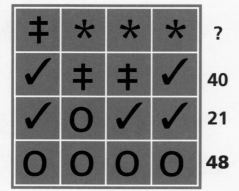

35	47		24
‡	*	*	*	?
✓	‡	‡	✓	40
✓	O	✓	✓	21
O	O	O	O	48

SOLUTION ON PAGE 290

180 CLOCK CONUNDRUM

Can you work out what the blank clock face should look like?

SOLUTION ON PAGE 290

181 PHONE FREAK

The diagram represent an old–fashioned telephone dial with letters as well as numbers. Below is a list of numbers representing 10 American towns or cities. Can you decode them?

A. 214417
B. 7217742
C. 1331135
D. 534918422
E. 53552165437
F. 65674152
G. 2276537
H. 1741571
I. 1351355173
J. 352315165437

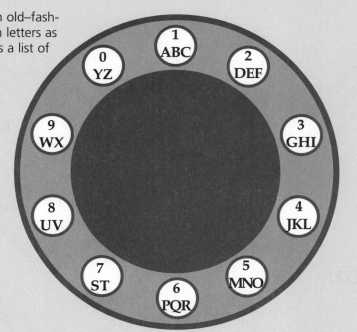

SOLUTION   ON PAGE 290

183 CLOCK FACES

Look at the clock faces shown in the top line below. Choose one from the second row to continue the series.

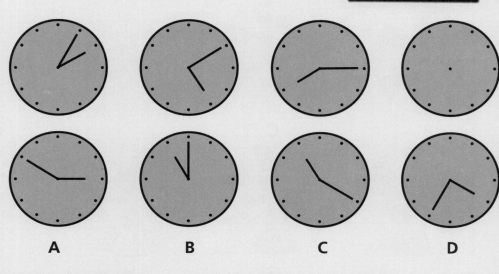

A   B   C   D

SOLUTION   ON PAGE 290

182 ODD ONE OUT

Which is the odd one out?

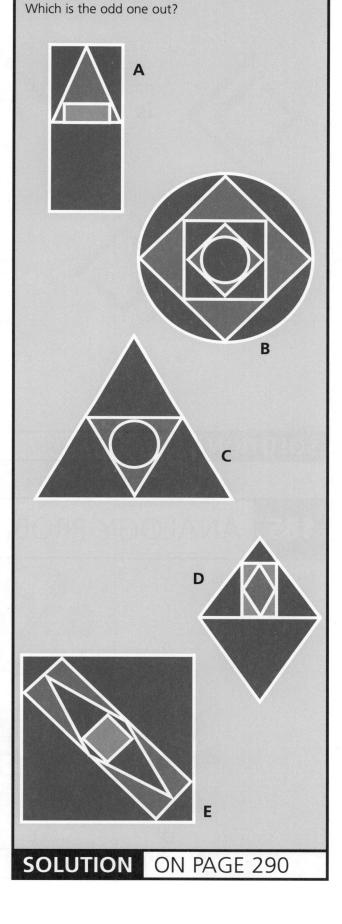

A

B

C

D

E

SOLUTION   ON PAGE 290

184 ANALOGY PROBLEM

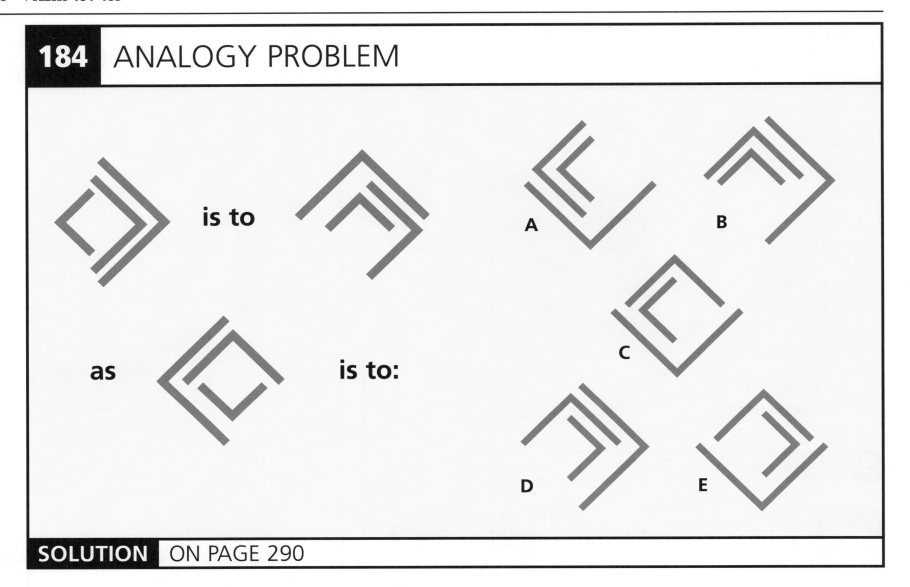

is to

as

is to:

A

B

C

D

E

SOLUTION ON PAGE 290

185 ANALOGY PROBLEM

A is to B as C is to ?

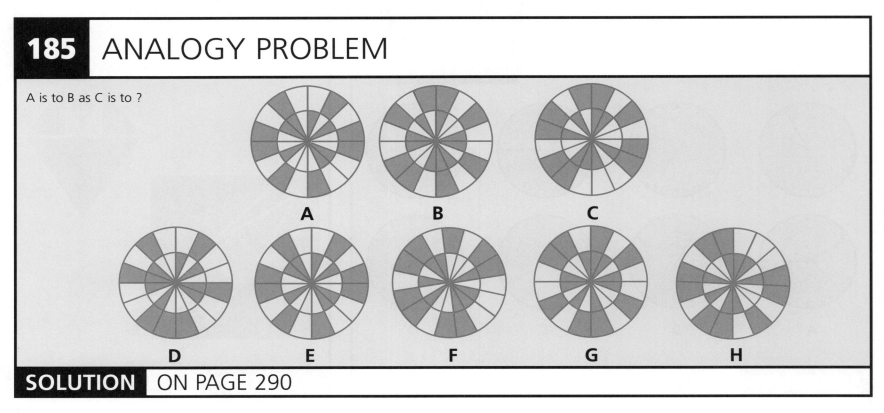

A

B

C

D

E

F

G

H

SOLUTION ON PAGE 290

186 | TORN TRIANGLES

Which of the following forms a perfect triangle when combined with the picture on the right?

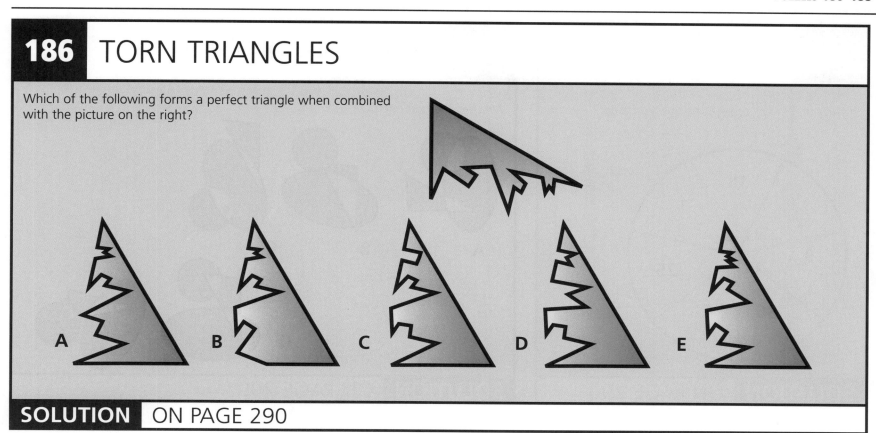

A   B   C   D   E

SOLUTION | ON PAGE 290

187 | CUT CORNERS

Which is the odd one out?

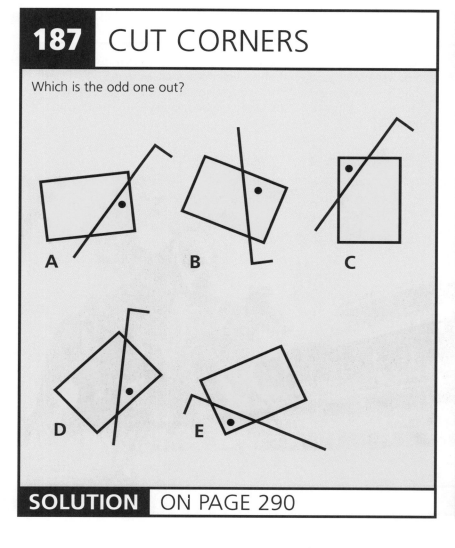

A   B   C

D   E

SOLUTION | ON PAGE 290

188 | MATCH PROBLEM

By taking away four matches from this diagram, leave eight small squares.

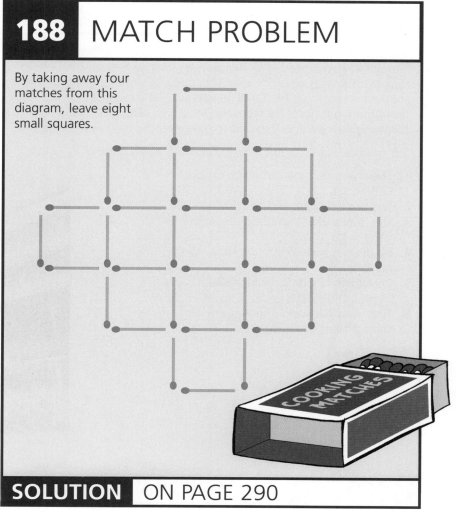

SOLUTION | ON PAGE 290

189 NUMBER PUZZLE

What number will replace the question mark?

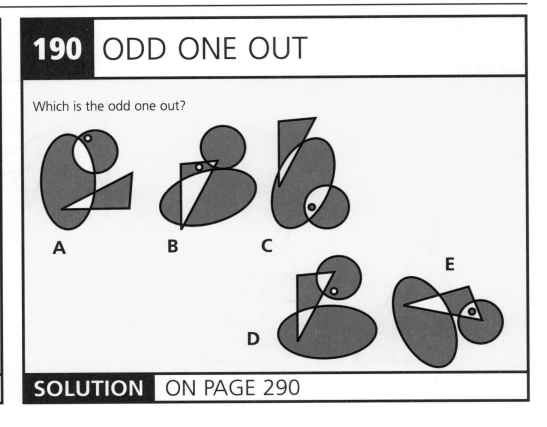

A. 46
B. 45
C. 47
D. 49
E. 0

SOLUTION ON PAGE 290

190 ODD ONE OUT

Which is the odd one out?

A   B   C

E

D

SOLUTION ON PAGE 290

191 TRACKSIDE JOE

Trackside Joe had been taken into hospital for a serious heart condition. The nurse who looked after him noticed that he had several betting slips in his pocket when he was admitted but she thought that these should be kept from him until he was well. The extra stress, she thought, might upset his recovery. After two weeks of total rest following his operation, the nurse gave him the daily newspaper and gave him his betting slips and wallet. Looking at his first betting slip and newspaper, he noted that his first horse had won at 50-to-1 and he had $50 to win on it. When he left hospital his first call was to collect his winnings of $2500. They refused to pay him, but do you know why?

1. There was no time restriction on the betting slip.
2. The bet was valid and he had paid $50.
3. The bookmaker had not disappeared or gone bust.
4. He did not owe $2500, or more, to the bookmaker.
5. He had not made a mistake when filling out his betting slip.
6. The horse had won and was not subject to disqualification.

SOLUTION ON PAGE 290

192 ANALOGY PROBLEM

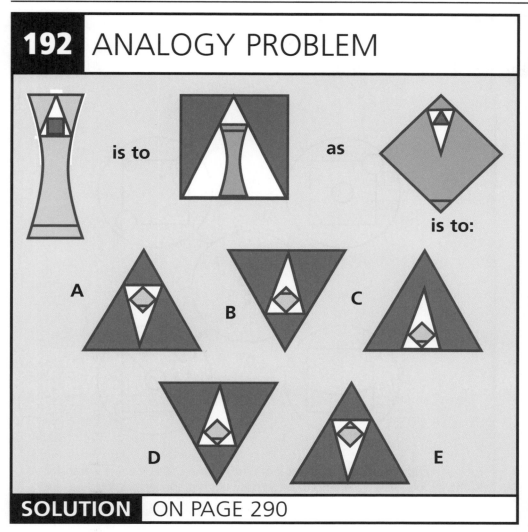

is to ... as ... is to:

A   B   C   D   E

SOLUTION ON PAGE 290

193 NUMBER WHEEL

What number should replace the question mark?

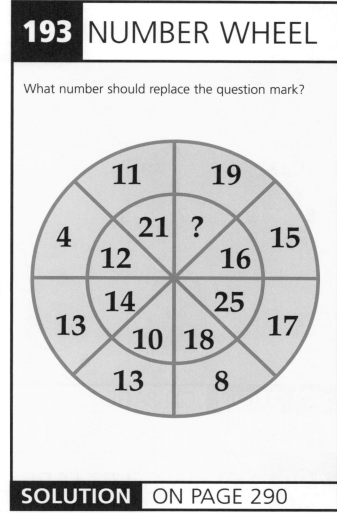

SOLUTION ON PAGE 290

194 MISSING LETTERS

If the missing letters in the circle below are correctly inserted they will form an eight-letter word. The word will not have to be read in a clockwise direction, but the letters are consecutive. What is the word and missing letters?

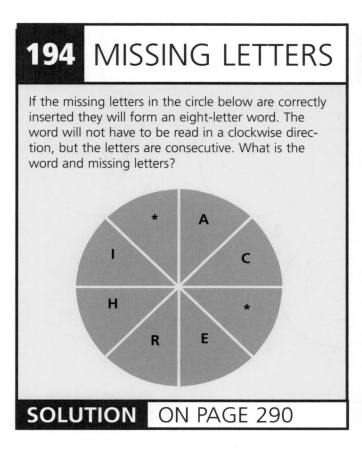

SOLUTION ON PAGE 290

195 WORD WHEELS

If the missing letters in the two circles below are correctly inserted they will form synonymous words. The words do not have to be read in a clockwise direction, but the letters are consecutive. What are the words and missing letters?

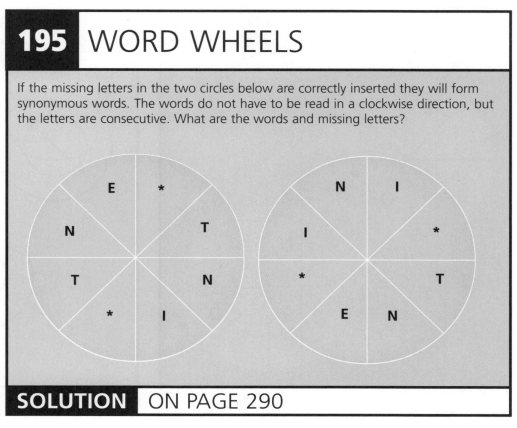

SOLUTION ON PAGE 290

196 MISSING NUMBER

What number should replace the question mark?

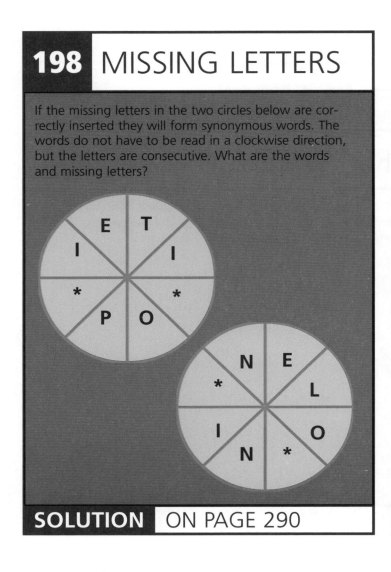

SOLUTION ON PAGE 290

197 PATTERN POSER

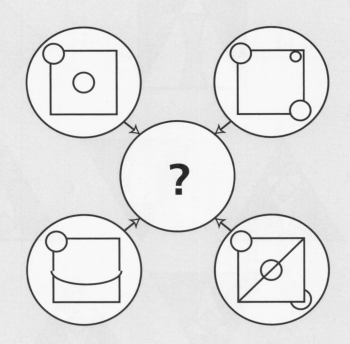

Each line and symbol that appears in the four outer circles, above, is transferred to the middle circle according to how many times it appears, as follows:

One time — it is transferred
Two times — it is possibly transferred
Three times — it is transferred
Four times — it is not transferred

Which of the circles below should appear in the middle circle?

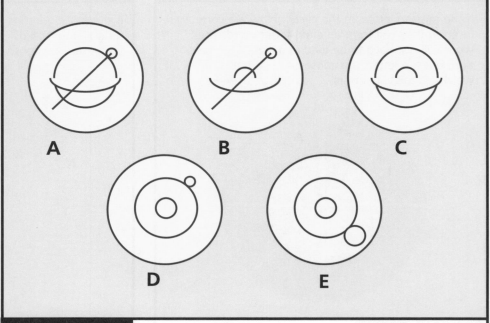

SOLUTION ON PAGE 290

198 MISSING LETTERS

If the missing letters in the two circles below are correctly inserted they will form synonymous words. The words do not have to be read in a clockwise direction, but the letters are consecutive. What are the words and missing letters?

SOLUTION ON PAGE 290

199 PATTERN PROBLEM

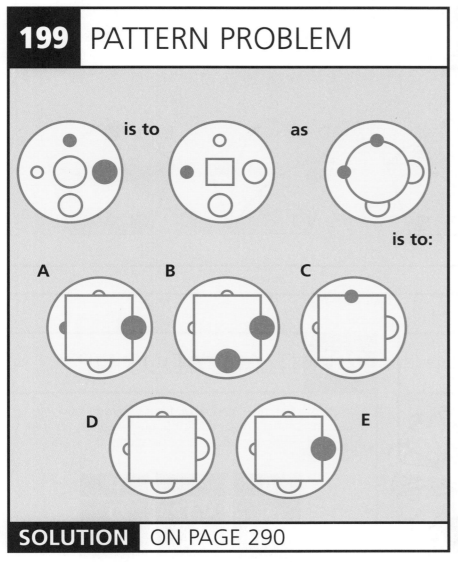

is to ... as ... is to:

A   B   C

D   E

200 MISSING NUMBER

What number should replace the question mark?

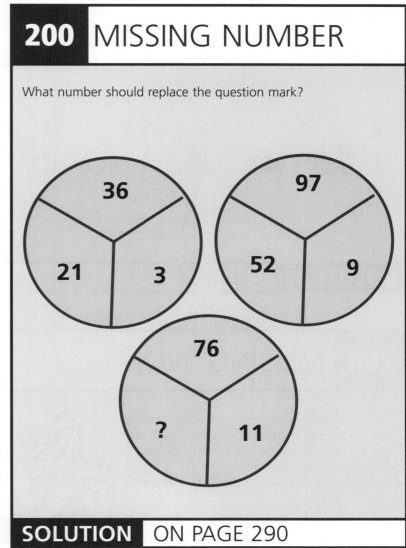

201 LETTER LOGIC

If the missing letters in the circle below are correctly inserted they will form an eight-letter word. The word will not have to be read in a clockwise direction, but the letters are consecutive. Can you figure out the word and the missing letters?

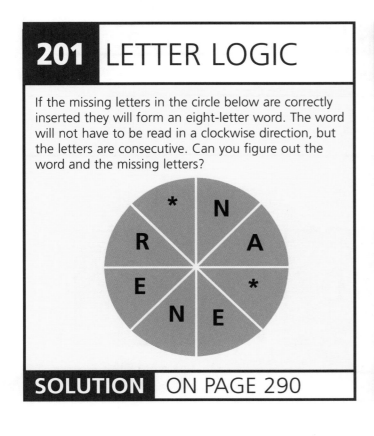

202 MISSING WORD

ANGER TENDER DIRECT
RENTED RANGE

What word is missing from above?

A. GREEN

B. FINAL

C. CREDIT

D. DETECT

203 PROBLEM PATTERN

Which of the following is the odd one out?

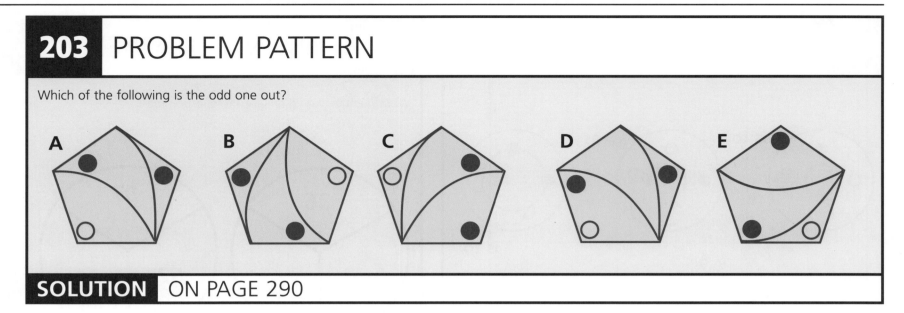

A B C D E

SOLUTION ON PAGE 290

204 MISSING WORD

Take three letters from the words either side of the brackets to create a new word. Just to make it interesting, however, if the first letter from the left word (T) is used then the first letter of the right one cannot. The missing word has no sound.

TENDON (• • • • • •) LILIES

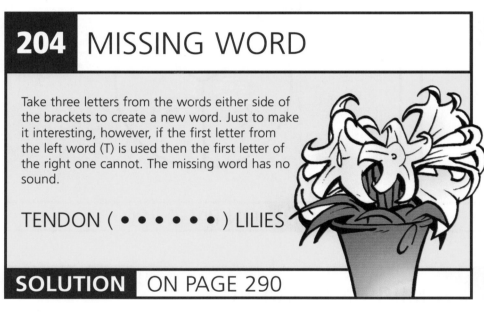

SOLUTION ON PAGE 290

205 IT ALL ADDS UP

Find the starting point and move from square to adjoining square, horizontally or vertically, but not diagonally, to spell a 12-letter word, using each letter once only. What are the missing letters?

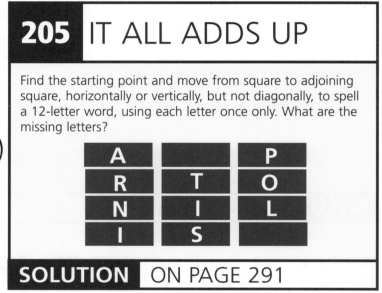

SOLUTION ON PAGE 291

206 SEQUENTIAL SQUARES

What number should replace the question mark?

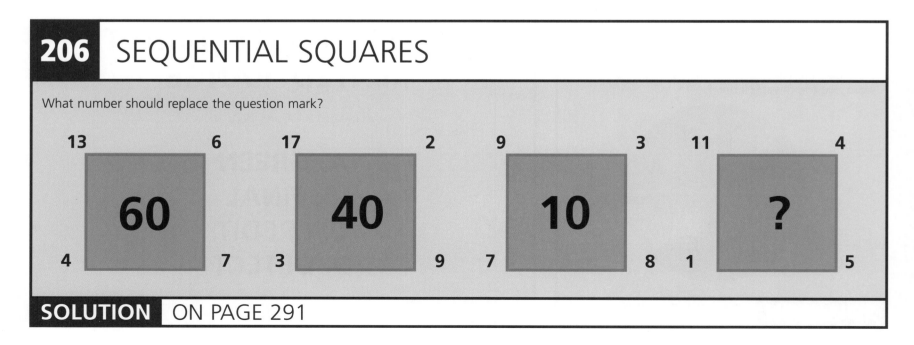

13	6	17	2	9	3	11	4
60		**40**		**10**		**?**	
4	7	3	9	7	8	1	5

SOLUTION ON PAGE 291

207 LOGICAL LETTERS

Which of the following is the odd one out?

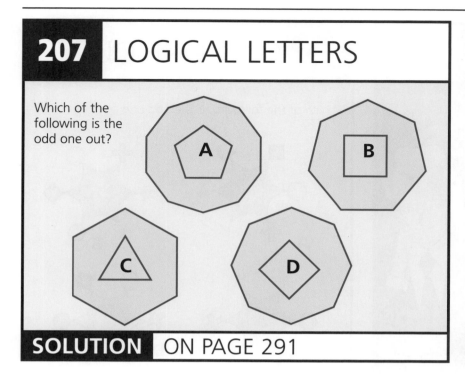

SOLUTION ON PAGE 291

208 NEXT PLEASE!

What comes next in this sequence?

L N Q U ?

SOLUTION ON PAGE 291

209 SHIELD SHUFFLE

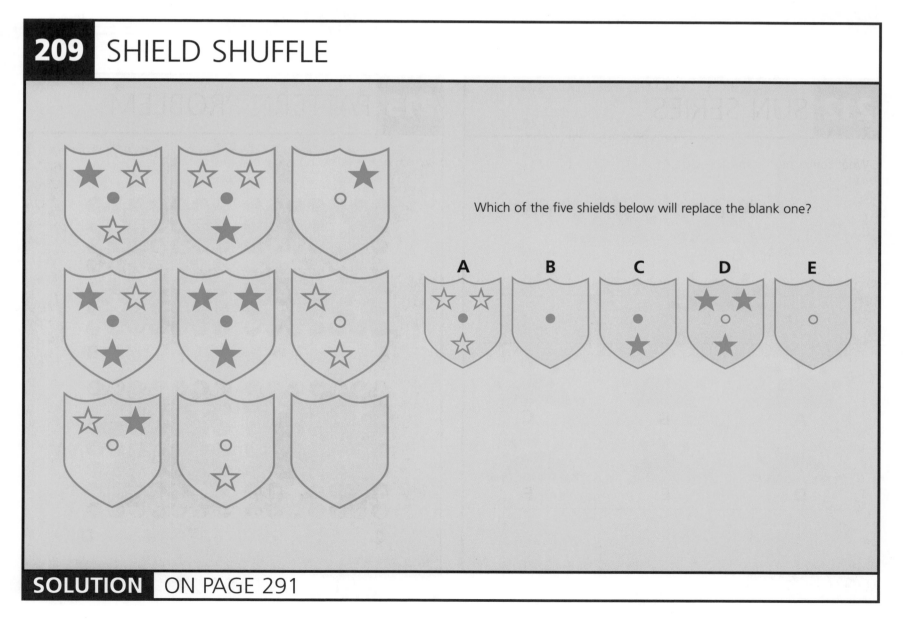

Which of the five shields below will replace the blank one?

A   B   C   D   E

SOLUTION ON PAGE 291

210 DIAMOND QUEST

Which one of these strings leads you to the diamond?

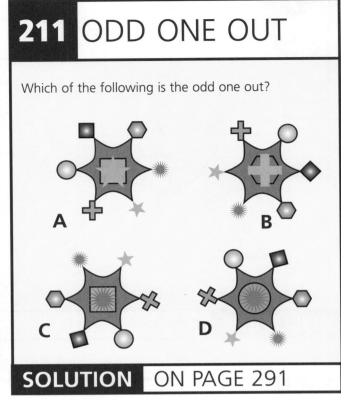

SOLUTION   ON PAGE 291

211 ODD ONE OUT

Which of the following is the odd one out?

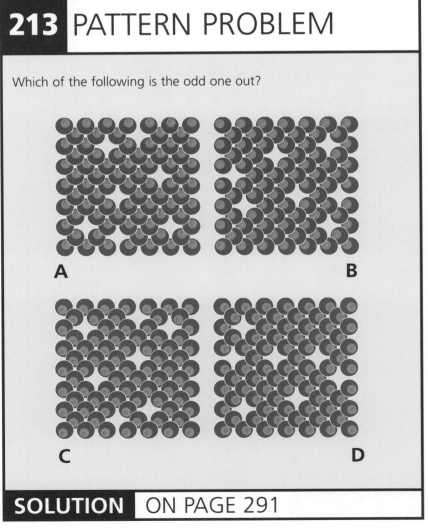

A

B

C

D

SOLUTION   ON PAGE 291

212 SUN SERIES

What comes next in the series?

?

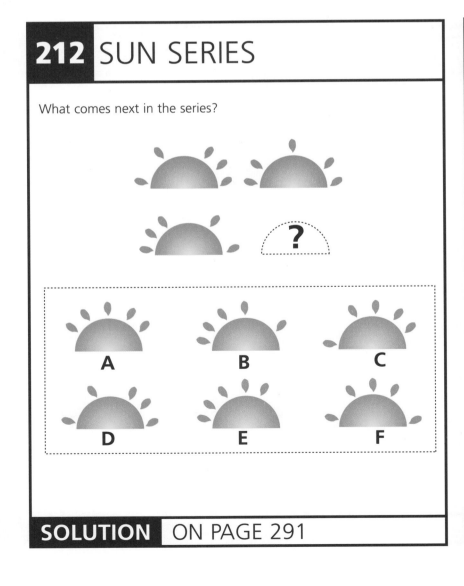

A

B

C

D

E

F

SOLUTION   ON PAGE 291

213 PATTERN PROBLEM

Which of the following is the odd one out?

A

B

C

D

SOLUTION   ON PAGE 291

214 ODD ONE OUT

Which set does not go with the other three?

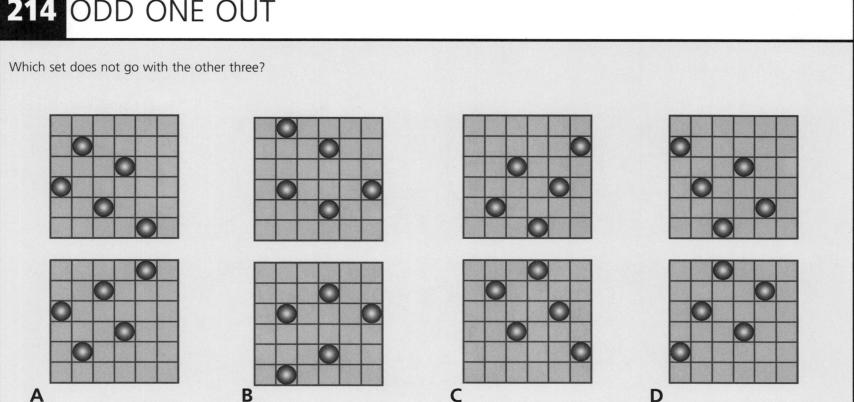

A   **B**   **C**   **D**

SOLUTION ON PAGE 291

215 MISSING PANEL

Which tile is missing from the following panel?

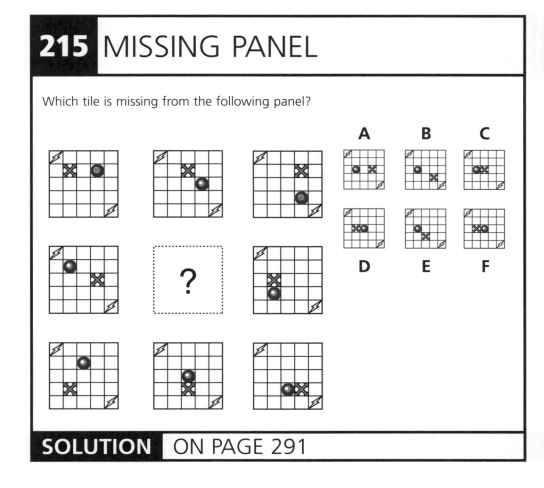

SOLUTION ON PAGE 291

216 SHARP THINKING

Which of the following is the odd one out?

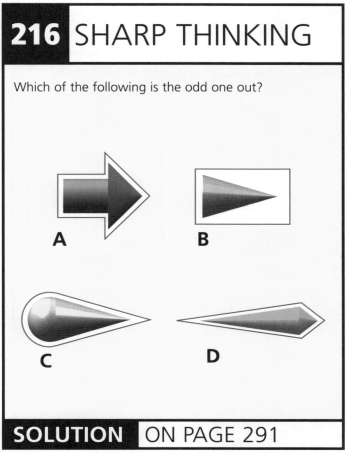

SOLUTION ON PAGE 291

217 PATTERN POSER

Which of the following is the odd one out?

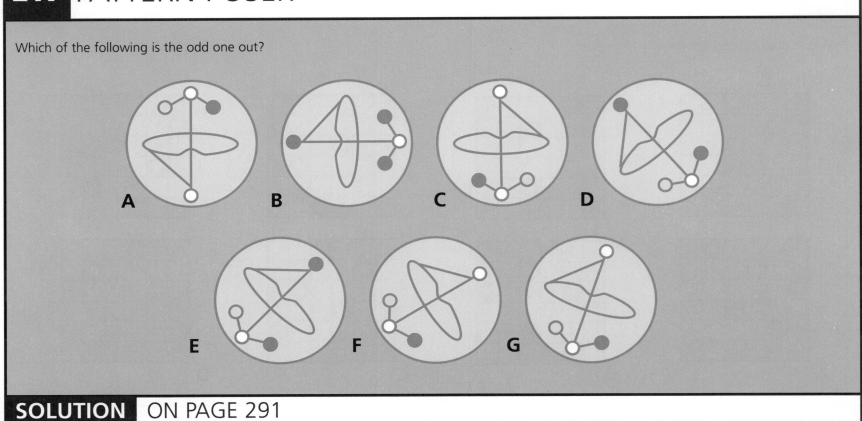

SOLUTION ON PAGE 291

218 LOST NUMBER

What number should replace the question mark?

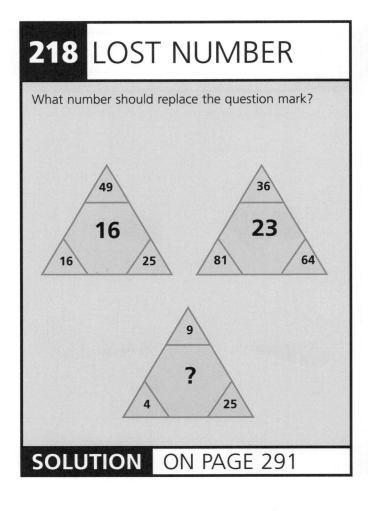

SOLUTION ON PAGE 291

219 WHAT COMES NEXT?

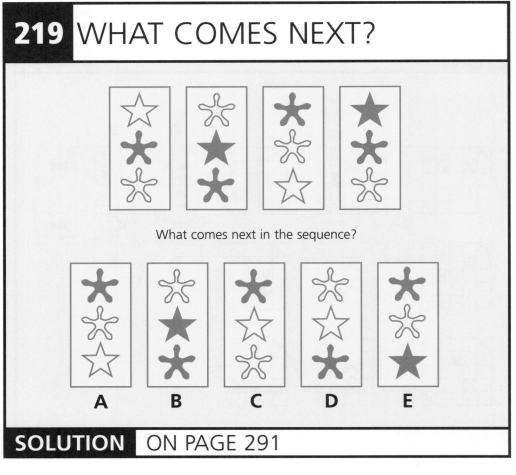

What comes next in the sequence?

SOLUTION ON PAGE 291

220 FOLDED FORMS

When the below is folded to form a cube, just one of the following can be produced. Which one is it?

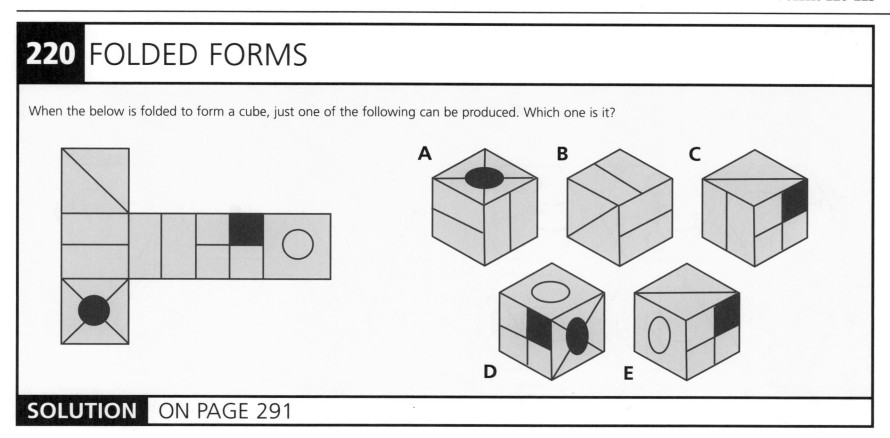

A B C

D E

SOLUTION ON PAGE 291

221 LOST NUMBER

What number should replace the question mark?

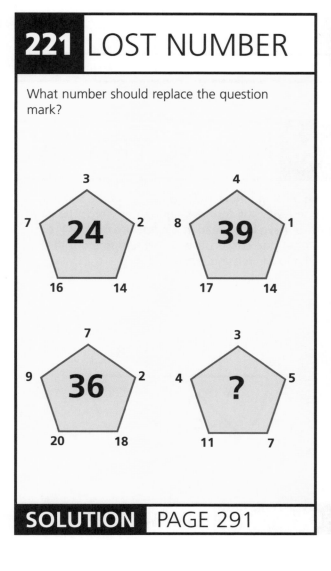

222 WORDS

If the missing letters in the circle below are correctly inserted they will form an eight-letter word. The word will not have to be read in a clockwise direction, but the letters are consecutive. Can you figure out the word and the missing letters?

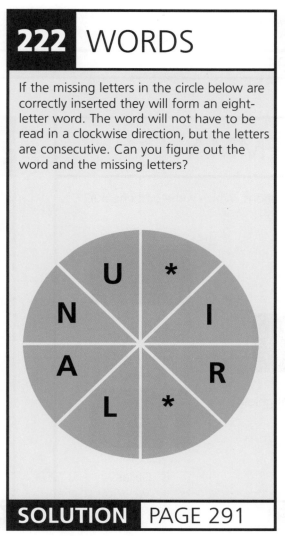

223 ODD ONE?

Which is the odd one out?

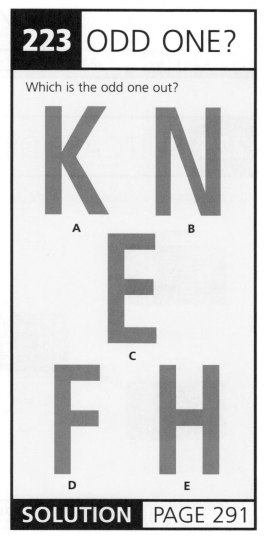

SOLUTION PAGE 291

224 PATTERN PUZZLE

Which of the hexagons on the right, A, B, C, D, or E, should replace the question mark below?

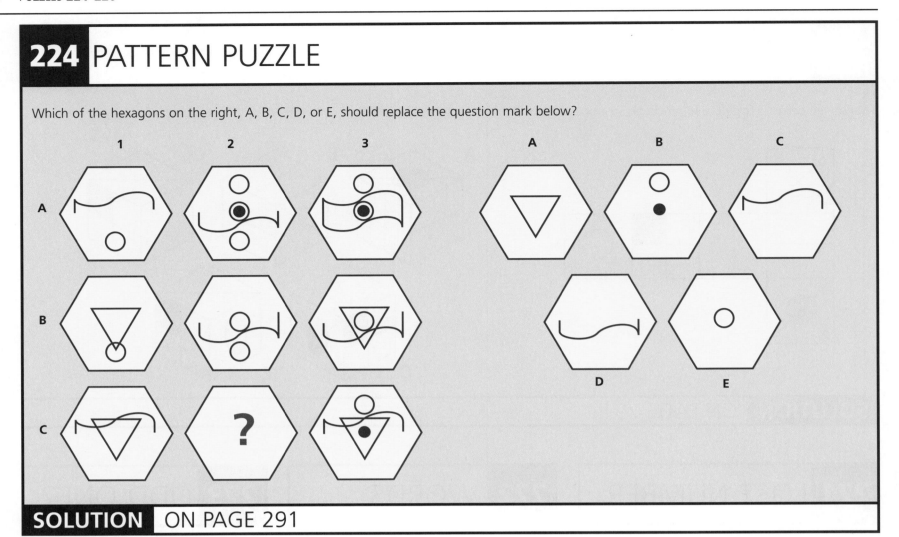

SOLUTION ON PAGE 291

225 SUITCASE DILEMMA

All the suitcases are shown with their destinations. Which is the odd one out?

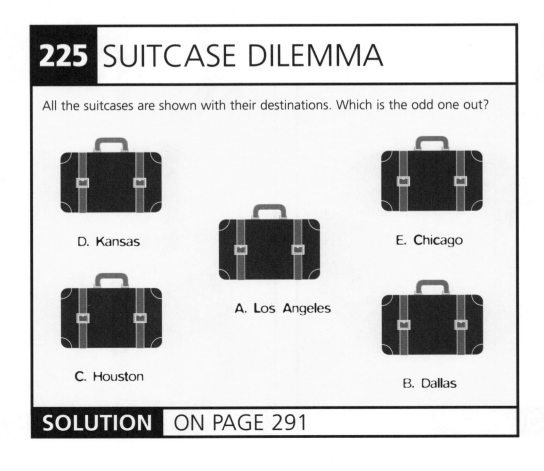

D. Kansas

A. Los Angeles

E. Chicago

C. Houston

B. Dallas

SOLUTION ON PAGE 291

226 MISSING LETTERS

If the missing letters in the circle below are correctly inserted they will form an eight-letter word. The word will not have to be read in a clockwise direction, but the letters are consecutive. Can you figure out the word and the missing letters?

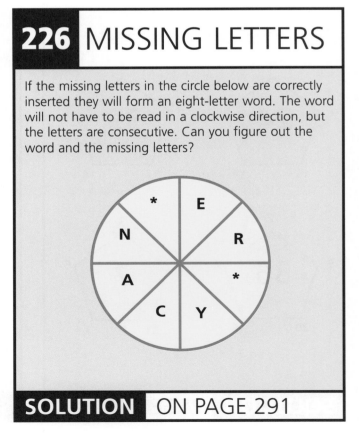

SOLUTION ON PAGE 291

227 BOX BOTHER

Which of the five boxes below is most like the box above?

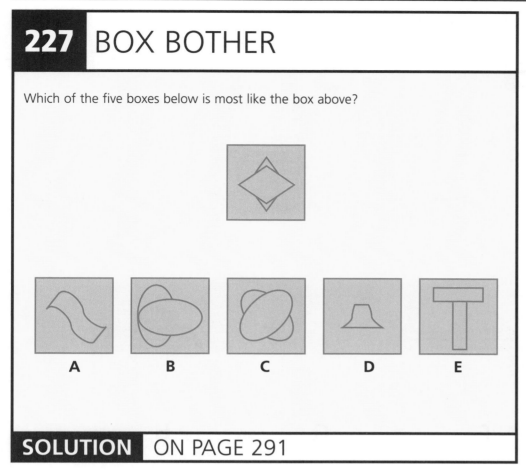

A   B   C   D   E

SOLUTION ON PAGE 291

228 MISSING LETTERS

If the missing letters in the two circles below are correctly inserted they will form synonymous words. The words do not have to be read in a clockwise direction, but the letters are consecutive. What are the words and missing letters?

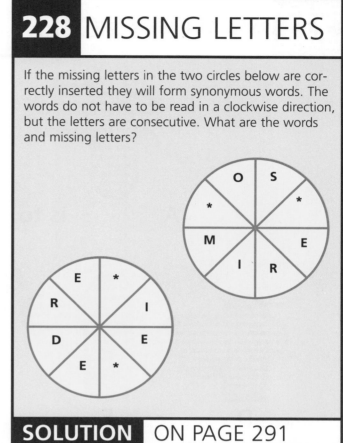

SOLUTION ON PAGE 291

229 LOST NUMBER

What number should replace the question mark?

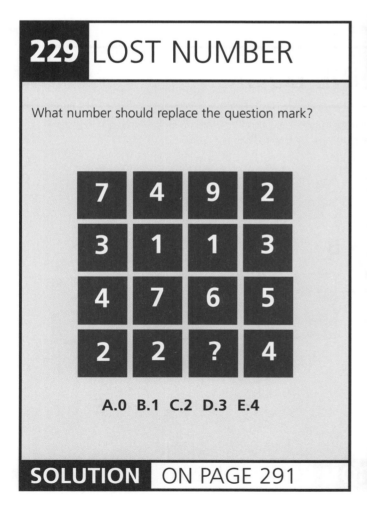

7	4	9	2
3	1	1	3
4	7	6	5
2	2	?	4

A.0   B.1   C.2   D.3   E.4

SOLUTION ON PAGE 291

230 CAKE CONUNDRUM

Someone has made a mistake decorating this cake. Can you correct the pattern?

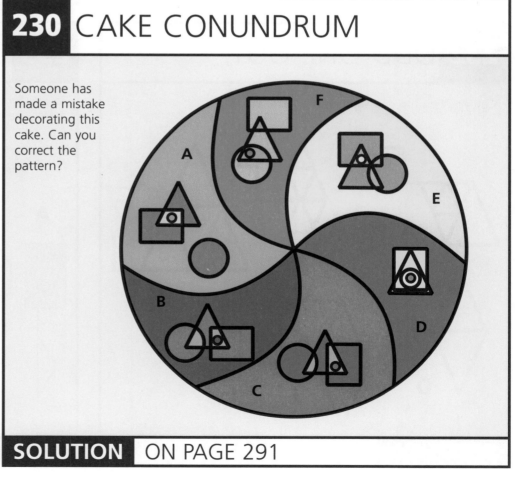

SOLUTION ON PAGE 291

231 ANALOGY POSER

A   is to   **B**   as   **C**   is to

D   **E**   **F**   **G**   **H**

SOLUTION   ON PAGE 291

232 ODD ONE OUT

Can you find the odd shape out?

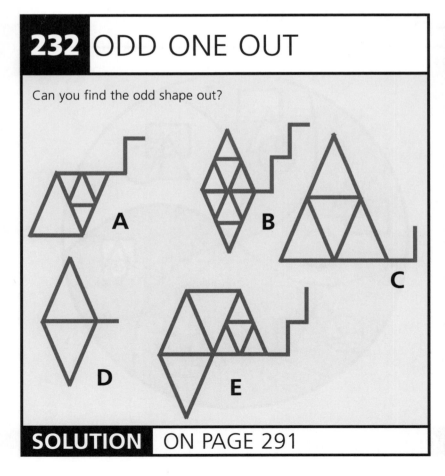

A   **B**   **C**   **D**   **E**

SOLUTION   ON PAGE 291

233 LINE LOGIC

To which of these diagrams could you add a single straight line to match the conditions of the topmost figure?

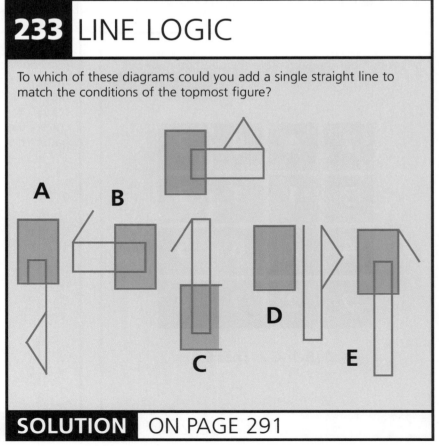

A   **B**   **C**   **D**   **E**

SOLUTION   ON PAGE 291

234 SIGNS MISSING

The four main mathematical signs have been left out of this equation.
Can you replace them?

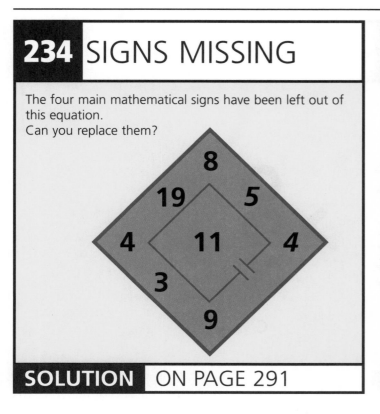

235 LETTER LOGIC

Can you unravel the logic behind this square and find the missing letter?

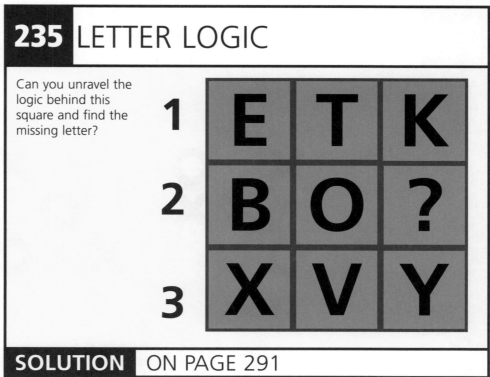

1	E	T	K
2	B	O	?
3	X	V	Y

236 ODD ONE OUT?

Which is the odd one out?

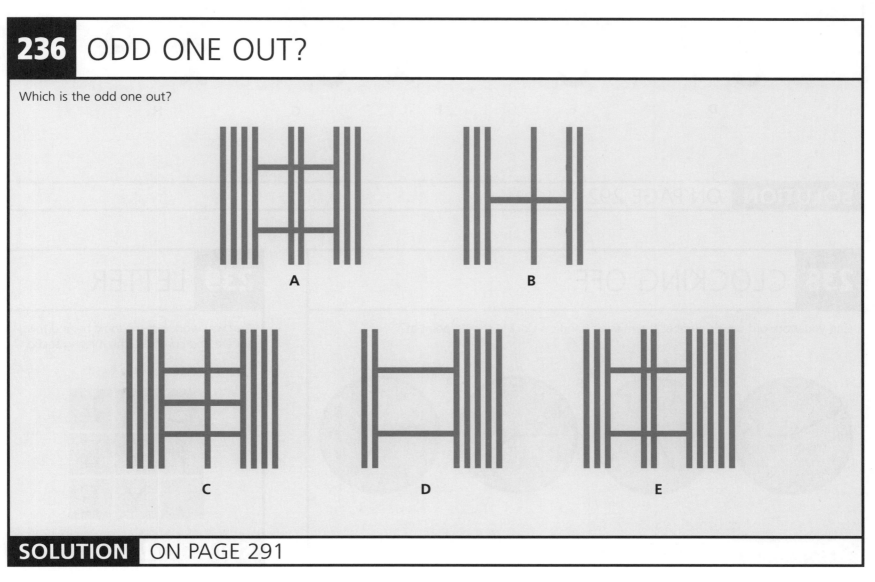

A

B

C

D

E

237 ANALOGY POSER

A is to B as C is to ?

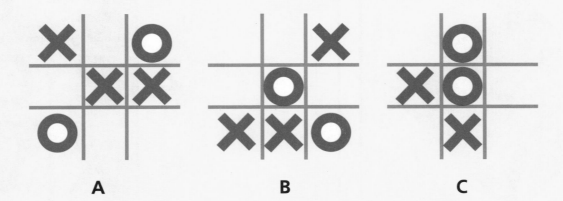

D   E   F   G   H

SOLUTION ON PAGE 292

238 CLOCKING OFF

Can you work out which number the missing hand on clock 4 should point at?

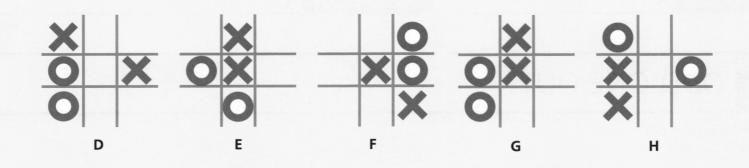

SOLUTION ON PAGE 292

239 LETTER

Can you work out the logic behind this square and complete the missing section?

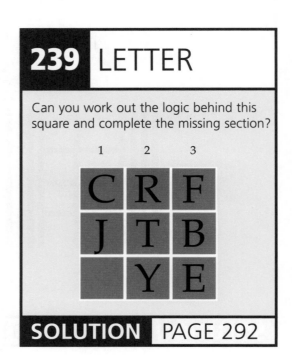

SOLUTION PAGE 292

240 DOTTY PUZZLE

Can you work out the logic behind this square and fill in the missing section?

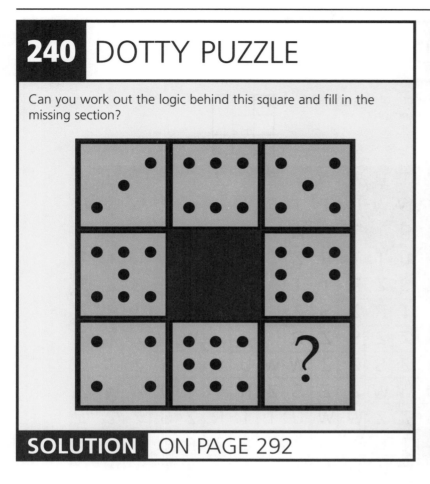

SOLUTION ON PAGE 292

241 NUMBER SQUARE

Can you work out the logic behind this square and find the missing number?

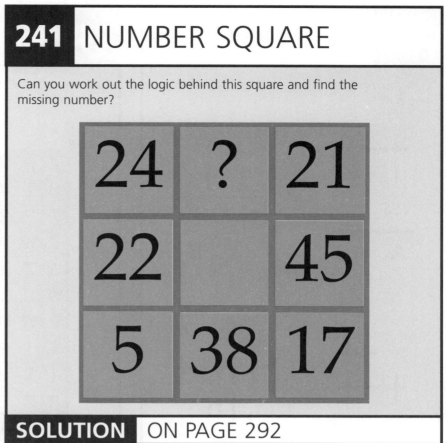

SOLUTION ON PAGE 292

242 STATE SEQUENCE

Pick up one letter from each bulb in numerical order. You should find the names of five US states and two dummy letters. What are they?

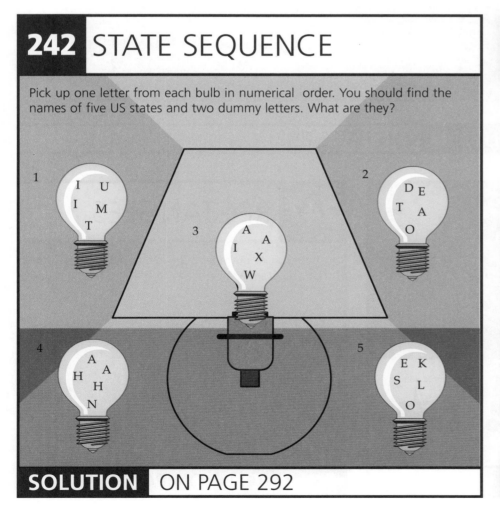

SOLUTION ON PAGE 292

243 CUBE FOLDING

Can you spot the cube that cannot be made from the layout above?

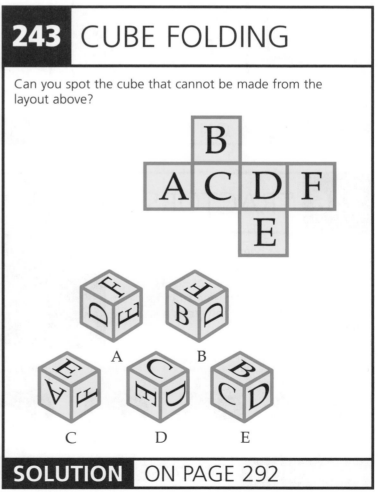

SOLUTION ON PAGE 292

244 LINE LOGIC

Can you work out which diagram is the odd one out?

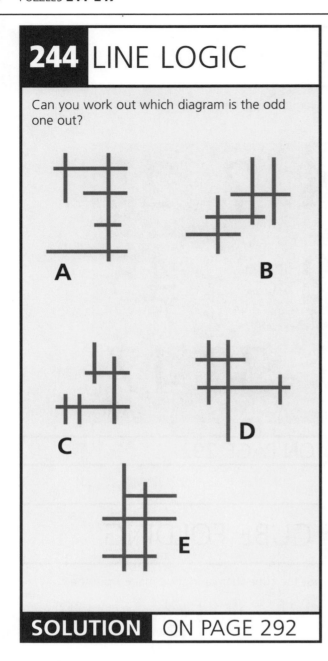

A

B

C

D

E

SOLUTION ON PAGE 292

245 GRID GRIPE

Can you spot the pattern of this grid and complete the missing section?

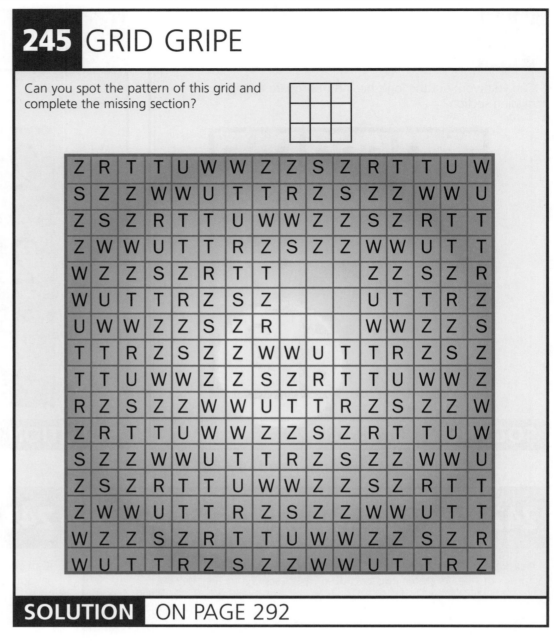

Z	R	T	T	U	W	W	Z	Z	S	Z	R	T	T	U	W
S	Z	Z	W	W	U	T	T	R	Z	S	Z	Z	W	W	U
Z	S	Z	R	T	T	U	W	W	Z	Z	S	Z	R	T	T
Z	W	W	U	T	T	R	Z	S	Z	Z	W	W	U	T	T
W	Z	Z	S	Z	R	T	T			Z	Z	S	Z	R
W	U	T	T	R	Z	S	Z			U	T	T	R	Z
U	W	W	Z	Z	S	Z	R			W	W	Z	Z	S
T	T	R	Z	S	Z	Z	W	W	U	T	T	R	Z	S	Z
T	T	U	W	W	Z	Z	S	Z	R	T	T	U	W	W	Z
R	Z	S	Z	Z	W	U	T	T	R	Z	S	Z	Z	W
Z	R	T	T	U	W	W	Z	Z	S	Z	R	T	T	U	W
S	Z	Z	W	W	U	T	T	R	Z	S	Z	Z	W	W	U
Z	S	Z	R	T	T	U	W	W	Z	Z	S	Z	R	T	T
Z	W	W	U	T	T	R	Z	S	Z	Z	W	W	U	T	T
W	Z	Z	S	Z	R	T	T	U	W	W	Z	Z	S	Z	R
W	U	T	T	R	Z	S	Z	Z	W	W	U	T	T	R	Z

SOLUTION ON PAGE 292

246 TRACTORS

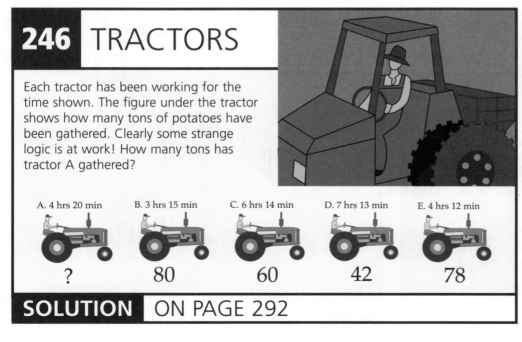

Each tractor has been working for the time shown. The figure under the tractor shows how many tons of potatoes have been gathered. Clearly some strange logic is at work! How many tons has tractor A gathered?

A. 4 hrs 20 min — ?

B. 3 hrs 15 min — 80

C. 6 hrs 14 min — 60

D. 7 hrs 13 min — 42

E. 4 hrs 12 min — 78

SOLUTION ON PAGE 292

247 RECTANGLES

Can you work out how many rectangles can be found in this diagram altogether?

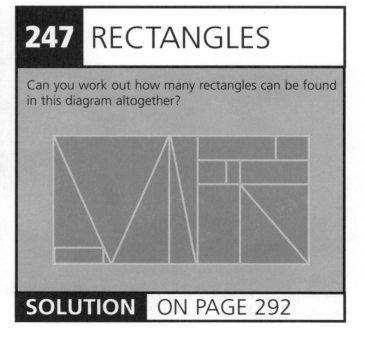

SOLUTION ON PAGE 292

248 ODD PROBLEM

Which is the odd one out?

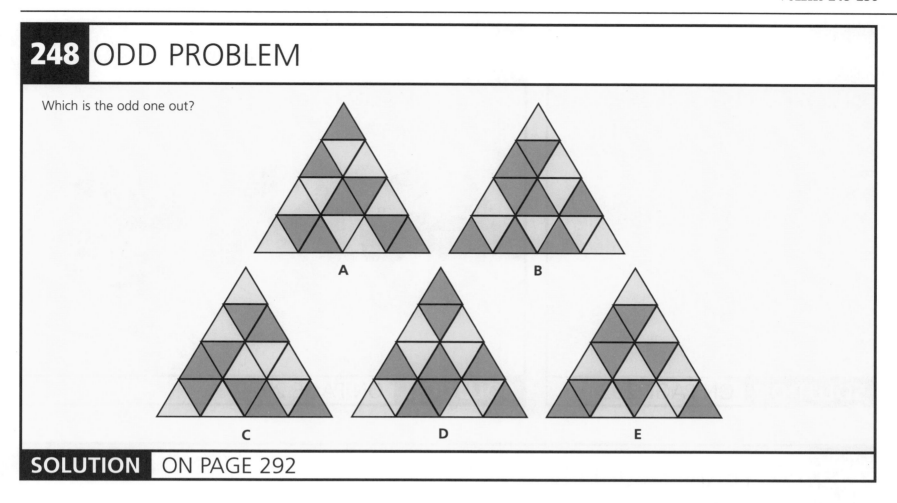

A

B

C

D

E

SOLUTION ON PAGE 292

249 CAR CONUNDRUM

These cars are all racing at famous circuits. Can you work out the number of the car at Indianapolis?

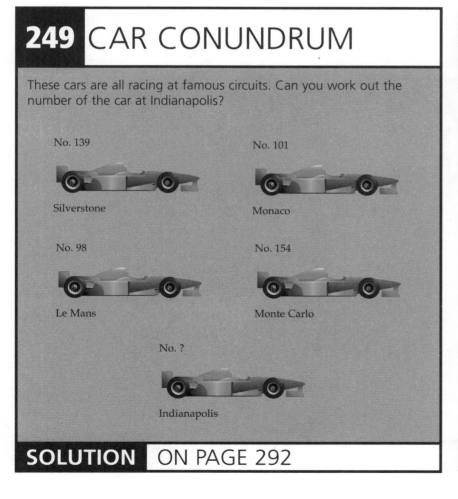

No. 139

Silverstone

No. 101

Monaco

No. 98

Le Mans

No. 154

Monte Carlo

No. ?

Indianapolis

SOLUTION ON PAGE 292

250 BALLOON BLAST

Each balloon has been sponsored by a famous newspaper. The number is somehow linked to the paper's name. What is the number of The Independent's balloon?

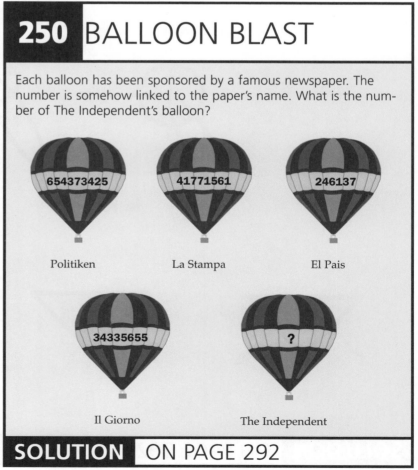

654373425

Politiken

41771561

La Stampa

246137

El Pais

34335655

Il Giorno

?

The Independent

SOLUTION ON PAGE 292

251 ODD ONE OUT?

Can you work out which symbol is the odd one out?

252 NUMBER WHEELS

Can you replace the question mark with a number?

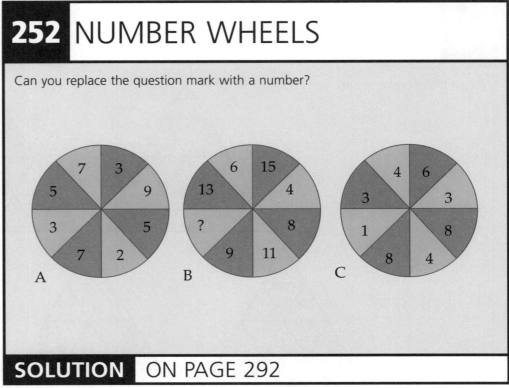

SOLUTION   ON PAGE 292

SOLUTION   ON PAGE 292

253 PATTERN PROBLEM

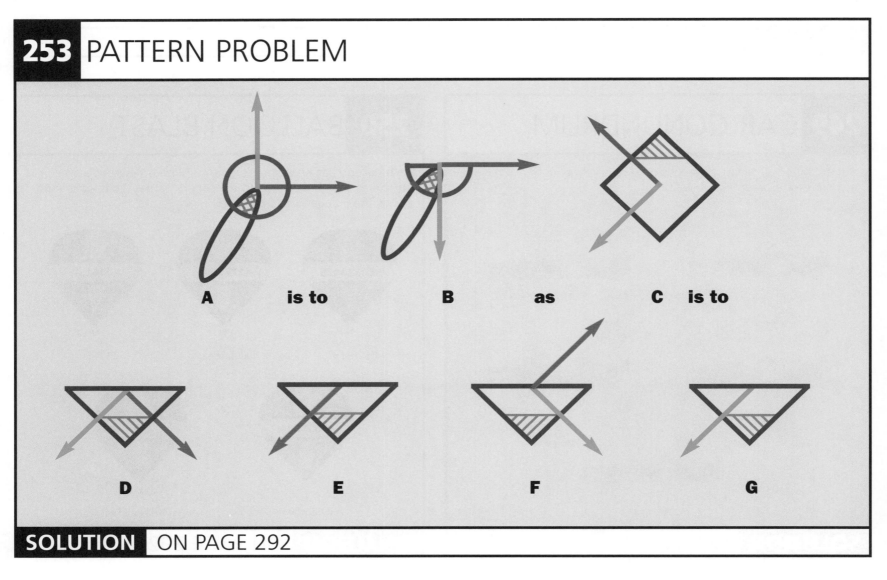

A   **is to**   **B**   **as**   **C**   **is to**

D   **E**   **F**   **G**

SOLUTION   ON PAGE 292

254 CUBE CHALLENGE

Which of these layouts could be used to make the cube below?

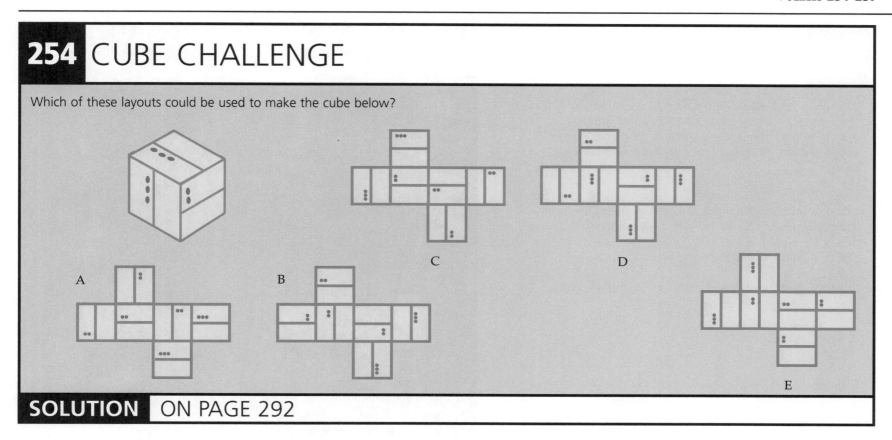

A   B   C   D   E

SOLUTION ON PAGE 292

255 CARD PUZZLE

If you know that the answer forms a well-known sequence, can you work out how much each shape is worth?

SOLUTION ON PAGE 292

256 WHEEL LETTERS

Can you replace the question mark with a letter?

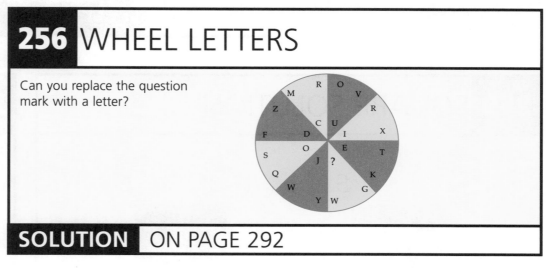

SOLUTION ON PAGE 292

257 COLOUR CHALLENGE

Find a number that could replace the question mark. Each colour represents a number under 10.

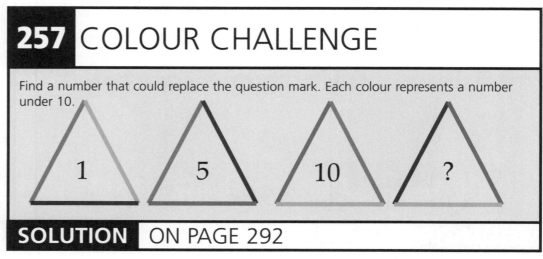

SOLUTION ON PAGE 292

258 NEW YEAR

It is August and a 26-year-old woman said that she had never missed a New Year celebration in her life. She also claimed to have seen "The New Year" in 51 times. How could she be telling the truth if she was born in June?

1. She only counted January the First as a New Year and other religious or cultural New Years were not counted.

2. She did not cheat by winding her clock back.

3. Her 26 years were using a modern calendar and she lived in modern times on the planet Earth.

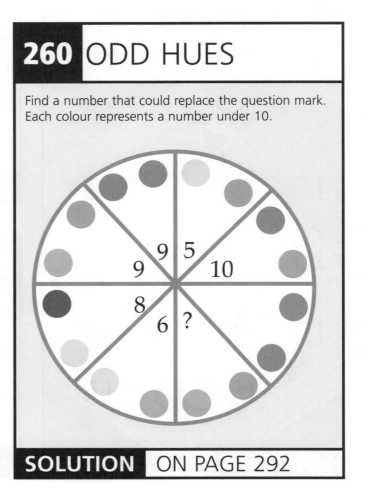

SOLUTION ON PAGE 292

259 SQUARE SOLUTION

Find the missing letter..

D	S	H	D
O	L	H	O
E	U	Q	?
Q	Z	O	D

SOLUTION ON PAGE 292

260 ODD HUES

Find a number that could replace the question mark. Each colour represents a number under 10.

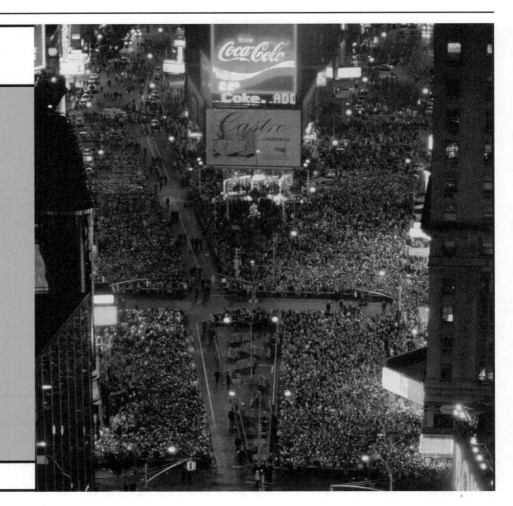

SOLUTION ON PAGE 292

261 TRIANGLE TROUBLE

Find a number that could replace the question mark. Each colour represents a number under 10.

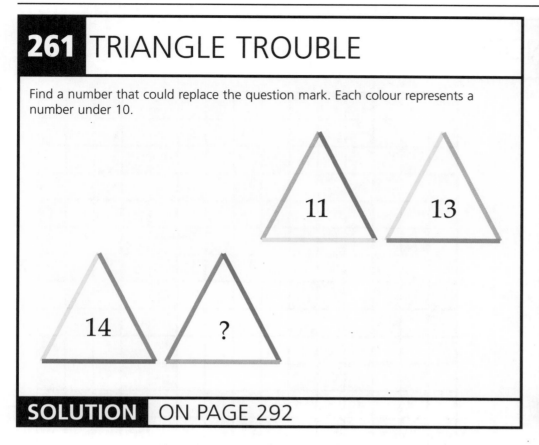

SOLUTION ON PAGE 292

262 SYMBOL PUZZLE

Can you work out which number should replace the question mark in this diagram?

SOLUTION ON PAGE 292

263 SQUARE SEQUENCE

What is the largest square you can make from the pieces given? You will not need all the pieces.

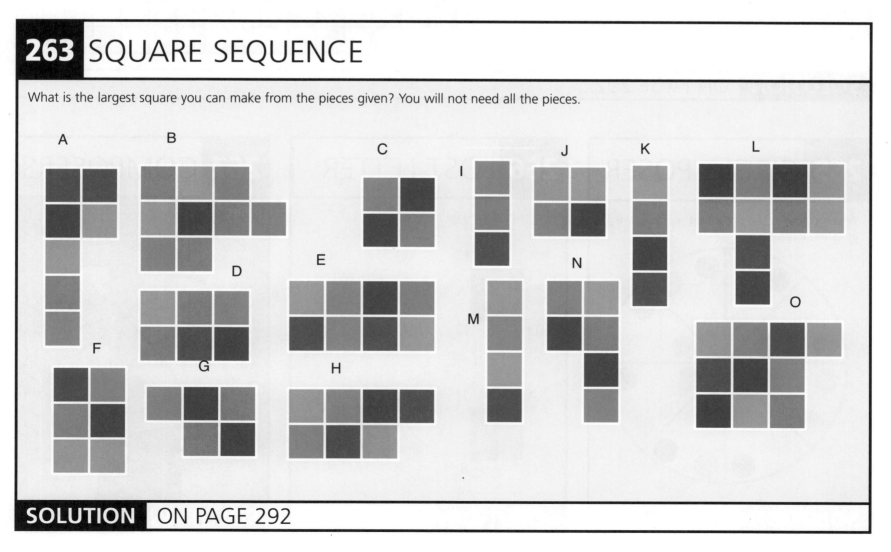

SOLUTION ON PAGE 292

264 COLOURED CONUNDRUM

This square is drawn according to a certain logic. If you can work out what the system is you should be able to fill in the missing area.

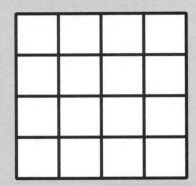

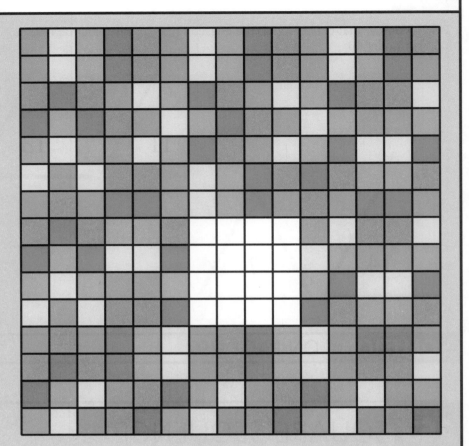

SOLUTION   ON PAGE 292

265 CIRCLE POSER

Which colour is the circle that replaces the question mark?

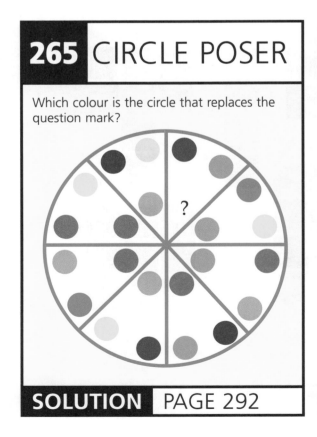

SOLUTION   PAGE 292

266 LOST LETTER

Find the missing letter.

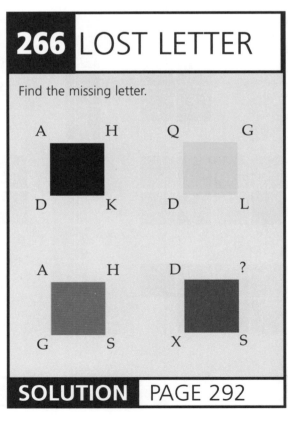

SOLUTION   PAGE 292

267 COMPOSERS

Pick one letter from each cloud in order. You should be able to make the names of five composers.

SOLUTION   PAGE 292

268 FANCY FISH

Can you work out what the next fish in this sequence should look like?

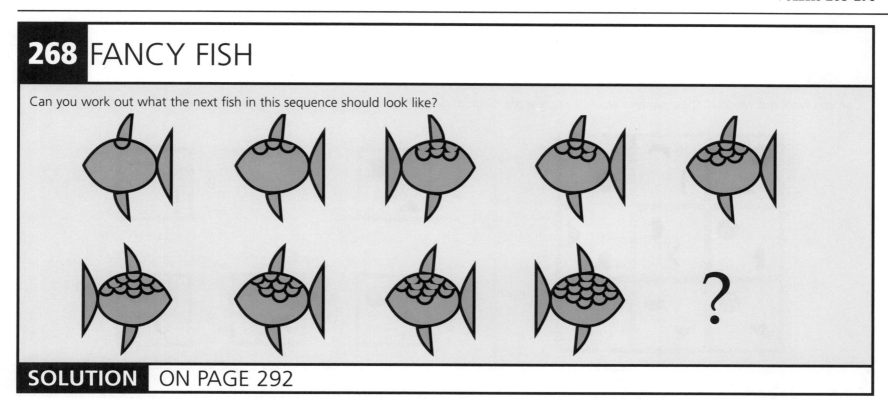

SOLUTION   ON PAGE 292

269 SUITCASE PUZZLE

The weight of each suitcase is shown. Which is the odd one out?

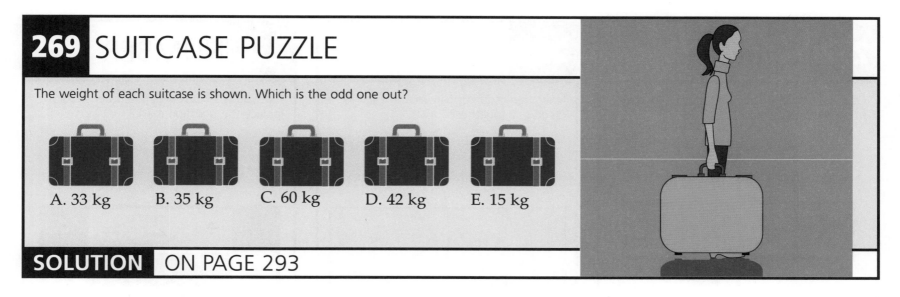

A. 33 kg   B. 35 kg   C. 60 kg   D. 42 kg   E. 15 kg

SOLUTION   ON PAGE 293

270 SEQUENCE POSER

Can you find the column that comes next in the sequence?

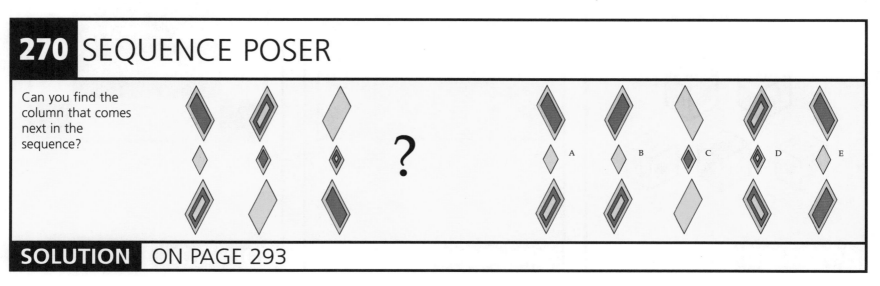

SOLUTION   ON PAGE 293

271 SQUARE COMPLETION

Can you work out which of these squares would complete the diagram below?

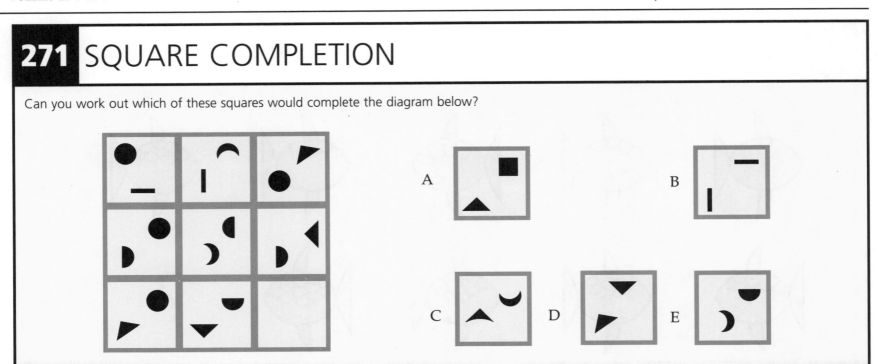

SOLUTION ON PAGE 293

272 CUBED

Can you spot the cube that cannot be made from the layout below?

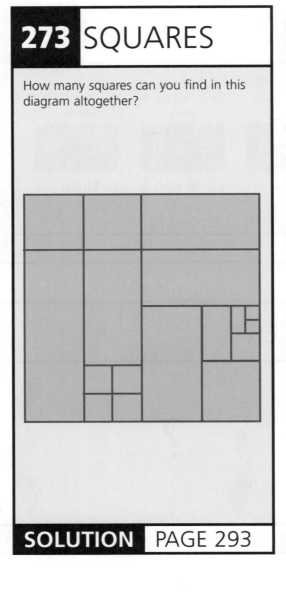

SOLUTION PAGE 293

273 SQUARES

How many squares can you find in this diagram altogether?

SOLUTION PAGE 293

274 NUMBER

Can you work out which number should replace the question mark?

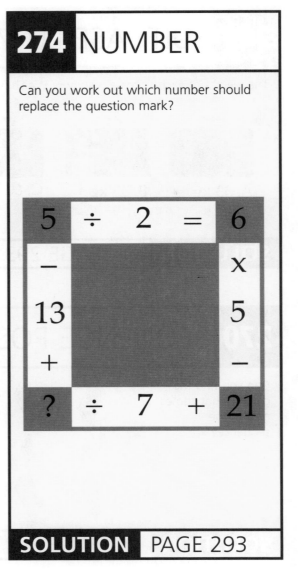

SOLUTION PAGE 293

275 BROKEN SHAPES

Can you work out which of these shapes would fit together with the shape above?

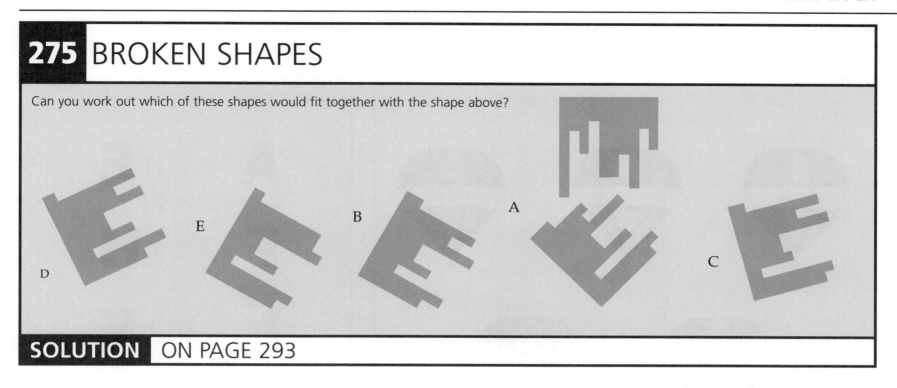

SOLUTION ON PAGE 293

276 SQUARE SEQUENCE

Can you work out the reasoning behind these squares and replace the question mark with a number?

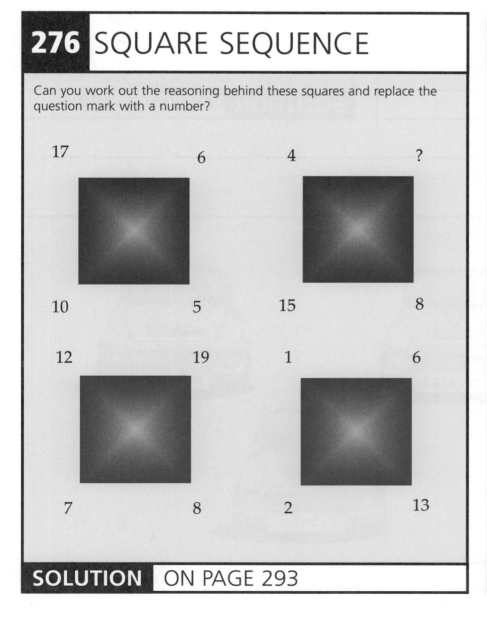

SOLUTION ON PAGE 293

277 NUMBER PROBLEM

Can you find the number that should replace the question mark?

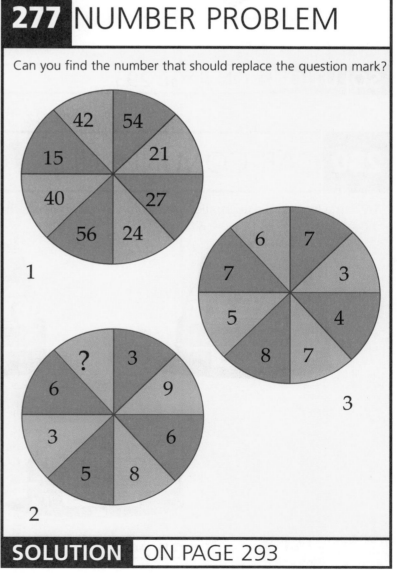

SOLUTION ON PAGE 293

278 BALLOON SPEEDS

The diagram gives the speed, number and distance covered for each balloon. Can you work out the distance for A?

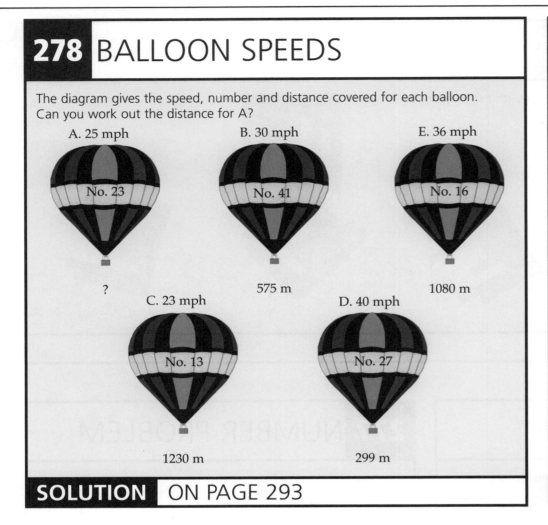

A. 25 mph
No. 23
?

B. 30 mph
No. 41
575 m

E. 36 mph
No. 16
1080 m

C. 23 mph
No. 13
1230 m

D. 40 mph
No. 27
299 m

SOLUTION ON PAGE 293

279 LETTER LOGIC

Can you find the letter that comes next in this series?

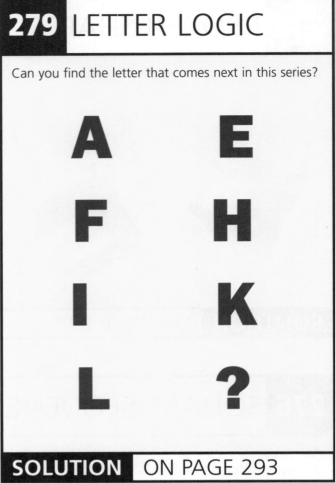

A   E

F   H

I   K

L   ?

SOLUTION ON PAGE 293

280 CAR CONUNDRUM

There is a logic to the registration plates of these cars. What is the plate on the last car?

LQN 1916

HMJ 1512

BGD 9611

GLI 1411

J ?

SOLUTION ON PAGE 293

281 NUMBER SQUARES

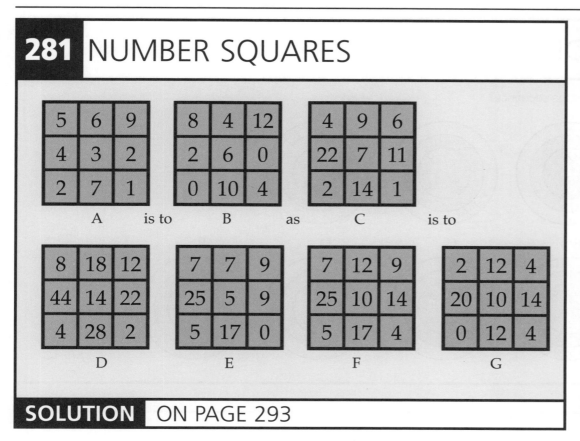

5	6	9
4	3	2
2	7	1

A

is to

8	4	12
2	6	0
0	10	4

B

as

4	9	6
22	7	11
2	14	1

C

is to

8	18	12
44	14	22
4	28	2

D

7	7	9
25	5	9
5	17	0

E

7	12	9
25	10	14
5	17	4

F

2	12	4
20	10	14
0	12	4

G

SOLUTION ON PAGE 293

282 WHEELS

Can you work out the reasoning behind this square and replace the question mark with the correct shape?

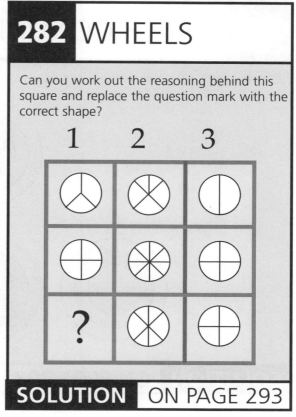

SOLUTION ON PAGE 293

283 FEEDING FRENZY

Take one letter from each bulb in order. You should be able to make five five-letter words related to food.

SOLUTION ON PAGE 293

284 DANCE BAND

Can you work out which of these musical terms is the odd one out?

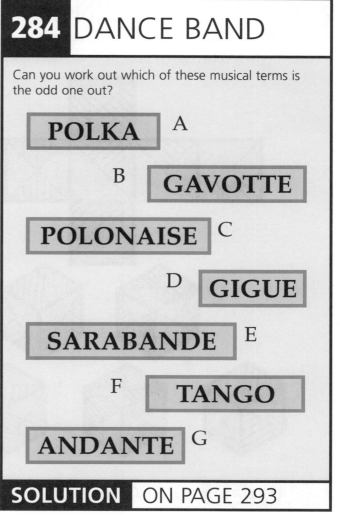

POLKA A

B **GAVOTTE**

POLONAISE C

D **GIGUE**

SARABANDE E

F **TANGO**

ANDANTE G

SOLUTION ON PAGE 293

285 CIRCLE CONUNDRUM

Can you work out which of these symbols follows the sequence?

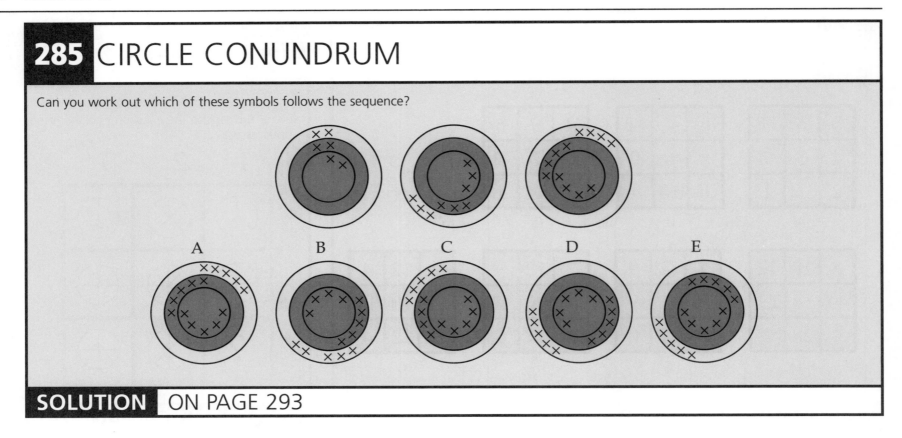

A   B   C   D   E

SOLUTION   ON PAGE 293

286 CUBE FOLDING

Which of these cubes can be made from the layout below?

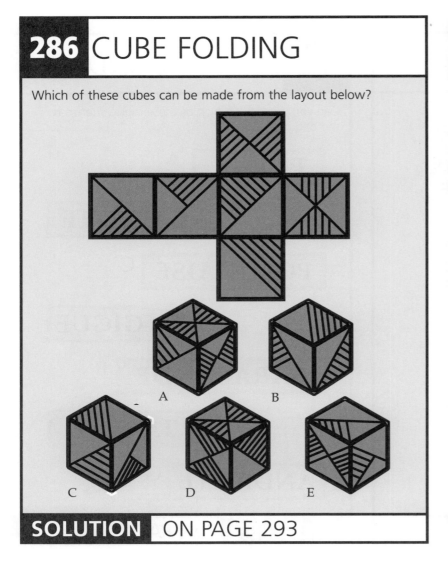

A   B

C   D   E

SOLUTION   ON PAGE 293

287 ANALOGY PUZZLE

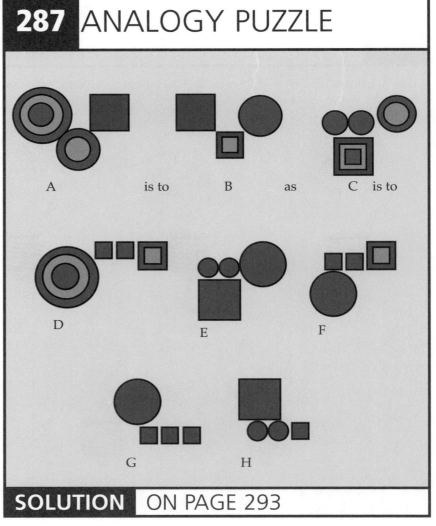

A   is to   B   as   C   is to

D   E   F

G   H

SOLUTION   ON PAGE 293

288 NUMBER NIGHTMARE

Can you work out the reasoning behind this grid and complete the missing section?

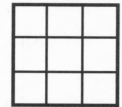

2	2	3	1	1	7	1	4	5	5	2	2	3	1	1	7
5	3	1	1	7	1	4	5	5	2	2	3	1	1	7	1
5	2	3	1	1	7	1	4	5	5	2	2	3	1	1	4
4	2	2	2	2	3	1	1	7	1	4	5	5	2	7	5
1	5	2	5	1	4	5	5	2	2	3	1	1	2	1	5
7	5	5	5	7	2	2	3	1	1	7	1	7	3	4	2
1	4	5	4	1	5	3	1	1	7	1	4	1	1	5	2
1	1	4	1	1	5	2	3	1	1	4	5	4	1	5	3
3	7	1	7	3	4	2	2	2	7	5	5	5	7	2	1
2	1	7	1	2	1	5	5	4	1	5	2	5	1	2	1
2	1	1	1	2	7	1	1	3	2	2	2	2	4	3	7
5	3	1	3	5	5	4	1	7	1	1	3	2	5	1	1
5	2	3	2	2	5	5	4	1	7	1	1	3	5	1	4
			2	5	5	4	1	7	1	1	3	2	7	5	
			4	1	7	1	1	3	2	2	5	5	4	1	5
			3	2	2	5	5	4	1	7	1	1	3	2	2

SOLUTION ON PAGE 293

290 BERMUDA TRIANGLES

Can you work out which letter should replace the question mark?

F
Y
O   T

A

I
X
V   Q

B

D
W
I   Z

C

N
?
U   Y

D

SOLUTION ON PAGE 293

289 WHEEL NUMBERS

Can you work out the reasoning behind this wheel and replace the question mark with a number?

5 3
6   5
8   4
40   15
7   56   42   6
3   27   54   9
24   **?**
3   9
6   7
8   7

SOLUTION ON PAGE 293

291 ORANGE POSER

Can you work out what the missing section in the last wheel should look like?

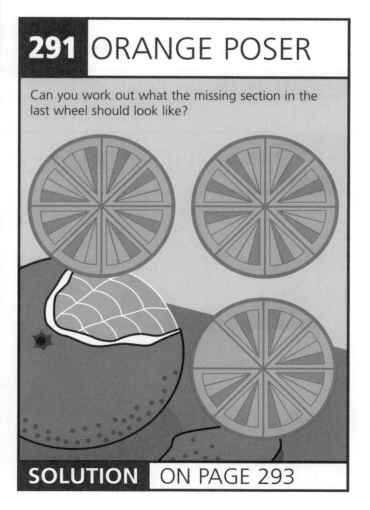

SOLUTION ON PAGE 293

292 ODD ONE OUT

Which is the odd one out?

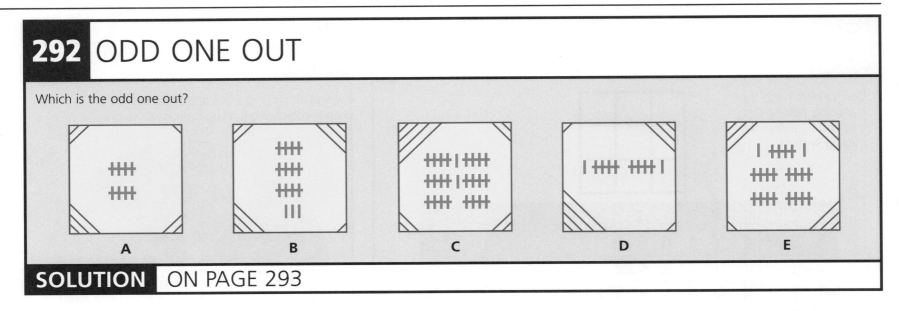

A   B   C   D   E

SOLUTION   ON PAGE 293

293 ANALOGY POSER

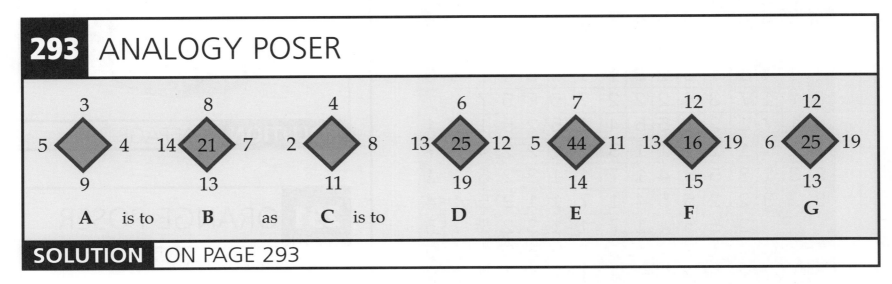

A   is to   B   as   C   is to   D   E   F   G

SOLUTION   ON PAGE 293

294 BERMUDA TRIANGLES

Can you find the letter that should replace the question mark?

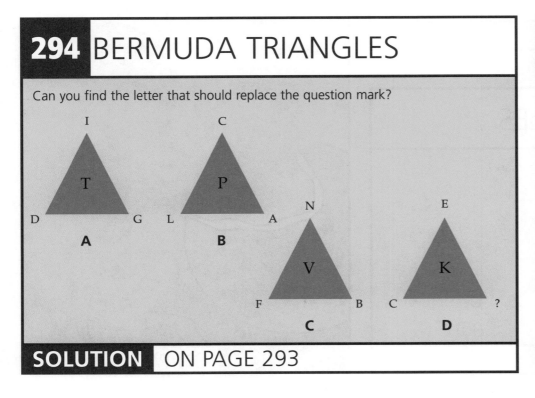

SOLUTION   ON PAGE 293

295 LETTER LOGIC

Can you find the letter which completes this diagram?

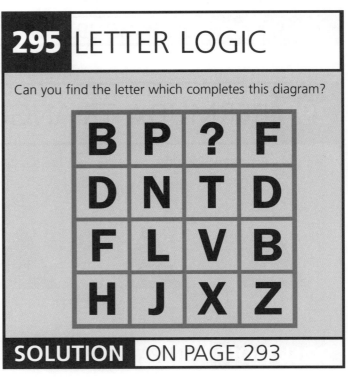

SOLUTION   ON PAGE 293

296 FOLDING FEVER

Can you work out which of these cubes cannot be made from the layout below?

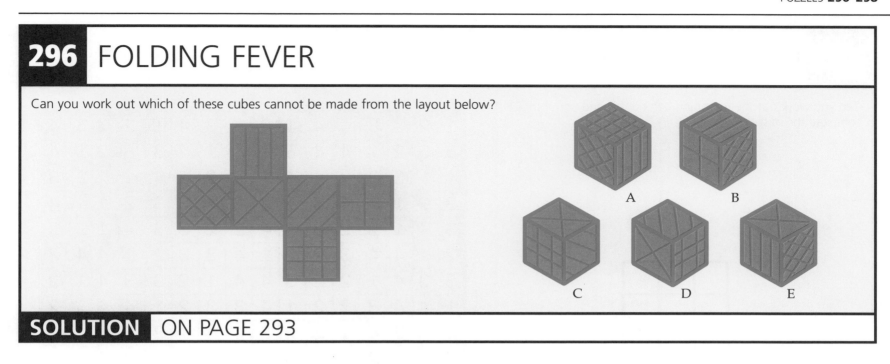

SOLUTION ON PAGE 293

297 SHAPE SERIES

Can you find the shape that would continue the series above?

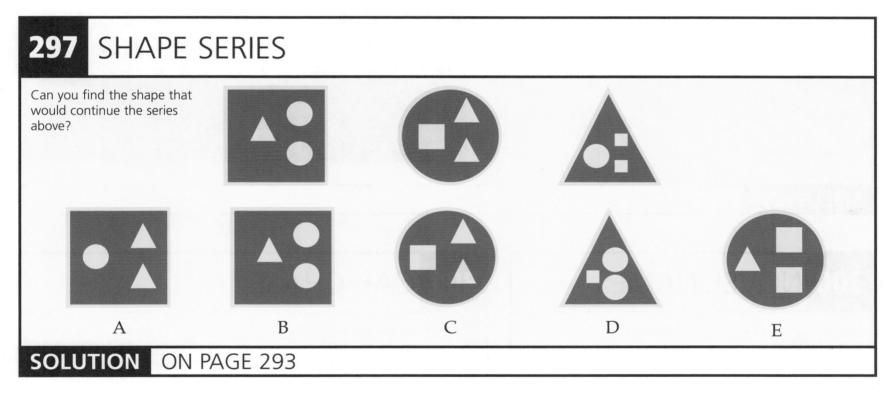

SOLUTION ON PAGE 293

298 HORSE RACE

Each horse carries a weight handicap. Can you work out the number of the final horse?

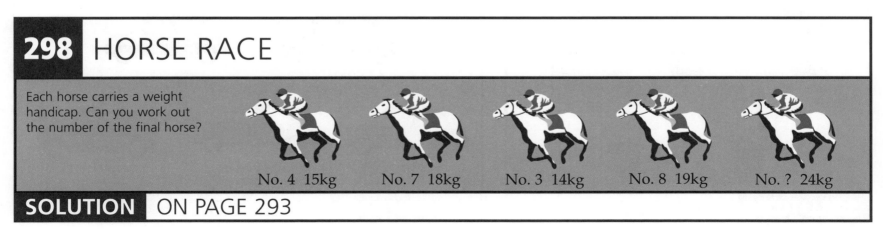

No. 4 15kg   No. 7 18kg   No. 3 14kg   No. 8 19kg   No. ? 24kg

SOLUTION ON PAGE 293

299 NUMBER NIGHTMARE

Can you work out the reasoning behind this grid and complete the missing section?

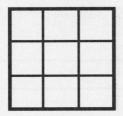

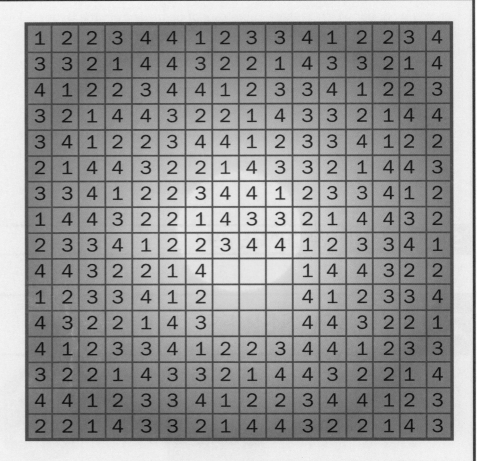

SOLUTION ON PAGE 293

300 NOVEL NAMES

Pick a letter from each bulb in turn and make the names of five novelists.

SOLUTION ON PAGE 293

301 CAR CHASE

All these cars started from the same place and drove to the cities indicated. The mileages shown on the trip meter seem to make no sense, but the logic comes from the names of the destinations. Can you work out what it is, and the mileage of the last car?

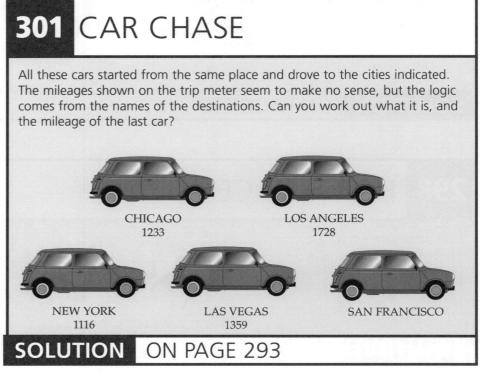

CHICAGO
1233

LOS ANGELES
1728

NEW YORK
1116

LAS VEGAS
1359

SAN FRANCISCO

SOLUTION ON PAGE 293

302 SCIENCE QUEST

Take one letter from each cloud in order.
You should be able to make the names of five scientists.

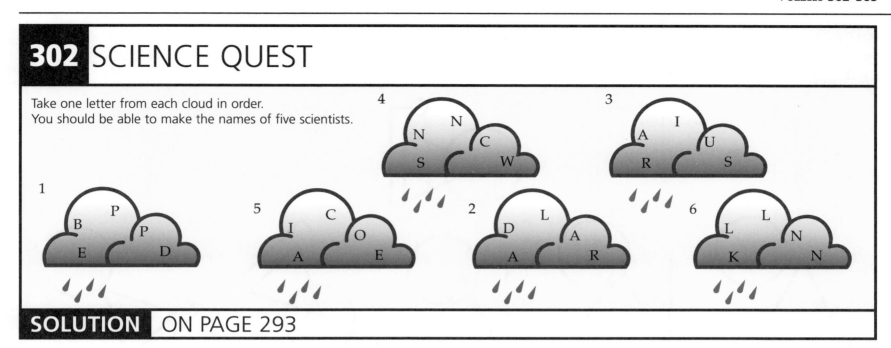

SOLUTION ON PAGE 293

303 SQUARE NUMBERS

Can you work out the reasoning behind these squares and find the missing number?

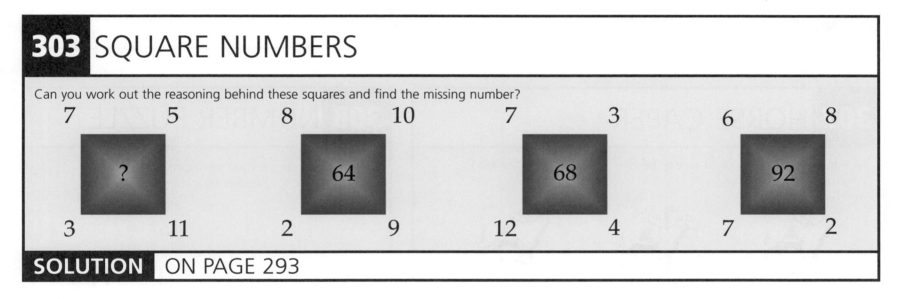

7		5	8		10	7		3	6		8
	?			64			68			92	
3		11	2		9	12		4	7		2

SOLUTION ON PAGE 293

304 CYCLE RACE

All these bikes took part in an overnight race. Something really weird happened! The start and finish times of the bike became mathematically linked. If you can discover the link you should be able to decide when bike D finished.

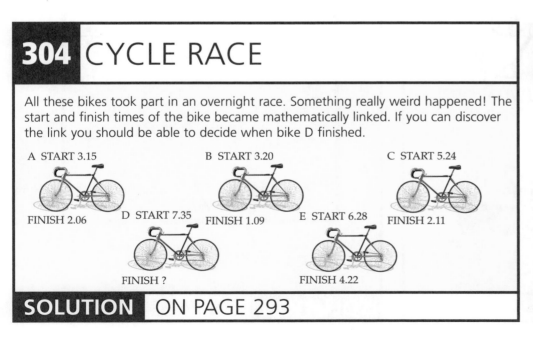

A START 3.15
FINISH 2.06

B START 3.20
FINISH 1.09

C START 5.24
FINISH 2.11

D START 7.35
FINISH ?

E START 6.28
FINISH 4.22

SOLUTION ON PAGE 293

305 MISSING LETTER

Can you work out which letter should replace the question mark in this square?

J	G	D	A
F	I	Z	?
A	L	U	F
U	P	O	J

SOLUTION ON PAGE 294

306 SHAPE SHIFTER

To which of the diagrams A–E could you add a circle to match the conditions of the figure below?

A   B   C   D   E

SOLUTION ON PAGE 294

307 HORSE CAPER

All these horses are about to race at famous courses around the world. Which is the odd one out?

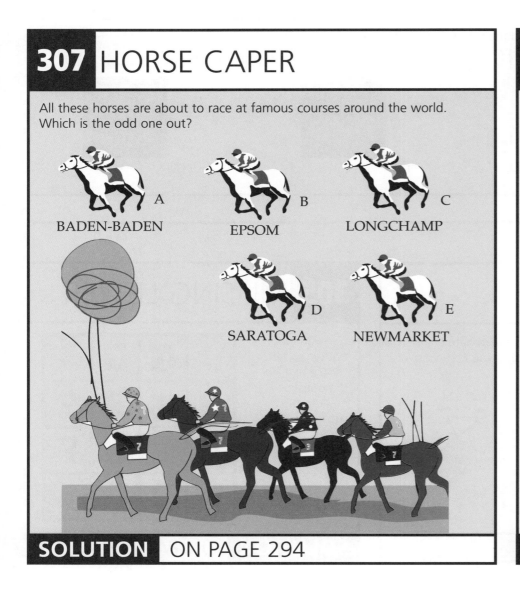

BADEN-BADEN   EPSOM   LONGCHAMP

SARATOGA   NEWMARKET

SOLUTION ON PAGE 294

308 NUMBER PUZZLE

Each symbol in this square represents a value. Can you find out which number should replace the question mark?

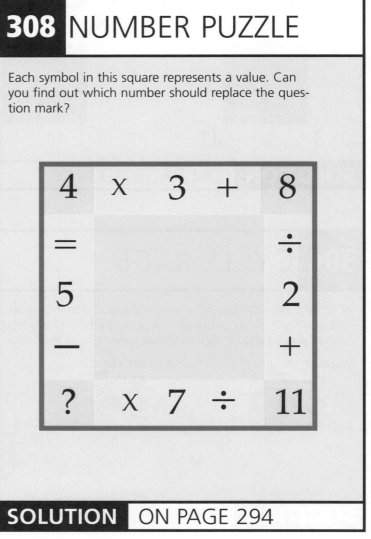

4	x	3	+	8
=				÷
5				2
−				+
?	x	7	÷	11

SOLUTION ON PAGE 294

309 TRACTOR TRIAL

Each farmer gets a different tonnage per acre. Somehow the amount of tons is related to the letters in his name. How many tons does Grimble get? You need to find two possible values for each letter.

FROGGIT
95

BLEASDALE
111

LUDLOW
56

WINTERBOTTOM
146

GRIMBLE
?

SOLUTION ON PAGE 294

310 NUMBER SQUARE

Each symbol in this square represents a value. Can you find out which number should replace the question mark?

?	− 5 x	4
÷ 14		÷ 6
+ 8	= 5 +	− 1

SOLUTION ON PAGE 294

311 SHAPE PROBLEM

Can you find the odd shape out?

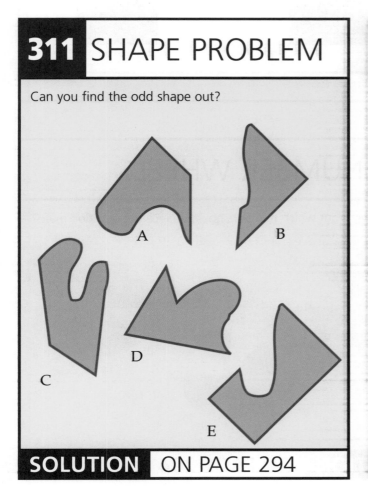

A

B

C

D

E

SOLUTION ON PAGE 294

312 SYMBOL LOGIC

A is to B as
C is to?

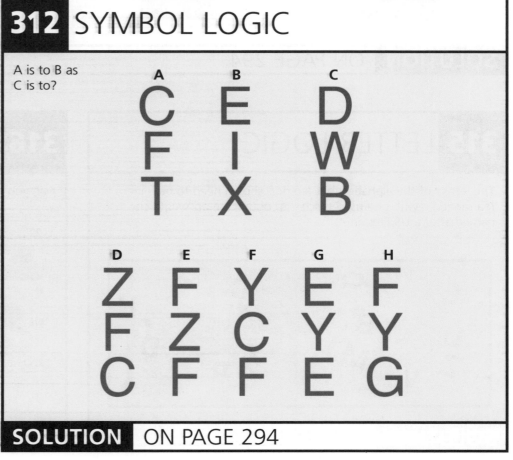

A
C
F
T

B
E
I
X

C
D
W
B

D
Z
F
C

E
F
Z
F

F
Y
C
F

G
E
Y
E

H
F
Y
G

SOLUTION ON PAGE 294

313 FISH CUBE

Which cube can be made from this layout?

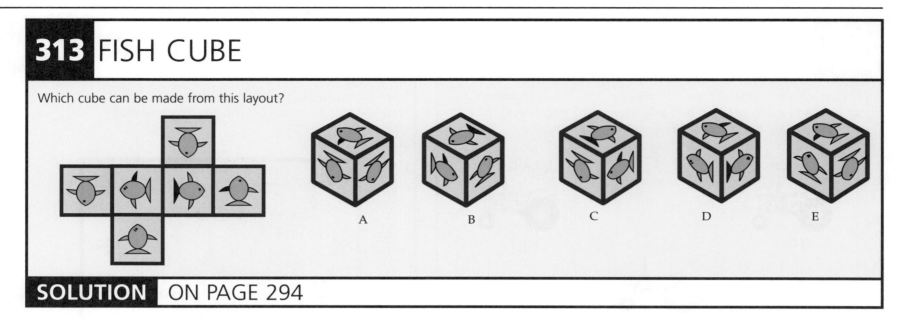

A   B   C   D   E

SOLUTION | ON PAGE 294

314 SQUARE SEQUENCE

Can you work out the reasoning behind these squares and find the number that should replace the question mark?

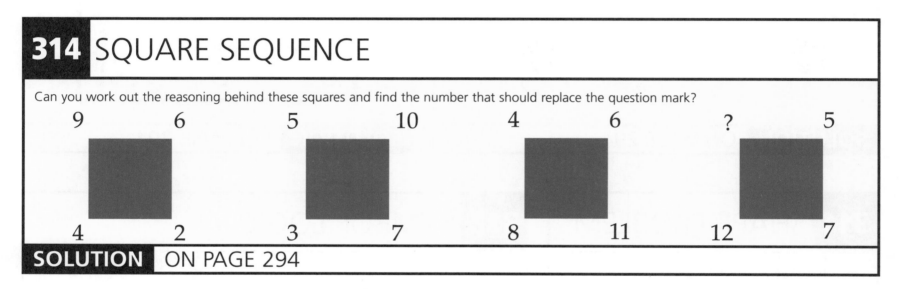

SOLUTION | ON PAGE 294

315 LETTER LOGIC

The letters of the alphabet that are *not* shown need to be rearranged – with one used twice – to obtain the answer (a city named after a US President).

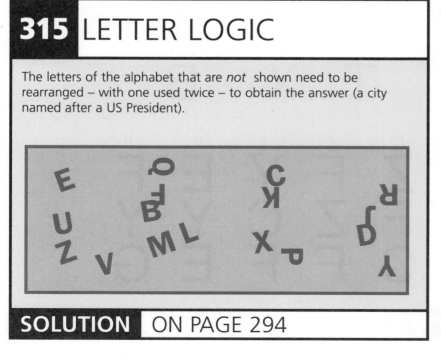

SOLUTION | ON PAGE 294

316 NUMBER WHEELS

Can you work out which number should replace the question mark?

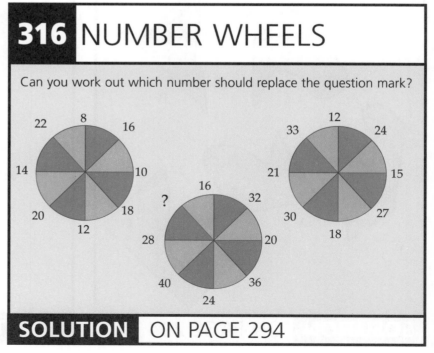

SOLUTION | ON PAGE 294

317 SHAPE SHENANIGANS

Can you find the odd shape out?

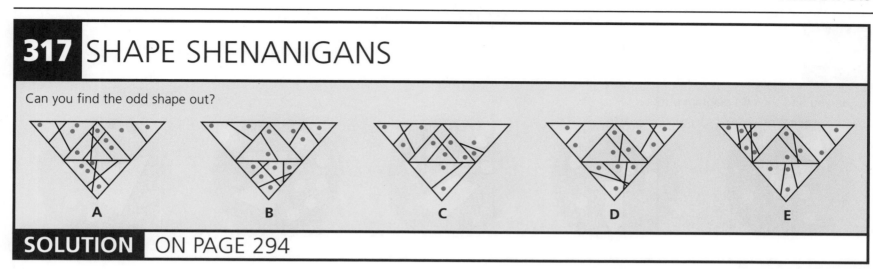

A **B** **C** **D** **E**

SOLUTION ON PAGE 294

318 ARTIST QUEST

Pick one letter from each bulb in order. You can make the names of five artists.

SOLUTION ON PAGE 294

319 PAPERCLIPS

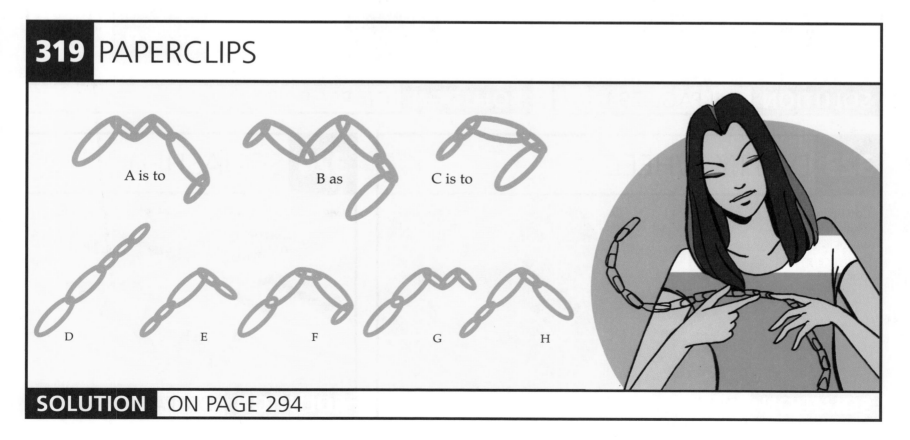

A is to   B as   C is to

D   E   F   G   H

SOLUTION ON PAGE 294

320 NUMBER SQUARE

Can you find the odd diagram out?

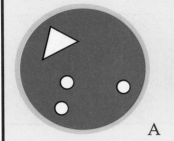    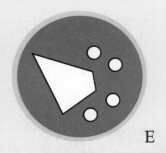

A   B   C   D   E

SOLUTION ON PAGE 294

321 PLANET PROBLEM

Can you work out the reasoning behind this square and replace the question mark with a number?

5	3	8	7
12	15	49	56
3	9	4	12
18	27	36	?

SOLUTION ON PAGE 294

322 SEQUENCE

The first interplanetary travellers are about to set off. Whose luggage is going to be put off at the wrong stop?

A   MARS   B   JUPITER   D   SATURN

C   VENUS   E   URANUS

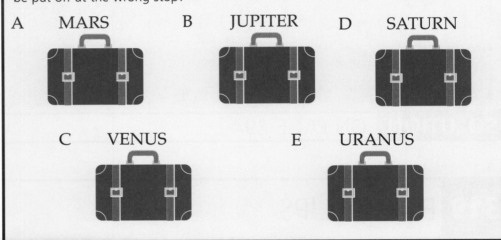

SOLUTION ON PAGE 294

323 DOTTY WHEEL

Can you work out what the next wheel in this sequence should look like?

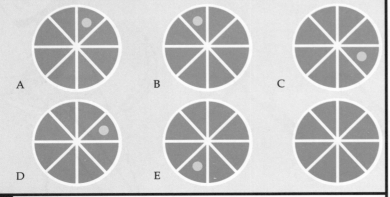

A   B   C

D   E

SOLUTION ON PAGE 294

324 SQUASHED

Can you work out which symbol is the odd one out?

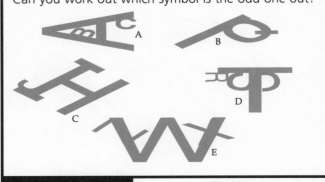

A
B
C
D
E

SOLUTION ON PAGE 294

325 ST. JOSEPH'S CHURCH

Daniel's family were very religious and always went to church on Sundays. Daniel's father had been asked to relocate because of a job promotion and they moved the family to a new city on the Saturday. The move was difficult and took all day and all of the family, except Daniel, slept in on the Sunday morning. Daniel felt tired but decided

he would find his local church and thank God for the safe move straightaway, and he would lead the others to church a little later in the day. The sign outside the church said St Joseph's Catholic Church. He entered to find a service was being conducted but he did not understand a word that was being said. Why?

1. It was nothing to do with accents.
2. They had not moved to a country outside the USA.
3. Daniel was only 10 years old.
4. The language used in the church was English and not Latin.
5. He did not have a problem with his ears. He could hear everything that was said.
6. The city they moved to was Washington.

SOLUTION | ON PAGE 294

326 NUMBER WHEEL

Can you work out which number should replace the question mark?

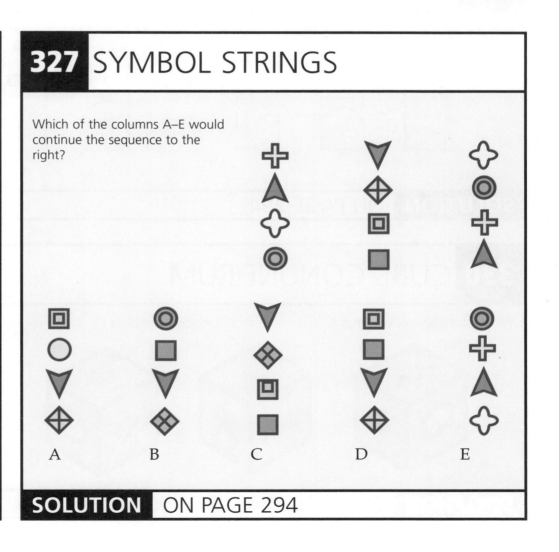

SOLUTION | ON PAGE 294

327 SYMBOL STRINGS

Which of the columns A–E would continue the sequence to the right?

A   B   C   D   E

SOLUTION | ON PAGE 294

328 SYMBOL SERIES

Can you work out which of these diagrams would continue the series?

A   B   C   D   E

SOLUTION ON PAGE 294

329 TILE TROUBLE

Can you work out which of the symbols A–E follows the sequence below?

        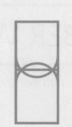 

A   B   C   D   E

SOLUTION ON PAGE 294

330 CUBE CONUNDRUM

Which of the shapes on cubes A, B, C and D should logically complete E?

A   B   C   D   E

SOLUTION ON PAGE 294

331 BERMUDA TRIANGLES

Can you work out the reasoning behind these triangles and replace the question mark with a number?

1804

1820   1812

A

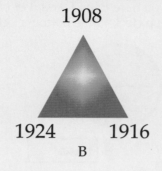

1908

1924   1916

B

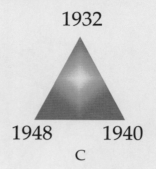

1932

1948   1940

C

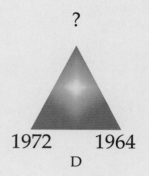

?

1972   1964

D

SOLUTION ON PAGE 294

332 TRAIN TRACKS

The number of each train and its destination are in some way related. Can you work out where train No. 428 is bound for?

A

No. 220
Denver

B

No. 47
Kansas City

C
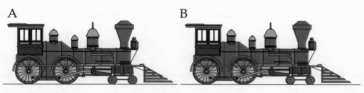
No. 25
Galveston

D

No. 363
Lafayette

E
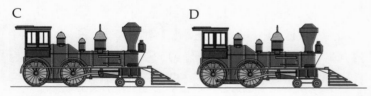
No. 428

a) Portland
b) Chicago
c) Nashville
d) Buffalo

SOLUTION ON PAGE 294

333 POET POSER

Take one letter from each of these bulbs in order. You will be able to make the names of five poets.

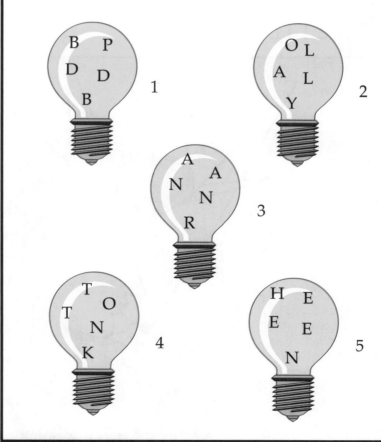

1
B P
D D
B

2
O L
A L
Y

3
A A
N N
R

4
T O
T N
K

5
H E
E E
N

SOLUTION ON PAGE 294

334 CYCLE RACE

Five cyclists are taking part in a race. The number of each rider and its arrival time are in some way related. Can you work out the number of the rider who arrives at 2.30?

No. 10
Arrives 2.15

No. 2
Arrives 3.02

No. ?
Arrives 2.30

No. 30
Arrives 2.45

No. 8
Arrives 3.08

SOLUTION ON PAGE 294

335 TIME TRIAL

Can you work out, using the amounts of time specified, whether you have to go forward or backward to get from the time on the top clock to the bottom clock?

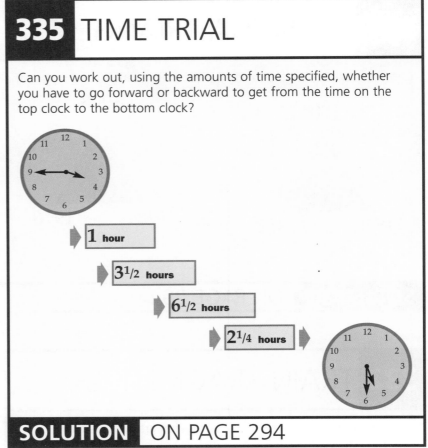

1 hour

3¹/₂ hours

6¹/₂ hours

2¹/₄ hours

SOLUTION ON PAGE 294

336 LETTER LOGIC

The phrase STATUE OF LIBERTY is concealed in this grid. It occurs only once in its entirety. Can you find it? It is written in straight lines with only one change of direction.

SOLUTION ON PAGE 294

337 LOST LETTER

Can you work out which letter should replace the question mark in this square?

B	Z	W	U
E	Q O R	R	
?	J	L	P
F	H	K	M

(grid letters: B Z W U / E Q O R / ? J L P / F H K M)

SOLUTION ON PAGE 294

338 CLOCK PUZZLE

The following clock faces are in some way related. Can you work out what the time on clock No. 3 should be?

SOLUTION ON PAGE 294

339 MISSING NUMBER

Can you work out which number should replace the question mark in this square?

?	−	9	x	5
=				÷
7				2
+				−
3	÷	12	+	4

SOLUTION ON PAGE 294

340 SQUARE SEQUENCE

Which diagram is the odd one out?

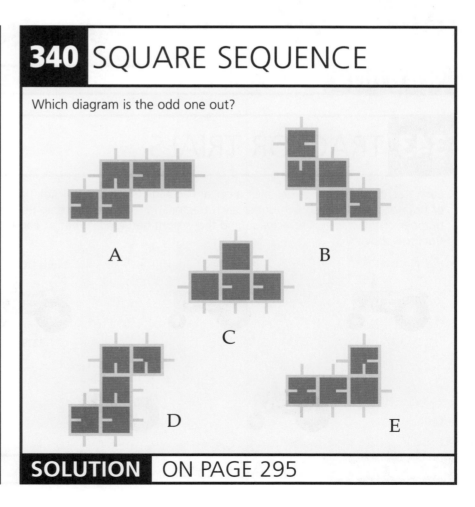

A

B

C

D

E

SOLUTION ON PAGE 295

341 SQUARE SOLUTION

Can you unravel the logic behind these squares and find the missing number?

10	5		4	7		9	1		6	2
	25			**10**			**17**			**?**
3	1		6	2		3	10		3	6

SOLUTION ON PAGE 295

342 CUBE PUZZLE

Can you work out which of these cubes is not the same as the others?

A   B   C   D   E

SOLUTION ON PAGE 295

343 TRACTOR TRIALS

Each tractor gathers potatoes over a certain acreage (shown in brackets). The weight of potatoes in kilos is shown under each tractor. There is a relationship between the number of the tractor, the acreage and the weight gathered. What acreage should tractor B show?

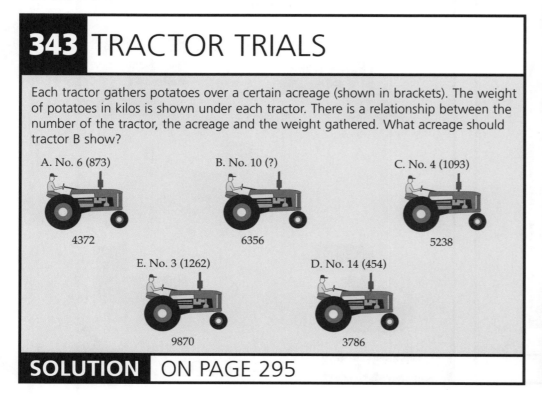

A. No. 6 (873)
4372

B. No. 10 (?)
6356

C. No. 4 (1093)
5238

E. No. 3 (1262)
9870

D. No. 14 (454)
3786

SOLUTION ON PAGE 295

344 TULIP TESTER

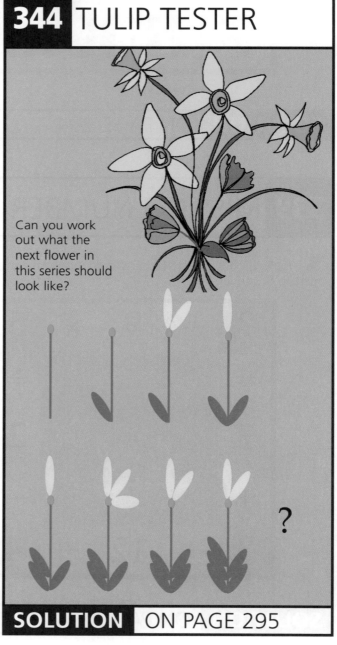

Can you work out what the next flower in this series should look like?

SOLUTION ON PAGE 295

345 LETTER LOGIC

The word SERPENTINE can be found in the grid only once. Can you spot it

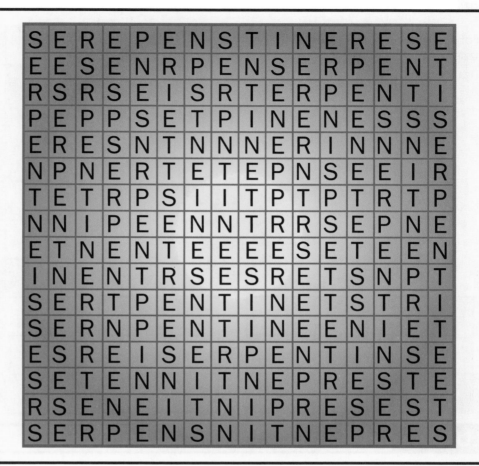

S	E	R	E	P	E	N	S	T	I	N	E	R	E	S	E
E	E	S	E	N	R	P	E	N	S	E	R	P	E	N	T
R	S	R	S	E	I	S	R	T	E	R	P	E	N	T	I
P	E	P	P	S	E	T	P	I	N	E	N	E	S	S	S
E	R	E	S	N	T	N	N	N	E	R	I	N	N	N	E
N	P	N	E	R	T	E	T	E	P	N	S	E	E	I	R
T	E	T	R	P	S	I	I	T	P	T	P	T	R	T	P
N	N	I	P	E	E	N	N	T	R	R	S	E	P	N	E
E	T	N	E	N	T	E	E	E	E	S	E	T	E	E	N
I	N	E	N	T	R	S	E	S	R	E	T	S	N	P	T
S	E	R	T	P	E	N	T	I	N	E	T	S	T	R	I
S	E	R	N	P	E	N	T	I	N	E	E	N	I	E	T
E	S	R	E	I	S	E	R	P	E	N	T	I	N	S	E
S	E	T	E	N	N	I	T	N	E	P	R	E	S	T	E
R	S	E	N	E	I	T	N	I	P	R	E	S	E	S	T
S	E	R	P	E	N	S	N	I	T	N	E	P	R	E	S

SOLUTION ON PAGE 295

346 LOST NUMBER

Can you find the missing number in this square?

1536	48	96	3
384	192	24	12
768	96	48	6
192	?	12	24

SOLUTION ON PAGE 295

347 CYCLE PROBLEM

Five cyclists are taking part in a race. The number of each rider and his cycling time are related to each other. Can you work out the number of the last cyclist?

No. 9

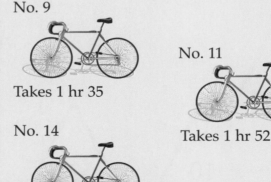

Takes 1 hr 35

No. 11

Takes 1 hr 52

No. 10

Takes 1 hr 43

No. 14

Takes 2 hr 27

No. ?

Takes 2 hr 33

SOLUTION ON PAGE 295

348 COLOUR CONUNDRUM

Which of the sections shown would logically complete the puzzle?

A   B   C

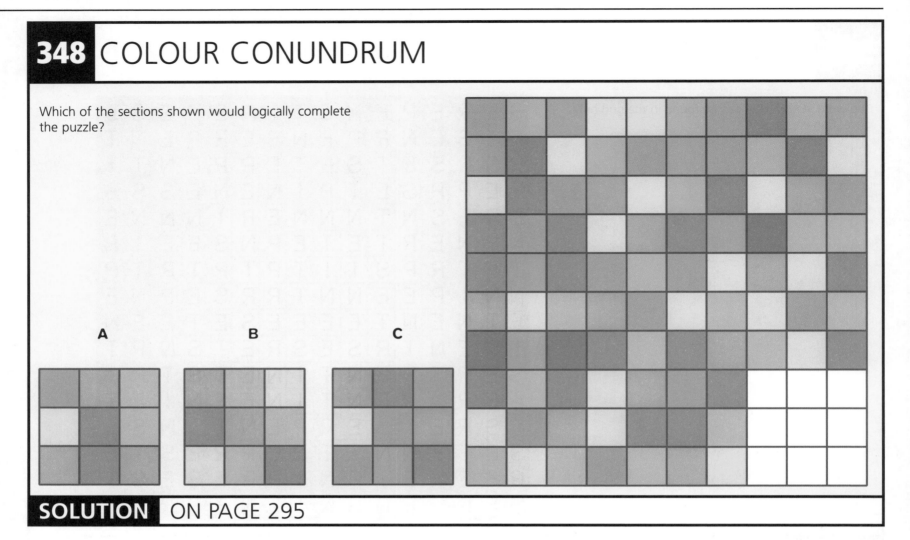

SOLUTION ON PAGE 295

349 TRIANGLE TROUBLE

Find a number that could replace the question mark. Each colour represents a number under 10.

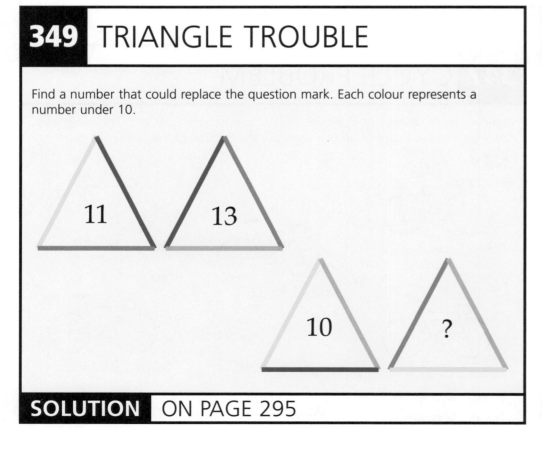

SOLUTION ON PAGE 295

350 DISC PROBLEM

Find a number that could replace the question mark. Each colour represents a number under 10.

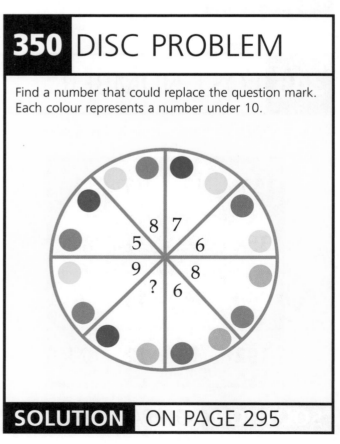

SOLUTION ON PAGE 295

351 LOST LETTER

Can you work out which are the two odd letters out in these triangles?

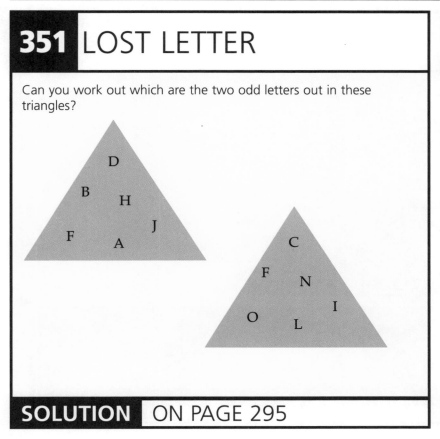

SOLUTION ON PAGE 295

352 TILE TROUBLE

Can you work out what should replace the question mark?

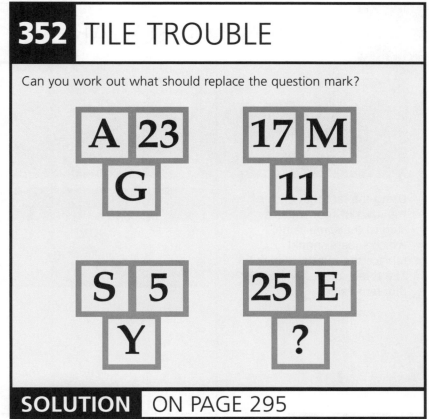

SOLUTION ON PAGE 295

353 COMPOSITIONS

Take a letter from each cloud in the given order. You will find the names of five composers and one extra name. Who is it?

SOLUTION ON PAGE 295

354 TRIANGLES

Can you work out the reasoning behind this diagram and fill in the last square?

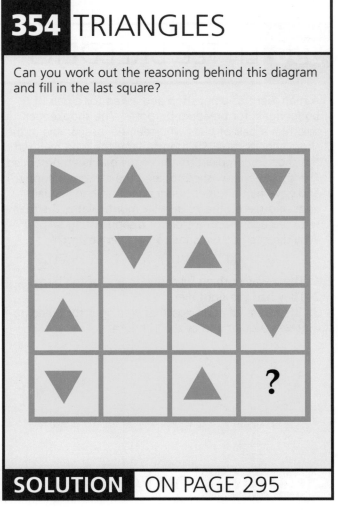

SOLUTION ON PAGE 295

355 SEQUENTIAL SQUARES

Using the fact that each of the rows of four squares sum to the same value, which square should replace the question mark? The three squares all have a different value.

?

SOLUTION ON PAGE 295

356 LITTLE BREEDERS

A man went to a pet shop and asked for a pair of budgerigars for breeding purposes. The shopkeeper sold him a pair of birds who seemed inseparable in the shopkeeper's cage. Six months later the man revisited the shop to complain that no eggs had been produced. The shopkeeper wished to keep the customer happy and gave him another budgerigar that had just laid eggs and reared the young. Six months later, the man returned again with a story of disappointing failure. Why did the hen birds fail to lay a fertile egg?

1. There was nothing wrong with any of the birds.
2. They had the right diet.
3. They were all at an age that was right for breeding.
4. It was a quiet and peaceful house.

SOLUTION ON PAGE 295

357 CLOCKS

Can you work out what number the missing hour hand on clock 4 should point at?

SOLUTION PAGE 295

358 STAR

Can you unravel the reasoning behind this star and fill in the missing letter?

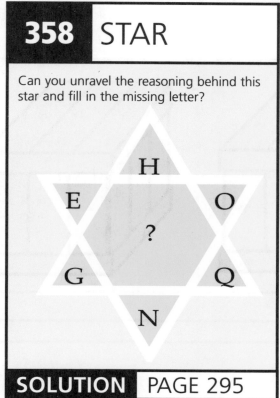

SOLUTION PAGE 295

359 TILE TRIAL

Can you work out which number should replace the question mark?

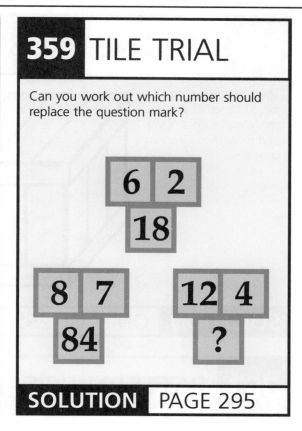

SOLUTION PAGE 295

360 SQUARE SOLUTION

Can you find the number that should replace the question mark?

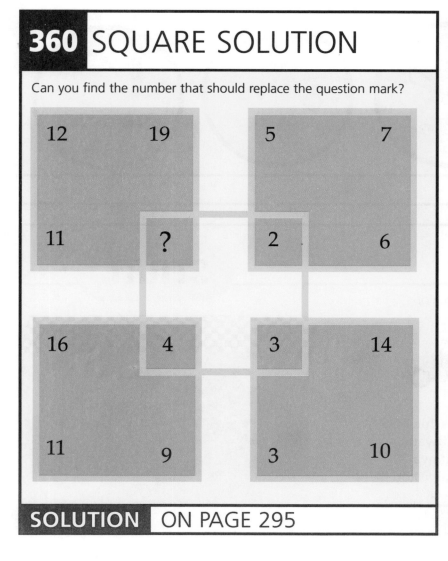

SOLUTION ON PAGE 295

361 DOTTY PROBLEM

Can you work out what numbers should replace A, B and C?

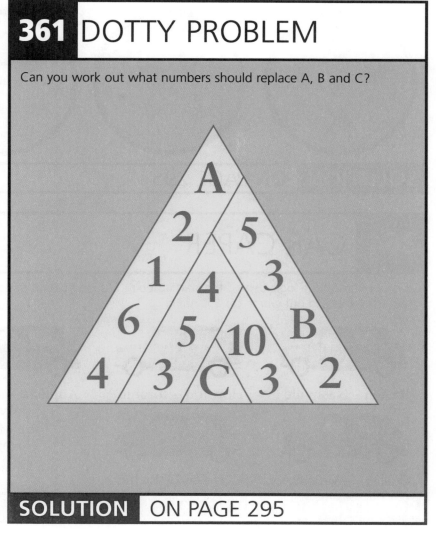

SOLUTION ON PAGE 295

362 PACKING PROBLEM

These letters, when joined together correctly, make up a novel and its author. Can you spot it?

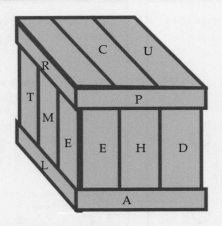
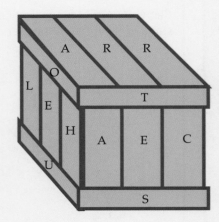
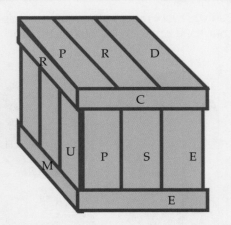

SOLUTION ON PAGE 295

363 PATTERN POSER

Can you find the odd one out?

A 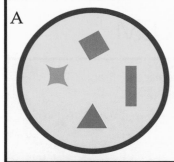 B  C  D 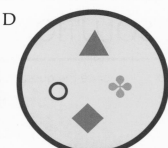 E

SOLUTION ON PAGE 295

364 CAR CAPER

START

Can you unravel the logic behind the starting point and destination of each of these cars and find out where car E is going?

A
Boston – Nashville

B
Chicago – Vancouver

C
Houston – Toronto

D
Cleveland – Richmond

E
Augusta – ?
a) Washington
b) Milwaukee
c) Ottawa
d) Galveston

SOLUTION ON PAGE 295

365 MISSING

What letter should replace the question mark?

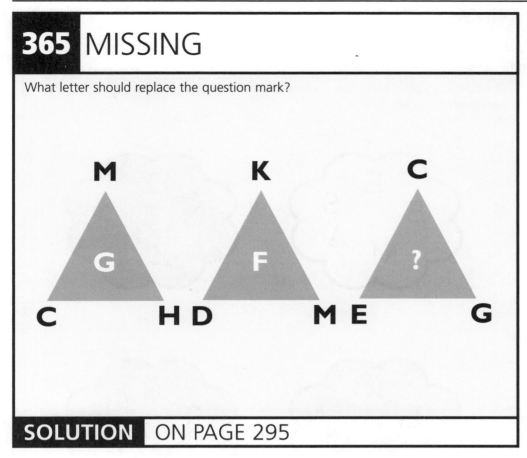

366 MISSING

What letter should replace the question mark?

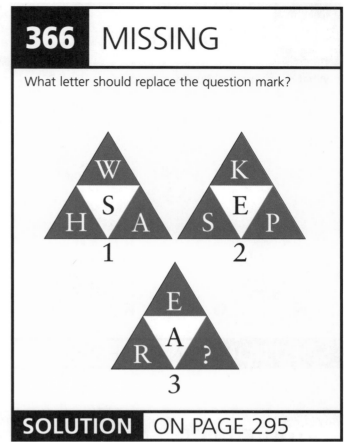

SOLUTION ON PAGE 295

367 TILE TROUBLE

Can you unravel the reasoning behind these domino pieces and find the missing letter?

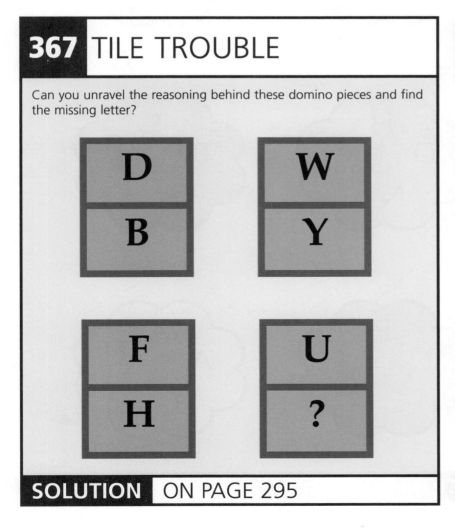

SOLUTION ON PAGE 295

368 LOST NUMBER

Can you work out which number should replace the question mark?

SOLUTION ON PAGE 295

369 MISSING

What number should replace the question mark?

H

45

R   R   S   T

39   ?

N   G   K   L

SOLUTION ON PAGE 295

370 LETTER LOGIC

Can you work out which number fits underneath letter E?

H E Y

14

?

29

SOLUTION ON PAGE 295

371 DEAD POLITICIANS

Pick one letter from each flower in the order shown. You will get the names of five politicians. Who are they?

E
E   S
M   A
3

T
N   R
Z   P
4

R
I   D
H   O
2

R
R   I
V   U
8

H
D   E
N   U
6

T
B   P
A   D
1

E
E   E
L   O
7

A
A   H
C   I
5

SOLUTION ON PAGE 296

372 TILE TANGLE

Can you work out which letter fits the square with the question mark?

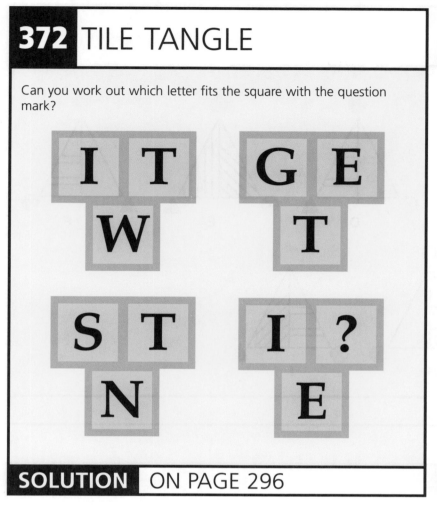

SOLUTION ON PAGE 296

373 LOST LETTER

Can you work out which letter does not belong in the second circle?

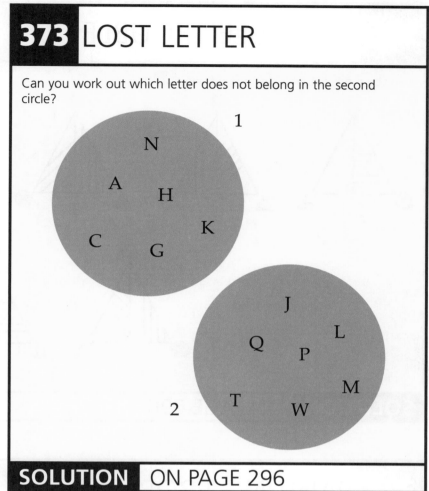

SOLUTION ON PAGE 296

374 JUGGLING

Can you unravel the reasoning behind this juggler and find the missing letter?

SOLUTION ON PAGE 296

375 FUNNY FACES

Can you unravel the reasoning behind this grid and complete the missing square?

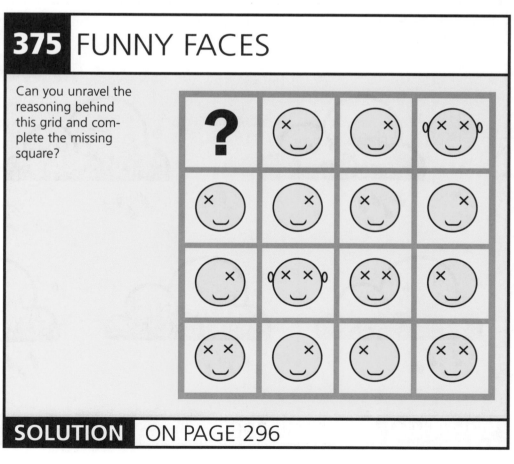

SOLUTION ON PAGE 296

376 TRIANGLE TROUBLE

Can you work out which is the odd one out?

SOLUTION ON PAGE 296

377 PAINTING PROBLEM

Take a letter from each cloud in turn. You should find the names of five painters and one extra name. What is it?

1
V
H M
G H E

2
A
O O
A R E

3
U
G A
C T R

4
I M
G A
S K

5
S
E N
U M R

6
I
E E
T
U S

7
Y
H S
R
E N

SOLUTION ON PAGE 296

378 MISSING LETTER

Can you unravel the logic behind these diagrams and find the missing letter?

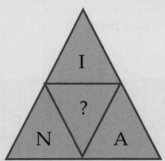

379 NUMBER WHEEL

Can you find the missing number in this wheel?

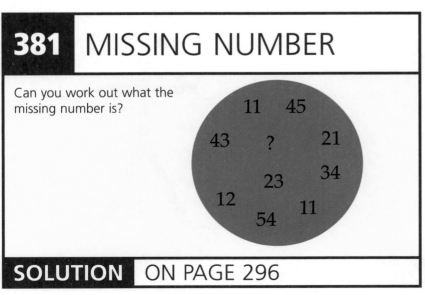

SOLUTION ON PAGE 296

380 TILE TROUBLE

Can you unravel the reasoning behind these domino pieces and find the missing letter? Think pink and musical!

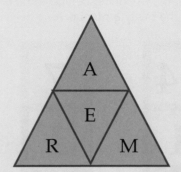

SOLUTION ON PAGE 296

SOLUTION ON PAGE 296

381 MISSING NUMBER

Can you work out what the missing number is?

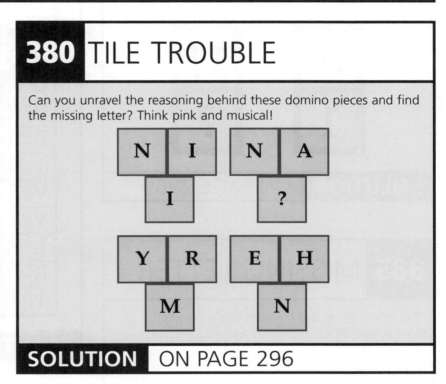

SOLUTION ON PAGE 296

382 STAR TURN

What letter should replace the question mark?

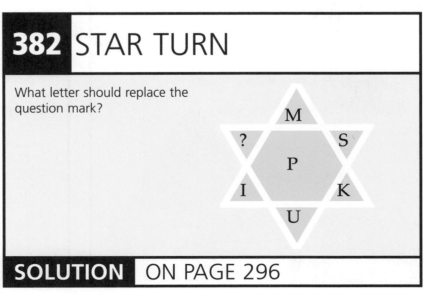

SOLUTION ON PAGE 296

383 DOMINO POSER

Can you unravel the reasoning behind these domino pieces and find the missing number?

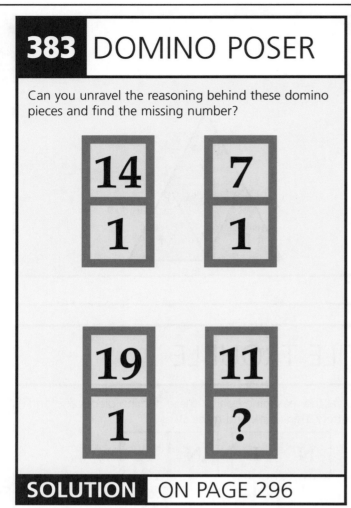

SOLUTION ON PAGE 296

385 MISSING LETTER

The letters in the two triangles below have some connection. Which is the odd one out?

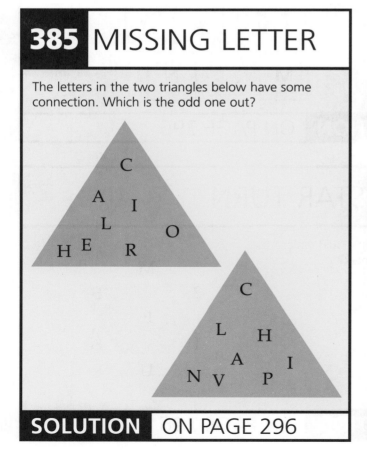

SOLUTION ON PAGE 296

384 VERDI SEARCH

In this grid the name VERDI appears in its entirety only once in a straight line. Can you spot it? However, there is also another word hidden which involves one change of direction. What is it? It might have been one of the composer's famous last words.

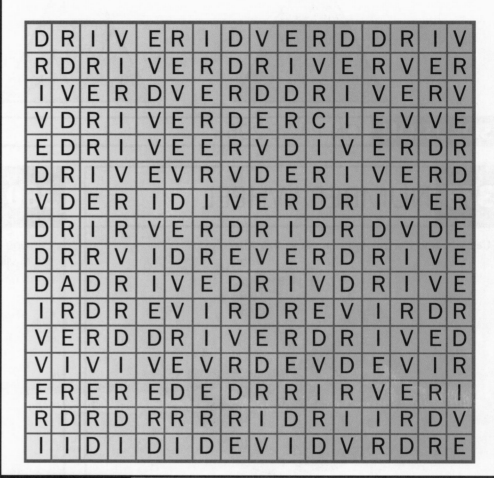

SOLUTION ON PAGE 296

386 LOST LETTER

Can you replace the question mark with a letter?

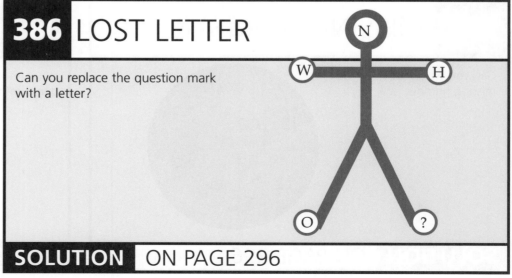

SOLUTION ON PAGE 296

387 THE PLAY'S THE THING

Pick one letter from each cloud in the order shown. You will find the names of five playwrights plus one extra name. Who is it?

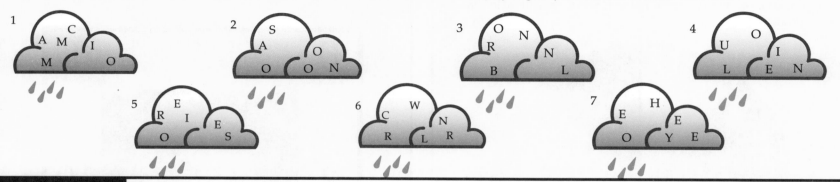

SOLUTION ON PAGE 296

388 DOMINO POSER

Can you unravel the reasoning behind these diagrams and find the missing letter?

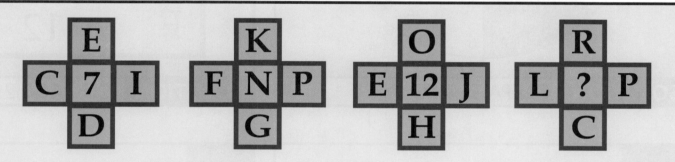

SOLUTION ON PAGE 296

389 CAR CRISIS

Each of the cars was filled with fuel. Can you unravel the connection between the registration mark and amount of fuel and work out what amount the last car was filled with?

A) 30 units   B) 72 units
C) 36 units   D) 78 units

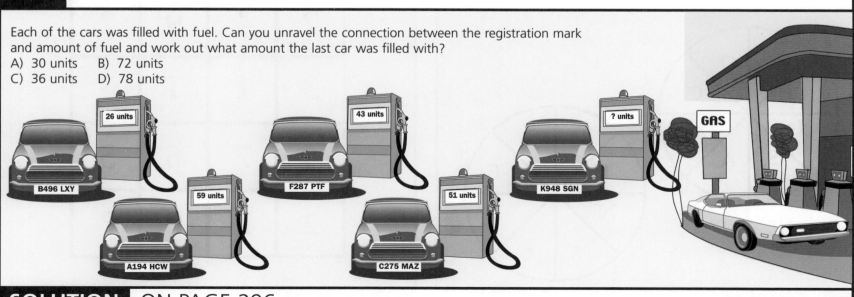

SOLUTION ON PAGE 296

390 NUMBER WHEEL

Can you work out the reasoning behind this wheel and fill in the missing number?

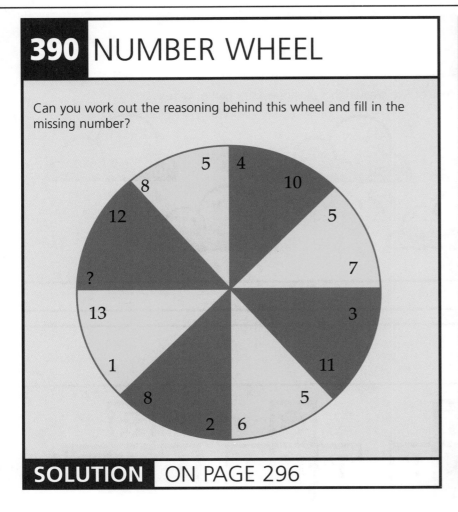

SOLUTION ON PAGE 296

391 NO NUMBER?

What number should replace the question mark?

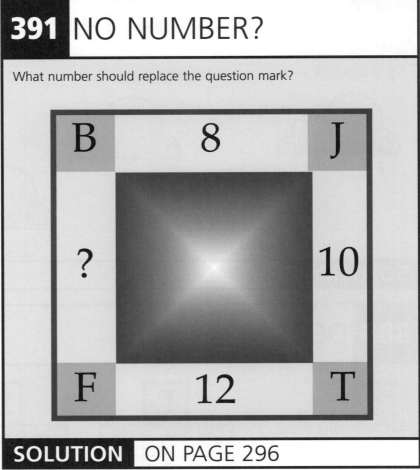

SOLUTION ON PAGE 296

392 LOST LETTERS

If the missing letters in the two circles below are correctly inserted they will form synonymous words. The words do not have to be read in a clockwise direction, but the letters are consecutive. What are the words and missing letters?

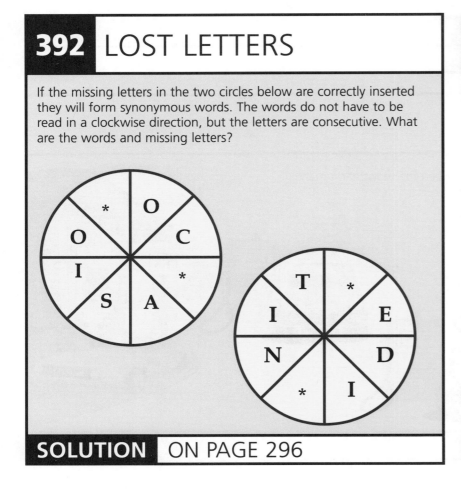

SOLUTION ON PAGE 296

393 NUMBER PUZZLE

What number should replace the question mark?
A. 0 B. 1 C. 2 D. 3 E. 4

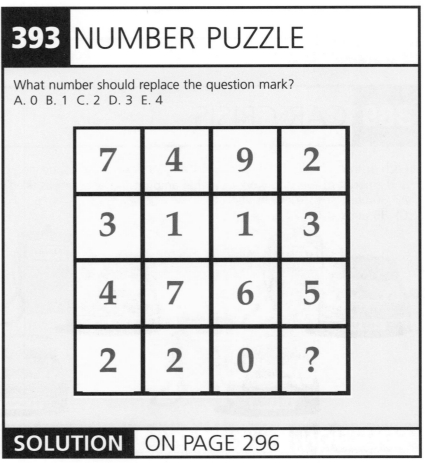

SOLUTION ON PAGE 296

394 PATTERN POSER

Which is the odd one out?

A   B   C   D   E

SOLUTION ON PAGE 296

395 SERIES SOLUTION

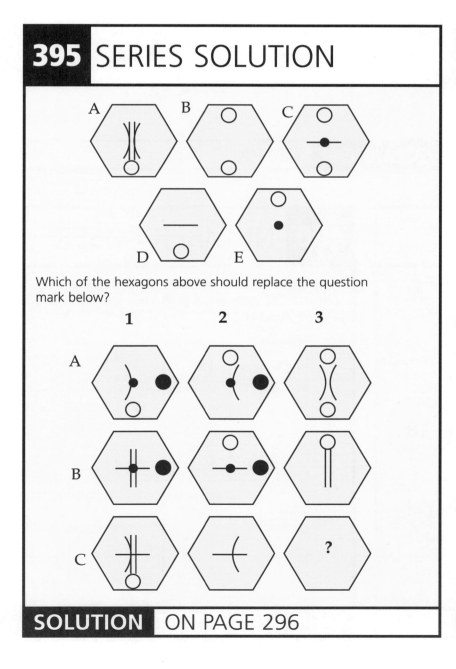

Which of the hexagons above should replace the question mark below?

1   2   3

A

B

C

SOLUTION ON PAGE 296

396 SHAPE SHIFTER

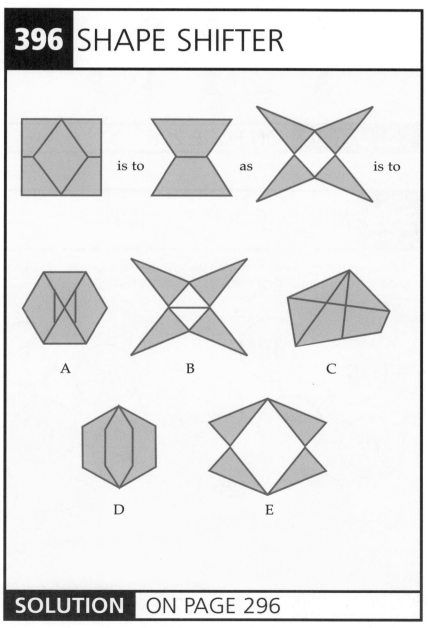

is to   as   is to

A   B   C

D   E

SOLUTION ON PAGE 296

397 MISSING NUMBERS

There is a relationship between the columns of numbers in this diagram. The letters above the grid are there to help you. Which number should be placed in the empty squares?

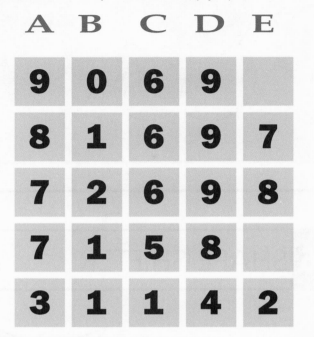

A	B	C	D	E
9	0	6	9	
8	1	6	9	7
7	2	6	9	8
7	1	5	8	
3	1	1	4	2

SOLUTION ON PAGE 296

398 NUMBER NOTION

Place six three-digit numbers of 100 plus at the end of 451 so that six numbers of six digits are produced. When each number is divided by 61 six whole numbers can be found. In this case, the first numbers are given. Which numbers should be placed in the grid?

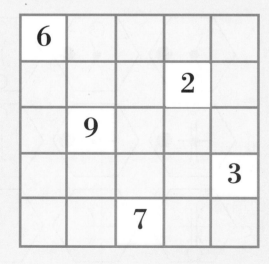

4 5 1 →

1
3
4
4
6
9

SOLUTION ON PAGE 296

399 MATHS MYSTERY

Insert the missing numbers. In each pattern the missing number has something to do with the surrounding numbers in combination.

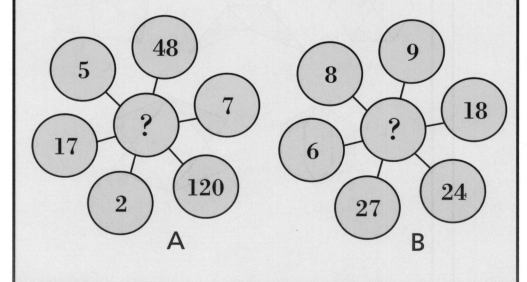

A

B

SOLUTION ON PAGE 296

400 NUMBER POSER

Using only the numbers already used, complete this puzzle to make all the rows, columns, and long diagonals add to 27.

6				
			2	
	9			
				3
		7		

SOLUTION ON PAGE 297

401 DOTTY PROBLEM

What number should replace the question mark?

$$\square + \square - \square = 6$$

$$\square - \square + \square = 3$$

$$\square \times \square \times \square = 140$$

$$\square + \square + \square = ?$$

SOLUTION ON PAGE 297

402 BINARY BOTHER

The panel below, when complete, contains the binary numbers from 1 to 25. Does binary patch A, B, C or D complete the panel?

1	1	0	1	1	1	0	0	1	0	1
1	1	0	1	1	1	1	0	0	0	1
0	0	1	1	0	1	0	1	0	1	1
1	1	0						1	1	1
0	1	1		?			0	0	1
0	0	0					0	1	0
0	1	1	1	0	1	0	0	1	0	1
0	1	1	0	1	1	0	1	0	1	1
1	1	1	0	0	0	1	1	0	0	1

1	0	1	1	1
1	1	1	1	0
1	1	1	0	0

A

0	1	1	0	1
1	1	1	0	0
0	1	0	0	1

B

1	1	0	1	1
1	1	0	1	1
0	0	1	0	1

C

0	1	1	0	1
1	1	1	0	0
1	1	0	0	1

D

SOLUTION ON PAGE 297

403 DIAMOND DILEMMA

What number should replace the question mark?

289

256   196

225

441

?   324

361

SOLUTION ON PAGE 297

404 MAGIC SQUARE

When the shaded sections of this puzzle are brought together, one of the green patches is inserted into the middle to make a magic square in which all rows, columns and long diagonals add to 49. Is it patch A, B, C or D?

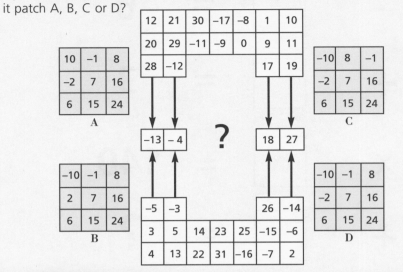

12	21	30	−17	−8	1	10
20	29	−11	−9	0	9	11
28	−12				17	19

10	−1	8
−2	7	16
6	15	24

A

−10	8	−1
−2	7	16
6	15	24

C

−13	−4

?

18	27

−10	−1	8
2	7	16
6	15	24

B

−10	−1	8
−2	7	16
6	15	24

D

−5	−3			26	−14
3	5	14	23	25	−15	−6
4	13	22	31	−16	−7	2

SOLUTION ON PAGE 297

405 PATTERN POSER

Each shape is made up of two items, and each same shape has the same value, whether in the foreground or background. What number should replace the question mark?

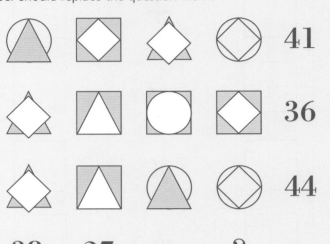

41

36

44

38   27   ?

SOLUTION ON PAGE 297

406 LETTERS LOST

Which letters, based on the alphanumeric system, should go into the blank boxes?

6	1	7	3				5	1	3	9				2	2	9	2			
1	3	5	4	A	H	B	2	8	6	4	F	B	C	4	3	0	9			
7	7	0	9				8	6	2	6				7	1	7	8			

SOLUTION ON PAGE 297

407 WEIGHTY PROBLEM

If each large ball weighs one and a third times the weight of each little ball, what is the minimum adjustment that will make the scales balance?

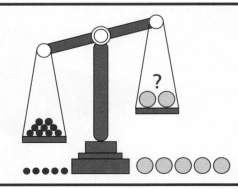

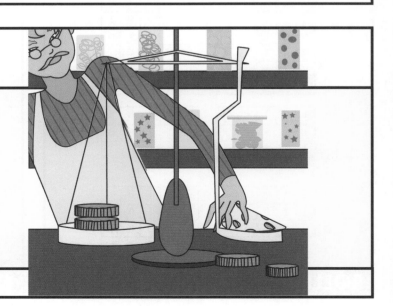

SOLUTION ON PAGE 297

408 ROSETTE ENIGMA

How many rosettes are missing from the blank circle?

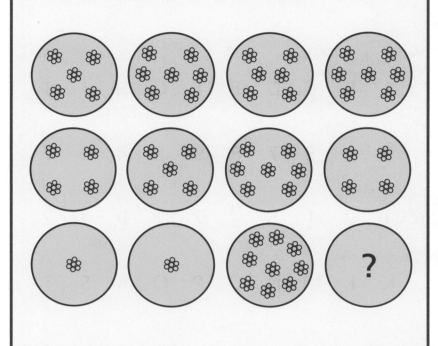

SOLUTION ON PAGE 297

409 FAMILY FUN

Present at Juan's birthday party were a father-in–law, a mother-in-law, a daughter-in-law, two sons, two daughters, two sisters and a brother, four children, three grandchildren, two fathers, two mothers, a grandfather, and a grandmother. However, family relationships can be complicated. One man's brother can, of course, be another man's brother-in-law, and at the same time, someone's son. With that in mind, what is the smallest number of people needed at the party for the above relationships to exist?

SOLUTION ON PAGE 297

410 NUMBER NOTION

Find a route from the top of this puzzle to the bottom that arrives at the total 353, always going down and to an adjoining hexagon.

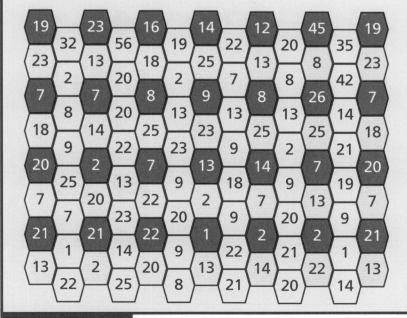

SOLUTION ON PAGE 297

411 RIGHT ROUTE

Insert the supplied rows of numbers into the appropriate places in the grid to make all rows, columns and long diagonals add to 175. Example: C goes into location A.

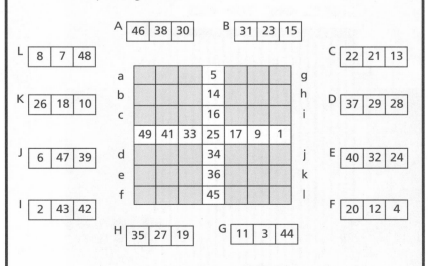

SOLUTION ON PAGE 297

412 PATTERN PROBLEM

Use logic to discover which shape has the greatest perimeter.

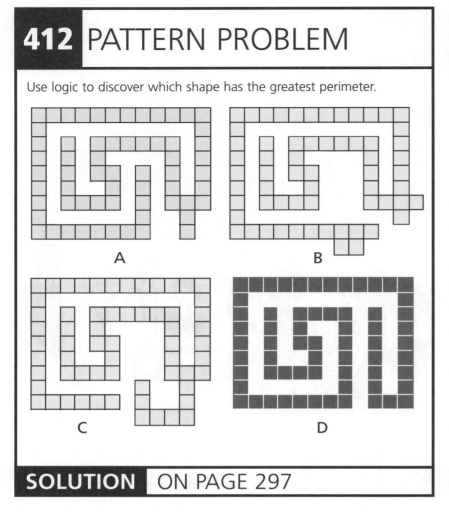

413 CODE CORNER

Crack the code to find the missing number.

A	B	C	D	E	F	G	H	I	J
9	3	8	7	8	9	2	8	5	7
1	2	1	5	?	7	1	0	1	2
K	L	M	N	O	P	Q	R	S	T

SOLUTION ON PAGE 297

SOLUTION ON PAGE 297

414 ANIMAL CRACKERS

Which number replaces the question mark? What is the value of each animal?

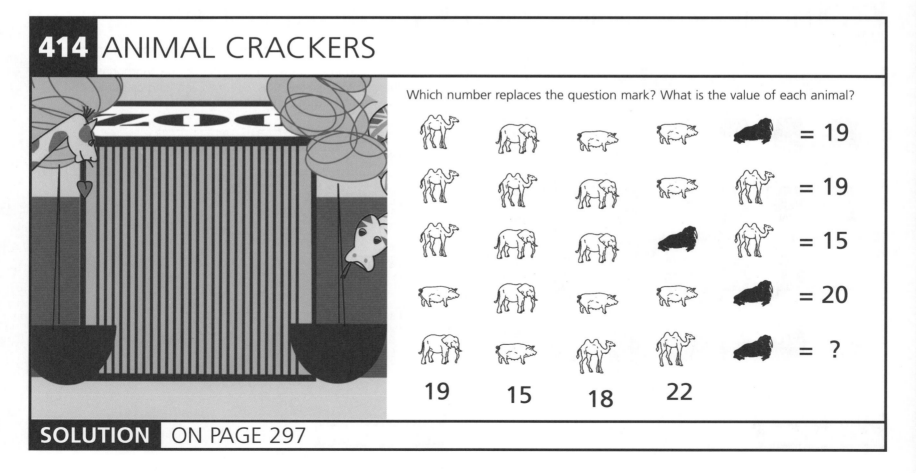

SOLUTION ON PAGE 297

415 NUMBER PUZZLE

What number should replace the question mark?

A	B	C	D	E
3	11	7	4	18
2	12	7	5	19
5	17	11	6	?

SOLUTION ON PAGE 297

416 STAR SHINE

Put the right number in the blank star.

SOLUTION ON PAGE 297

417 CENTRAL NUMBERS

Insert the central numbers.

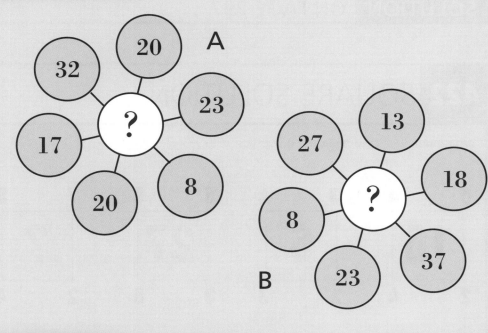

SOLUTION ON PAGE 297

418 SYMBOL VALUES

Which number should replace the question mark?

$$\star + \maltese - \ast = 6$$

$$\star \times \maltese \times \ast = 30$$

$$\star - \maltese - \ast = 0$$

$$\star + \maltese + \ast = ?$$

SOLUTION ON PAGE 297

419 SQUARE POSER

What number should replace the question mark in the blank square?

9   3   4   3

57   **18**

5   6   3   2

6   1   2   8

24   **?**

9   2   3   1

SOLUTION ON PAGE 297

420 BULL BRAIN BENDER

Four ramblers walked down the lane, past the stream, over the hills to the edge of a field. The field was full of cattle. Before the ramblers managed to reach the other side of the field they were charged by a Bull. Why did the ramblers make a formal complaint when none of them suffered an injury?

1. They did not run to safety.
2. They were not scared.
3. The cattle took no notice of the ramblers.
4. Bulls had charged others in the past but not for a period of time.
5. The charging Bull was fully fit and fully grown.

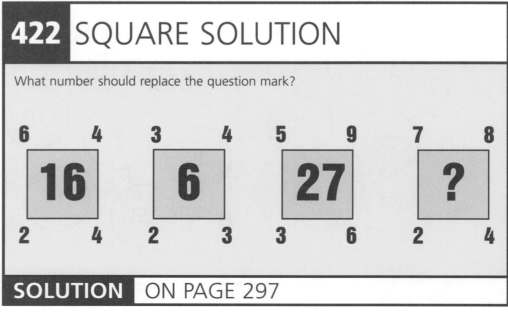

SOLUTION ON PAGE 297

421 NUMBER MAGIC

Insert the central numbers.

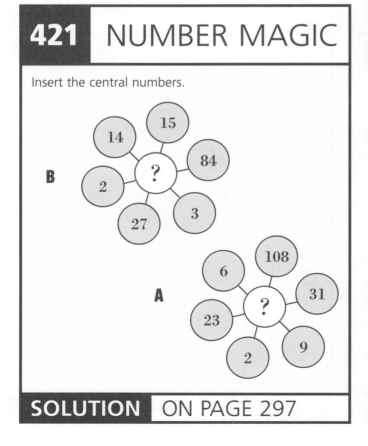

B

14   15
2   **?**   84
27   3

A

6   108
23   **?**   31
2   9

SOLUTION ON PAGE 297

422 SQUARE SOLUTION

What number should replace the question mark?

6   4   3   4   5   9   7   8

16   **6**   **27**   **?**

2   4   2   3   3   6   2   4

SOLUTION ON PAGE 297

423 NUMBER CROSSWORD

Insert the numbers supplied into the puzzle grid. There is only one correct way.

ACROSS

118	916	3052	9481
155	951	3184	9857
200	0193	5056	16659
277	0360	5119	35677
293	1048	5832	51719
390	1066	6073	56151
653	1918	7176	76891
724	2390	7775	6036300
915	2983	8885	~~7424361~~

DOWN

08	5667	72612	897511
49	7900	87333	965853
63	8659	95138	3704058
66	8890	116765	4756628
69	10875	215810	6754451
90	50713	353637	229137152
4920	62817	675856	248143773
5086			

SOLUTION ON PAGE 297

---

424 SQUARE SOLUTION

The black, white and shaded rings of this square target always have the same value, irrespective of their position, and each target is worth 44. Which of the targets, A, B, C or D, will replace the question mark?

SOLUTION ON PAGE 297

---

425 CROSS PROBLEM

What number replaces the question mark?

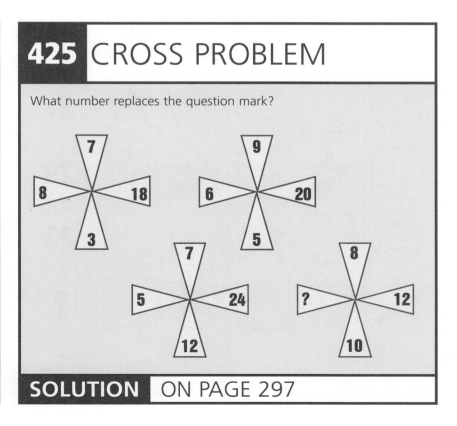

SOLUTION ON PAGE 297

426 TILE TROUBLE

Insert the missing number in the blank square.

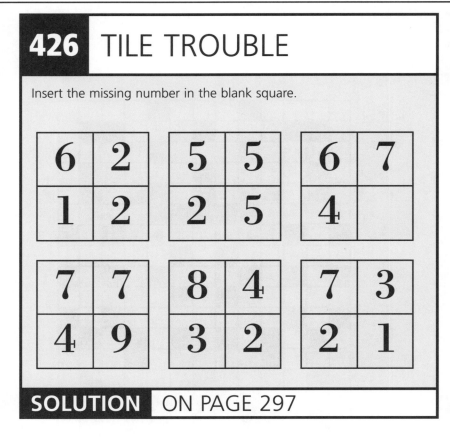

SOLUTION ON PAGE 297

427 NUMBER NONSENSE

Find the missing number.

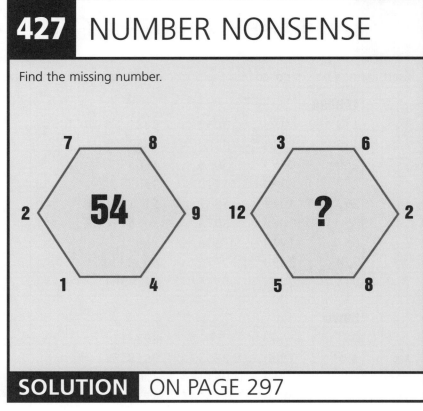

SOLUTION ON PAGE 297

428 SHAPE SHIFTER

Each same shape has the same value. What number should replace the question mark

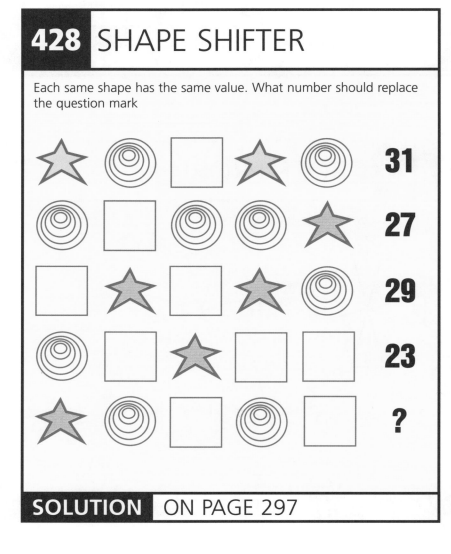

SOLUTION ON PAGE 297

429 LINE LOGIC

What three-digit number should replace the question mark?

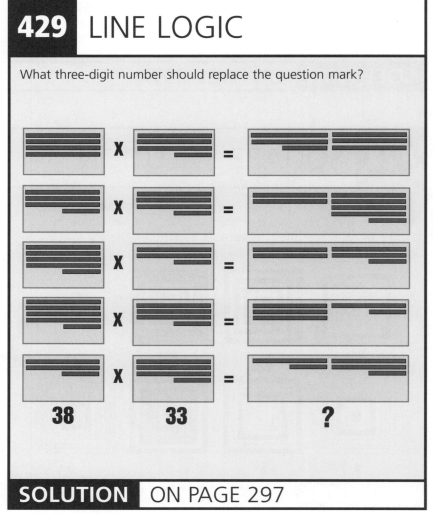

SOLUTION ON PAGE 297

430 BALL BALANCE

The three balls at the top of each hexagon should contain numbers that, when added together and subtracted from the total of the numbers in the three balls at the bottom of each hexagon, equal the number inside each relevant hexagon. Insert the missing numbers.

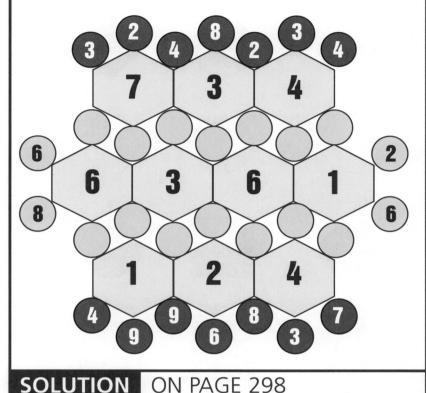

SOLUTION ON PAGE 298

431 RANDOM DOTS?

This is a time puzzle. Which symbol is missing ?
Is it A, B, C, D, E or F?

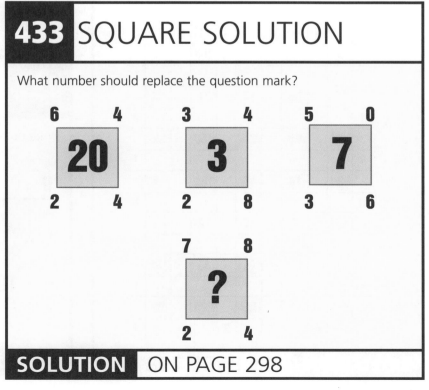

SOLUTION ON PAGE 298

432 CLOCKING OFF

This clock has been designed for a planet that rotates on its axis once every 16 hours. There are 64 minutes to every hour, and 64 seconds to the minute. At the moment, the time on the clock reads a quarter to eight. What time, to the nearest second, will the clock say the time after the next time the hands appear to meet?

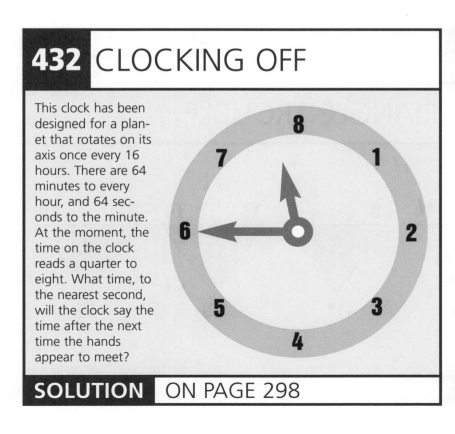

SOLUTION ON PAGE 298

433 SQUARE SOLUTION

What number should replace the question mark?

6 **20** 4	3 **3** 4	5 **7** 0
2 4	2 8	3 6

7   8
?
2   4

SOLUTION ON PAGE 298

434 TIME TROUBLE

What time will it be, to the nearest second, when the hands of this clock next appear to meet?

SOLUTION ON PAGE 298

436 NUMBER MAGIC

Insert in the boxes at the corner of each shaded number-square the digits which are multiplied together to give the numbers in the shaded boxes. For example, in the bottom left corner, 144 is derived from 3 x 6 x 8 (and another multiplier – here 1), but you also have to consider how this helps to make solutions for the surrounding numbers … and so on.

3		5		4		4		3		3
	90		120		64		144		54	
2										1
	48		96		16		72		36	
1										2
	160		80		20		150		30	
4										1
	180		10		40		100		15	
9										3
	27		8		32		12		81	
3										9
	24		28		84		45		135	
8										1
	144		42		63		225		25	
3		6		1		3		5		1

SOLUTION ON PAGE 298

435 SYMBOL SOLUTION

Each like symbol has the same value. Supply the missing total.

31

29   37   24   ?

SOLUTION ON PAGE 298

437 TRIANGLE TROUBLE

What number should replace the question mark?

9	14	6	6	11	14	12	10
	2		3		4		?
19		11		19		15	

SOLUTION ON PAGE 298

438 NUMBER SNAKE

What number should replace the question mark?

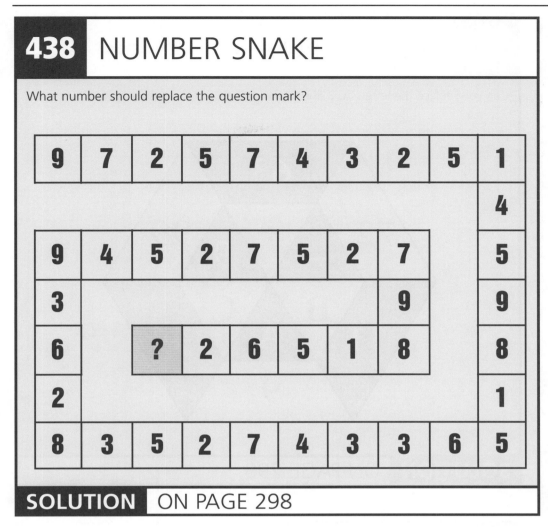

SOLUTION ON PAGE 298

439 DIAMONDS

What number should replace the question mark?

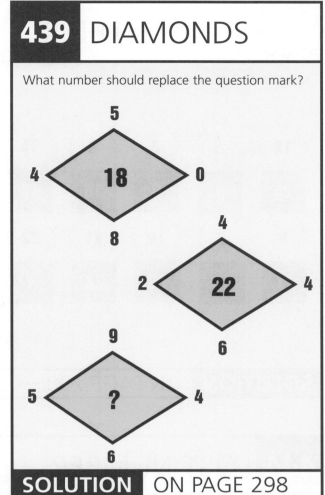

SOLUTION ON PAGE 298

440 SQUARE ENIGMA

What number should replace the question mark?

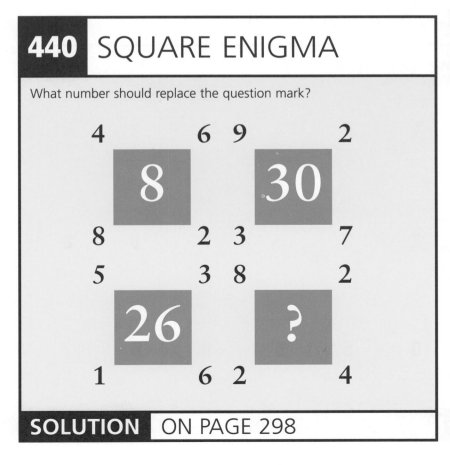

SOLUTION ON PAGE 298

441 NUMBER NOTION

What number should replace the question mark?

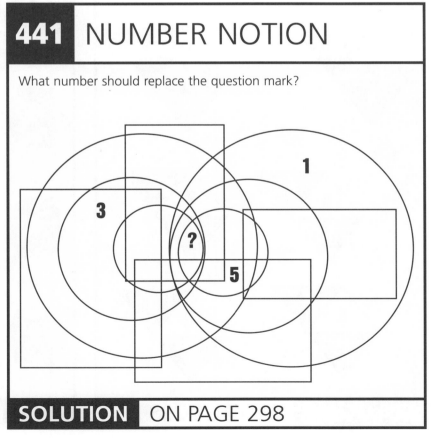

SOLUTION ON PAGE 298

442 SHAPE SHIFTER

Insert the missing numbers in the blank hexagons.

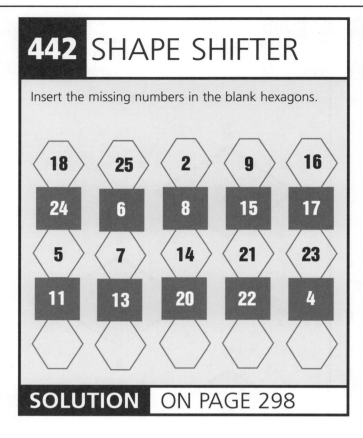

SOLUTION ON PAGE 298

443 SYMBOL POSER

Can you replace the letters A, B and C with the correct number or symbol?

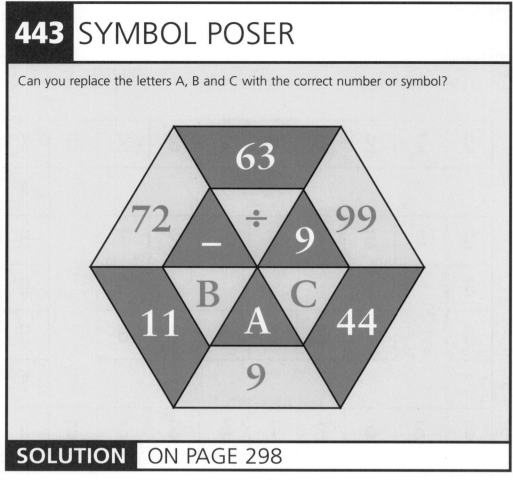

SOLUTION ON PAGE 298

444 LOST NUMBER

What number should replace the question mark?

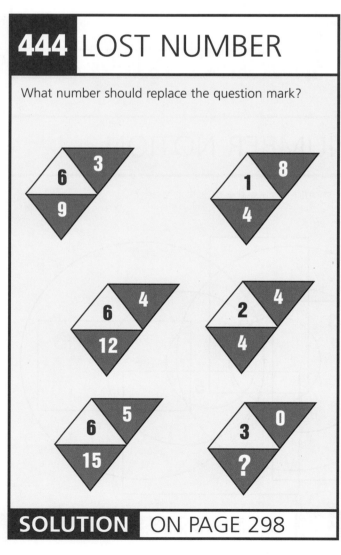

SOLUTION ON PAGE 298

445 HEXAGON ENIGMA

What number should replace the question mark?

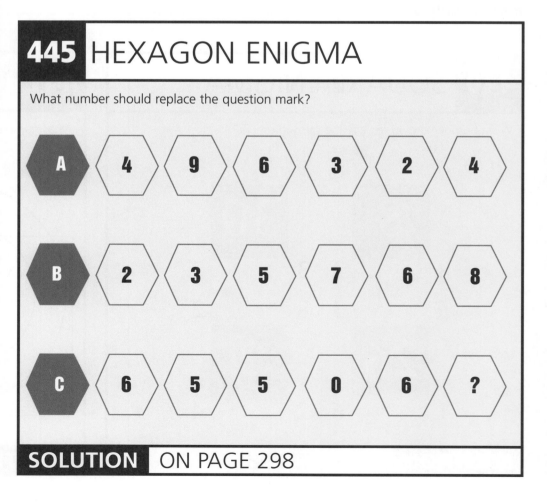

SOLUTION ON PAGE 298

446 KING CONUNDRUM

How many different ways is it possible to arrange the order of these four kings?

SOLUTION ON PAGE 298

447 SQUARES

$$2 \times \sqrt{2} = \sqrt{8}$$

$$3 \times \sqrt{5} = \sqrt{45}$$

What number should replace the question mark?

$$4 \times \sqrt{6} = \sqrt{?}$$

SOLUTION ON PAGE 298

448 WATCH PUZZLE

Previous to the time shown, when were all four of the digits on this watch last on display?

SOLUTION ON PAGE 298

449 BUSH FIRE

There was a forest fire in Australia. After the firefighters had managed to extinguish the fire, the search for bodies began. After two days of searching they found a man in complete scuba diving gear. Although he was dead, he had not been burned at all. The forest is 20 miles from any water. How did he get there?

1. The man had not walked to where he was found.
2. The man had not been murdered. It was an accidental death.
3. His wet suit was not burned or melted.
4. The man had several broken bones.

SOLUTION ON PAGE 298

450 NUMBER POSER

Find within the number below, two numbers, one of which is double the other, and which when added together make 10743.

57162383581

SOLUTION ON PAGE 298

451 HEXAGON

What number should replace the question mark in the third hexagon pattern?

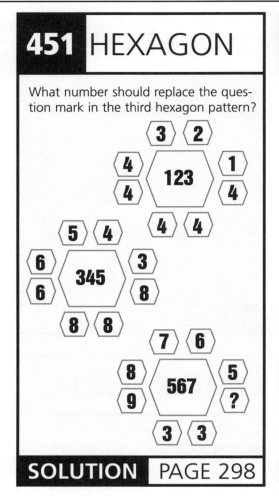

SOLUTION | PAGE 298

452 ODD ONE OUT

Which is the odd one out?

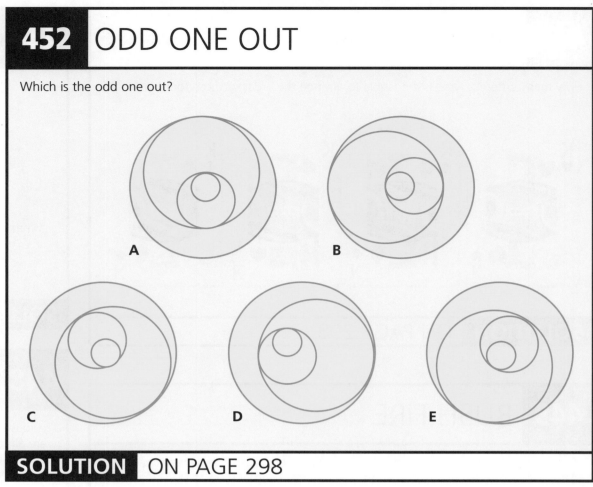

SOLUTION | ON PAGE 298

453 BALANCE BEAM

This system is balanced. How heavy is the black weight (ignoring leverage effects)?

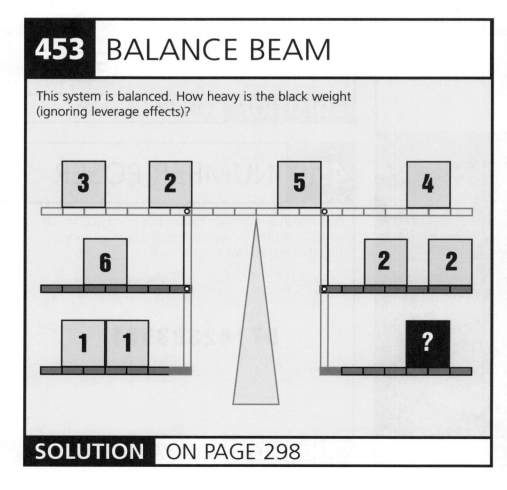

SOLUTION | ON PAGE 298

454 SQUARE SOLUTION

A is to B as C is to?

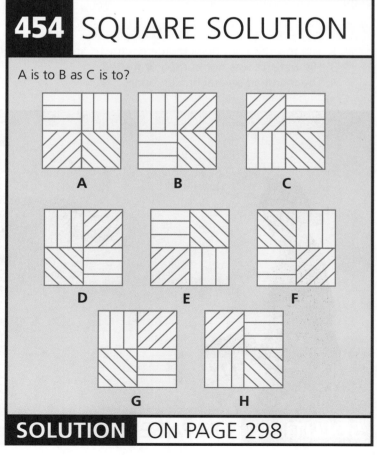

SOLUTION | ON PAGE 298

455 ZERO ORBIT

The squares of the times it takes planets to go round their sun are proportional to the cubes of the major axes of their orbits. With this in mind, if CD is four times AB, and a year on the planet Zero lasts for six earth years, how long is a year on the planet Hot?

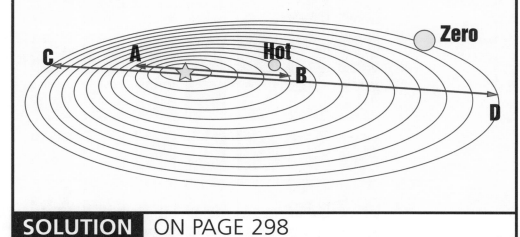

SOLUTION ON PAGE 298

456 ODD NUMBER

Which is the odd number out?

Thirty-six
Sixty-four
Seventy-two
Twenty-five
Eighty-one

SOLUTION ON PAGE 298

457 STAR BOXES

Put the stars into the boxes in such a way that each row is double the row below.

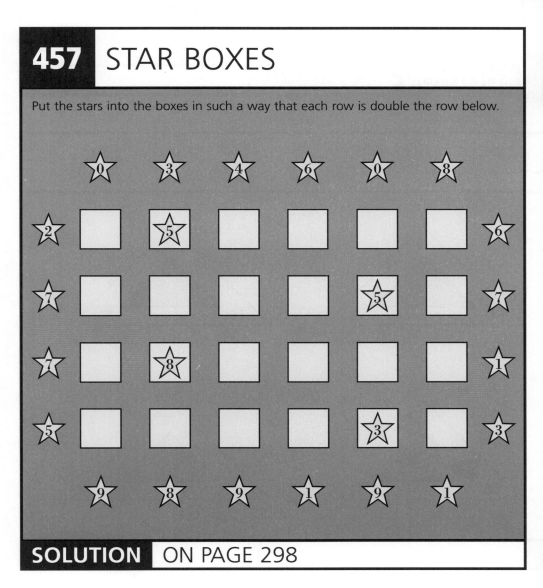

SOLUTION ON PAGE 298

458 DIAMONDS

What number should replace the question mark?

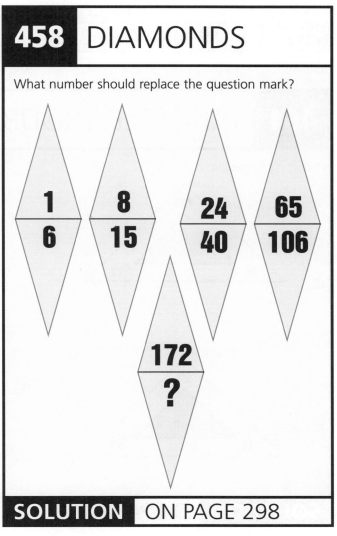

SOLUTION ON PAGE 298

459 FAMILY PUZZLE

Jon is Lorraine's brother. Diane married Jon. Diane is John's sister. Lorraine married John. Diane and Jon had seven grandchildren. Diane and Jon had three children. Lorraine and John had two children. Lorraine and John had seven grandchildren. Ricardo, one of Diane and Jon's children, and a cousin to Lorna-Jane and Frazier, did not marry, and had no offspring. Diane and Jon had two other children – Juan and Suzi. Lorraine and John had two children – Lorna-Jane and Frazier. Lorna-Jane married Juan, and had four children. Frazier married Suzi and had three children. Lorraine and John had twins. Frazier and Juan were cousins. Suzi and Lorna-Jane were cousins. Ricardo had a sister. Lorna-Jane had a brother. Frazier had a sister. Suzi had two brothers. For the above relationships to exist, how many were there, grand-parents, parents, children, cousins and siblings in all?

SOLUTION ON PAGE 298

460 SQUARE POSER

Insert the missing numbers to make each row, column, and long diagonal add to 189.

24	23	15	7	48	40	32
33		17	16	8		41
42	34		18		9	50
51	43	35		19	11	3
4	45		36		20	12
13		46	38	37		21
22	14	6	47	39	31	30

SOLUTION ON PAGE 298

461 TRIANGLE TROUBLE

What is the missing number?

137
36   27

92
47   61

50
16   134

28
132   40

43
85   72

79
21   ?

SOLUTION ON PAGE 298

462 DOTTY POSER

What is the missing number?

△ + △ + △ = 1368

△ − △ − △ = 210

△ + △ − △ = 1122

△ − △ + △ = ?

SOLUTION ON PAGE 298

463 WHICH NUMBERS?

Five of these numbers interact together to give the number 1 as a solution. Which five numbers, and in which order?

+ 19	**x 9**	**+ 29**	**x 7**	**− 999**
− 94	**+ 173**	**+ 65**	**− 236**	**x 8**
+ 122	**x 5**	**x 212**	**+ 577**	**− 567**
+ 190	**x 6**	**x 4**	**− 435**	**x 22**
x 13	**− 87**	**x 12**	**− 172**	**+ 117**

SOLUTION ON PAGE 298

464 NUMBER POSER

What is the missing number?

	27	
9		9
	18	

	51	
17		39
	12	

	60	
20		48
	12	

	45	
15		?
	18	

SOLUTION ON PAGE 299

465 NUMBER PROBLEM

What number should replace the question mark?

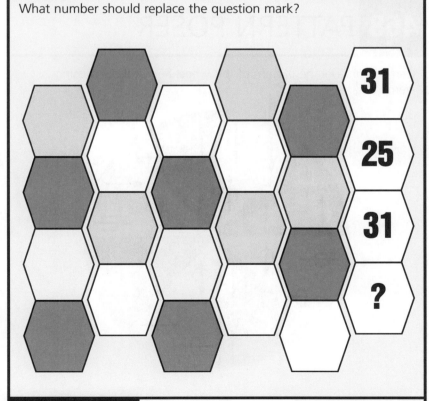

31

25

31

?

SOLUTION ON PAGE 299

466 TILE TROUBLE

Can you find the letter that would replace the question mark?

C
E G I

K

J
H L P

N

L
N P R

T

?
X B D F

B

D

SOLUTION ON PAGE 299

467 SHAPE SHUFFLE

These pieces, put together correctly, form a disc. However, two extra pieces got mixed up with them which are not part of the disc. Can you find them?

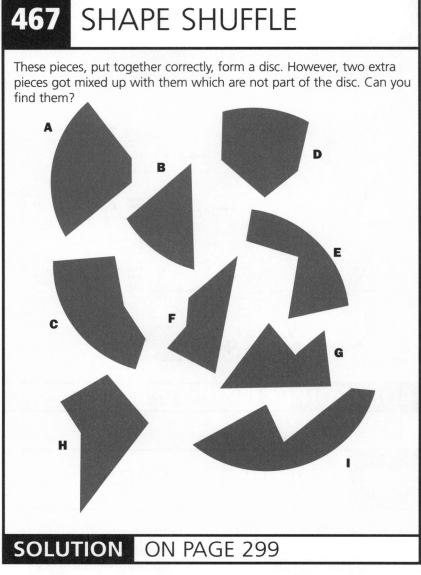

A B D E C F G H I

SOLUTION ON PAGE 299

468 PATTERN POSER

Can you unravel the pattern of this wheel and find the missing element?

SOLUTION ON PAGE 299

469 DOTTY DIAGRAM

Can you work out what the square with the question mark should look like?

?

SOLUTION ON PAGE 299

470 MISSING NUMBER

What number replaces the question mark?

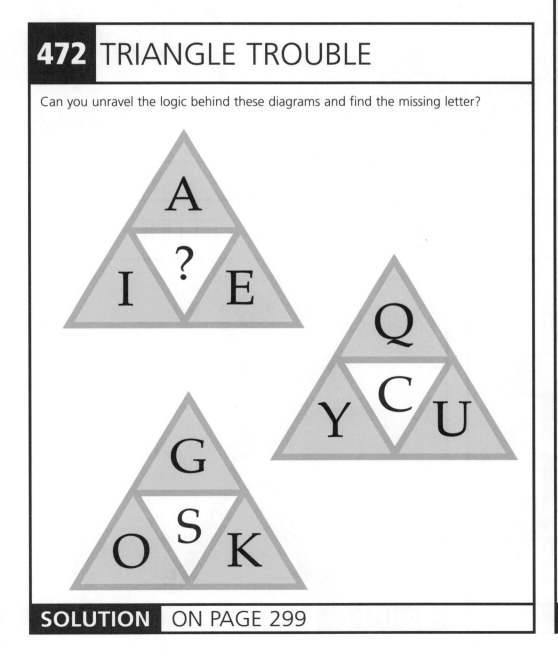

SOLUTION ON PAGE 299

472 TRIANGLE TROUBLE

Can you unravel the logic behind these diagrams and find the missing letter?

SOLUTION ON PAGE 299

471 SQUARE THINGS

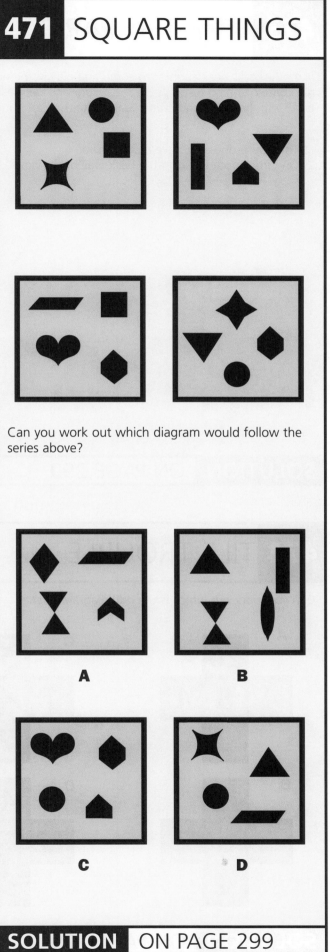

Can you work out which diagram would follow the series above?

SOLUTION ON PAGE 299

473 THE TEA PARTY

A mother calls her daughter to come and play in the house. The little girl comes running through the front door and decides to have a tea party with her dolls and teddy bears. After half an hour she is bored with this game, and decides to go back outside to play with her ball in the front garden. To get to the front garden she has to go through two front doors. Why?

1. The house does not have a porch door.
2. One front door is facing the back wall of the house.

SOLUTION ON PAGE 299

474 TILE TROUBLE

Can you work out which is the odd diagram out?

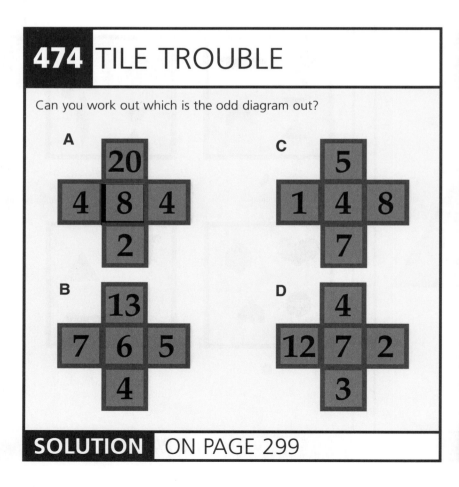

A
20
4 8 4
2

B
13
7 6 5
4

C
5
1 4 8
7

D
4
12 7 2
3

SOLUTION ON PAGE 299

475 MISSING LETTER

Can you work out which is the missing letter?

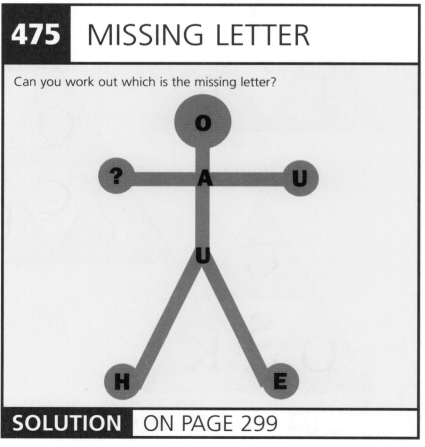

O

? A U

U

H E

SOLUTION ON PAGE 299

476 SHAPE SHUFFLE

The above pieces make up a disc when put together correctly. However, one piece is missing. Which is it?

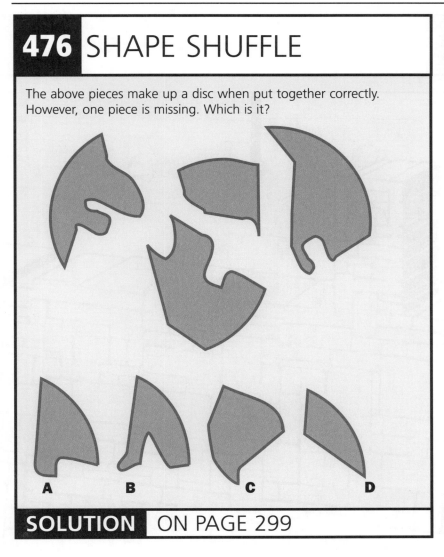

A   B   C   D

SOLUTION   ON PAGE 299

477 TILE TROUBLE

Can you unravel the reasoning behind these diagrams and find the missing shape?

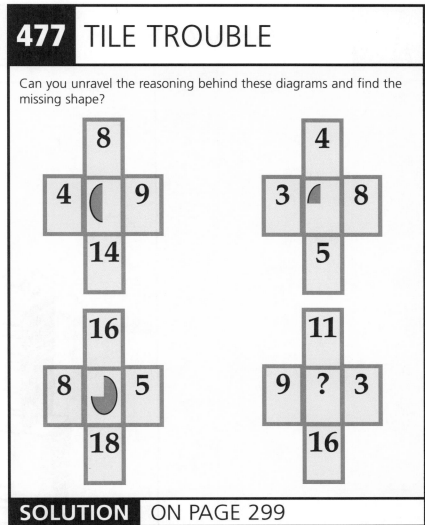

SOLUTION   ON PAGE 299

478 STAR MYSTERY

What letter should replace the question mark?

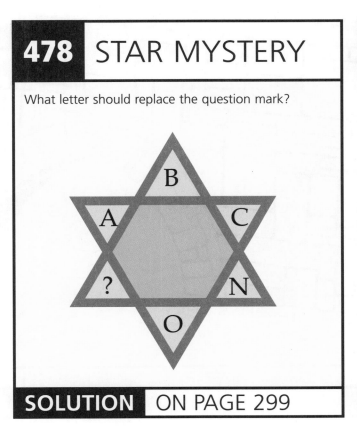

SOLUTION   ON PAGE 299

479 MISSING NUMBER

What number should replace the question mark?

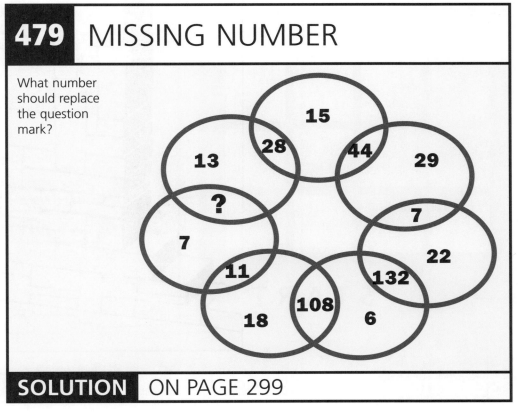

SOLUTION   ON PAGE 299

480 BRIDGE MAZE

START

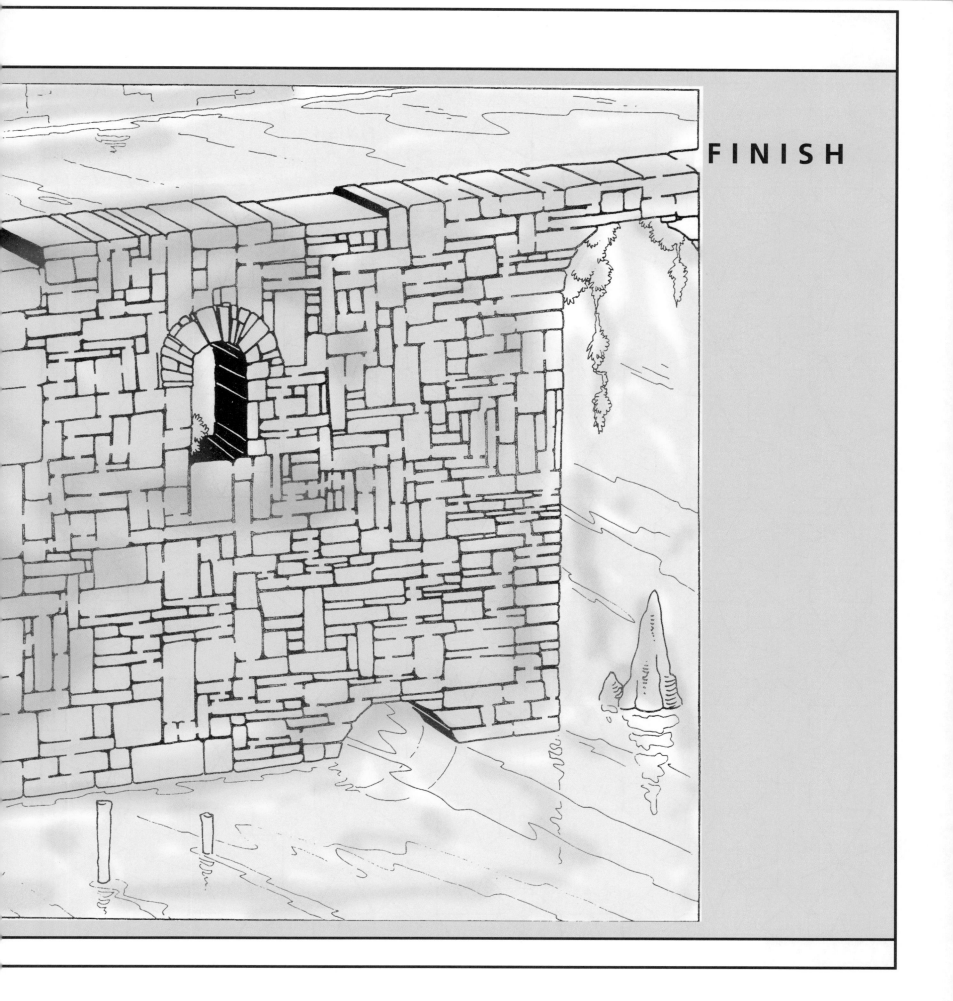

FINISH

481 CHINESE CONUNDRUM

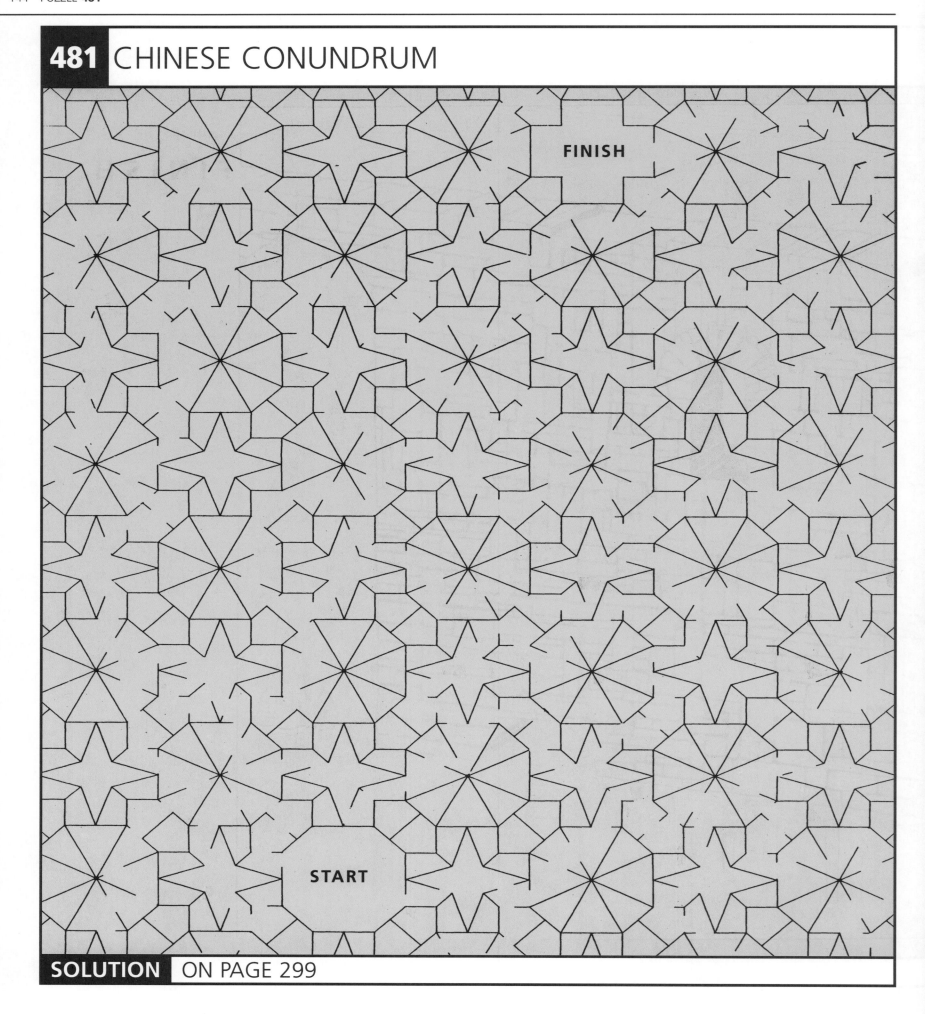

482 MAZE MURDER

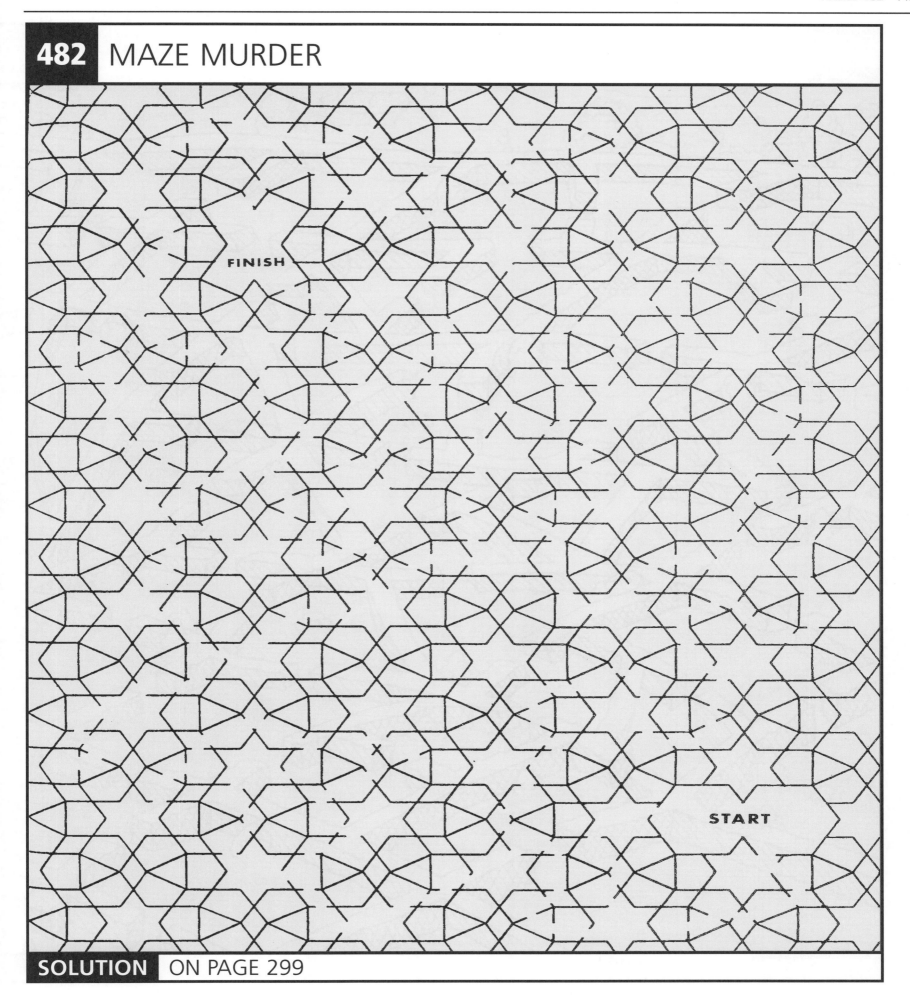

483 GARDEN QUEST

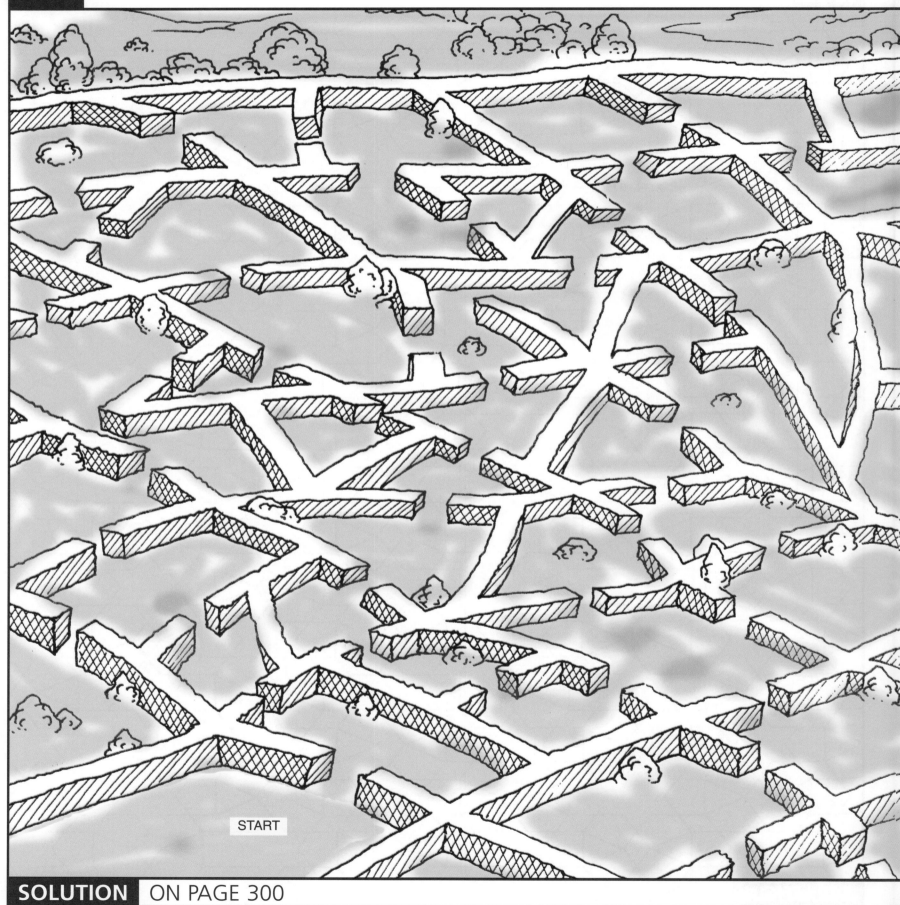

START

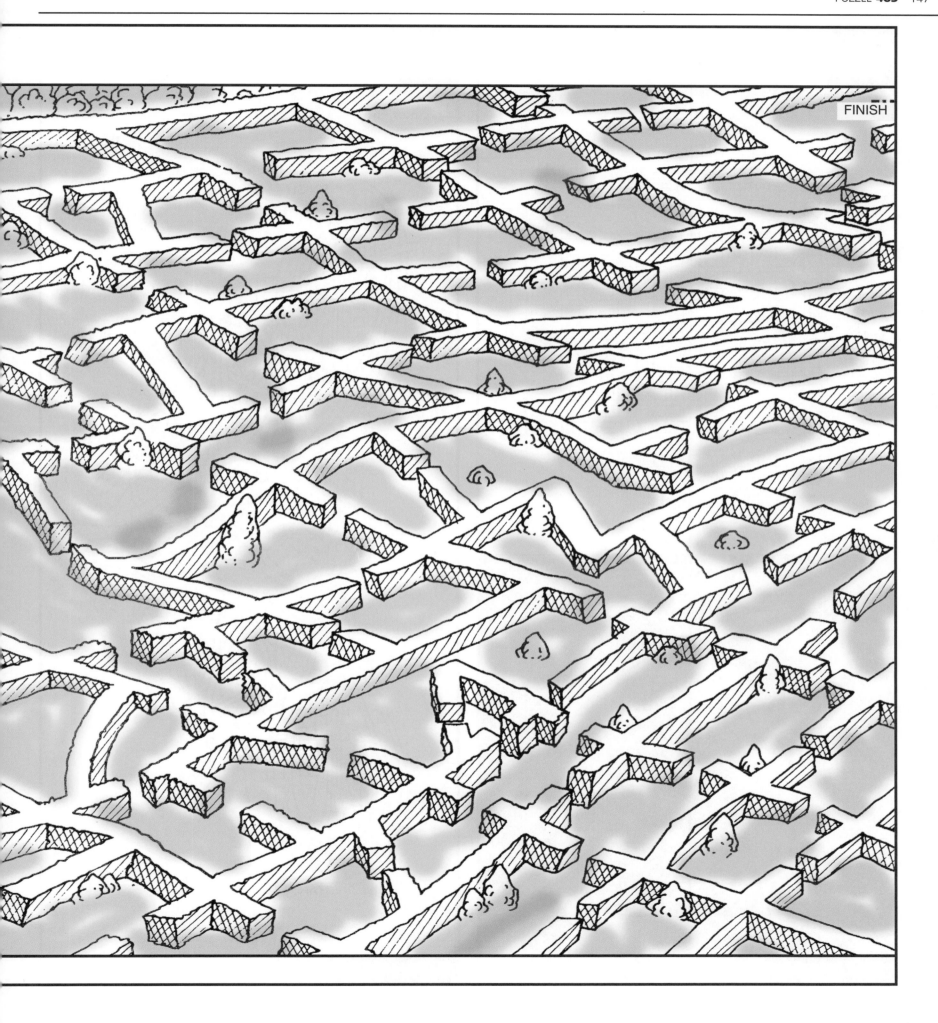

FINISH

484 ORIENTAL MAZE

SOLUTION ON PAGE 300

485 KNOTTY CELTS

SOLUTION ON PAGE 300

486 ALL AT SEA

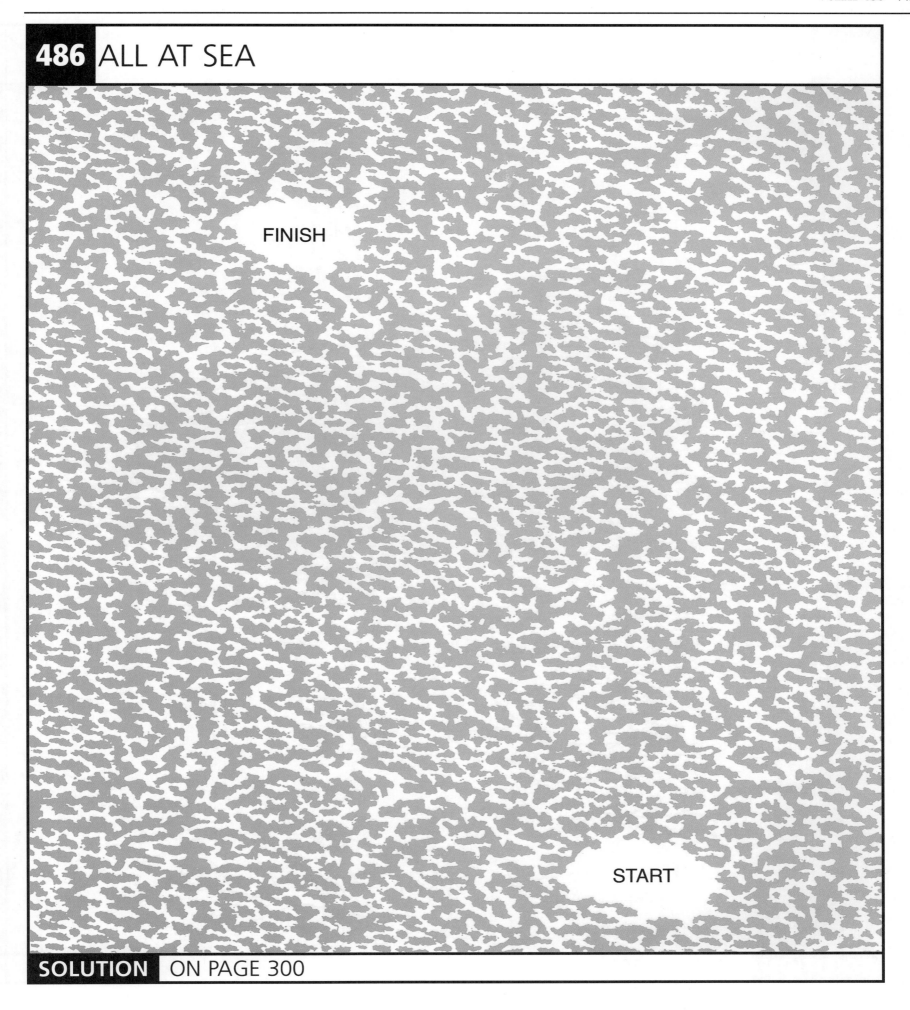

SOLUTION ON PAGE 300

487 PAINT PERPLEXITY

FINISH

START

488 NUMBER LOGIC

Can you unravel the logic behind this diagram and find the missing number?

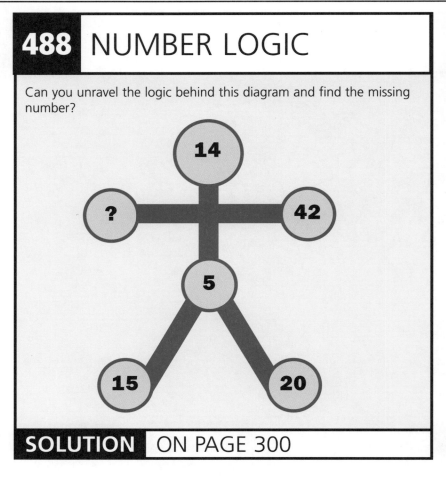

SOLUTION ON PAGE 300

489 MATH WHEEL

Can you unravel the reasoning behind this wheel and replace the question mark with a number?

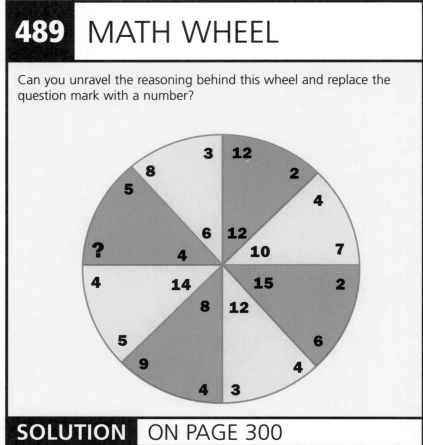

SOLUTION ON PAGE 300

490 LETTER LOGIC

Fit the 12 six-letter words in the spaces around each number so that they all interlink with the two adjoining ones. Words may be entered either clockwise or anti- (counter) clockwise.

ASPIRE
DELUGE
LADDER
PASSER
PERUSE
PLEADS
REPAST
SATIRE
STALKS
SURELY
TIPPLE
TREATS

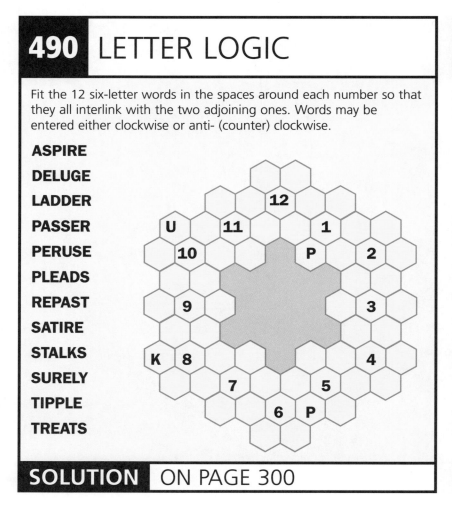

SOLUTION ON PAGE 300

491 PACKING POSER

A well known work of literature and its author are concealed in these crates. What are they?

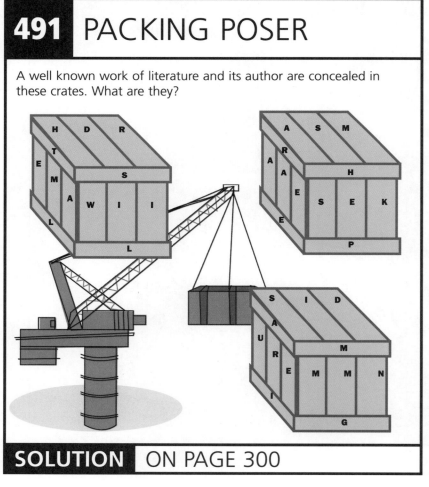

SOLUTION ON PAGE 300

492 PATTERN PROBLEM

Which of the following is the odd one out?

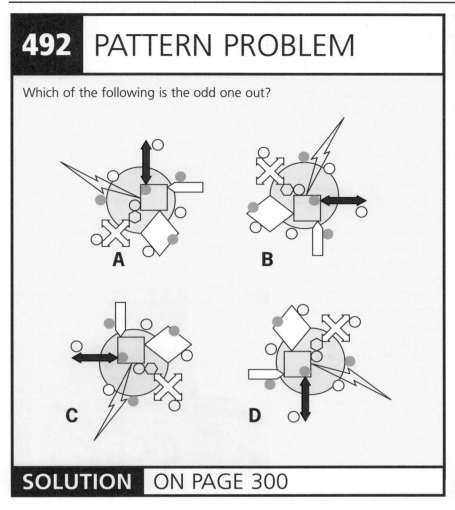

A B

C D

SOLUTION ON PAGE 300

493 WHEELIE DIFFICULT

If the wheel at A is turned as indicated, will the load first rise, or fall?

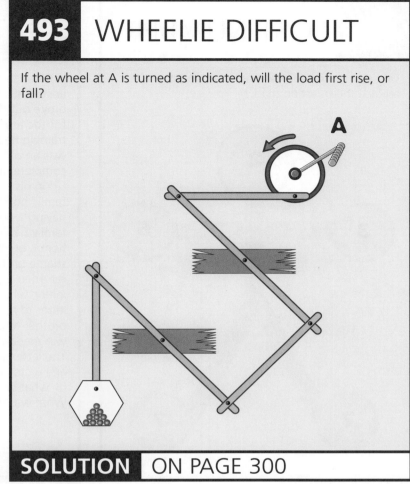

SOLUTION ON PAGE 300

494 SQUARE SOLUTION

Can you work out which diagram is the odd one out?

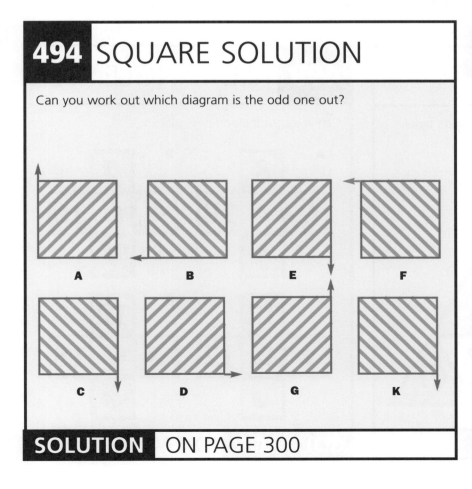

A B E F

C D G K

SOLUTION ON PAGE 300

495 SHAPE SHUFFLE

These pieces, when fitted together correctly, make up a square. However, one piece is not needed. Can you work out which one it is?

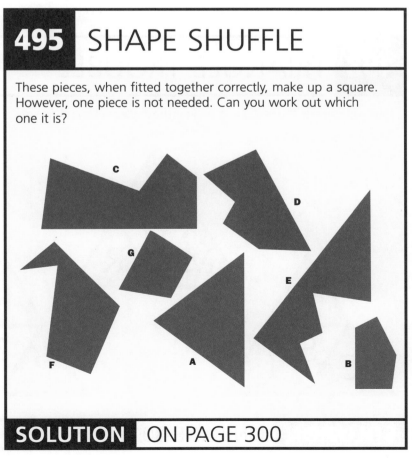

SOLUTION ON PAGE 300

496 LOST NUMBER

Can you work out which number would replace the question mark?

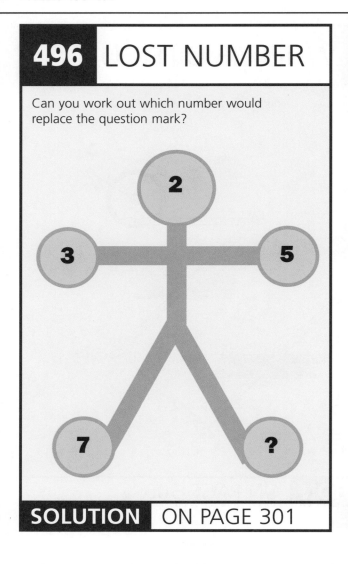

SOLUTION ON PAGE 301

497 TWO BROTHERS

In 1914 there were two brothers of an aristocratic family in England. When war broke out the first brother volunteered for the army without delay. After basic training he was sent to the front line. He was an officer and led his unit with complete distinction for over 12 months. Upon his return for a rest he went to his family home to find his brother just having a good time. For generations his family had served their country with honor, but his brother was bringing shame on the family name. The officer returned to the front and suffered an injury; while in the hospital he sent a letter to his brother, which caused his brother to enlist as a foot-soldier and win medals of distinction and bravery. The letter sent did not contain a letter or any words from his brother. Yet he knew by what was in there what it meant. What was in the letter?

1. The handwriting on the envelope was not his brother's.
2. It had a postmark that could not be read.
3. His brother did not speak to him to cause him to change his mind.
4. The envelope contained something that weighed no more than the envelope itself.
5. There was no message on the envelope.

SOLUTION ON PAGE 301

498 TRIANGLE TROUBLE

Can you unravel the reasoning behind these diagrams and find the missing letter?

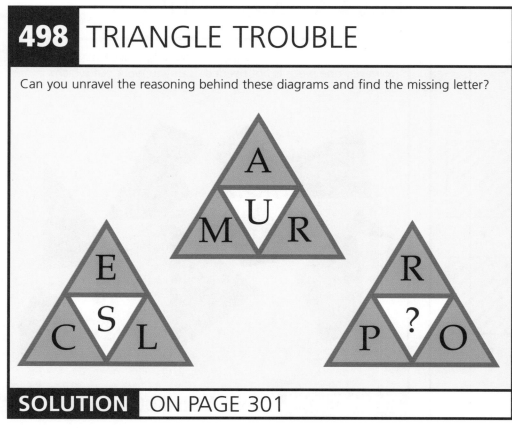

SOLUTION ON PAGE 301

499 TILE TANGLE

Can you spot the odd one out?

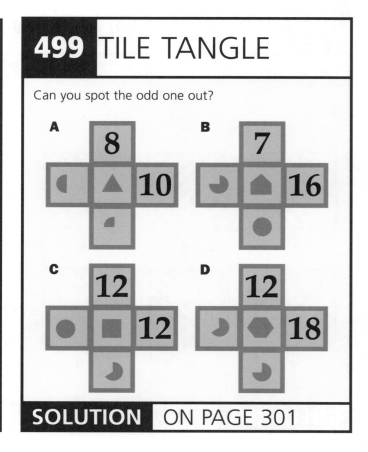

SOLUTION ON PAGE 301

500 ODDBALL?

Can you find the odd number out?

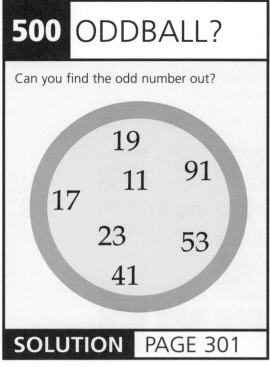

19
91
11
17
23
53
41

SOLUTION PAGE 301

501 LOST DIGIT

This square follows a pattern. Can you unravel it and replace the question mark with a number?

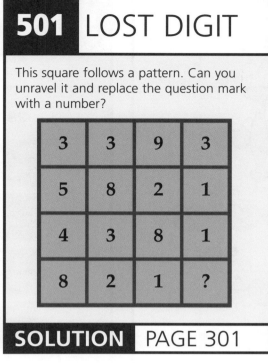

3	3	9	3
5	8	2	1
4	3	8	1
8	2	1	?

SOLUTION PAGE 301

502 SQUARES

Find a letter that could replace the question mark.

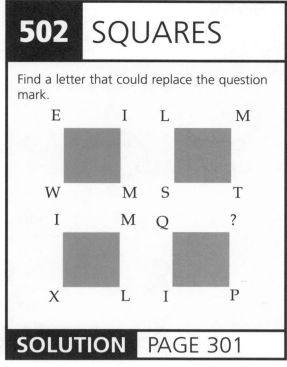

E   I   L   M

W   M   S   T

I   M   Q   ?

X   L   I   P

SOLUTION PAGE 301

503 COLOUR CODED

Find a number that could replace the question mark. Each colour represents a number under 10.

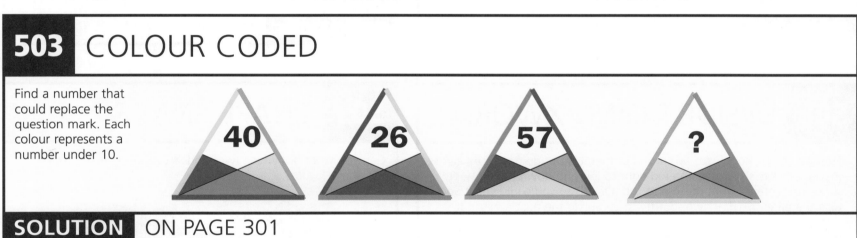

40   26   57   ?

SOLUTION ON PAGE 301

504 SQUARE SOLUTION

Find a number that could replace the question mark. Each colour represents a number under 10

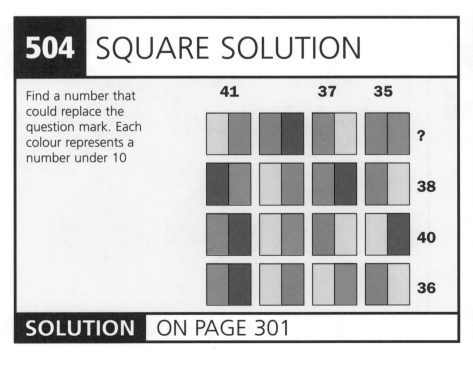

41   37   35

?
38
40
36

SOLUTION ON PAGE 301

505 COLOUR QUESTION

Find a number that could replace the question mark. Each colour represents a number under 10.

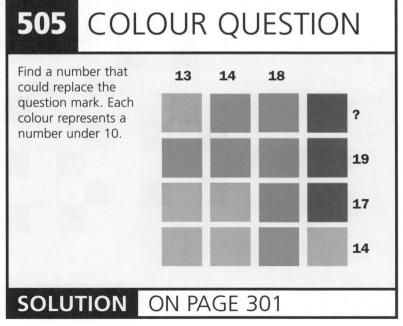

13   14   18

?
19
17
14

SOLUTION ON PAGE 301

506 SHAPE SHUFFLE

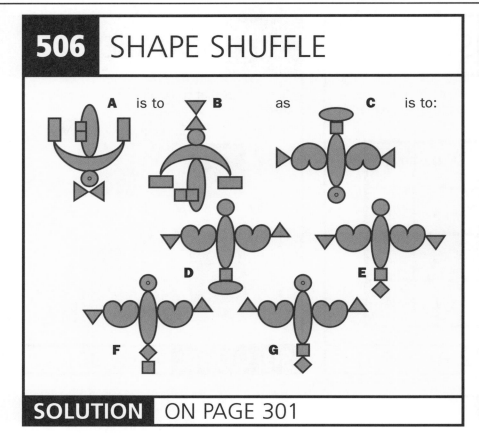

A is to B as C is to:

D E F G

SOLUTION ON PAGE 301

507 COOL COLOURS

Find a number that could replace the question mark. Each colour represents a number under 10.

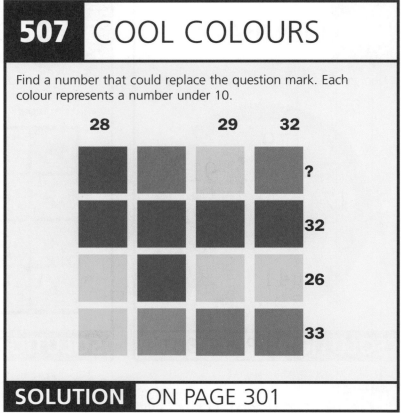

28   **29**   **32**

?

32

26

33

SOLUTION ON PAGE 301

508 UPSIDE DOWN XWORD

This is a conventional crossword except that it is upside-down. All across (back) answers should be entered right to left and down (up) answers should be entered from bottom to top. Of course you could cheat and turn the page upside-down, but try to complete the puzzle without doing that.

Back

3 The bony cavity of the eye (5)
6 Two-masted sailing vessel (4)
7 Backless chair (5)
8 A large cask for wine (4)
10 All separately (5)
14 Large book or volume (4)
15 Berate (5)
16 In Greek mythology, a man of superhuman powers (4)
17 Goodbye (5)

Up

1 A graceful and slender girl (5)
2 To swing at or through (5)
4 Large receptacle (6)
5 Image of religious figure (4)
9 Unfold (6)
11 Type of Swiss shout or cry (5)
12 Wading bird (5)
13 Sharp to the taste (4)

SOLUTION ON PAGE 301

509 SHAPE SNAKE

Can you work out which two models cannot be made from the above layout?

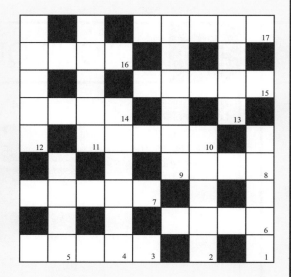

A   B   C

D   E   F

SOLUTION ON PAGE 301

510 DIGIT DILEMMA

Find a number that could replace the question mark. Each colour represents a number under 10.

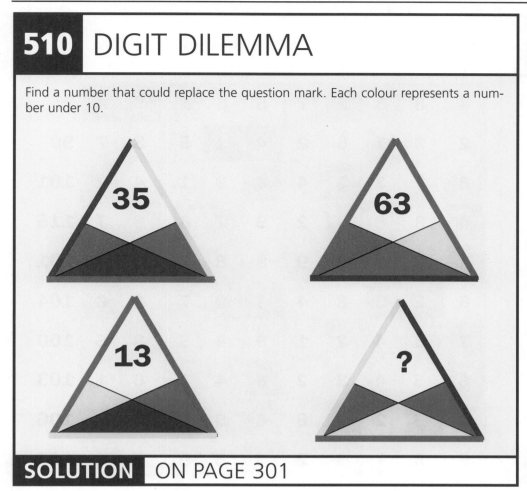

SOLUTION ON PAGE 301

511 COLOUR CODED

Find a number that could replace the question mark. Each colour represents a number under 10

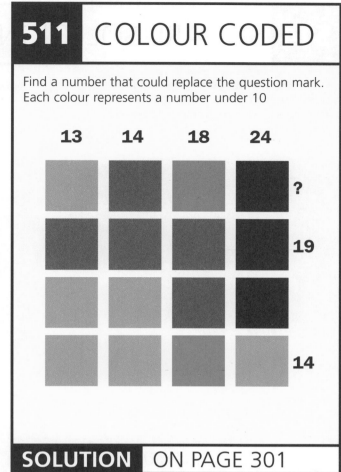

SOLUTION ON PAGE 301

512 LINE LOGIC

Which is the odd one out?

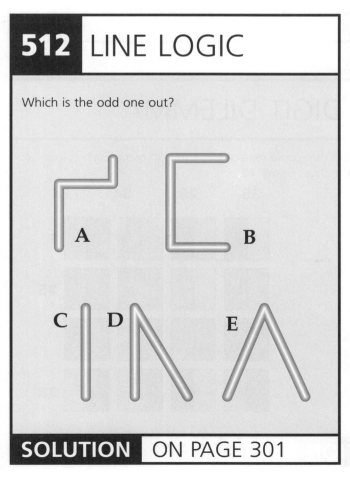

SOLUTION ON PAGE 301

513 BOOK BONANZA

The circles of letters below contain the names of three works of literature (one French, one from the Middle East, one American). Can you unravel them?

SOLUTION ON PAGE 301

514 SQUARE SOLUTION

Find a number that could replace the question mark. Each colour represents a number under 10. Some may be minus numbers.

4	8	3	2	7	5	6	1	9	4	?
2	3	7	6	2	4	1	5	3	7	90
8	7	3	2	4	6	9	1	4	2	101
4	3	6	8	2	9	7	6	8	7	115
3	2	1	6	9	8	8	7	3	4	101
6	2	3	8	4	1	9	7	2	6	104
7	3	4	2	1	9	4	5	3	5	100
6	5	4	3	2	8	4	7	6	1	103
3	5	2	1	8	6	9	4	3	7	106
6	8	7	3	2	4	5	9	5	6	109
103	98	99	100	81	117	121	109	99	107	

SOLUTION ON PAGE 301

515 LETTER TEASER

Using all 26 letters of the alphabet, once only, fill in the blanks to complete the crossword with good English words.

A B C
D E F
G H I
J K L
M N O
P Q R
S T U
V W X
Y Z

SOLUTION ON PAGE 301

516 DIGIT DILEMMA

Find a number that could replace the question mark. Each colour represents a number under 10.

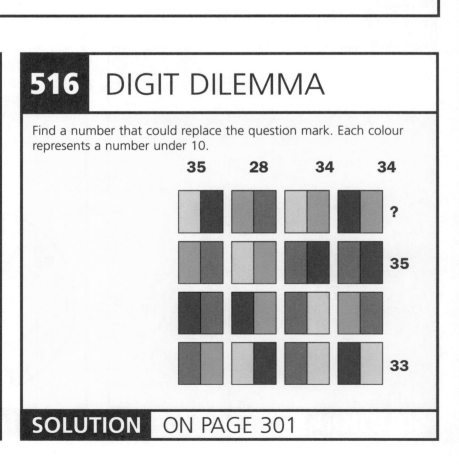

35	28	34	34
			?
			35
			33

SOLUTION ON PAGE 301

517 TIME TROUBLE

Have a look at these strange watches below. By cracking the logic which connects them you should be able to work out what time should be shown on the face of the fifth watch.

15.14.01

12.18.00

08.26.58

03.42.55

SOLUTION ON PAGE 301

518 EGGXACTLY!

Which of the following forms a perfect circle when combined with the diagram on the right?

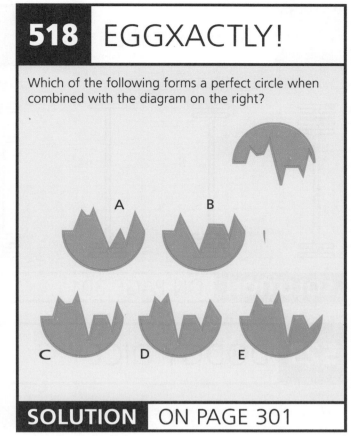

A   B

C   D   E

SOLUTION ON PAGE 301

519 MATCHES

Take 9 matches and lay them out in three triangles. By moving three matches try to make five triangles.

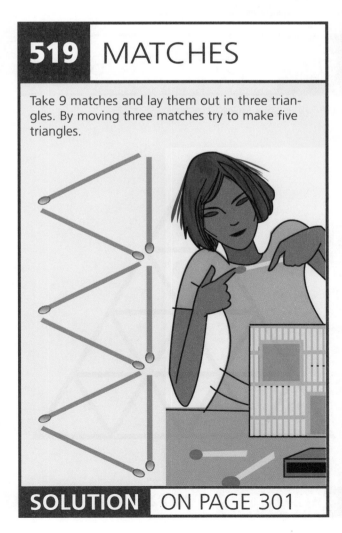

SOLUTION ON PAGE 301

520 STAR SOLUTION

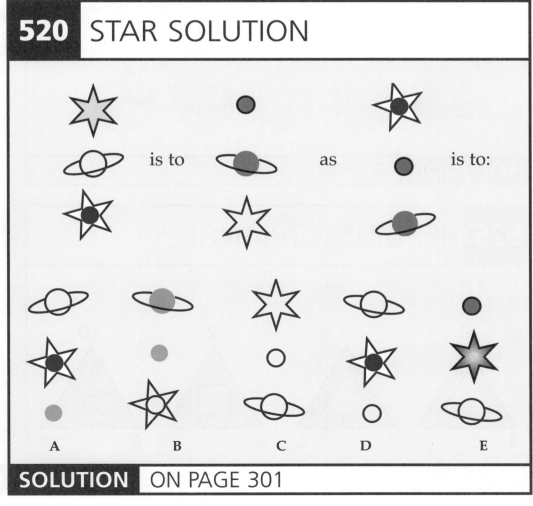

is to   as   is to:

A   B   C   D   E

SOLUTION ON PAGE 301

521 LINE LOGIC

Which is the odd one out?

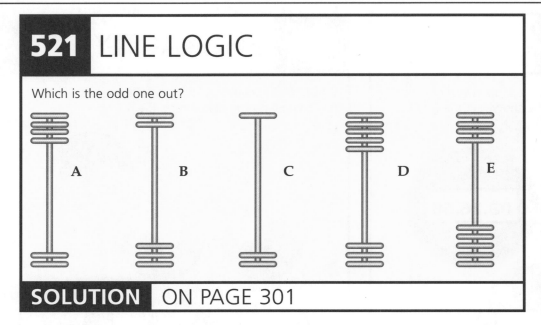

A B C D E

SOLUTION ON PAGE 301

523 DODGY DICE

Which cube can be made using:

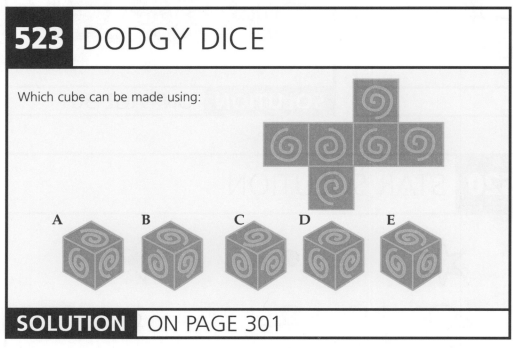

A B C D E

SOLUTION ON PAGE 301

525 BERMUDA TRIANGLES

Look at the triangles above. What geometrical shape should logically be placed in the fourth triangle?

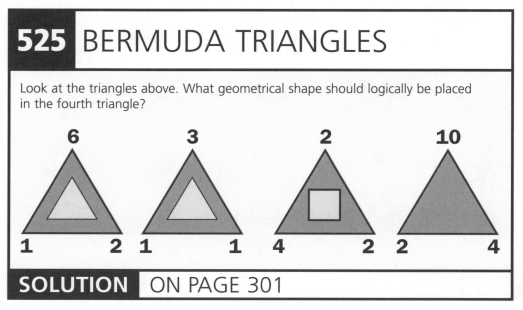

SOLUTION ON PAGE 301

522 DIGIT DODGE

The values of the segments are 3 consecutive numbers under 10. The yellow is worth 7 and the sum of the segments equals 50. What do the blue and green segments equal?

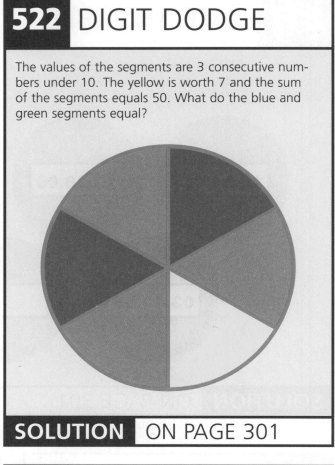

SOLUTION ON PAGE 301

524 DOTTY PROBLEM

Where should another dot belong?

SOLUTION ON PAGE 301

526 | AIRPORT PUZZLE

If you look at the grid carefully you will be able to find the names of three international airports cunningly concealed. The names wind through the grid like a snake so, once you have discovered one of them, it should be possible to discover the others.

SOLUTION | ON PAGE 302

527 | ANAGRAM XWORD

Each clue is an anagram of the answer. Take care, though, as some anagrams can produce more than one word. Make sure you enter the correct solution in the grid.

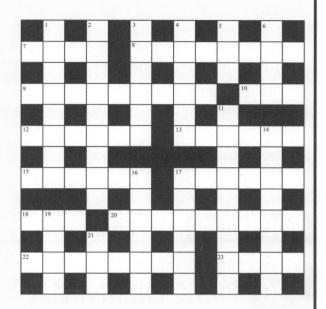

Across

7   PETS
8   MINE MINT
9   ROUT SATAN
10 SAP
12 RAT PEN
13 LET ANT
15 TO SLAM
17 SEE CUR
18 PAL
20 TOO MENIAL
22 ALL PALER
23 ELBA

Down

1   ALSO SANE
2   MOTOR SORE
3   INK PAD
4   OUT MAN
5   NED
6   SPAN
11 LOCAL TREE
14 MANY ROLL
16 PET ELM
17 LET SET
19 DALE
21 TEA

SOLUTION | ON PAGE 302

528 | BATH OF LIQUID

A woman fell into a full bath of liquid at work. When she got out she was dry, but she was taken straight to a hospital. Can you explain why she was dry and why she was taken to hospital?

1. The liquid in the bath was at room temperature.
2. There were warning signs to keep clear.
3. It was an accident that caused her to fall into the bath.
4. She had fallen gently and had not suffered a concussion or any severe blows.
5. The liquid in the bath was 4 feet deep, and little was lost when she fell in.
6. She was not wearing any protective clothing.
7. She had not ingested any of the liquid.
8. She was required to burn her clothes.

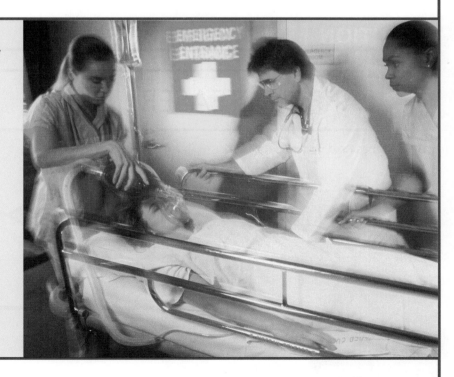

SOLUTION | ON PAGE 302

529 CAR PARKING OVERCROWDING

A company had a car park where all of the 10 spaces were allocated to its managers. They expanded the business and a new manager joined them. Part of his contract was to have a car-park space, just like the other managers. How was this achieved if nobody was asked to double-park?

1. The cars could not obstruct either of the access roads.
2. All of the spaces between the cars had to remain the same.
3. The extra car could not be parked in a location away from the front office wall, and all of the other managers kept their slot.
4. All of the cars needed to be parked at the same time.

SOLUTION   ON PAGE 302

530 DISK DILEMMA

Try to work out the fiendish logic behind this series of disks and decide which of A – E should go next.

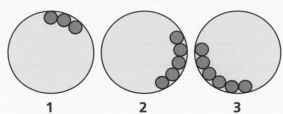

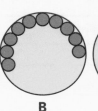

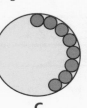

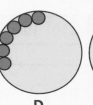

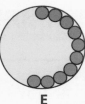

SOLUTION   ON PAGE 302

531 ARROW TEASER

What comes next in the sequence?

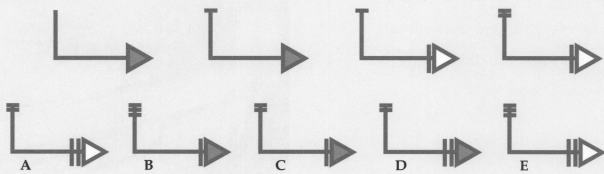

SOLUTION   ON PAGE 302

532 MISFIT?

Given that U in example D is incorrect, would C, I, M or X make it correct?

APDS   OYJC   HTBL   BLVU   ZGPF

A   B   C   D   E

SOLUTION ON PAGE 302

533 SYMBOL PUZZLE

Insert a basic mathematical symbol in between each number below to make the equations valid. No symbol is used more than once in each equation.

a) 3 4 5 6 = 13

b) 7 8 9 10 = 125

c) 11 12 13 14 = 140

SOLUTION ON PAGE 302

534 TRIANGLE TROUBLE

Which comes next in the sequence?

A   B   C   D

SOLUTION ON PAGE 302

535 CUBE CONUNDRUM

The pictures illustrate different views of one cube. What does the hidden side indicated by the X look like?

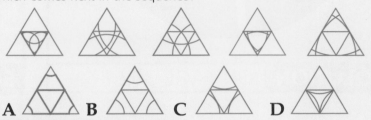

A   B   C   D   E

SOLUTION ON PAGE 302

536 STAR SOLUTION

Which is the odd one out?

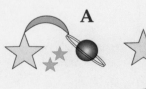   

A   B   C   D   E

SOLUTION ON PAGE 302

537 LOST NUMBER

How much is the question mark worth?

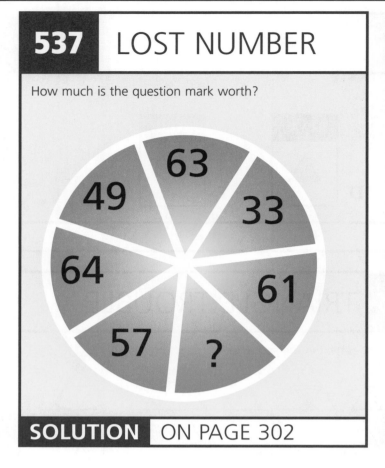

SOLUTION ON PAGE 302

538 STAR SEQUENCE

Which of the following comes next in the sequence?

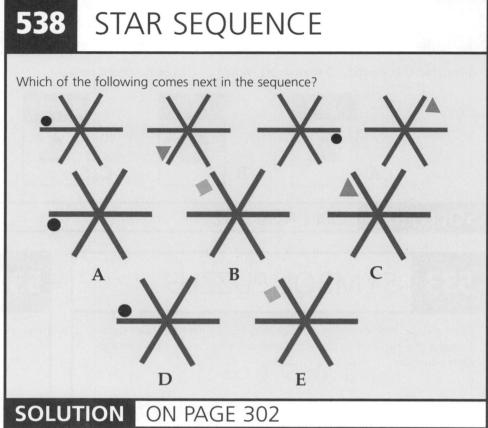

SOLUTION ON PAGE 302

539 THE COURIER'S WAIT

The courier phoned his customer to say that the crate that he had brought with him weighed one ton, and that they would need lifting equipment to unload it. He was less than a mile from the delivery point but it would be 6 hours before he could get there. He had covered the 20 miles from the collection point in just over one hour. Why would it take so much longer to reach the delivery point given the following clues?

1. He was not taking a detour, and there was no traffic between his current position and the delivery point.
2. He was not being held up because of other meetings or people.
3. The delay was not caused by unloading or loading any other products.
4. If it was 5¾ hours later, he could make the same journey in 15 minutes.
5. The roads in the area were free from traffic congestion and road works.
6. The reason was not due to anything anyone did.

SOLUTION ON PAGE 302

540 UNFOLDING DRAMA

Which of these is the odd one out? Think triangles.

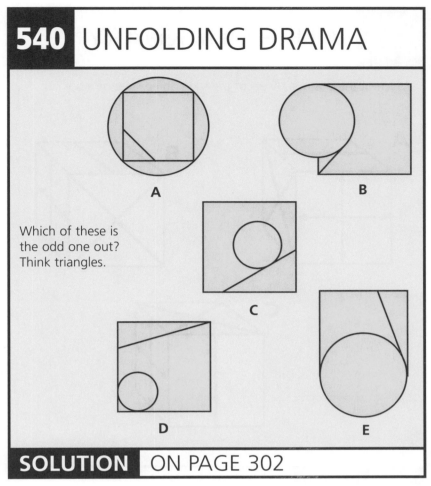

541 PATTERN POSER

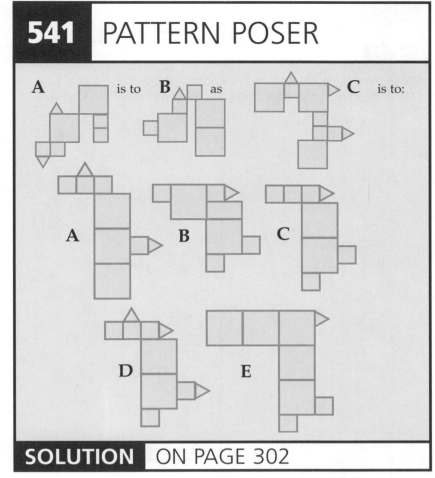

SOLUTION ON PAGE 302

SOLUTION ON PAGE 302

542 SEQUENCE SOLUTION

What comes next in the sequence?

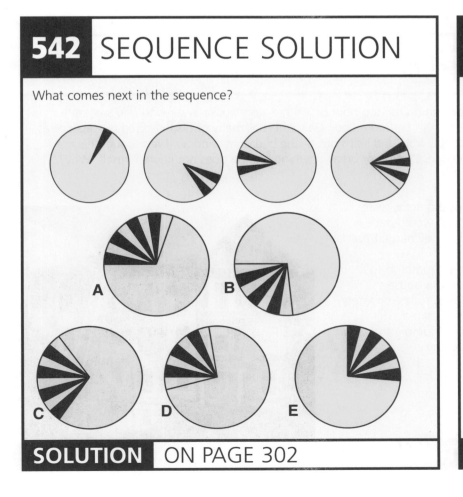

543 AIRPORT QUEST

Hidden in this grid are 11 international airports. The names follow each other and meander in a snake-like route through the grid. When you discover the first name you should be able to find the other 10.

SOLUTION ON PAGE 302

SOLUTION ON PAGE 302

544 DING DONG PUZZLE

Move from circle to touching circle collecting the letters of BELL. Always start at the B. How many different ways are there to do this?

SOLUTION ON PAGE 302

545 CUBE QUANDARY

Which of these is not a view of the same three sides of a box?

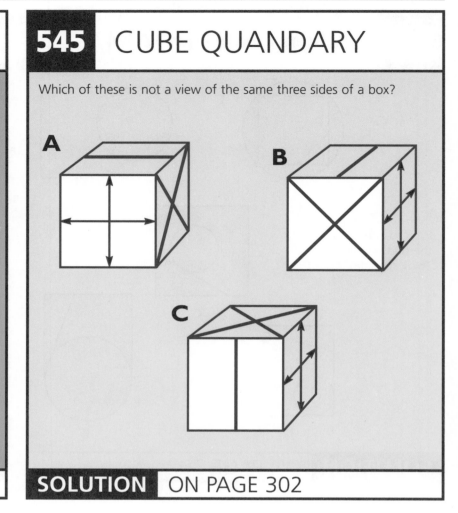

SOLUTION ON PAGE 302

546 WORD LADDER

Change the second letter of each word to the left and the right. Two other words must be formed. Place the letter used in the empty section. When this has been completed for all the words another word can be read down. What is the word?

GLOW			BEAT
CONE			DOME
HAVE			MACE
SHOW			ITCH
IRIS			ILEX
READ			LIVE
STAG			SLAB

SOLUTION ON PAGE 302

547 LEAP TO SAFETY

A man sleeping on the top floor of a three-story house awakes to find smoke coming under his bedroom door. He gathers as many of his treasured possessions as he can possibly hold and leaps out of the bedroom window. Even though his arms are full, he doesn't drop or break anything and he does not injure himself. Why?

1. Some of the items were fragile and would have broken if they had hit the ground.
2. He did not jump on to a ledge on the house.
3. No ladders, ropes, or safety nets were employed.
4. He did not jump into water or soft snow.

SOLUTION ON PAGE 302

548 BALLOON BUST

Which of the numbers on these balloons is the odd one out?

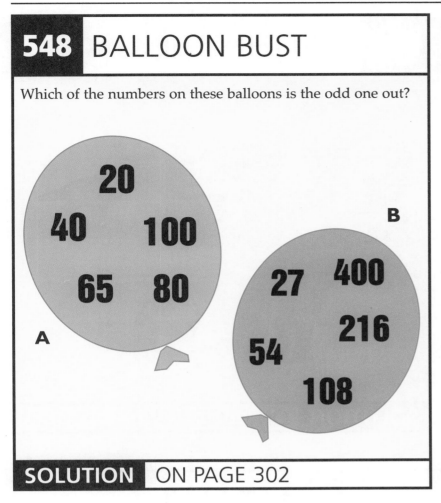

20
40 100
65 80
A

B
27 400
216
54
108

SOLUTION   ON PAGE 302

549 BOX BONANZA

Which two boxes in this diagram are similar?

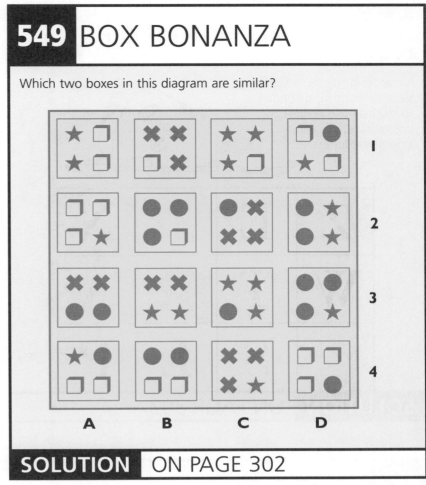

A   B   C   D

SOLUTION   ON PAGE 302

550 KID CONUNDRUM

These kids' ages are in some way related to their names. How old is Andrew?

Harry
Ronald

8

18

Nicola
Andrew
Caroline

14   ?

3

SOLUTION   ON PAGE 302

551 CLOCK PUZZLE

What time should the fourth clock show?

SOLUTION   ON PAGE 302

552 COUNTRY CONCERN

Move from square to touching square, including diagonals, to discover the longest possible country name from these letters.

Z	E	D	N
W	T	R	A
I	S	L	P

SOLUTION ON PAGE 302

553 CRITTER CLUE

Four of these animals have something in common. Which is the odd one out? (Clue: think diets)?

SOLUTION ON PAGE 302

554 CODE CORNER

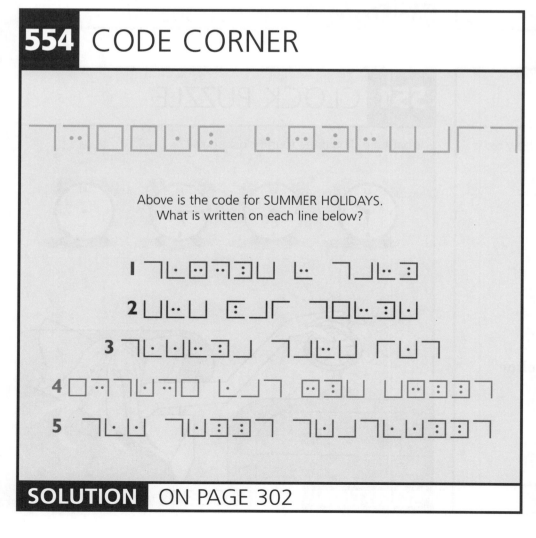

Above is the code for SUMMER HOLIDAYS. What is written on each line below?

1

2

3

4

5

SOLUTION ON PAGE 302

555 STICKY!

Remove eight of these straight lines to leave only two squares. How can this be done?

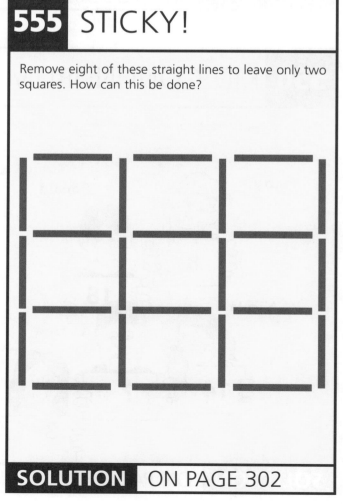

SOLUTION ON PAGE 302

556 DISC DILEMMA

Which one of the following numbers is the odd one out?

68 **50** **31** **24** **18**

SOLUTION ON PAGE 302

557 NAUTICAL BUT NICE

All across answers are nautical terms.

Across
1 Ship's cook house (6)
4 Cargo thrown overboard (6)
9 Type of navigation method (4,9)
12 Rise and fall of the sea (4)
14 Carry by the wind (4)
16 Timber support (4)
17 Left side (4)
24 Instrument for seizing ship (9,4)
25 Beach (6)
26 Distance to be made up away from the wind (6)

Down
1 Trick of the trade (6)
2 Mineral (4)
3 Make money (4)
5 Famous English public school (4)
6 Satirical piece (4)
7 Attractive metal (6)
8 Perform (3)
10 Units in sport (5)
11 Exchanges (5)
13 Frozen water (3)
15 A long distance (3)
16 Boats carrying goods (6)
18 Number (6)
19 Human "fur" (4)
20 Extend from side to side (4)
20 Taste (3)
22 Amorous glance (4)
23 Bird (4)

SOLUTION ON PAGE 302

558 BUNNY HUTCH

In row A–A there are three rabbits. Another three rabbits are in row C–C. In row B–B there are two rabbits. How many rows are there of three rabbits and how many of two? Remove three rabbits and arrange the remaining six in three rows of three rabbits each. How can this be done?

SOLUTION ON PAGE 302

559 PARCEL POSER

There is a different pattern on each side of the box. Which of these is not a view of the same box?

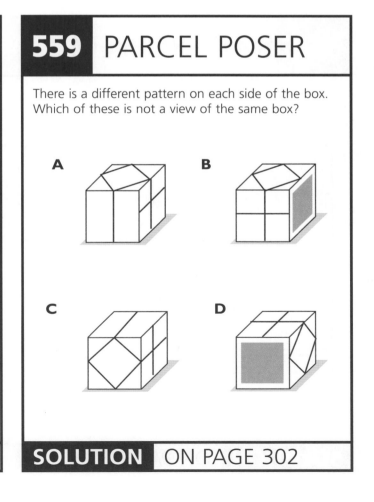

A   B   C   D

SOLUTION ON PAGE 302

560 SYMBOL SOLUTION

Each shape in the diagram has a value. Work out the values to discover what number should replace the question mark.

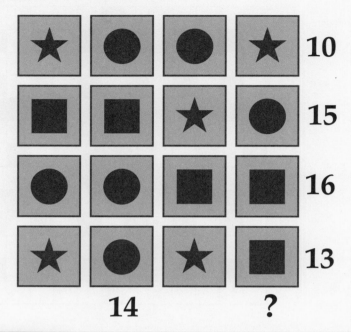

10
15
16
13
14   ?

SOLUTION   ON PAGE 302

561 TRIANGLES

What number should replace the question mark in the fourth triangle?

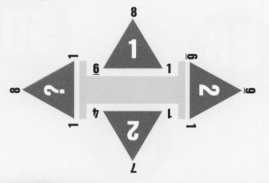

SOLUTION   ON PAGE 302

563 TIME TEASER

What time should the fourth clock show?

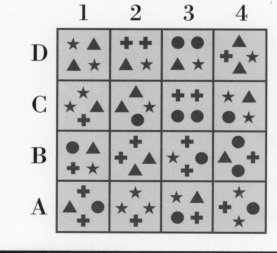

SOLUTION   ON PAGE 302

562 BOX PROBLEM

Should box A, B, C or D come next in this series?

A   B   C   D

SOLUTION   ON PAGE 302

564 BRAIN BOX

Which two boxes are similar?

SOLUTION   ON PAGE 302

565 THE CLASS

James trudges off to school each morning with his books but he rarely does homework, and he doesn't achieve high marks in tests either. There are 36 children in his class and 35 of them are good students. Why does James never get into trouble?

1. James is always polite.
2. James has been sent to the head's office on a number of occasions.
3. James is not related to anyone at the school and he is not a special student.

SOLUTION ON PAGE 302

566 COLOUR BLIND

Match each of the colours shown with one of the words from the list. Each pair will comprise a well-known expression.

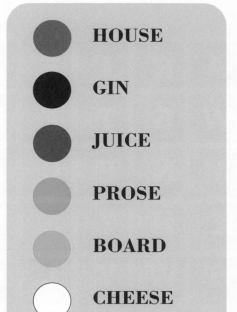

HOUSE

GIN

JUICE

PROSE

BOARD

CHEESE

SOLUTION ON PAGE 302

567 X WORD

A straightforward crossword, but with only 21 blank spaces.

Across
1 Bag made of netting (5)
6 Water bottles (7)
13 Stay (6)
14 Dormant (6)
15 Warning call (5)
16 Dye (7)
17 One thought likely to gain office (9)
19 Delve (3)
20 Hoax (3)
21 Strong wind (4)
22 Present (4)
23 Throw (4)
24 Employer (5)
26 The two (4)
27 Vessels (4)
28 Away (5)
30 Thaw (4)
32 Trick (4)
33 Circumvent (4)
34 Plan (3)
36 Mimic (3)
37 Carriage (9)
39 Painting (7)
41 Extend (5)
42 Lure (6)
43 Minor (6)
44 Canopies (7)
45 Exploits (5)

Down
1 Course (5)
2 Put down again (6)
3 Correct (5)
4 Custody (4)
5 Go to law (8)
7 Having wings (5)
8 Fury (4)
9 Devoured (3)
10 Metal guards (7)
11 Whole (6)
12 Old hands (7)
16 Barley for brewing (4)
18 Elan (4)
22 Suggest slightly (4)
23 Body of laws (4)
24 Fastened up with rope (8)
25 Low wall (7)
26 Cuts in two (7)
27 Nuisance (4)
29 Indolent (6)
30 Absolutely (4)
31 Notched (6)
33 For making holes (5)
34 Minister's house (5)
35 Nobles (5)
37 Hue (4)
38 Demolish (4)
40 Bird (3)

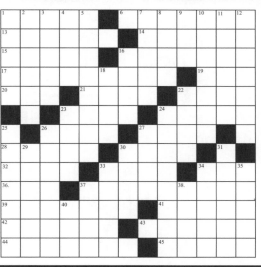

SOLUTION ON PAGE 303

568 STYLE SOLUTION

Five of the words in the diagram are associated for some reason. Find the words and then work out whether STYLE belongs to the group.

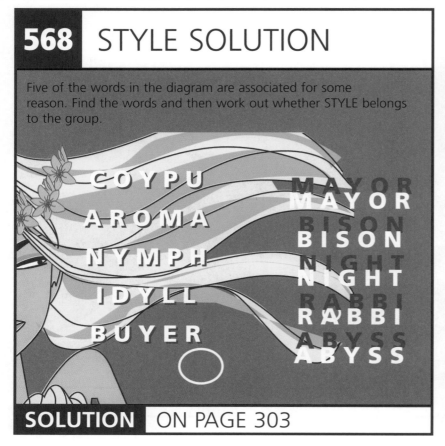

COYPU
AROMA
NYMPH
IDYLL
BUYER

MAYOR
BISON
NIGHT
RABBI
ABYSS

SOLUTION ON PAGE 303

569 WORD LADDER

Which is the odd one out?

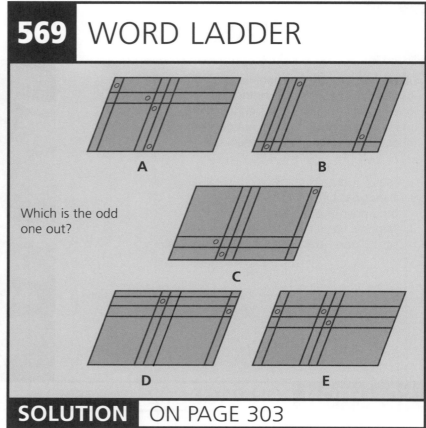

A   B

C

D   E

SOLUTION ON PAGE 303

570 WORD

A is to **B** as **C** is to:

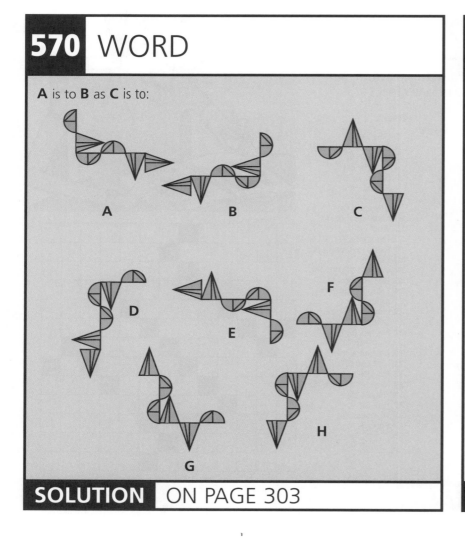

A   B   C

D   E   F

G   H

SOLUTION ON PAGE 303

571 QUOTE UNQUOTE

A quotation has been written in this diagram. Find the start letter and move from square to touching square until you have found it. What is the quotation and to whom is it attributed?

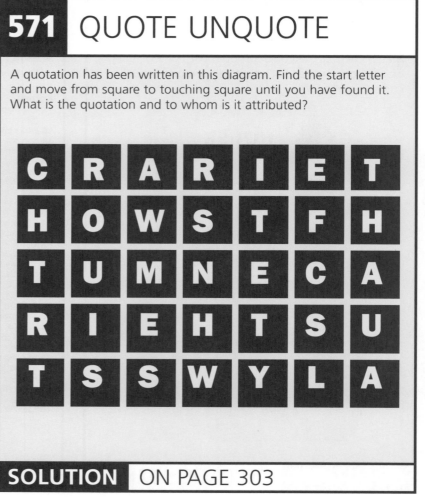

C	R	A	R	I	E	T
H	O	W	S	T	F	H
T	U	M	N	E	C	A
R	I	E	H	T	S	U
T	S	S	W	Y	L	A

SOLUTION ON PAGE 303

572 PONY & TRAP?

Complete the word ladder by changing one letter of each word per step. The newly created word must be found in the dictionary. What are the words to turn PONY to CART?

P O N Y

C A R T

573 CAROUSEL PROBLEM

The name given to this puzzle is the old fairground name for the roundabout ride on horses, now more familiarly known as the carousel. Complete the words in each column, all of which end in G. The scrambled letters in the section clockwise of each column are an anagram of a word that will give you a clue to the word that should be put in the column. The first letter of the answer is given each time, and one other is also provided.

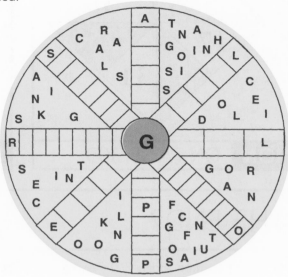

574 FEEDING FRENZY

The names of three foods are to be found in the diagram. The letters of the names are in the order they normally appear. What are the foods?

575 WORD WHEEL

Select one letter from each of the segments.
When the correct letters have been found a word of eight letters can be read clockwise. What is the word?

576 DIAMOND

Study the diamond to work out which number should replace the question mark.

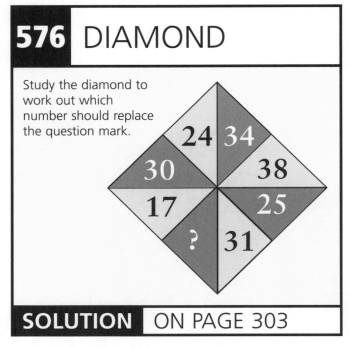

SOLUTION ON PAGE 303

577 DISTANCE DISASTER

This is a meaningless signpost but there is a twisted form of logic behind the figures. Discover the logic and find the distance.

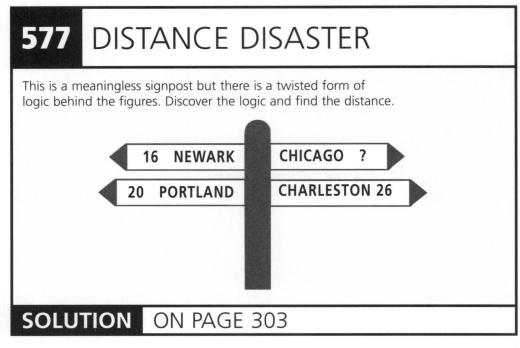

16 NEWARK   CHICAGO ?

20 PORTLAND   CHARLESTON 26

SOLUTION ON PAGE 303

578 THE END?

Which four-letter word can be added to the end of the six words below to create half a dozen new eight-letter words?

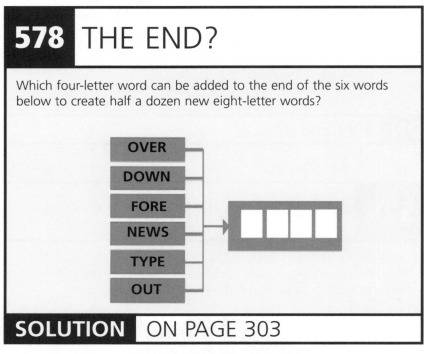

OVER

DOWN

FORE

NEWS

TYPE

OUT

SOLUTION ON PAGE 303

579 BALLET ENIGMA

Start at the letter B and move from circle to touching circle to the A at the top right. How many different ways are there of collecting the nine letters of BALLERINA?

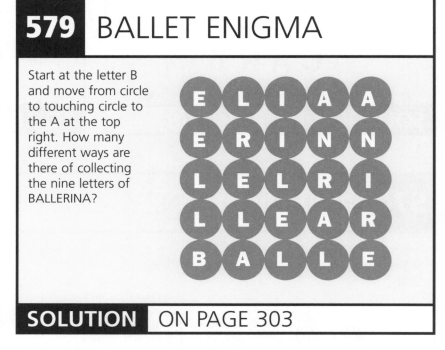

SOLUTION ON PAGE 303

580 NUMBER

Which shape replaces the question mark?

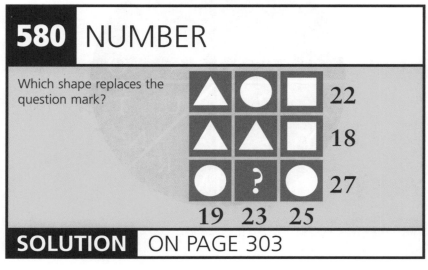

SOLUTION ON PAGE 303

581 WORD HEAP

Place the letters shown into the diagram in such a way that three words can be read across and one down the middle. What are the words?

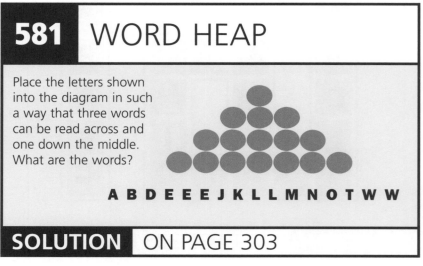

A B D E E E J K L L M N O T W W

SOLUTION ON PAGE 303

582 FRUIT FIESTA

A woman has a small collection of artificial fruits on the windowsill. The apple is rosy red on one side and bright green on the other side, and there is a little white stalk sticking out from the top. The peach is a lovely soft warm shade of pinky-orange, with a larger white stalk. There is also a pear and a deep burgundy-coloured plum. The woman leaves them on the windowsill and goes out of the room. When she returns half an hour later she cannot see the fruits at all. Why? Nobody else has been in the room. Nobody has moved them. There is nothing blocking her view; the room is clear, and there is no mist.

1. They had not been stolen.
2. They had not been eaten.
3. A telltale clue had been left.
4. The room had an unusual smell about it when she returned.
5. Animals and insects had nothing to do with the disappearance.

SOLUTION ON PAGE 303

583 LETTER LOGIC

Take the letters and arrange them correctly in the column under which they appear. Once this has been done a movie title will appear.
What is the movie?

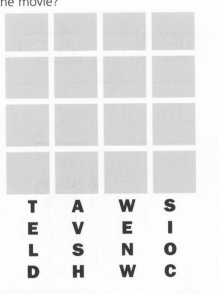

T	A	W	S
E	V	E	I
L	S	N	O
D	H	W	C

SOLUTION ON PAGE 303

584 CROSSWORD

Insert the words provided into the grid to complete the crossword. There is just one problem: in the list provided are two red-herring words, which do not fit in the grid.

AUDIO
AXIS
COMB
COOL
CROCHET
CUPID
DAB
DEER
DEFY
DEMOCRAT
DETERGENT
HEWER
LIBRA
MICRO
OCCUPY
OCTET

PANDORA
PIT
RHETORIC
SHORTHAUL
SIMMER
SPOKESMAN
STIFLE
SYMBOLIC
THORN
WAFER
WOOLLY
ZERO HOUR

SOLUTION ON PAGE 303

585 WORD WHEEL

Place one letter in the middle of this diagram. Four five-letter words can now be rearranged from each straight line of letters. What is the letter and what are the words?

SOLUTION ON PAGE 303

586 TILE TROUBLE

Arrange the tiles in this diagram so that they form a square. When this is done correctly four words can be read down and across. What are the words?

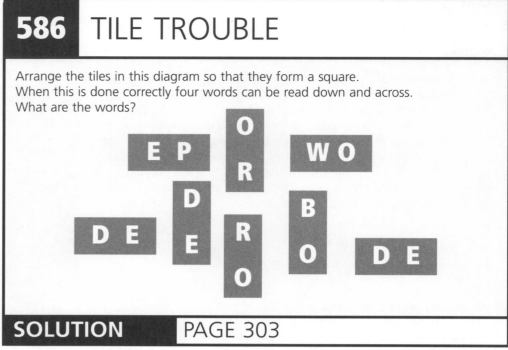

SOLUTION PAGE 303

587 WORDFRAME

Select one of the two letters from the grid, in accordance with the reference shown, and place it in the wordframe. When the correct letters have been chosen a 16-letter word can be read. What is the word?

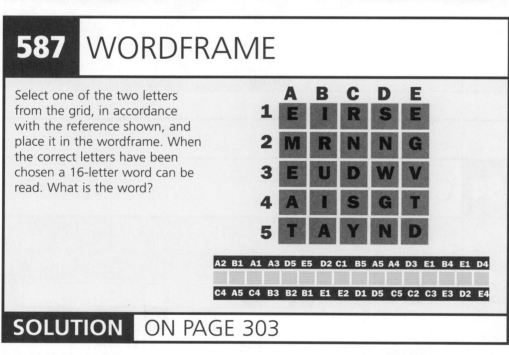

SOLUTION ON PAGE 303

588 MIDDLE MUDDLE

Place a word of four letters in the empty space. This word, when added to the end of the three words to the left and to the beginning of the three words to the right, will form six other words. What is the word?

BELL   MAN

BLUE   BATH

JAIL   LIME

SOLUTION ON PAGE 303

589 WORD WEDGE

Make a circle out of these shapes. When the correct circle has been found a word can be read clockwise. What is the word?

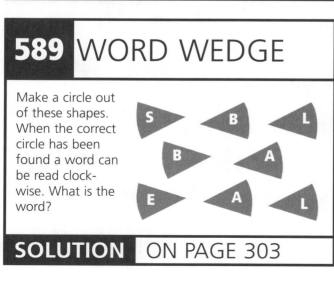

SOLUTION ON PAGE 303

590 SILK SOLUTION

Move from circle to touching circle collecting the letters of SILK. Always start at the S. How many different ways are there to do this?

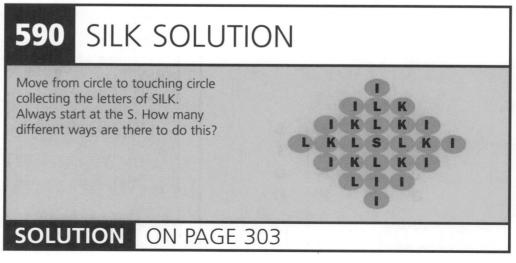

SOLUTION ON PAGE 303

591 WORD LADDER

Change the first letter of each word to the left and the right. Two other words must be formed. Place the letter used in the empty section. When this has been completed for all the words another word can be read downwards. What is the word?

PANG		DREW
OVEN		OVER
RING		DEED
MAKE		BENT
INTO		KNIT
BEST		CAGE
CARS		OMIT

SOLUTION ON PAGE 303

592 CROSSWORD

This is a straightforward crossword, almost! There is just one problem; the answers to the clues might need to be entered forward or back, down or up. For instance, the across answer "play" may appear as play or yalp, and a down answer "work" may appear as either

w or k
o r
r o
k w

Across

3 Blaze with unsteady flame (5)
6 Develop gradually (6)
7 Elephant tusk material (5)
8 Discount (6)
12 Large bang (6)
13 Roll of tobacco for smoking (5)
14 Combined (6)
15 Coverings for feet (5)

Down

1 Move stealthily (5)
2 Orb (5)
3 Reticent (9)
4 Always (4)
5 Spoken (4)
9 Ruin (5)
10 Quarrel (5)
11 Pile (4)
12 Rise and fall of sea (4)

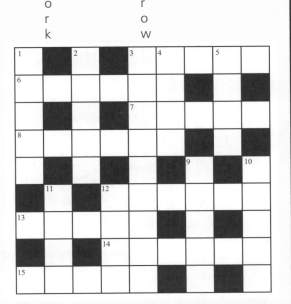

SOLUTION ON PAGE 303

593 DISAPPEARING TREAT

At a candy store a young boy was allowed to choose what he wanted. He came out of the shop happily clutching a full bag. He made a hole in the top of the bag and began eating. He only ate a small amount of the contents but within half an hour his bag was virtually empty. He did not drop the bag or its contents. He did not give any away, throw any away, or transfer the contents into anything else. Where did the contents of the bag go?

1. Only about 5% of the content of the bag had been consumed.
2. The hole in the bag did not let any of the contents out.
3. The contents were not eaten by insects or anything else.

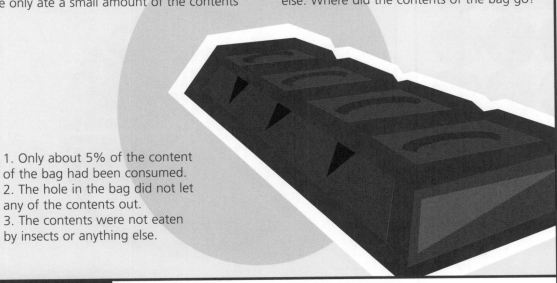

SOLUTION ON PAGE 303

594 CAT CRISIS

Complete the word ladder by changing one letter of each word per step. The newly created word must be found in the dictionary. What are the words to turn LION to PUMA?

LION

PUMA

SOLUTION PAGE 303

595 WORD GRID

Select one of the two letters from the grid, in accordance with the reference shown, and place it in the wordframe. When the correct letters have been chosen a 16-letter word can be read. What is the word?

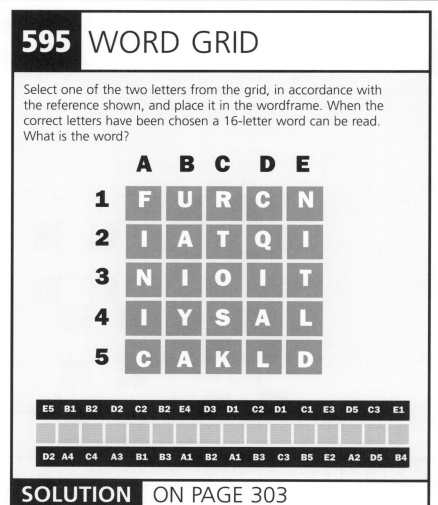

	A	B	C	D	E
1	F	U	R	C	N
2	I	A	T	Q	I
3	N	I	O	I	T
4	I	Y	S	A	L
5	C	A	K	L	D

E5	B1	B2	D2	C2	B2	E4	D3	D1	C2	D1	C1	E3	D5	C3	E1
D2	A4	C4	A3	B1	B3	A1	B2	A1	B3	C3	B5	E2	A2	D5	B4

SOLUTION ON PAGE 303

596 FLUTE PUZZLE

Five of the words in the diagram are associated for some reason. Find the words and then work out whether FLUTE belongs to the group.

EPOCH   TULIP

SWINE   EXILE

OKAPI   ABBEY

DECOY   HIPPO

STEAM   BLOND

SOLUTION ON PAGE 303

597 WALKABOUT

Start at the bottom letter A and move from circle to touching circle to the E at the top right. How many different ways are there of collecting the nine letters of ABORIGINE?

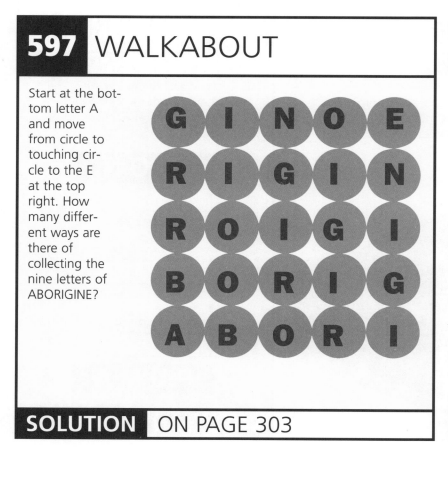

G I N O E
R I G I N
R O I G I
B O R I G
A B O R I

SOLUTION ON PAGE 303

598 WORD WHEEL

Select one letter from each of the segments. When the correct letters have been found a number of eight letters can be read clockwise. What is it?

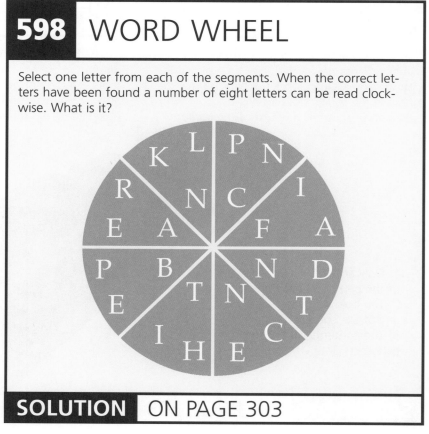

SOLUTION ON PAGE 303

599 FIRST THREE

Which word of three letters can be attached to the front of the words shown in the diagram to create six other words?

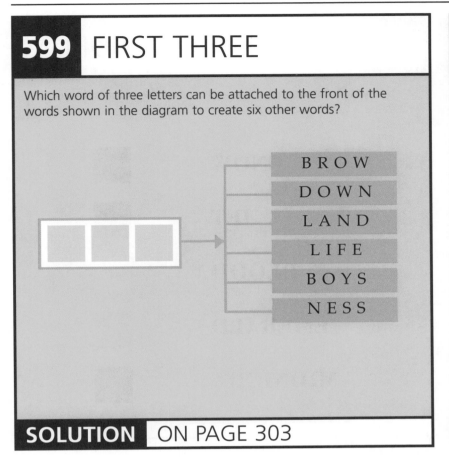

BROW
DOWN
LAND
LIFE
BOYS
NESS

SOLUTION ON PAGE 303

600 TREE SNAKE

The names of three trees can be found in the diagram. They are in the order they normally appear. What are the trees?

SOLUTION ON PAGE 303

601 LETTER LOGIC

Puzzle over the squares below to determine the true values of A, B and C. This is not a magic square but all the horizontal and vertical lines add up to the same number.

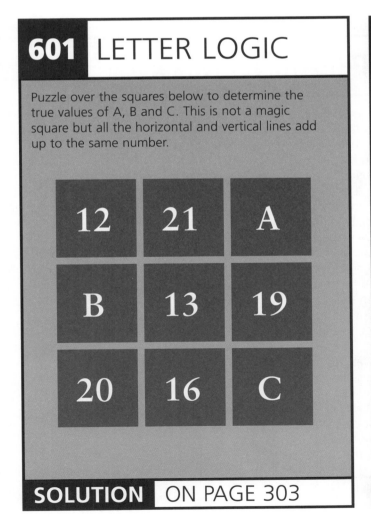

| 12 | 21 | A |
| 20 | 16 | C |

12	21	A
B	13	19
20	16	C

SOLUTION ON PAGE 303

602 WORDSEARCH

The blanks squares in this crossword have been replaced by spurious letters. You have to find them and fill in the blanks to create a completed crossword.

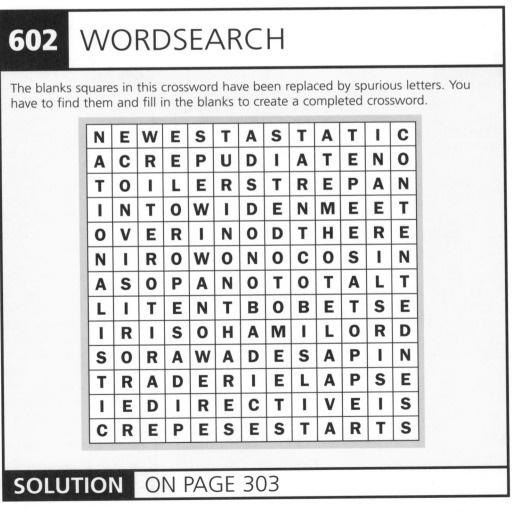

N	E	W	E	S	T	A	S	T	A	T	I	C
A	C	R	E	P	U	D	I	A	T	E	N	O
T	O	I	L	E	R	S	T	R	E	P	A	N
I	N	T	O	W	I	D	E	N	M	E	E	T
O	V	E	R	I	N	O	D	T	H	E	R	E
N	I	R	O	W	O	N	O	C	O	S	I	N
A	S	O	P	A	N	O	T	O	T	A	L	T
L	I	T	E	N	T	B	O	B	E	T	S	E
I	R	I	S	O	H	A	M	I	L	O	R	D
S	O	R	A	W	A	D	E	S	A	P	I	N
T	R	A	D	E	R	I	E	L	A	P	S	E
I	E	D	I	R	E	C	T	I	V	E	I	S
C	R	E	P	E	S	E	S	T	A	R	T	S

SOLUTION ON PAGE 303

603 SAFE SOLUTION

There is only one way to open this safe. You must press each button once only, in the correct order, to reach OPEN. Each button is marked with a direction, U for up, L for left, D for down, R for right. The number of spaces to move is also marked on each button. Which button must you press first to open the safe?

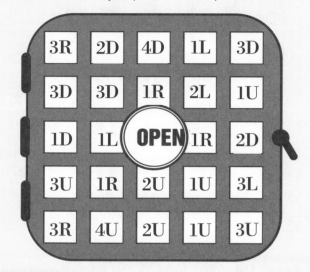

SOLUTION ON PAGE 303

604 COLOUR CONUNDRUM

Match each of the words shown with one of the colours. Each pair will make a well-known expression.

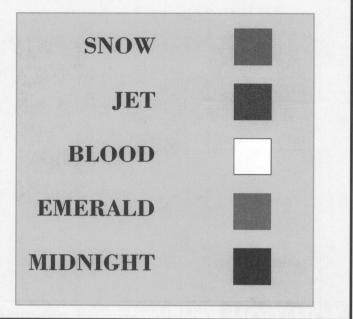

SOLUTION ON PAGE 303

605 CLOUDED ISSUE

There are five 5-letter words to be made. It will help your search considerably when you're told that they all have something to do with the arts.

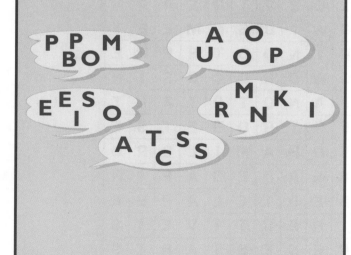

SOLUTION ON PAGE 303

606 DISAPPEARING MAN

One cold winter morning Jayne was walking down a narrow country lane. On either side of the lane there were four houses. Jayne noticed that each house had a different-coloured front door and different-coloured cars parked in the driveways. Outside one of the houses she noticed a man standing in the garden. He was very well dressed with a hat and scarf on to keep him warm. She waved at the gentleman and shouted, "Hello!" and he smiled at her. Later that day when she came back along the lane she noticed the man again. She waved to him and said, "It certainly is getting warmer, it doesn't feel as cold as it was this morning." The gentleman smiled at her and she went on her way, counting the cars that passed her as she went. The next day when Jayne went down the lane she noticed the gentleman had gone. Where?

1. He had not gone inside the house or any other house.
2. He had not walked down the lane in any direction.
3. He had not driven anywhere by car.

SOLUTION ON PAGE 303

607 SQUARE PUZZLE

Each shape in this diagram has a value. Work out the values to discover what numbers should replace the question marks.

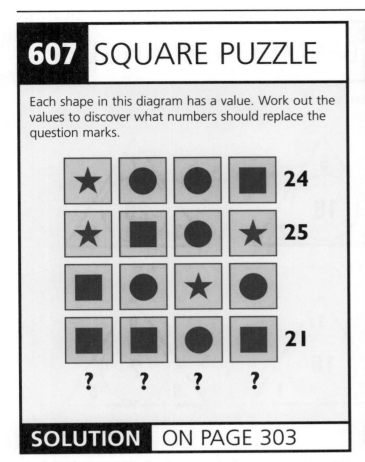

SOLUTION ON PAGE 303

608 CUBE CROSSWORD

Each cube contains three faces. Only one face on each cube will fit correctly into the grid. Select the nine correct faces and fit them correctly into the grid to form a symmetrical crossword.

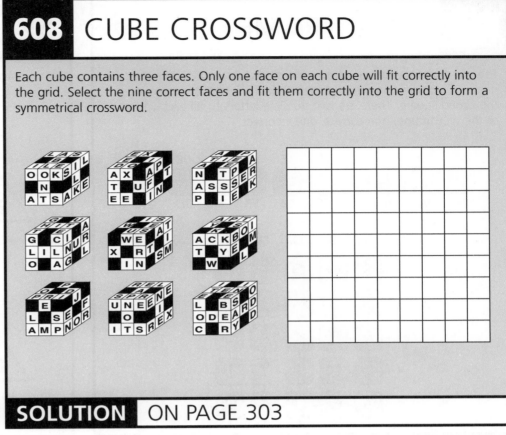

SOLUTION ON PAGE 303

609 DISTANCE DISASTER

On this strange signpost how far should it be to Aberdeen?

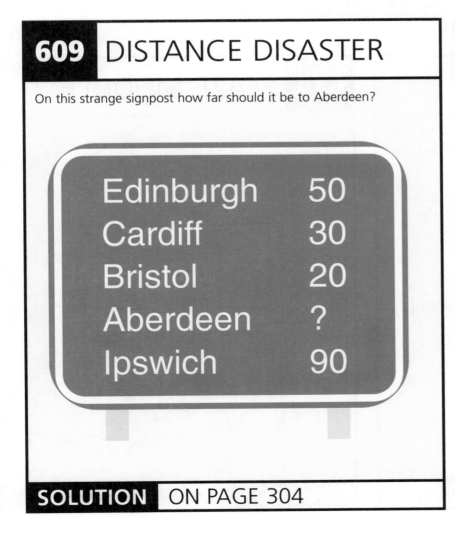

Edinburgh 50
Cardiff 30
Bristol 20
Aberdeen ?
Ipswich 90

SOLUTION ON PAGE 304

610 DISC PROBLEM

Which of these discs is the odd one out?

SOLUTION ON PAGE 304

611 WORDFRAME

The wordframe, when filled with the correct letters will give the name of a city in England and Alabama. The letters are arranged in the coded square. There are two possible letters to fill each square of the wordframe, one correct, one incorrect.

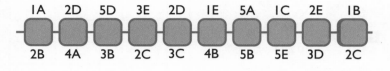

1A	2D	5D	3E	2D	1E	5A	1C	2E	1B
2B	4A	3B	2C	3C	4B	5B	5E	3D	2C

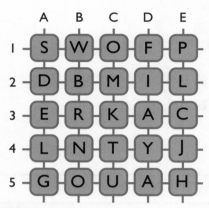

	A	B	C	D	E
1	S	W	O	F	P
2	D	B	M	I	L
3	E	R	K	A	C
4	L	N	T	Y	J
5	G	O	U	A	H

SOLUTION ON PAGE 304

612 BERMUDA TRIANGLES

What number should replace the question mark?

Triangle 1: 5 (top), 2 (left), 2 (right), circle 18
Triangle 2: 7 (top), 3 (left), 4 (right), circle 28
Triangle 3: 1 (top), 6 (left), 1 (right), circle 16
Triangle 4: 9 (top), 8 (left), 5 (right), circle ?

SOLUTION ON PAGE 304

613 DIAMOND DILEMMA

Start at the far left circle and move, to the right only, along the lines to the far right circle, collecting numbers and shapes as you go. Each shape has a value of −41. How many routes give 0?

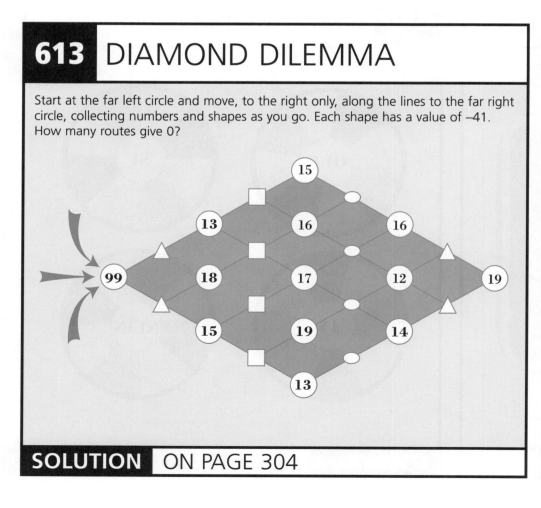

SOLUTION ON PAGE 304

614 MAZE MUDDLE

Which route should the bear take to get to the woods?

SOLUTION ON PAGE 304

615 TILE TROUBLE

Arrange the pieces to form a square where the numbers read the same horizontally and vertically

SOLUTION ON PAGE 304

616 SAFE SOLUTION

Here is an unusual safe. Each button must be pressed once only, in the correct order, to reach OPEN. The direction to move, i for in, o for out, c for clockwise, and a for anti-clockwise (counterclockwise) is marked on each button. The number of spaces to move is also shown on each button. Which button is the first you must press to open the safe?

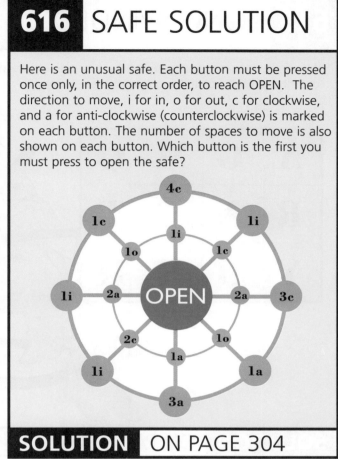

SOLUTION ON PAGE 304

617 WORDS

Find five five-letter words by taking one letter from each bubble.

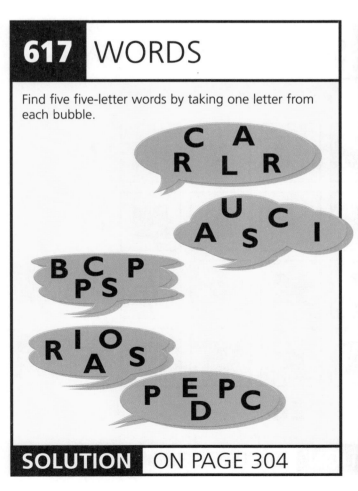

SOLUTION ON PAGE 304

618 INITIAL PROBLEMS

Choose the odd one out on each line and write its initial in the space alongside. When completed these initials will give a word reading downwards. What is the word?

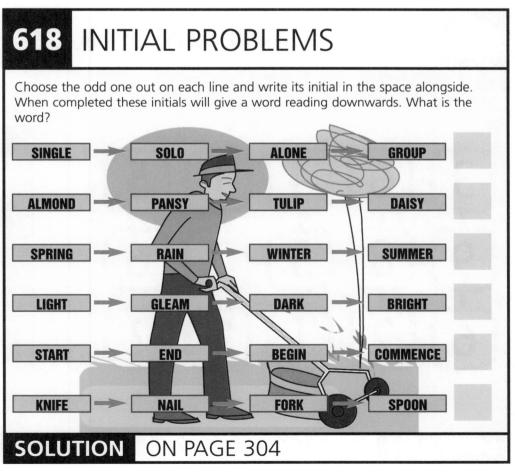

SINGLE	SOLO	ALONE	GROUP	
ALMOND	PANSY	TULIP	DAISY	
SPRING	RAIN	WINTER	SUMMER	
LIGHT	GLEAM	DARK	BRIGHT	
START	END	BEGIN	COMMENCE	
KNIFE	NAIL	FORK	SPOON	

SOLUTION ON PAGE 304

619 LONG WINDED

Move from square to touching square – including diagonals – to discover the longest possible word from these letters.

SOLUTION ON PAGE 304

620 SIMILAR BOXES

Which two boxes in this diagram are similar?

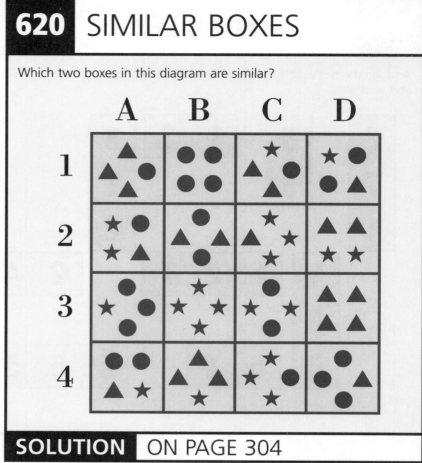

SOLUTION ON PAGE 304

621 DIAGRAM ENIGMA

Find a number to replace the question mark.

SOLUTION ON PAGE 304

622 SQUARE SOLUTION

What number should replace the question mark?

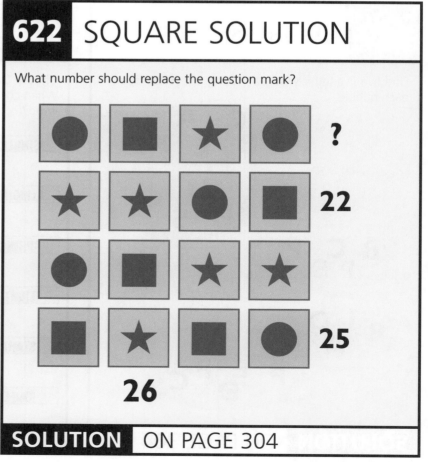

SOLUTION ON PAGE 304

623 PATTERN PROBLEM

Should A, B, C or D come next in the series?

 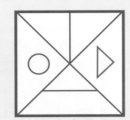  

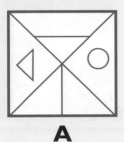 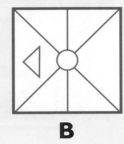 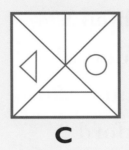 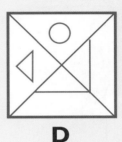

A   **B**   **C**   **D**

SOLUTION | ON PAGE 304

624 WASHING DISHES

A married couple in New York had six children and each night of the week one child would wash the dishes. This task was performed by a different child every night. On Sundays all of the children would draw lots to see who would have the sad privilege. One of the children figured that it was best to be left the last lot and not pick at all. She calculated that the first pick would have a 1 : 5 choice, the next a 1 : 4 choice, the next 1 : 3, etc until she was left with the last lot. The child added all of the previous factors together and decided that it would be unlikely that it would be the worst lot left. Was this trick likely to work?

SOLUTION | ON PAGE 304

625 BOX ENIGMA

Which of the below is not a view of the same three sides of a box?

A   **B**

C

SOLUTION | ON PAGE 304

626 TRAIN TROUBLE

The fares for these train rides all relate to the place names in England. What is the fare to Oxford?

| Bath £17 |
| Brighton £34 |
| London £24 |
| Taunton £26 |
| Oxford ? |

SOLUTION ON PAGE 304

627 KENTUCKY JOURNEY

The distances on this fictitious signpost relate to the states' place names. How far is it to Kentucky?

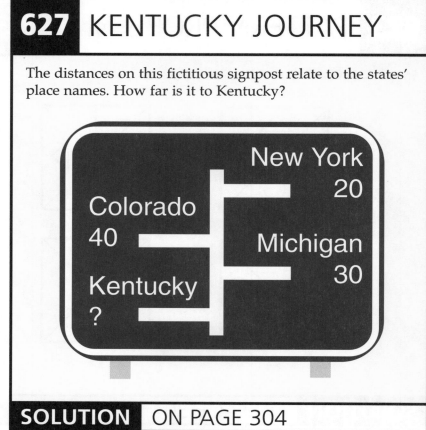

New York 20
Colorado 40
Michigan 30
Kentucky ?

SOLUTION ON PAGE 304

628 TENNIS TANGLE

These jumbled letters spell the names of two tennis stars. Who are they?

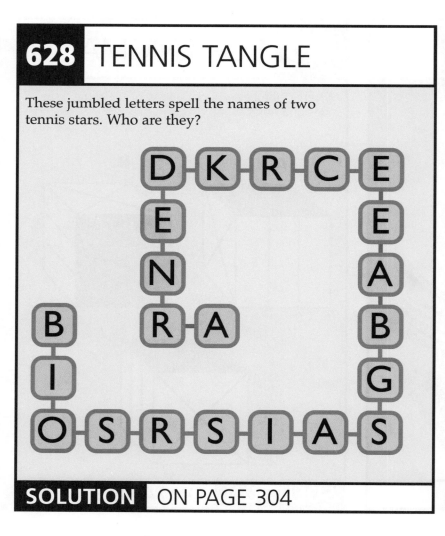

SOLUTION ON PAGE 304

629 DART DILEMMA

On this unusual dartboard how many different ways are there to score 30 with three darts? Every dart must land in a segment (more than one dart may land in each), and all must score. The same three scores in a different order do not count as another way.

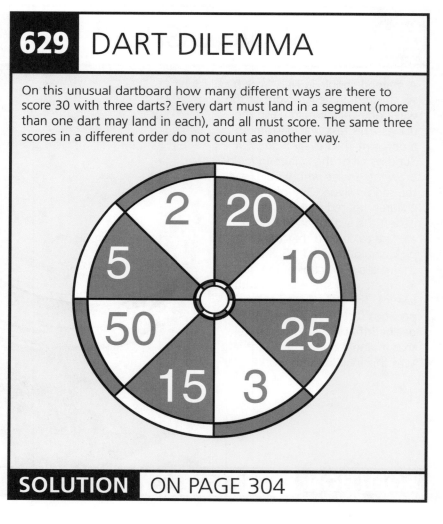

SOLUTION ON PAGE 304

630 PATTERN POSER

Which two patterns do not go with the other three?

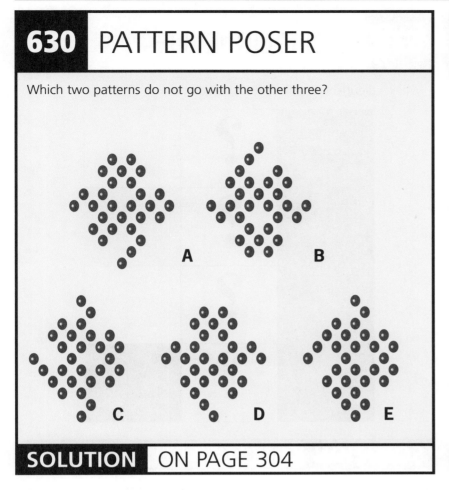

631 COUNTRY PUZZLE

If you go from square to touching square – including diagonals – which country will you find using all the letters only once?

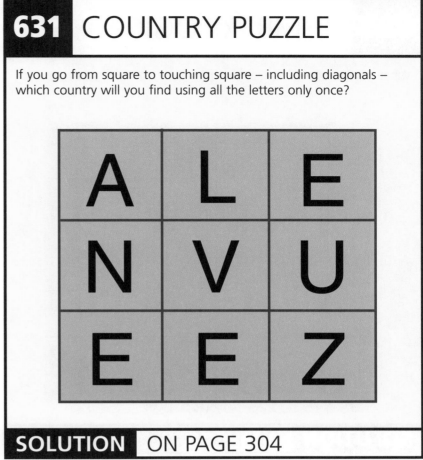

SOLUTION ON PAGE 304

632 DODGY DIAMOND

The ovals are worth –13. Travelling from start to finish what are the lowest and highest totals you can make?

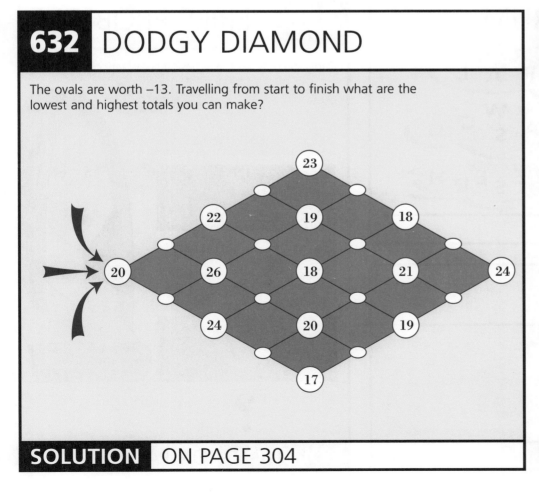

SOLUTION ON PAGE 304

633 TIME TEASER

The minute and hour hands move separately on these strange clocks. What time should the fourth clock show?

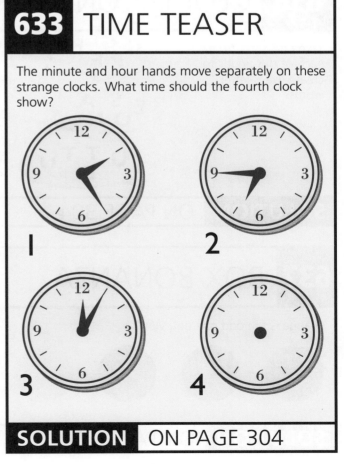

SOLUTION ON PAGE 304

634 NUMBER LOGIC

What number should replace the question mark?

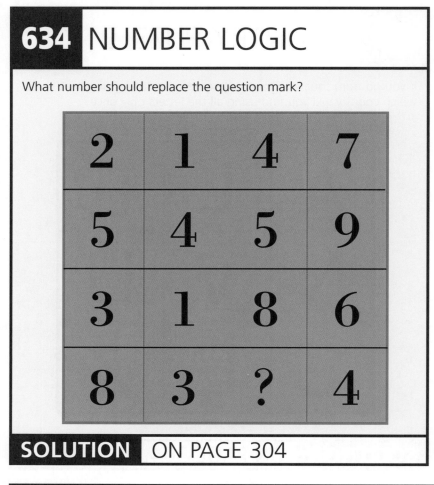

2	1	4	7
5	4	5	9
3	1	8	6
8	3	?	4

SOLUTION ON PAGE 304

635 COLOUR CLUE

Which colour could replace the question marks?

SOLUTION ON PAGE 304

636 CLOUD CONUNDRUM

Take one letter from each of the clouds to create five 6-letter words?

SOLUTION ON PAGE 304

637 BOX BONANZA

Orange is the odd one out. Why?

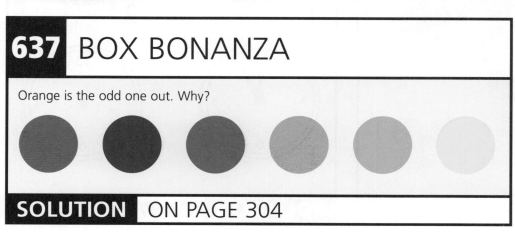

SOLUTION ON PAGE 304

638 SERIES PROBLEM

Can you continue this series? If so, what colour is next?

?

SOLUTION ON PAGE 304

639 DANGEROUS NEIGHBOURS?

The Price family were regarded by their neighbours in Quietsville as complete undesirables. At least one of the family would always be terrorizing some neighbour. The neighbours were too frightened to speak to the police because of their fear of reprisals based on a long history of previous events. One day the situation escalated into a much more serious problem when one of the Price family set fire to a neighbour's home. The police questioned all of the neighbours, but even though some knew who did the deed they would not say. One neighbour handed a note to a policeman, and he went straight to the right member of the family. If the family names were Mr Tom Price (father), Mrs Julie Price (mother), and the children were James, David, Mark and Chuck, which family member was arrested?

SOLUTION ON PAGE 304

640 WHITE IN OR OUT?

Does white belong with group A or B?

A   B

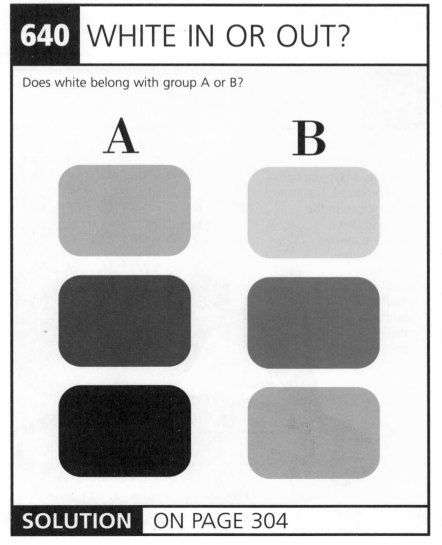

SOLUTION ON PAGE 304

641 LOST NUMBER

What number should replace the question mark?

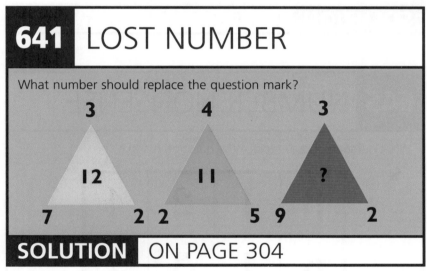

3
12
7   2

4
11
2   5

3
?
9   2

SOLUTION ON PAGE 304

642 SHAPE SQUARE

Each shape in the diagram has a value. Work out the values to discover what number should replace the question mark.

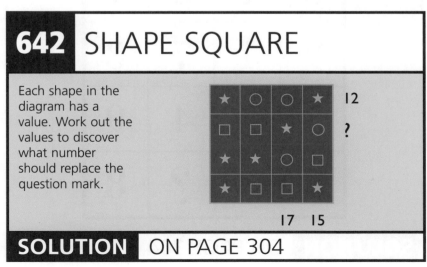

★ ○ ○ ★   12
□ □ ★ ○   ?
★ ★ ○ □
★ □ □ ★

17 15

SOLUTION ON PAGE 304

643 TRIANGLE TROUBLE

What number should replace the question mark?

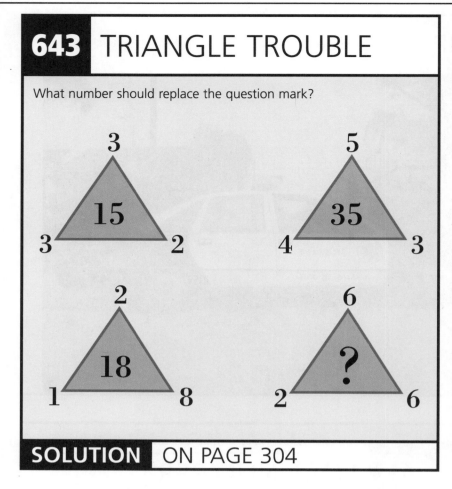

644 LOST NUMBER

What's the missing number?

SOLUTION ON PAGE 304

645 NUMBER NONSENSE

What numbers should replace the question marks?

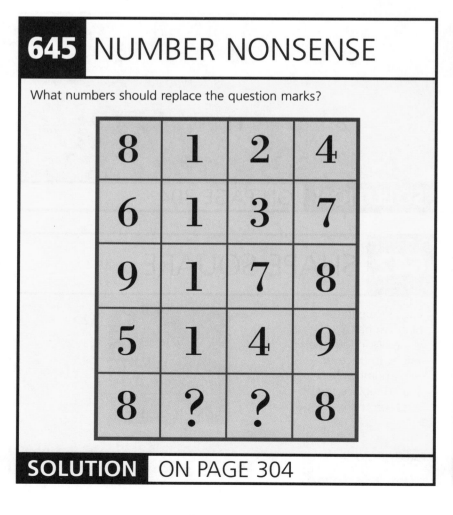

SOLUTION ON PAGE 304

646 WORDFRAME

The wordframe below, when filled with the correct letters, will give the name of a composer. The letters are arranged in the coded square. There are two possible letters to fill each square of the wordframe, one correct, the other is wrong each time. Who is the composer?

SOLUTION ON PAGE 304

647 SQUARE SHAPES

Each shape in the diagram has a value. Work out the values to discover what number should replace the question mark.

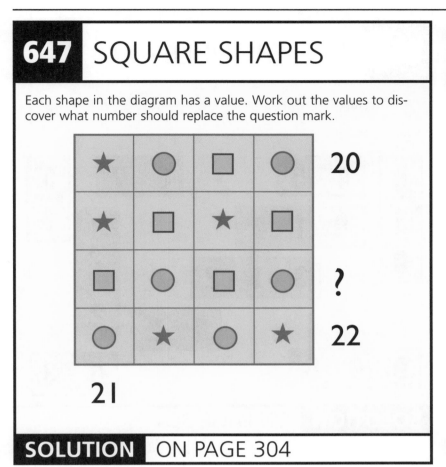

20

?

22

21

SOLUTION ON PAGE 304

648 NUMBER PROBLEM

What number should replace the question mark?

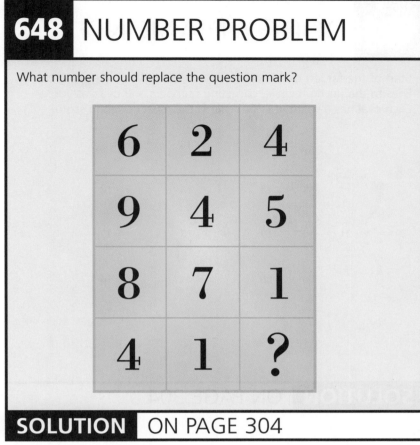

SOLUTION ON PAGE 304

649 TIME TRIAL

What time should the fourth clock show?

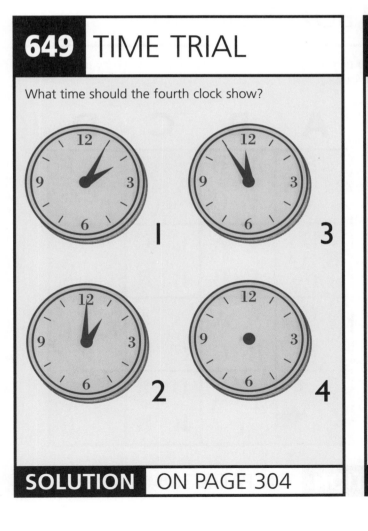

1

3

2

4

SOLUTION ON PAGE 304

650 1930s FLIGHT FRIGHT

On one early transatlantic flight in the 1930s a plane carrying 20 passengers had very low fuel reserves when approaching New York from England. It was a very windy day when the plane arrived, but it could not land where it was supposed to because of the wind. It was, however, able to land only a few miles away where the wind had a slightly higher speed. Why was this possible?

1. The wind direction for landing at the second landing point was less favourable. It was more of a crosswind than the wind at the first landing point.
2. The first arrival area had no other vehicles on it and no other air traffic was involved.
3. Air traffic control did not advise of anything being wrong with the plane, and indeed nothing was wrong with the plane.
4. The plane was not diverted because of the low fuel situation.
5. The pilot could see why he should divert the plane.

SOLUTION ON PAGE 304

651 DODGY DIAMOND

Start at the far left circle and move – to the right only – along the lines to the far right circle, collecting numbers and ovals as you go. Each oval has a value of –20. What is the most common score?

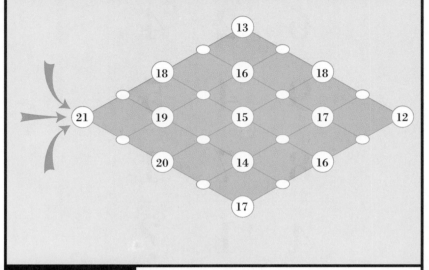

SOLUTION ON PAGE 304

652 TILE TROUBLE

Arrange the pieces to form a square where the numbers read the same horizontally and vertically. What will the finished square look like?

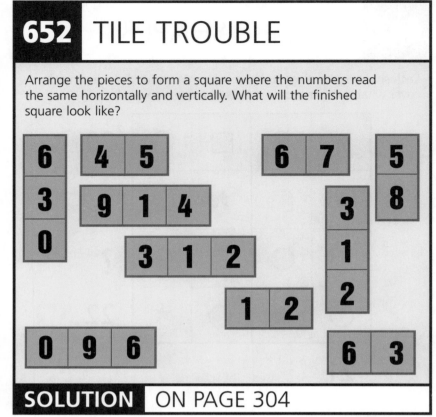

SOLUTION ON PAGE 304

653 CODE CORNER

Three artists, Michelangelo, Constable and Leonardo Da Vinci are hidden in this coded message. Who are the five artists below them?

1
2
3
4
5
6

SOLUTION ON PAGE 304

654 BOX PROBLEM

Which two boxes contain exactly the same letters? (They may be in a different order.)

	A	B	C	D
1	B B A A	A B A C	A A A A	B B A C
2	B B B A	A A A B	C C B B	A C A C
3	C C C C	B A B C	A A C C	B B B C
4	B C C A	A A A C	B B B B	C A C B

SOLUTION ON PAGE 305

655 TRAIN TROUBLE

A man went to the railway station to catch the 12:47 train. When he arrived, he realized that he was not wearing his watch. As he walked past the ticket machines, he saw a clock. The man then thought that he was an hour and a half early, so he walked away from the platform. A short while later, he realized his mistake when he missed the train. The clock was correct, so why did the man think he had been early?

1. His watch was showing the correct time.
2. He did not ask anyone any questions.
3. He had not read anything about delays.
4. His train was on time and had not been re-scheduled.

SOLUTION ON PAGE 305

656 MUSIC MAYHEM

Move from square to touching square – including diagonals – and, using all the letters, find a musical instrument.

G	C	E	N
O	L	K	S
L	E	I	P

SOLUTION ON PAGE 305

657 HOW FAR?

This strange signpost shows the distances to motor-racing destinations. How far is it to Hockenheim?

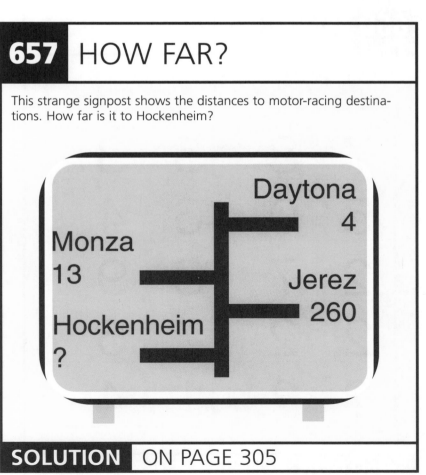

Daytona 4

Monza 13

Jerez 260

Hockenheim ?

SOLUTION ON PAGE 305

658 COMMON CENTS?

In her piggy bank, Jane has $5.24. The sum is made up of an equal number of four coins from 1¢, 5¢, 10¢, 25¢, 50¢ and $1, Which four coins does she have and how many of each of them?

SOLUTION   ON PAGE 305

659 SPORT SEQUENCE

This grid contains three sports all spelled in the correct order, but mixed with the other two. Which are they?

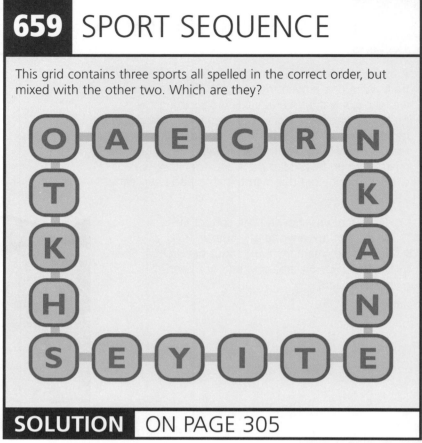

SOLUTION   ON PAGE 305

660 DOUBLE DIGITS

Which two digits will replace the question marks?

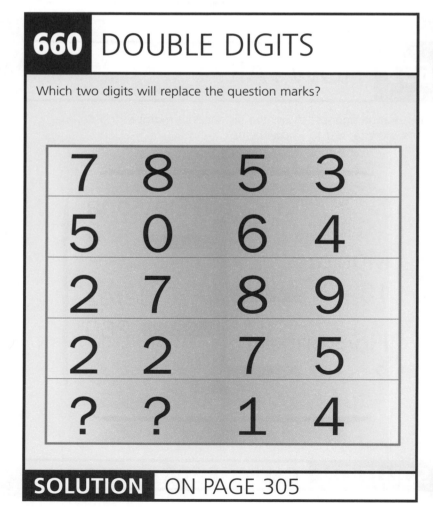

SOLUTION   ON PAGE 305

661 CODE CORNER

The codes for these letters are shown below. Who are these famous historical scientists?

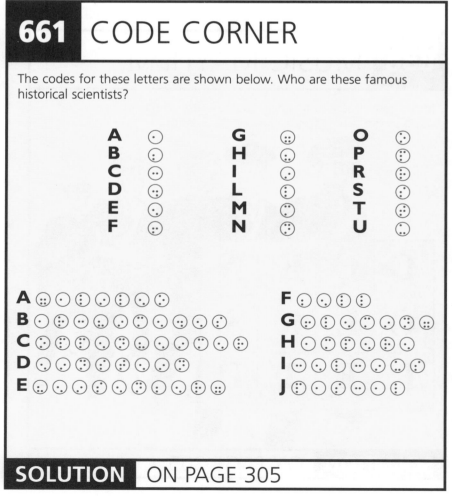

SOLUTION   ON PAGE 305

662 LOCK PROBLEM

A locksmith was called to an exclusive bank and asked to change the lock on a room that was used to store valuable documents. The door was to be activated only by the breaking of two low-power laser beams in front of the door. This would release a steel plate that covered the lock, and the owner could then use the new special key to open the lock. The system was to be automatic and re-set itself after use. Just before he had completed his clearing up, the manager of the bank wanted to check it out and after helping the locksmith to clear his tools from the storeroom, he was locked into the storeroom. The locksmith could not get him out. Why?

1. The door had closed by accident or by design.
2. The police and fire department had to release the manager.
3. The locksmith had to change the lock again.
4. The locksmith still had the key but he could not make it work, even though he had tested it before clearing up.
5. The laser beams were only 3 feet apart.

SOLUTION | ON PAGE 305

663 DODGY DIRECTIONS

Starting from the top left corner, follow the arrows in a continuous down and up route. Which direction, north, south, east or west, should go in the empty space?

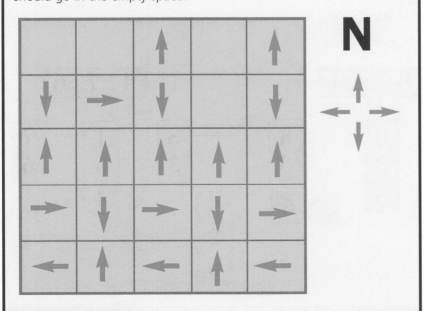

N

SOLUTION | ON PAGE 305

664 LOST DIGIT

Which number should replace the question mark in the bottom left sector?

SOLUTION | ON PAGE 305

665 BRAIN BALANCE

Scales 1 and 2 are in perfect balance. How many diamonds will balance scale 3?

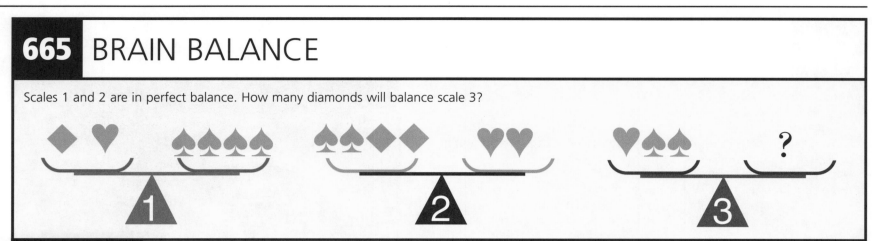

SOLUTION ON PAGE 305

666 DEVIL'S DICE

Which of these diagrams is the odd one out?

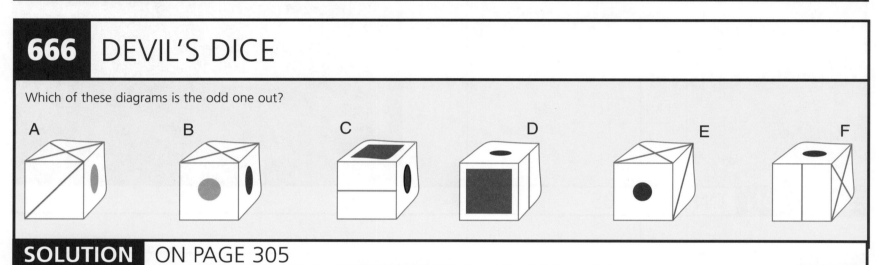

A   B   C   D   E   F

SOLUTION ON PAGE 305

667 TRIANGLE TEASER

There is a simple logic to the numbers in and around these triangles. Which numbers should replace the question marks?

```
      1              2

      5              6
   5     6        6     ?

      3              4

      7              ?
   7    10        8     ?
```

SOLUTION ON PAGE 305

668 TILE TROUBLE

Arrange these pieces to form a square where the numbers read the same horizontally and vertically. What will the finished square look like?

```
  8 6 4              4 7 6

3      0      3      3      1      7
8      8      5      3      5      6
       5                    4
        2 6           5
                      2
                      0
```

SOLUTION ON PAGE 305

669 WORDFRAME

The wordframe below, when filled with the correct letters, gives the name of a famous boxer. However, to make things interesting, you have to decide which of the two options from the grid are correct.

5A	4E	2B	1E		1C	4D	5C	1B	4B
ID	3D	IE	1C		1B	3A	4C	4E	IE

	A	**B**	**C**	**D**	**E**
1	G	R	T	J	E
2	P	K	C	B	W
3	Y	X	F	I	H
4	U	N	Z	A	O
5	M	D	S	V	L

SOLUTION ON PAGE 305

670 TRIANGLES

What letter completes the third triangle?

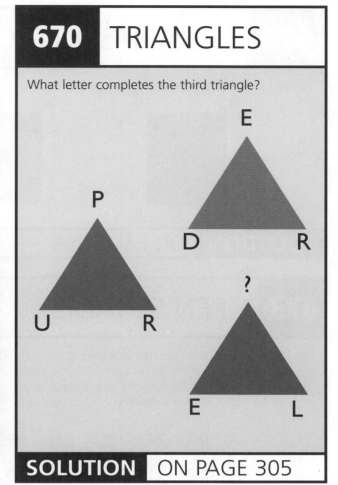

SOLUTION ON PAGE 305

671 GLASS HEAD

In recognition of the President's services to his country and for his contribution to world peace, a huge, two-ton polished glass head of his likeness was commissioned, the base of which was to be flat to ensure that it did not move on its plinth. The top of the plinth matched the neck of the glass head perfectly. An overhead crane with specially padded ropes was used to lift the head on to the plinth, but then a problem occurred. The two parts had to be positioned exactly, and the workers could not drag the ropes, since this would chip the head or base. How did they do it?

1. They could not use wooden wedges or anything that might scratch the glass.
2. They could not use compressed air since the compressor did not have the power.
3. The ropes had to pass under the neck in 4 places.
4. The ropes were made of nylon, which covered a stainless steel core. They were 2 inches in diameter.
5. They could not use suckers or rubber props.

SOLUTION ON PAGE 305

672 SQUARE SOLUTION

Can you find a letter to replace the question mark?

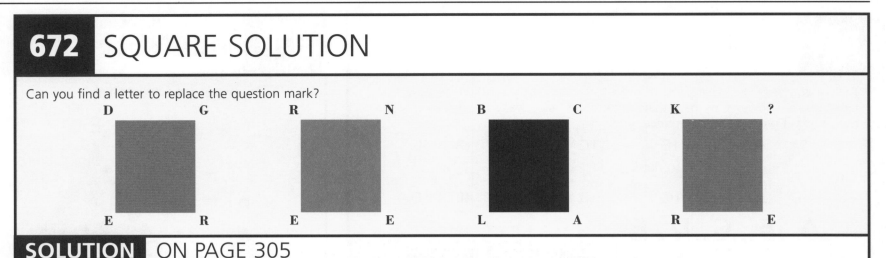

D   G   R   N   B   C   K   ?

E   R   E   E   L   A   R   E

SOLUTION ON PAGE 305

673 OPEN SESAME!

This is an unusual safe. To open it you must press the OPEN button, but you must press all the other buttons in the correct order. This can only be done by following the directions and the number of steps to be taken. Which is the first button you should push?

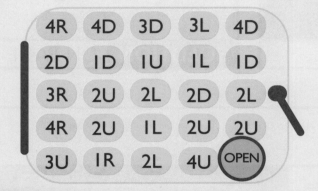

SOLUTION ON PAGE 305

675 DODGY DARTS

You have three darts to throw at this dartboard. All must land in a segment to score – even 0 – and none can miss. Although more than one dart can land in the same segment only one order for each set of three can count. How many different ways are there to score 32?

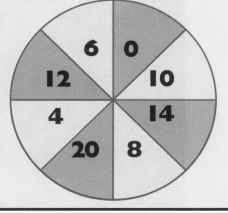

SOLUTION ON PAGE 305

674 TIME TEASER

The hands on these clocks move in a strange but logical way. What is the time on the fourth clock?

SOLUTION ON PAGE 305

676 MAZE MAYHEM

This is an unusual maze. There are a few ways of completing it, but the aim is to collect as few points as possible. What is the lowest possible score?

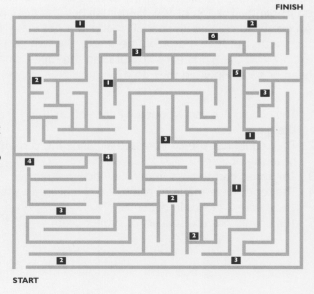

SOLUTION ON PAGE 305

677 SURVIVAL OF THE WEAKEST?

Three men were passionately in love with a lady. The woman loved them all equally, but the passion boiled over and the men agreed that they should have a duel using pistols. To the victor, the hand of the lady; to the vanquished and defeated, death, injury, or disappointment. After agreeing to duel, the odds were stacked against one and in favour of the other two. As Count Nevermiss was an expert and a perfect shot, he had won every duel even against better opposition than he was to face that fateful day. Lord Bullseye was a good shot and a military man. He could be relied on to hit his target two out of every three shots, while Captain Missalot could only be relied upon to hit his target once every three shots.

They were, however, men of honour and decided that the rules of the duel gave the poorer shots a chance. They decided that they would stand and face each other from three points of a triangle. There was no limit to ammunition, but they would shoot in turn at either of the opponents with the worst shot going first and the best shot shooting last.

You are put in Captain Missalot's position. How do you maximize your chances of survival with honour? It is you who will shoot first. Who are you going to go for? Survival depends on good lateral and deductive reasoning.

SOLUTION ON PAGE 305

---

678 UP OR DOWN?

Does pink go above or below the line?

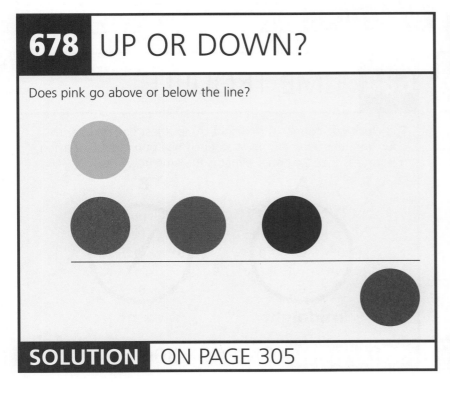

SOLUTION ON PAGE 305

---

679 ABOVE OR BELOW?

Does black go above or below the line?

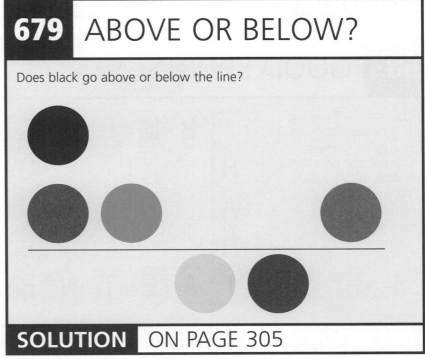

SOLUTION ON PAGE 305

680 A PROBLEM FOR THE FERRYMAN

A man leaves his 5 children with the ferryman and is told that they must all be taken to the other side of the river in a minimum number of crossings, such that each of the children has an identical number of one-way trips. The children are all of different ages and the ferryman can only take himself plus a maximum of 2 children at any time. No pair of children of neighbouring ages can be left in the absence of the ferryman. Only the ferryman can row the boat. How many trips are needed and what is the sequence?

SOLUTION ON PAGE 305

681 FAN FRENZY

Madonna's fan club has 1500 members, Mariah Carey's fan club is 1101 strong and there are 1201 Metallica fans. How many members are there in Michael Jackson's fan club?

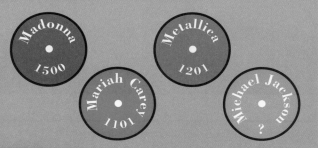

Madonna 1500

Metallica 1201

Mariah Carey 1101

Michael Jackson ?

SOLUTION ON PAGE 305

682 LOST NUMBER

Which numbers replace the question marks?

4	7	4	9	5
8	5	1	3	6
3	7	6	?	?

SOLUTION ON PAGE 306

683 GOOD SPORTS

The names of one former baseball star and one former American football star have been hidden in this frame. Who are they?

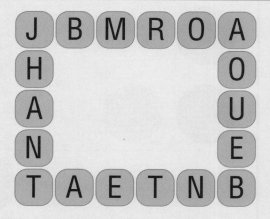

J B M R O A
H   O
A   U
N   E
T A E T N B

SOLUTION ON PAGE 306

684 TIME TROUBLE

This clock was correct at midnight (A), but lost one minute per hour from that moment on. It stopped one hour ago (B), having run for less than 24 hours. What is the time now?

A   B

midnight   a.m.

SOLUTION ON PAGE 306

685 STAR SOLUTION

Scales 1 and 2 are in perfect balance. How many stars are required to balance scale 3?

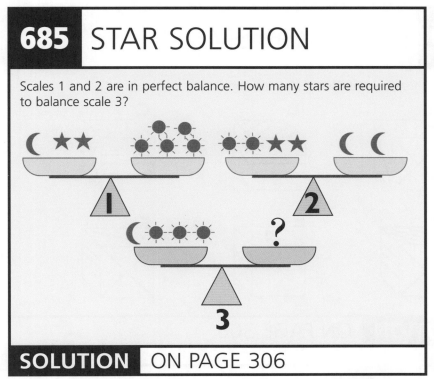

SOLUTION | ON PAGE 306

686 POINTER PROBLEM

The arrows from this grid go from the top left corner in a logical sequence. In which direction should the arrow go in the empty box and what is the order?

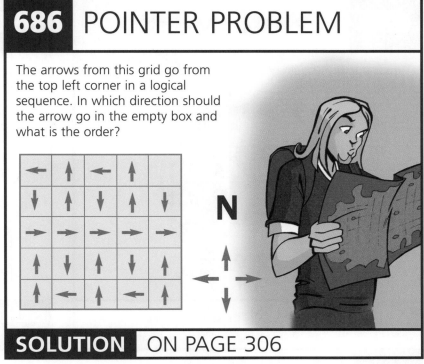

SOLUTION | ON PAGE 306

687 TIME TEASER

The hands on these clocks move in a strange but logical way. What time should replace the question mark?

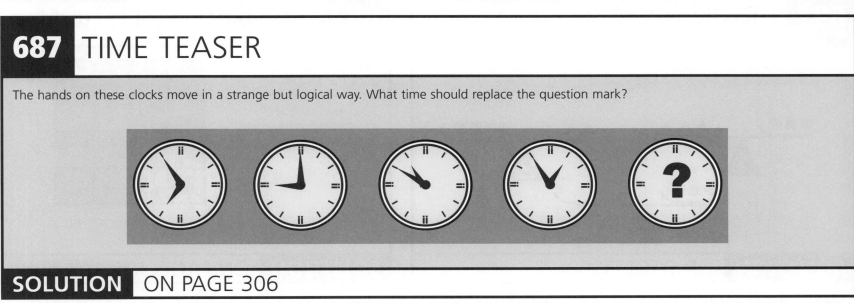

SOLUTION | ON PAGE 306

688 BRAIN BALANCE

Each shape has a value. Scales 1 and 2 are in perfect balance. How many squares are needed to balance scale 3?

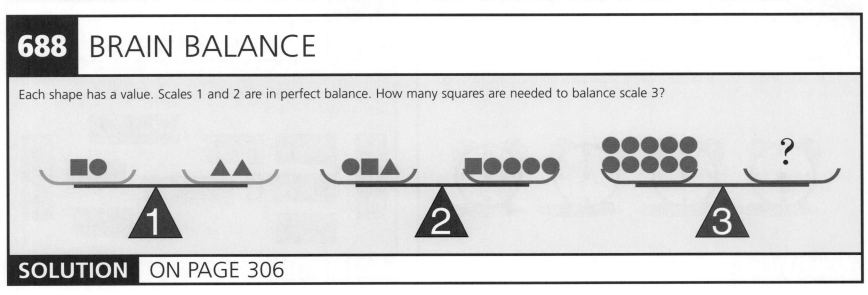

SOLUTION | ON PAGE 306

689 LOST NUMBER

Which number should replace the question mark?

SOLUTION ON PAGE 306

690 BOX PROBLEM

Which of these is not a view of the same box?

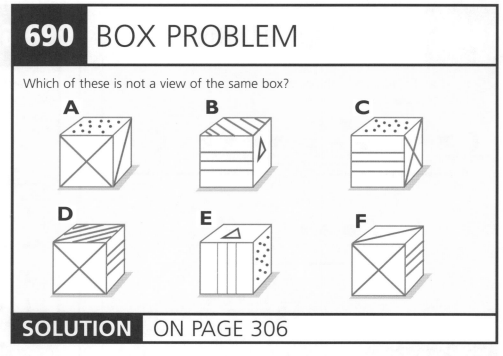

A   B   C

D   E   F

SOLUTION ON PAGE 306

691 BRAIN BALANCE

Each shape has a value. Scales 1 and 2 are in perfect balance. How many squares are needed to balance scale 3?

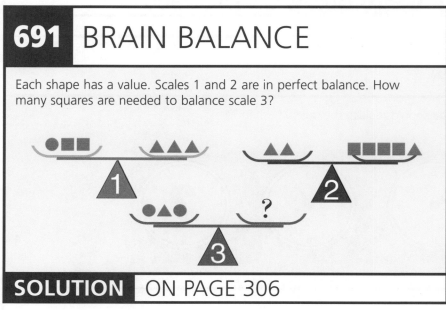

SOLUTION ON PAGE 306

692 SQUARE SOLUTION

Each shape in the diagram has a value. Work out the values to discover what number should replace the question mark.

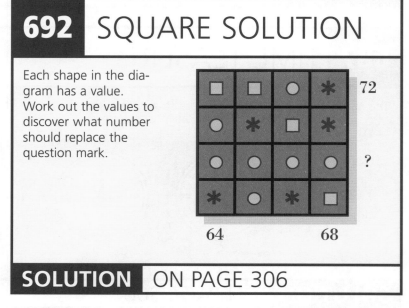

SOLUTION ON PAGE 306

693 TIME TEASER

The minute and hour hands are moving separately on these weird clocks. What time will the fourth clock show?

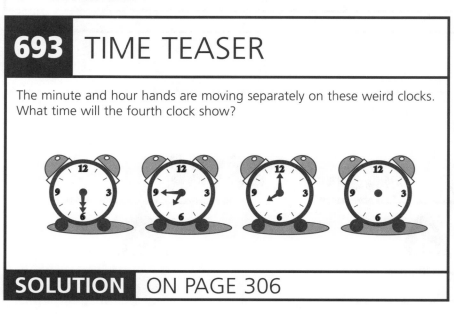

SOLUTION ON PAGE 306

694 TILE TROUBLE

Arrange the pieces to form a square where the numbers read the same vertically and horizontally. What will the finished square look like?

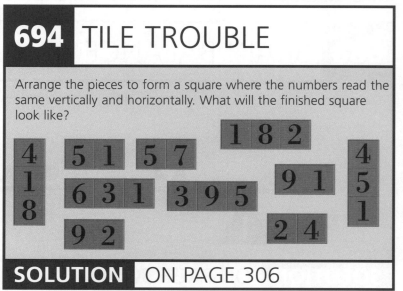

SOLUTION ON PAGE 306

695 TOMB TEASER

Long ago, in the days of the Pharaohs, the Puzzle King was a very favoured man – so much so that one of the Pharaohs allowed him to design the entrance to his tomb. The Pharaoh said that his tomb must not be plundered after his death so the design had to deter his people from trying to enter. He would also have 200 of his strongest soldiers entombed with him in case he revived and needed to be released. The design for the entrance is shown below. The magic cube would seal the entrance. How did the cube go together before it was moved into position in the pyramid so that the Pharaoh could get out?

1. The cube was solid and made from stone. It was made in two halves as shown.
2. Dovetail joints were on the faces that you cannot see and are in central positions. The cube looks the same from each side view. Each side has the same dovetail joint showing.
3. 200 men could move half of the cube but they would not be able to move the entire cube. It took 400 men to move the cube into place.
4. No outside help was needed.
5. No hinges or tricks were employed.

SOLUTION ON PAGE 306

696 LOST DIGIT

What number should replace the question mark?

3	1	4	2	7
5	6	6	5	0
7	8	9	6	9
1	9	4	1	5
2	6	?	2	5

SOLUTION ON PAGE 306

697 DODGY DIAMOND

Start at the far left circle and move along the lines to the far right circle, collecting the numbers, the diamonds and the ovals as you go. Each oval has a value of minus 10. Each diamond has a value of minus 15. What are the minimum and maximum totals possible?

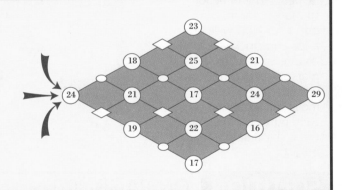

SOLUTION ON PAGE 306

698 SQUARE SOLUTION

Which two boxes in the diagram are similar?

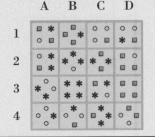

SOLUTION ON PAGE 306

699 SHAPE SHOCK

Each shape in the diagram has a value. Work out the values to discover what number should replace the question mark.

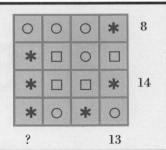

SOLUTION ON PAGE 306

700 PULLEY PROBLEM

In this system of levers and rollers the black spots are fixed swivel points and the shaded spots are non-fixed swivel points. With this in mind, if the lever is pushed as shown, will the load rise or fall?

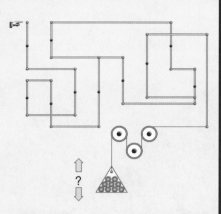

SOLUTION ON PAGE 306

701 SHAPE SHIFTER

Should A, B, C or D come next in this series?

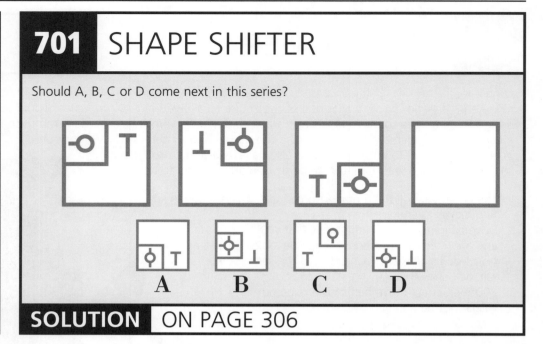

A   B   C   D

SOLUTION ON PAGE 306

702 OPEN SECRET

Here is an unusual safe. Each button must be pressed once only, in the correct order, to reach "Open". The direction to move, i for in, o for out, c for clockwise and a for anti-clockwise (or counterclockwise) is marked on each button. The number of spaces to move is also shown on each button. Which button is the first you must press?

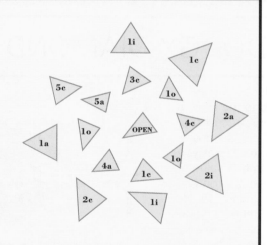

SOLUTION ON PAGE 306

703 LOST NUMBER

What number should replace the question mark?

6	7	4	8
2	3	0	0
4	5	2	4
5	6	3	?

SOLUTION ON PAGE 306

704 COLOUR CONUNDRUM

Which of these letters is the odd one out?

P   B   R   P   G

SOLUTION ON PAGE 306

705 MISSING DIGITS

What number should be on the bottom line in this diagram?

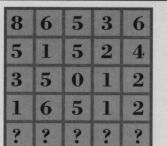

8	6	5	3	6
5	1	5	2	4
3	5	0	1	2
1	6	5	1	2
?	?	?	?	?

SOLUTION ON PAGE 306

706 PLUG PROBLEM

Sally goes to the bathroom to have a wash. She wants to run a full basin of water so that she can get a nice lather on the soap, but unfortunately the plug for the basin has been lost. She cannot find another plug anywhere and cannot find anything else to fill the plughole. She knows, however, that while the water from the one faucet will not stay in the basin, the water from the other faucet will not run away. Why is this?

1. She does not jam the soap in the plughole.
2. The plughole can let out water more quickly than both faucets on full.
3. A few days before and a few days later she could not have used this idea.
4. She had to run the other faucet to clean the basin.

SOLUTION ON PAGE 306

707 MINUSCULE MALE?

Which well known character is represented by this rebus?

boy

SOLUTION ON PAGE 306

708 JUICY PROBLEM?

What does this rebus represent?

JUICE

SOLUTION ON PAGE 306

709 BOX BONANZA

Which of these is not a view of the same box?

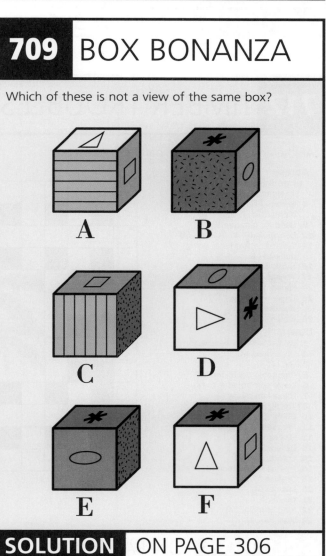

A   B

C   D

E   F

SOLUTION ON PAGE 306

710 DIAMOND DILEMMA

Start at the far left circle and move along the lines to the far right circle, collecting the numbers and shapes as you go. Each oval means divide by 2, each square means multiply by 3, and each triangle means add 13. What are the maximum and minimum totals possible?

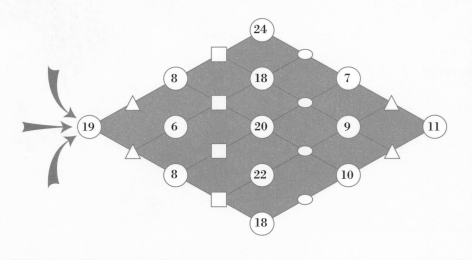

SOLUTION   ON PAGE 306

711 TRIANGLES

What numbers should surround the fourth triangle?

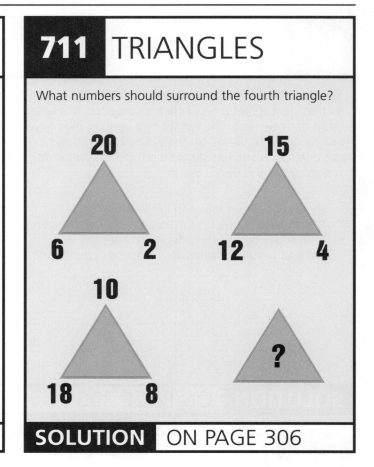

SOLUTION   ON PAGE 306

712 TIMBER TROUBLES

All the answers across are names of trees.

Across
1 Has evergreen leaves and black berries (6)
4 Eastern origin used as canes (6)
9 Used for furniture (5-3,5)
12 Sounds like two together (4)
14 Tree you might fancy going out with (4)
16 Bottle stopper (4)
17 Very hard wood (4)
24 Found near streams (7,6)
25 Used in tanning and dyeing (6)
26 Indian tree (6)

Down
1 Women's indoor headwear (6)
2 Underdone (4)
3 Girl (4)
5 Charitable donations (4)
6 Large soft bread rolls (4)
7 Unspoken threat (2,4)
8 Tinting material (3)
10 Hikes (5)
11 Prepares a book (5)
13 Self-esteem (3)
15 Beverage (3)
16 Entertainers (6)
18 He has information (6)
19 Organism (4)
20 Mineral (4)
21 Ovum (3)
22 Kind of music (4)
23 Walk heavily (4)

SOLUTION   ON PAGE 306

713 TIME TRAVEL

Time is moving strangely again on these clocks. What time should the fourth clock show?

1

2

3

4

SOLUTION   ON PAGE 306

714   WATER JET?

Why did the men fill the transatlantic passenger jet's fuselage with water?

1. It was safe to do so.
2. The jet was not on fire or a fire risk.
3. Passengers were at risk prior to this being done.
4. It was not an emergency procedure after landing on water.
5. It was not a safety drill.

SOLUTION   ON PAGE 306

715   WORDFRAME

The wordframe, right, when filled with the correct letters, will give the name of a Caribbean island. The letters are arranged in the coded square. There are two possible letters to fill each square of the wordframe, one correct, the other incorrect. What is the island?

2B	1B	2E	3A	3C	5C	2D	1A

3E	4A	3D	1D	1B	4E	1C	4B

	A	B	C	D	E
1	H	A	O	B	F
2	V	B	W	T	R
3	E	U	K	M	J
4	U	S	P	A	I
5	G	Z	D	G	X

SOLUTION   ON PAGE 306

716   CROSSWORD

Clues 1 down and 12 across (both three words) are not given. You have to discover them by solving the remaining clues.

Across

2 Everything (3)
4 Once more (5)
5 Playing card (3)
8 More than one (3)
10 Make a mistake (3)
13 Increase (3)
14 An outcome worked toward (3)
15 Female person (3)
17 Tapering blade or pinnacle (5)
18 Devoured (3)

Down

2 High-ranking Turkish officer (3)
3 Recline (3)
6 Aroused (5)
7 Prevailing tendency (5)
8 Definite article (3)
9 Mineral (3)
10 Female sheep (3)
11 Scarlet (3)
15 Mineral spring (3)
16 Before (3)

SOLUTION   ON PAGE 306

717 TIME TEASER

The clocks move in a special way. What time should be on the blank face?

SOLUTION ON PAGE 306

718 TRIANGLE TROUBLE

Which number can replace the question mark?

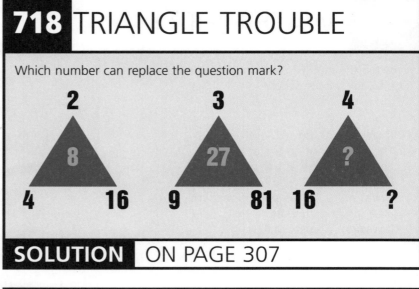

SOLUTION ON PAGE 307

720 LOST LAKE

The distances on this signpost to the Great Lakes have something to do with their names. What is the distance to Lake Superior?

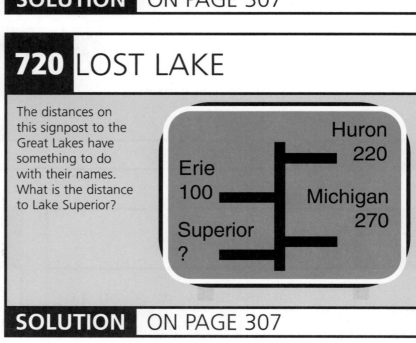

SOLUTION ON PAGE 307

719 FIVES

Place the 36 five-letter words in the grid to complete the crossword.

ABOUT
ADDER
APPLE
ARENA
ARISE
DELTA
DRILL
DUNCE
EARED
HIRED
KNOWN
LINEN
MADAM
MANGO
MANIA
MANOR
MEDIA
MULES

MUTED
NOUNS
OKAPI
PANEL
PLANE
PLUSH
RATES
REBEL
REMIT
ROWAN
SMEAR
SNAIL
SPORE
SPRAT
THERE
TINGE
TRIBE
UNDER

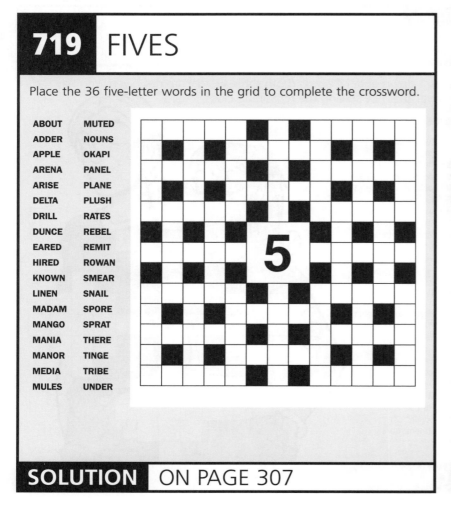

SOLUTION ON PAGE 307

721 CUBE CONUNDRUM

Which of these is not a view of the same box?

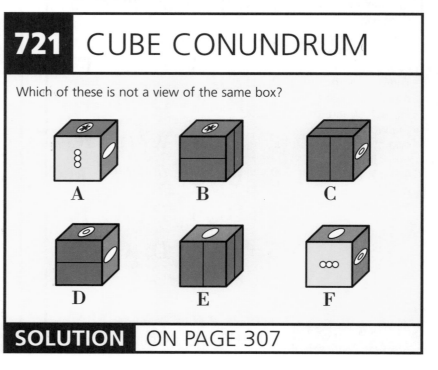

SOLUTION ON PAGE 307

722 THE INHERITED HOUSE

Jamie did not know his uncle had left him Sea View House when he passed away. He knew that it was a mansion built about 200 yards back from the cliffs overlooking the sea. He had been there when he was a child, some 30 years ago. Jamie was not close to his uncle, but he was the last surviving relative. It had taken legal investigators some years to find Jamie, as he worked overseas. When he saw the mansion again, he was very disappointed. Why?

1. It had been well maintained and was in good order.
2. No building had been placed between the house and sea.
3. The gardens were still in good order.
4. The nearby town had prospered.
5. It was not sentimental disappointment.
6. His uncle had lived there until he died.

SOLUTION ON PAGE 307

723 DODGY DARTS

You have three darts to throw at this strange dartboard. Each dart must score and more than one dart can land in the same segment, but separate scoring rounds may not contain the same three values in a different order. How many different ways are there to score 32?

SOLUTION ON PAGE 307

725 OPEN SECRET

There is only one way to open this safe. You must press each button once only, in the correct order, to reach "Open". Each button is marked with a direction, U for up, L for left, R for right, and D for down. The number of spaces to move is also marked on each button. Which is the first button you must press?

4D	4D	1L	3L	OPEN
2R	1D	1U	2L	4L
4R	1L	2D	1U	2L
4R	2R	2L	1D	2U
4R	1U	1U	4U	4U

SOLUTION ON PAGE 307

724 CROSSWORD

Answers run from the lower number in the direction of the next one, ending on that number.

Clues

1 – 2: To scatter or break up (9)
2 – 3: The act of spying (9)
3 – 4: Narcissistic (9)
4 – 5: Large two-edged broadsword (8)
5 – 6: Data on which to base truth (8)
6 – 7: To hold spellbound (7)
7 – 8: Direct descent from an ancestor (7)
8 – 9: Perpendicular (5)
9 – 10: The apparent passage of a celestial body across the meridian (7)
10 – 11: Brouhaha (7)
11 – 12: A place where clothes are washed (7)
12 – 13: Shriek (4)
13 – 14: A strong, fine cotton thread or fabric (5)
14 – 15: Age (3)
15 – 16: High European mountains (4)
16 – 17: Staunch (4)
17 – 18: Coalesce (3)

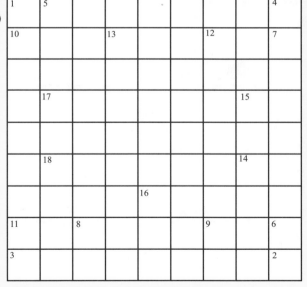

SOLUTION ON PAGE 307

726 CODE CORNER

If the semaphore codes above are for Michael Jackson and Paul McCartney, who are the people shown below?

Michael Jackson =

Paul McCartney =

1

2

3

4

5

SOLUTION ON PAGE 307

727 FRUIT FIESTA

Each like symbol in the diagram has the same value – one of which is a negative number. Can you work out the logic and discover which number should replace the question mark and the values of the symbols?

10

13

15   ?

SOLUTION ON PAGE 307

728 HEAVY PROBLEM

Scales 1 and 2 are in perfect balance. How many pairs of cherries will balance scale 3?

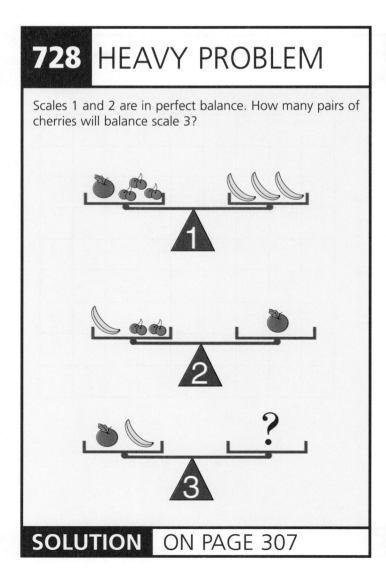

SOLUTION ON PAGE 307

729 AMAZING DISCOVERIES

There is more than one way to complete this maze, so the aim is to complete it by collecting as few points as possible. What is the route and how many points are collected?

SOLUTION ON PAGE 307

730 A BARGAIN

Why did the multi-millionaire decide to buy land that was over 200 yards from the seashore?

1. It was under the sea.
2. It did not contain any mineral rights and it had nothing to do with mining.
3. There was no oil for hundreds of miles.
4. It was not a port or going to be a port or harbor.
5. It had nothing to do with swimming rights.
6. It was a bargain.

SOLUTION ON PAGE 307

731 CLOCK CATASTROPHE

This clock was correct at midnight (A), but began to lose 3.75 minutes per hour from that moment. It stopped half an hour ago (B), having run for less than 24 hours. What is the correct time now?

A

midnight

B

p.m.

SOLUTION ON PAGE 307

732 CUBE PUZZLE

There is a different symbol on each side of the box. Which of these is not a view of the same box?

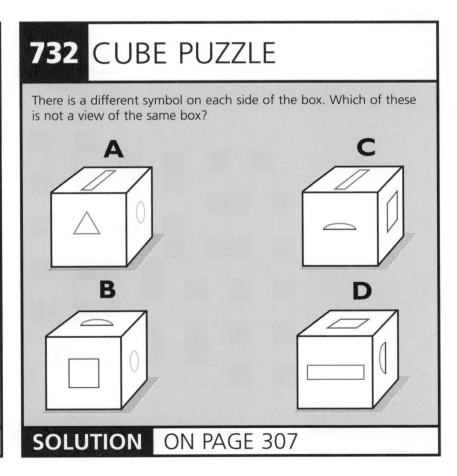

A

C

B

D

SOLUTION ON PAGE 307

733 RIVER RUSE

The 10 longest rivers in Europe are hidden in this grid. Each is spelled in a straight line with no letters missed nor any gaps, up, down, across or diagonally, forward or backward. Can you find them?

G	X	R	V	F	S	H	P	L	A
D	A	N	U	B	E	Q	F	Z	K
R	P	N	E	N	I	H	R	W	Q
C	Y	F	A	J	N	M	F	J	D
Z	K	E	B	I	E	B	L	E	H
E	B	M	B	U	D	G	E	T	H
R	D	U	S	R	Y	N	Q	V	F
I	Z	E	Q	W	O	J	A	P	X
O	N	P	J	H	T	A	G	U	S
L	Y	G	R	X	V	N	N	B	G

They are: Danube, Ebro, Elbe, Guandiana, Loire, Meuse, Rhine, Rhone, Seine, Tagus.

SOLUTION ON PAGE 307

734 TIME TEASER

This clock was correct at midnight (A), but began to lose 10 minutes per hour from that moment. It stopped 2½ hours ago (B), having run for less than 24 hours. What is the correct time now?

A

midnight

B

p.m.

SOLUTION ON PAGE 307

735 CROSSWORD

A straightforward crossword puzzle.

Across
1 Mitigate (9)
7 Penetrating photograph (1–3)
8 Tedium (5)
10 Crosswise (8)
11 A sudden major computer failure (5)
12 Relating to the stars (6)
14 Communication code word for the letter "S" (6)
17 Similar (5)
18 Examiner (8)
19 Straight edge (5)
22 Son of Isaac who sold his birthright to his brother Jacob (4)
23 Pure (4–5)

Down
1 The first lady (3)
2 Convert hide to leather (3)
3 Not one or the other (7)
4 Domesticated animal of Peru (6)
5 Duration (6)
6 Rickety (10)
9 Egocentrism (10)
13 Small brownish bird (7)
15 Regretful (6)
16 Descend a steep drop with the aid of rope (6)
20 Garland (3)
21 Type of grain (3)

SOLUTION ON PAGE 307

736 ODD XWORD

Find 25 words in the grid that can be paired up with one of the words below, for example, "Lateral Thinking."

AIRCRAFT
AMUSEMENT
ANIMATED
BINOMIAL
BIRTHDAY
BURNING
CIRCUIT
CONSCIENCE
COUNTER
DAYLIGHT
HONEYCOMB
INTERIM
JOINT
LATERAL
MOLECULAR
NUMBER
PATHETIC
PENCIL
ROCKET
ROUND
SATURATION
SHIP'S
SHUTTLE
SLEEP
SLEEPING

S	F	C	S	W	S	L	T	J	R	V	H	Y	G
T	A	D	Z	Z	H	A	R	E	N	T	R	A	P
A	L	N	I	Q	O	S	S	K	M	E	T	E	G
R	L	E	L	P	U	O	X	E	B	M	H	N	U
V	A	D	H	D	L	P	R	B	G	O	I	B	P
A	C	I	C	U	D	O	O	S	N	N	N	I	T
T	Y	V	T	A	E	R	M	H	I	E	K	S	E
I	F	I	I	H	R	P	S	A	H	Y	I	C	D
O	O	D	T	Q	E	R	R	R	C	T	N	U	A
N	R	C	S	T	D	T	I	P	N	Y	G	I	C
A	V	I	N	O	I	T	S	E	U	Q	F	T	R
W	E	I	G	H	T	F	I	N	R	R	E	Q	A
N	O	O	T	R	A	C	A	E	C	K	O	X	W
P	O	V	R	K	S	A	P	R	E	S	E	N	T

SOLUTION ON PAGE 307

737 LOST LETTERS

Here is the alphabet with some letters omitted. When you have found all the missing ones, they will spell the name of a German city. Which is it?

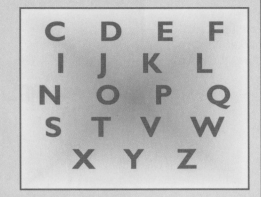

C D E F
I J K L
N O P Q
S T V W
X Y Z

SOLUTION ON PAGE 307

738 TRIANGLES

Find a number to replace the question mark.

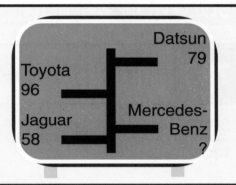

3
10
2 4

5
11
4 3

2
?
2 7

SOLUTION ON PAGE 307

739 CARD CONUNDRUM

Each same symbol in the diagram has the same value – one of which is a negative number. Can you work out the logic and discover which number should replace the question mark and the values of the symbols?

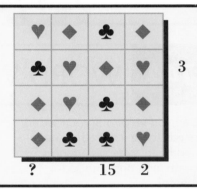

3

? 15 2

SOLUTION ON PAGE 307

740 LACKING DIRECTION

Can you tell how far it is to the Mercedes-Benz garage on this weird signpost?

Datsun 79
Toyota 96
Jaguar 58
Mercedes-Benz ?

SOLUTION ON PAGE 307

741 REMOVAL MEN

The removal men had been asked to pack and move the contents of a very expensive house to another even more exclusive area. The house contents included fine silver and gold cutlery, rare pieces of art and very expensive collections of stamps. One of the removal men found the temptation too much and stole a page from the stamp collection. It was the homeowner who was jailed. How could this be?

1. It was not an insurance scam.
2. The removal man did not know the homeowner.
3. The removal man lost his job and was arrested.
4. The value of each of the stamps was over $10,000 each.

SOLUTION ON PAGE 307

742 CHEAP SHOPPER

A man on low income wanted more for his family than he could provide. He devised a scheme that he thought might help him achieve this. He was useful with a computer and understood how the supermarket system worked. After going to the supermarket he implemented his scheme. He had a full trolley of goods and was prepared to pay the price on the register for all of the goods, yet he was arrested. Why?

1. The register asked for $120.25, which he offered to pay.
2. All of the goods bought were in tins, jars, or packets. He did not buy any fruit or vegetables.
3. He had planned this very well and had not been noticed as doing anything wrong by security cameras in the store.
4. He declared everything at the register and kept nothing in the trolley or on his person.

SOLUTION ON PAGE 307

743 CROSSWORD

Answers 2 to 9 contain the same letters as the word above plus one other letter. Clues 10 to 17 contain the same letters as the word above minus one letter.

1 Alpha
2 An indefinite article
3 Convert hide into leather
4 Small, biting dipteran fly
5 Something of great size
6 Playing a part
7 Allocating a part
8 Someone who neither believes or disbelieves in God
9 Yearning for past times
10 Finding a particular spot
11 Covering
12 Deed
13 Major division of a long poem
14 Outer garment
15 Small bed
16 In the direction of
17 Omega

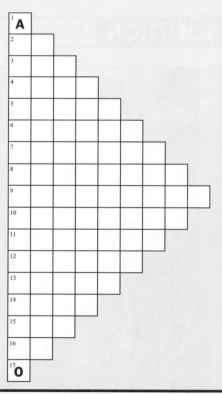

SOLUTION ON PAGE 307

744 WORD WHEEL

Can you work out what letter needs to be inserted in the middle to form four dances by combining opposite segments?

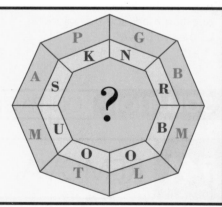

SOLUTION ON PAGE 308

745 OT PROBLEM

By taking a segment and finding its pair the names of four books from the Old Testament can be made. What are they?

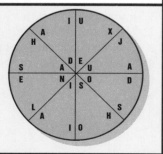

SOLUTION ON PAGE 308

746 COOK CAPER

The names of the following ten chefs can be found in this grid on either vertical, horizontal or diagonal lines. Can you find them?

Raymond Blanc
Paul Bocuse
Robert Carrier
Keith Floyd
Rosamund Grant
Ken Hom
Bruno Loubet
Gary Rhodes
Albert Roux
Anthony Tobin

T	N	A	R	G	D	N	U	M	A	S	O	R
B	Y	N	L	K	L	Q	O	X	C	B	O	A
Q	W	T	F	Z	P	H	K	U	J	B	G	Y
Y	G	H	V	S	N	X	E	O	E	R	C	M
D	V	O	W	E	M	D	I	R	S	U	K	O
J	K	N	K	D	B	P	T	T	U	N	O	N
P	M	Y	S	O	S	C	H	R	C	O	P	D
P	F	T	Y	H	A	Y	F	E	O	L	J	B
Z	W	O	U	R	Z	G	L	B	B	O	C	L
F	C	B	R	Y	Q	K	O	L	L	U	F	A
Y	V	I	D	R	J	F	Y	A	U	B	R	N
W	E	N	V	A	Y	Q	D	P	A	E	W	C
R	G	K	P	G	R	Z	B	Y	P	T	P	Q

SOLUTION ON PAGE 308

747 STATE SECRET

Collect one letter from each segment to give the name of an American state. What is it?

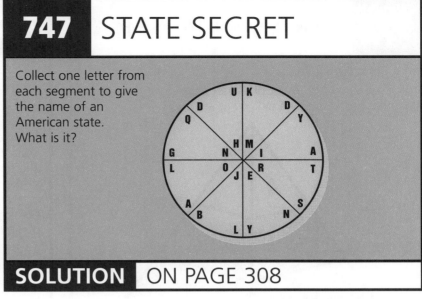

SOLUTION ON PAGE 308

748 DIFFICULT WHEEL

Can you work out what letter needs to be inserted in the middle to form four famous composers by combining opposite segments?

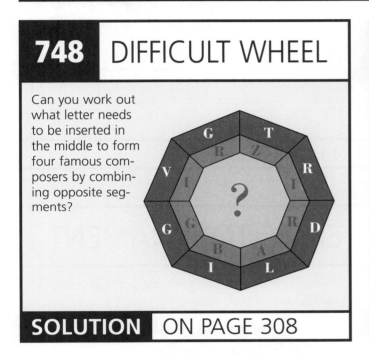

SOLUTION ON PAGE 308

749 WORDFRAME

The wordframe below, when filled with the correct letters, will give the name of a pop singer. The letters are arranged in the coded square below. There are two possible alternatives to fill each square of the wordframe, one correct, the other incorrect. Who is the singer?

2B	5D	4A		3A	1D	1B	4E	5E	1A
1E	3E	2E		2C	5B	4C	3B	1C	2D

	A	B	C	D	E
1	Y	R	V	N	B
2	P	F	M	Q	G
3	J	L	Y	W	O
4	B	U	K	C	S
5	D	A	T	H	E

SOLUTION ON PAGE 308

750 NUMBING NUMBERS

What number should replace the question mark?

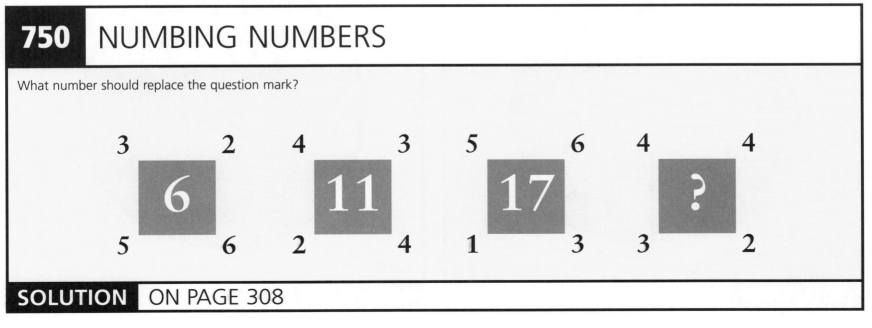

3 2   4 3   5 6   4 4

6   **11**   **17**   **?**

5 6   2 4   1 3   3 2

SOLUTION ON PAGE 308

751 PYRAMID POSER

Two sides of this pyramid can be seen, but the other two are obscured. Two eight-letter country names are written round the pyramid. What are they?

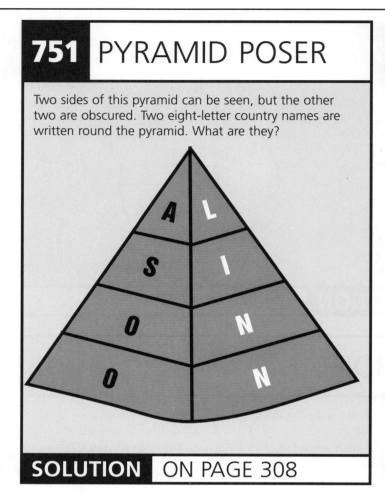

SOLUTION ON PAGE 308

752 WORDFRAME

The wordframe below, when filled with the correct letters, will give the name of a tennis player. The letters are arranged in the coded square right. There are two possible alternatives to fill each square of the wordframe, but one is correct, the other is a red herring. Who is the tennis player?

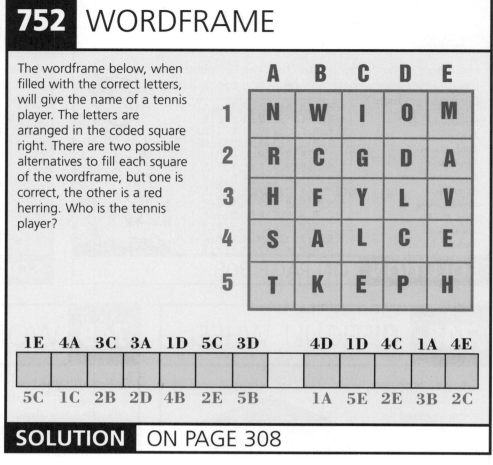

SOLUTION ON PAGE 308

753 CAPITAL PUNISHMENT

Can you work out what letter needs to be inserted in the middle to form four capital cities by combining opposite segments?

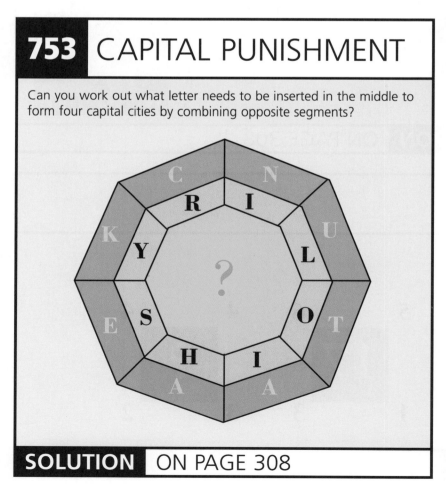

SOLUTION ON PAGE 308

754 TENNIS TOURNAMENT

By taking a segment and finding its pair the names of four tennis stars can be found. Who are they?

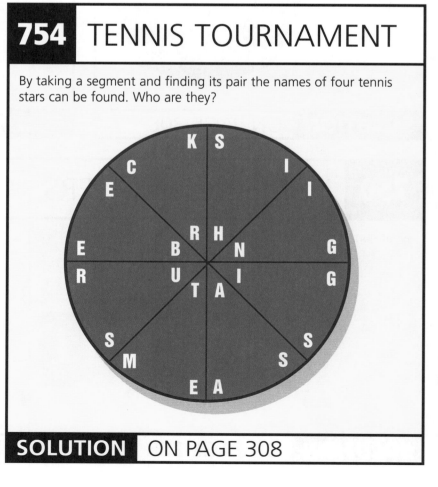

SOLUTION ON PAGE 308

755 WORD WONDER

The letters in this grid can be used to make two words, one connected with chemistry and the other with music. Every letter is used once only and the two words are of equal length. What are they?

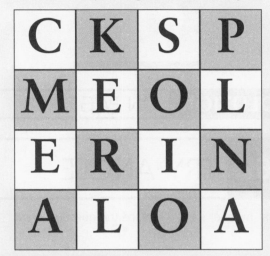

SOLUTION ON PAGE 308

756 CROSSWORD

A cryptogram is a coded message in which each letter of the alphabet has been substituted for another. In this crossword every letter has been substituted for another. For example, "E" has been substituted by "X" and "B" by "S" as shown. Can you decode the crossword and enter the correct words in the grid to the right?

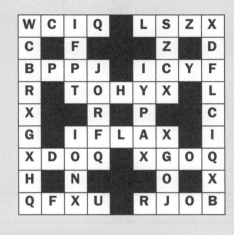 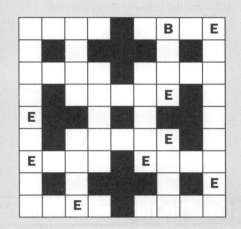

SOLUTION ON PAGE 308

757 FIZZY FUN

The names of the following 10 champagnes can be found in this grid on vertical, horizontal and diagonal lines. Can you find them?

D	G	J	B	F	H	C	L	G	B
D	E	U	T	Z	E	A	A	O	M
C	T	V	H	W	N	P	L	S	F
P	R	V	E	S	R	L	A	S	H
S	A	L	O	N	I	Q	Y	E	K
K	N	N	J	N	O	X	A	T	D
B	I	W	G	V	T	G	Q	B	W
D	U	E	Z	K	F	X	E	Y	G
F	R	E	G	O	R	L	O	P	Y
Q	G	X	V	C	H	X	Z	O	D

Ayala Bollinger De Venoge
Deutz Gosset Henriot Lanson
Pol Roger Ruinart Salon

SOLUTION ON PAGE 308

758 CROSSWORD

Each clue is an anagram of the answer. Take care, though, as some anagrams can produce more than one word. Make sure you enter the correct solution in the grid.

Across

1 EMU IS LION
7 TRACED SET
10 CHET
11 MODE
12 A VETO
14 PERSIA
15 MOB PAL
16 AN TIDY
18 CEDARS
19 HATER
20 A NET
22 CAME
23 LILY TIBIA
24 MORE MONET

Down

2 CHIN
3 TO CAVE
4 TIE ASS
5 EDEN
6 DAMNED GIN
7 SPLICE CAT
8 CREAMY COD
9 FOND BRIDE
12. OR TEA
13 COP HE
17 BY BEAR
18 LET SON
21 MITE
22 TO MA

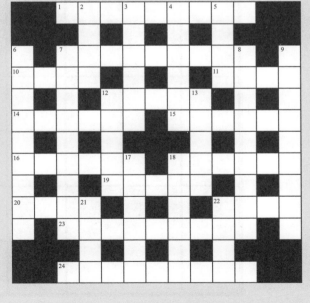

SOLUTION ON PAGE 308

759 CODE CORNER

If the name **WOODROW WILSON** is

⊘ ⊕ ⊕ ⊘ ⊖ ⊕ ⊘
⊘ ⊘ ⊕ ⊗ ⊖ ⊖

Who are the other U.S. presidents?

1. ⊘ ⊘ ⊕ ⊕   ⊘ ⊘ ⊖ ⊘ ⊕ ⊖
2. ⊘ ⊘ ⊖ ⊘ ⊖ ⊘ ⊖   ⊕ ⊘ ⊖ ⊘ ⊕ ⊖
3. ⊘ ⊗ ⊕ ⊖ ⊖ ⊕ ⊗   ⊘ ⊘ ⊗ ⊖ ⊖ ⊖ ⊕ ⊕ ⊕ ⊖
4. ⊖ ⊘ ⊖ ⊖ ⊘   ⊗   ⊘ ⊖ ⊘ ⊘ ⊘ ⊖
5. ⊘ ⊕ ⊖ ⊖   ⊕   ⊕ ⊗ ⊖ ⊖ ⊖ ⊗ ⊘ ⊘
6. ⊘ ⊕ ⊖ ⊘ ⊗ ⊗ ⊖   ⊗   ⊕ ⊖ ⊘ ⊖ ⊗

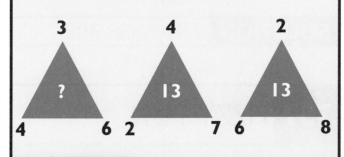

SOLUTION ON PAGE 308

761 LUVVIE LOGIC

Rearrange the order of these six famous actors' second names to give the name of another famous actor in the shaded diagonal line.
Steve MARTIN, Andy GARCIA,
Gary COOPER, Eddie MURPHY, Keanu REEVES, Lee MARVIN.

Who is the actor given in the diagonal?

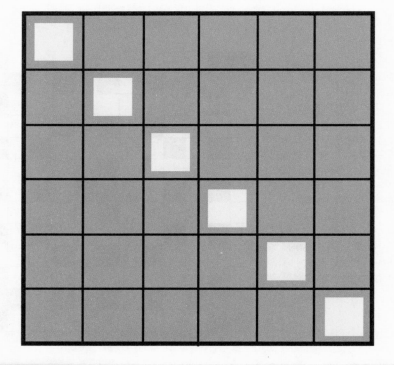

SOLUTION ON PAGE 308

760 LINE LOGIC

Which well-known expression is represented by this rebus?

P<u>IN</u>K

SOLUTION ON PAGE 308

762 TRY ANGLE

What number should replace the question mark?

```
    3            4            2
   /?\         /13\         /13\
  4   6       2   7       6   8
```

SOLUTION ON PAGE 308

763 ODD SHADE?

Which of these groups of colours is the odd one out?

A □ ▣ ▪ ▣

B ▪ ▣ ▣ □

C ▪ ▪ ▪ □

SOLUTION ON PAGE 308

764 FATHER vs SON

Joe's son was very fit and worked out every day but he was not the brainiest of individuals. Joe had seen his youth come and go and he was now in his late 40s and not in good health. He felt that he could still beat his son even if he gave his son a small start. Joe's son, who would never throw a chance to beat his father, took up the challenge, but still lost. How?

1. Joe was never any good as an athlete.
2. Joe never cheated and did not have any help.
3. It did not involve any motors or sails.
4. Joe's son did not let his father win deliberately.
5. The son had a 10-second start.

SOLUTION ON PAGE 308

765 CROSSWORD

This is a straightforward crossword, almost! There is just one problem; the answers to the clues might need to be entered forward or back, down or up. For instance, the across answer "play" may appear as play or yalp and a down answer "work" may appear as either w or k
o r
r o
k w

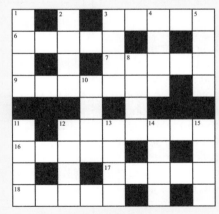

Across

3 Spending binge (5)
6 Slight error (5)
7 Pale mauve (5)
9 Suitcases (7)
12 Heading (7)
16 Extreme suffering (5)
17 Giving out voice (5)
18 Muffled (5)

Down

1 Soulful, sad shade (4)
2 European mountain range (4)
3 Mirth (4)
4 Make less distinct (4)
5 Unwell (4)
8 Native of Thailand (4)
10 Group of workmen (4)
11 Divisions of a week (4)
12 Garment (4)
13 Part of the hand (4)
14 Unit of measurement (4)
15 Dark blue (4)

SOLUTION ON PAGE 308

766 CROSSWORD

This puzzle has two grids and two sets of clues. The problem is that for each clue there are two clues, and it is up to you to work out which answer to each clue goes in which grid. The answers to clues 6 across have already been filled in.

Across

6 Hollow globe of liquid (6)
6 Short shrill sound (6)
7 Greek and Roman god of music and poetry (6)
7 Polite request (6)
8 Small amount (3)
8 Frequently (3)
9 Nickname of Jimmy Durante (9)
9 Blizzard conditions (9)
12 Large body of water (5)
12 Pat or Daniel (5)
13 In pieces (7)
13 Plot (7)
15 Department of university (7)
15 Pertaining to the state (7)
16 Male relative (5)
16 Forbidden (5)
18 Small carved ornament (9)
18 Committed to a cause (9)
19 Conclusion (3)
19 Excavate (3)
21 Group of six musicians (6)
21 Woman's headgear (6)
22 Terminate (6)
22 Trying experience (6)

Down

1 Use questionable language to mislead (10)
1 Adequate (10)
2 Fix in place (3)
2 Japanese sash (3)
3 Soft fruit (5)
3 Malodorous animal (5)
4 Belief (7)
4 Type of life jacket (3,4)
5 Elevated floor (9)
5 Constant (9)
10 Oratorical (10)
10 Attractiveness (10)
11 Annoy greatly (9)
11 The Holy Land (9)
14 Type of newspaper (7)
14 Secret behavior (7)
17 Pole or rod for support (5)
17 Greek teller of fables (5)
20 Increase by (3)
20 South African ox-like antelope (3)

SOLUTION ON PAGE 308

767 KNIGHT MOVES

A knight, which moves either one square horizontally and two vertically or two horizontally and one vertically, starts at the shaded square of this small chess board visiting each square without returning to the same square twice. Find the route which spells out four famous cartoon characters.

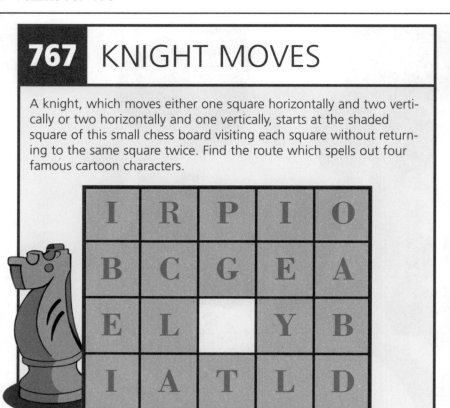

SOLUTION ON PAGE 308

768 CANADA CLUE

Take one letter from each segment to find the name of a Canadian city. What is it?

SOLUTION ON PAGE 308

769 TRIANGULAR TEASER

What number should replace the question mark?

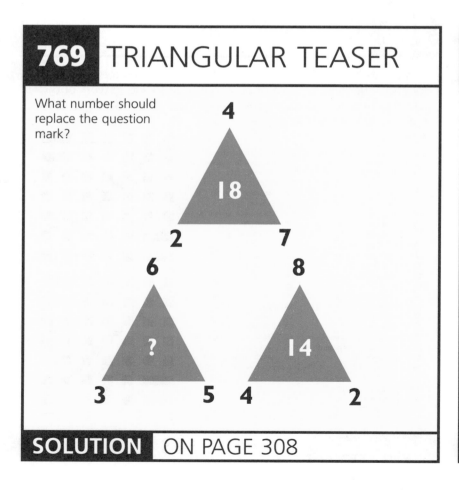

SOLUTION ON PAGE 308

770 ACTOR ENIGMA

The maze on the right contains four names of actors and actresses. Find four separate routes through the maze without any route crossing another, although they may merge. On each route collect six letters only to give you the names of the four actors and actresses.

FINISH

START

SOLUTION ON PAGE 308

771 KNIGHT MOVES

A knight, which moves either one square horizontally and two vertically or two horizontally and one vertically, starts at the shaded square of this small chess board visiting each square without returning to the same square twice. Find the route which spells out six names of books in the Old Testament.

L	N	H	A	R	D
U	I	E	A	S	S
I	E	O	A	H	E
J	A	E	A	I	D
S	S	X	U	H	M
E	L	T	U	O	S

SOLUTION ON PAGE 308

772 ATHLETIC CONTEST

This is an unusual maze. Find four separate routes through it without any route crossing another, although they may merge. On each route collect 7 letters only to give you four athletes.

SOLUTION ON PAGE 308

773 TRIANGLE TROUBLE

The letters surrounding each triangle are the consonants of a famous sports person's name. The letters inside the triangle have a connection with each person. What letter should replace the question mark in the fourth triangle?

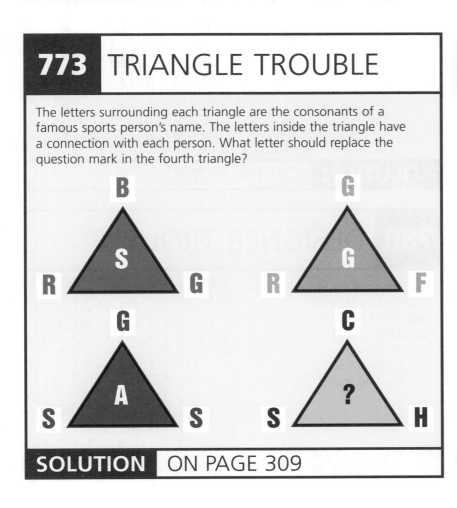

SOLUTION ON PAGE 309

774 CITY SEARCH

Take one letter from each segment to find the name of a city in the USA. What is it?

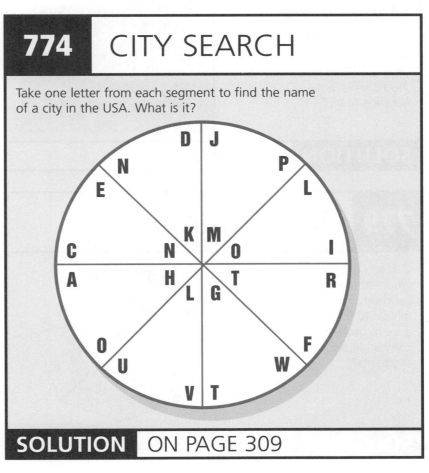

SOLUTION ON PAGE 309

775 CITY PUZZLE

By taking a segment and finding its pair the names of four cities of the USA can be made. What are they?

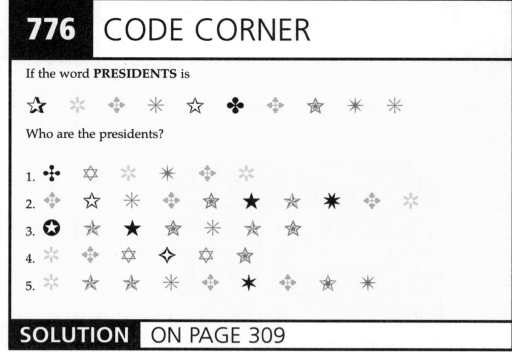

SOLUTION ON PAGE 309

776 CODE CORNER

If the word **PRESIDENTS** is

Who are the presidents?

1.
2.
3.
4.
5.

SOLUTION ON PAGE 309

777 LOST LETTER

Complete the square with the letters of B R Y A N. When completed no row, column or diagonal line will contain the same letter more than once and one horizontal line will spell the name correctly. What letter should replace the question mark?

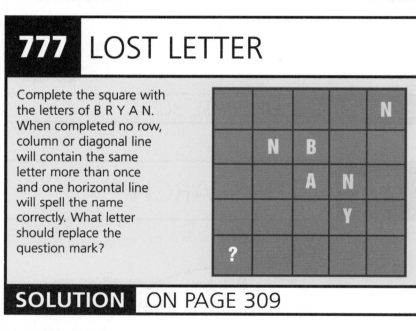

SOLUTION ON PAGE 309

778 MUSIC MAYHEM

The names of three musical terms have been merged together here. What are they?

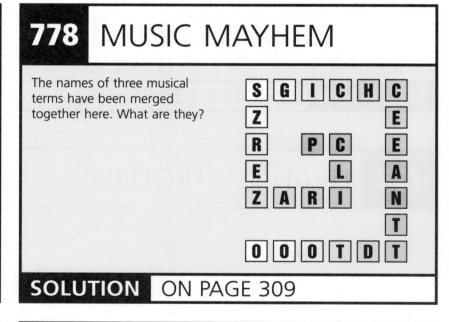

SOLUTION ON PAGE 309

779 GOD ENIGMA

Can you work out what letter needs to be inserted in the middle to form four ancient gods, by combining opposite segments?

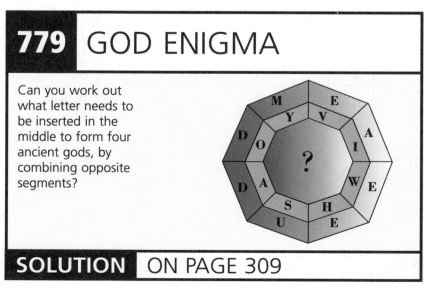

SOLUTION ON PAGE 309

780 DESIGNER TROUBLE

The names of the following 10 fashion designers can be found in this grid on vertical, horizontal and diagonal lines. Can you find them?

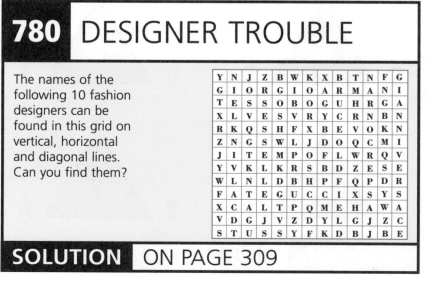

SOLUTION ON PAGE 309

781 AWKWARD PIANO

Alf was a bit of a practical joker and his workmates would always be under attack from him. One day they had to move a piano and some other items up the stairs in a department store. Although the piano was heavy, they decided that they could still put a few things on top of it before they carried it up the stairs. Alf was going backward and went up the stairs at the leading edge of the piano. Joe was at the bottom end and soon ran into a problem. Alf asked if Joe could hold the piano in place while he got help. Joe said, "Yes, but be quick." Alf rushed off and returned in under a minute pushing something into Joe's top pocket. "There," said Alf, "that should do it!" Joe was not amused. What had Alf done that he thought might have helped Joe so much? (Not!)

1. He used a literal translation of a need for help.
2. It did not help Joe at all and the piano was stuck.
3. Nobody else helped.

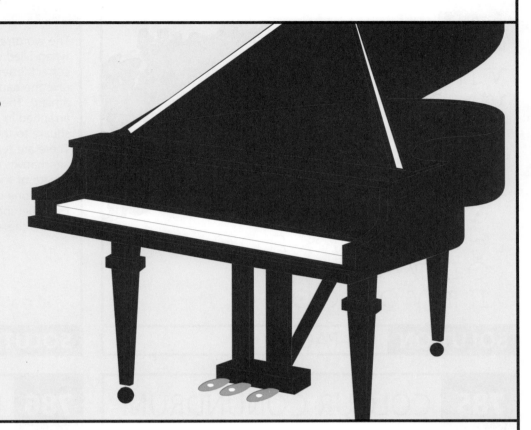

SOLUTION ON PAGE 309

782 CUBE CONUNDRUM

Each cube contains three faces. Only one face on each cube will fit correctly into the grid. Select the nine correct faces and fit them correctly into the grid to form a symmetrical crossword.

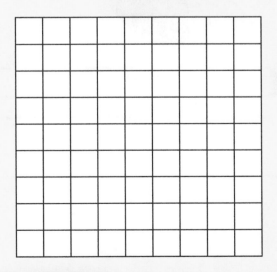

SOLUTION ON PAGE 309

783 STATE SECRETS

If the country **UNITED STATES** is

Which are these states?

1.
2.
3.
4.
5.
6.

SOLUTION ON PAGE 309

784 WORDFRAME

The wordframe below, when filled with the correct letters, will give the name of an athlete. The letters are arranged in the coded square to the right. There are two possible alternatives to fill each square of the word frame, one correct, the other incorrect. Who is the athlete?

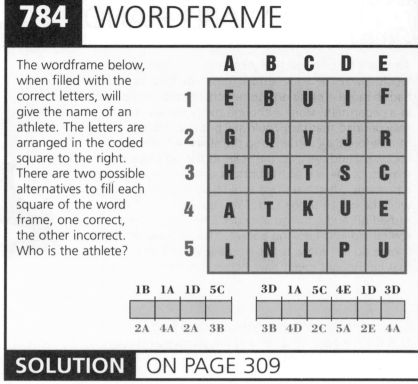

	A	B	C	D	E
1	E	B	U	I	F
2	G	Q	V	J	R
3	H	D	T	S	C
4	A	T	K	U	E
5	L	N	L	P	U

1B	1A	1D	5C
2A	4A	2A	3B

3D	1A	5C	4E	1D	3D
3B	4D	2C	5A	2E	4A

SOLUTION ON PAGE 309

785 COLOUR CONUNDRUM

One of these colours is wrong. Which is it and what should it be?

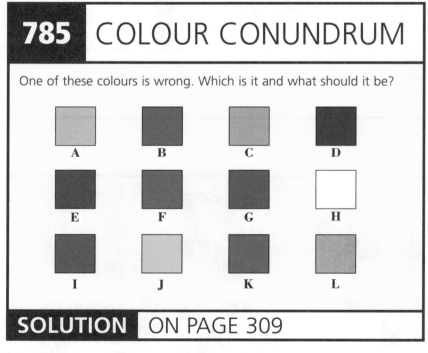

SOLUTION ON PAGE 309

786 HUE QUEST

What colour completes the series?

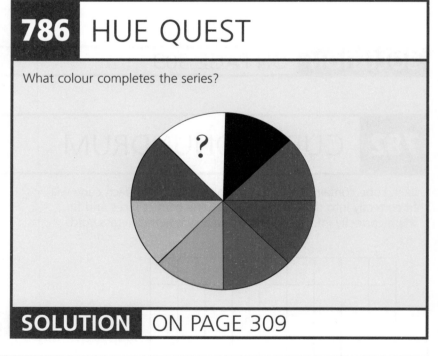

SOLUTION ON PAGE 309

787 SEQUENTIAL SQUARES

Find a number to replace the question mark.

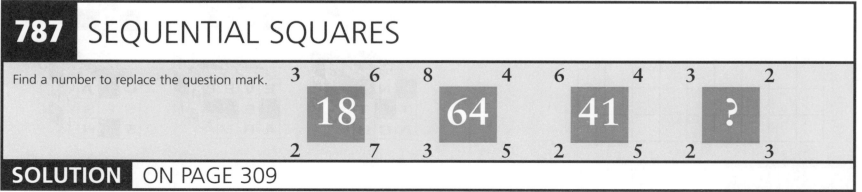

3	6	8	4	6	4	3	2
18		**64**		**41**		**?**	
2	7	3	5	2	5	2	3

SOLUTION ON PAGE 309

788 BOX BRAINBUSTER

What letter should replace the question mark in the box below?

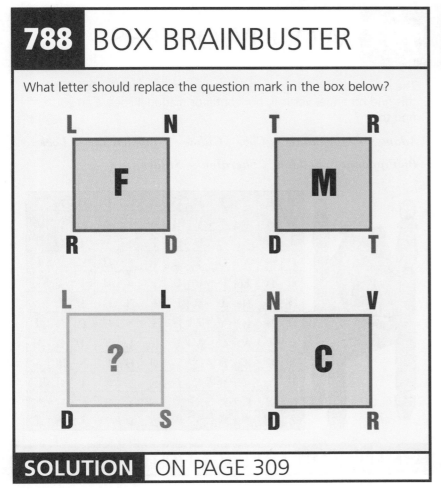

789 TILE TROUBLE

What number should replace the question mark?

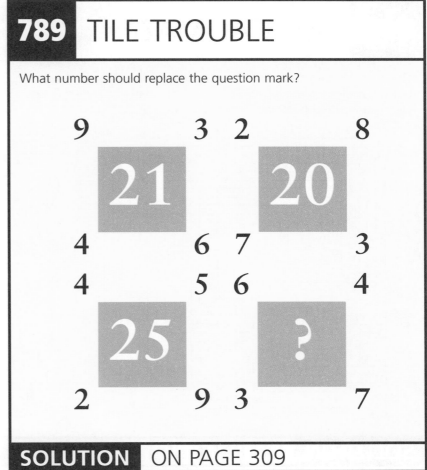

790 COLOUR PUZZLE

What is yellow worth?

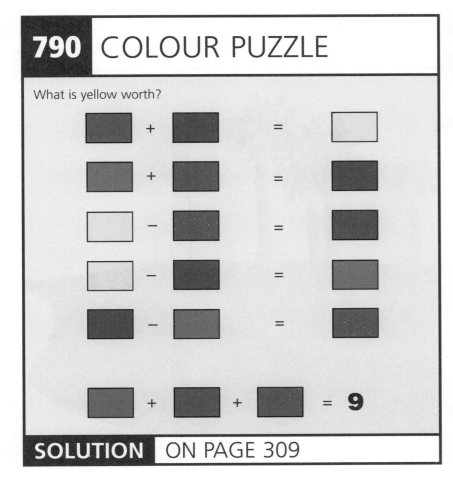

791 STAR SPIN

Take one letter from each segment to find the name of a film star. Who is it?

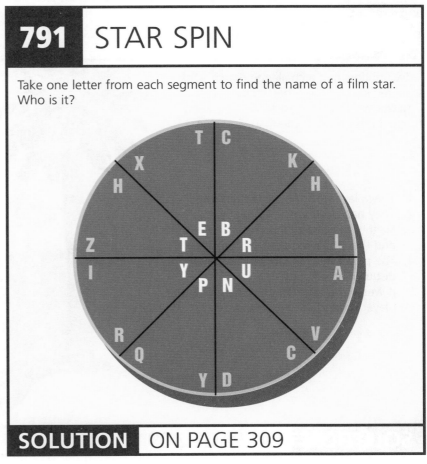

SOLUTION ON PAGE 309

SOLUTION ON PAGE 309

SOLUTION ON PAGE 309

SOLUTION ON PAGE 309

792 MUSICAL MAZE

This is an unusual maze. Find four separate routes through it without any route crossing another, although the paths may merge. On each route collect 6 letters to give you four musical terms.

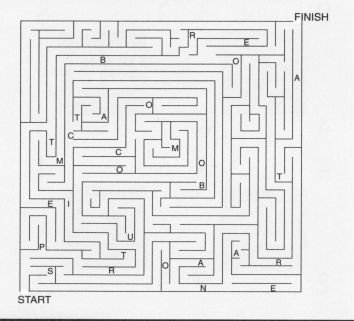

FINISH

START

SOLUTION ON PAGE 309

793 WOODWORKERS

The names of the following 10 furniture makers can be found in this grid on either vertical, horizontal or diagonal lines. Can you find them?

Adam   *Chippendale*   *Cob*   *Gillow*   *Hepplewhite*   *Lock*
Phillipponat   *Seddon*   *Sheraton*   *Stuart*

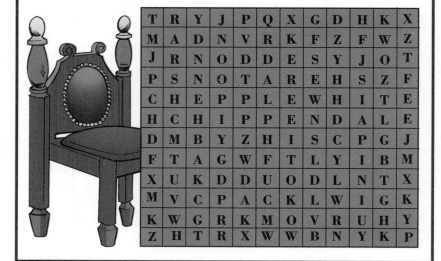

T	R	Y	J	P	Q	X	G	D	H	K	X
M	A	D	N	V	R	K	F	Z	F	W	Z
J	R	N	O	D	D	E	S	Y	J	O	T
P	S	N	O	T	A	R	E	H	S	Z	F
C	H	E	P	P	L	E	W	H	I	T	E
H	C	H	I	P	P	E	N	D	A	L	E
D	M	B	Y	Z	H	I	S	C	P	G	J
F	T	A	G	W	F	T	L	Y	I	B	M
X	U	K	D	D	U	O	D	L	N	T	X
M	V	C	P	A	C	K	L	W	I	G	K
K	W	G	R	K	M	O	V	R	U	H	Y
Z	H	T	R	X	W	W	B	N	Y	K	P

SOLUTION ON PAGE 309

794 GOLFERS

Two golfers had a challenge match. One scored 72 and the other scored 74. The player with the highest score won. How could this be given the following clues?

1. They played off the same handicap.
2. They had both scored correctly.
3. Neither player had incurred penalty shots and they followed the rules precisely.
4. The player with the lower score was not disqualified.
5. It was not a tournament where only the player scoring 74 was entered.

SOLUTION ON PAGE 309

795 IS THE DOCTOR WRONG?

A farm worker fell from his tractor and suffered bruising and what he thought might be a broken ankle. He was taken to the local hospital where the student doctor started to investigate his problems. Almost at once he shouted, "Cardiac arrest!" and revival equipment was rushed into the outpatients area. The diagnosis was correct and the farm worker went home in the next 5 hours. How could this be?

1. The farm worker was alive when he went home and he was discharged by qualified staff.
2. The student doctor did everything correctly.
3. The consultant physician thanked the doctor for his prompt action.
4. Neither the broken ankle, nor the bruising, caused the cardiac arrest.

SOLUTION ON PAGE 309

796 BIRD BRAIN

Rearrange the letters to form the names of six birds. Transfer the arrowed letters into the key anagram and then rearrange the letters to form the name of a seventh bird.

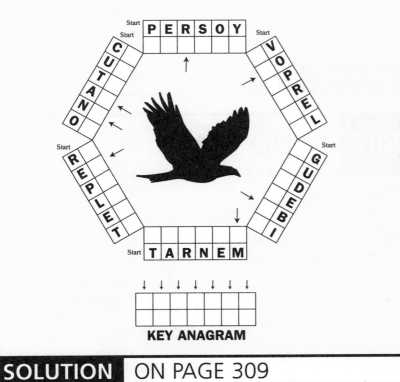

Start PERSOY
Start
Start VOPREL
CUTANO
REPLET
GUDEBI
Start TARNEM

KEY ANAGRAM

SOLUTION ON PAGE 309

797 WORD WONDER

The letters in the grid below can be rearranged to make a 16-letter word and concept that was practically unheard of a few decades ago. What is it?

B	A	R	D
E	A	L	G
T	O	I	I
D	Y	B	I

SOLUTION ON PAGE 309

798 KNIGHT MOVES

A knight, which moves either one square horizontally and two vertically or two horizontally and one vertically, starts at the shaded square of this small chess board visiting each square without returning to the same square twice. Find the route which spells out four famous writers.

A	E	W	N	S	K	L
R	N	M	N	I	E	H
H	I	A	R	P	D	I
E	A	E	S	J	A	A
L	P	E	S	A	N	E
C	T	T	I	O	U	K
E	L	S	S	E	W	G

SOLUTION ON PAGE 309

799 SCIENCE SEARCH

By taking a segment and finding its pair the names of three scientists can be found. Who are they?

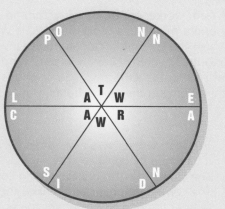

SOLUTION ON PAGE 309

800 IMAGE ENIGMA

From the information given, work out the missing total and the values of the different images.

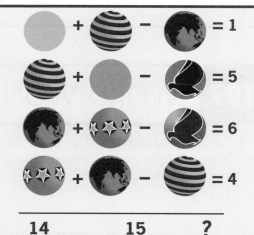

14	15	?

SOLUTION ON PAGE 309

801 CODE CORNER

If the names **DIEGO MARADONA** and **JACK CHARLTON** are

⊔⊓⌐⊓ ⊐⌐⊓⌐⊔⊓⌐⌐

and

⊓⊔⊔⊏ ⊔⊐⊔⌐⌐⊏⊓⌐

Who are the other footballers?

1. ⌐⊓⌐⌐⌐⊏⊓ ⌐⊔⊐⊐⊓⌐
2. ⊔⌐⌐⌐⊏⊏ ⌐⊏⊏⊏⌐⊓⌐
3. ⊏⌐<⊏⌐ ⊏⌐⌐⊐⌐
4. ⌐⌐⊏⊔ ⊔⊐⌐⌐⊓⌐
5. ⊔<⌐⊐⌐⌐ ⊏⊏⌐⌐⌐⊐⌐⌐

SOLUTION ON PAGE 309

802 WORDFRAME

The wordframe below, when filled with the correct letters, will give the name of a US city. There are two possible letters for each square, one right and one wrong. What is the city?

	A	B	C	D	E
1	I	D	B	F	T
2	Y	N	Q	G	C
3	V	J	H	R	X
4	M	A	E	K	P
5	C	Z	S	O	U

2E	3C	1A	4B	4B	2D	3A
1B	4D	2B	2E	2D	1E	5D

SOLUTION ON PAGE 309

803 MIND MAZE

This is an unusual maze. Find four separate routes through it without any route crossing another, although the paths may merge. On each route collect six letters to give you four scientists. Who are they?

SOLUTION ON PAGE 309

804 CUP OF COFFEE

A blind man went into a restaurant and ordered a cup of coffee. When it arrived he complained that the coffee was not hot enough and requested a fresh cup. When it arrived he complained that it was in the same cup. How did he know?

1. The cup did not have a crack or anything that distinguished it from the other cups that were used in the restaurant.
2. He could not tell by the temperature of the cup.
3. He had not left a sticky mark or cream on the outside of the cup.

SOLUTION ON PAGE 310

---

805 CROSSWORD

Answers are entered starting at the appropriate number, and running in a spiral into the middle. Each answer begins with one or more letters from the end of the previous word.

Clues

1 Four-speaker sound system (12)
2 To wink (9)
3 The 300th anniversary (12)
4 Suburb of New York (7)
5 Framework of an organ (6)
6 Figure of misspeech (11)
7 Teacher of mystical doctrines (10)
8 Visitor (5)
9 Vertical strut (9)
10 African pygmies (9)
11 Bird (6)
12 The green woodpecker (6)
13 A young bird (9)
14 Well versed in languages (8)
15 Family tree (6)
16 Small monkey (8)
17 Indian teatime (6)
18 Allusive remark (8)
19 A plane figure with 12 sides (9)
20 Venetian waterman (9)
21 Error in printing (7)
22 Desert plant (10)
23 Don Quixote's lady (8)
24 Living in trees (8)
25 Castle in Spain (8)
26 Women's undergarment (9)
27 Tear apart (6)

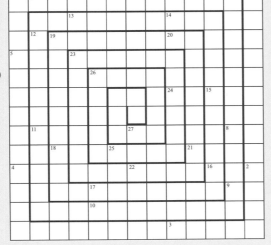

SOLUTION ON PAGE 310

---

806 CIRCLE XWORD

A crossword in a circle, so the clues are radial (going into the middle) or circular (going around one of the bands). The words end at a solid line.

Circular

1 Shape
12 Fabulous bird
15 Decorating
17 Pastel hue
18 Ballad
19 Disabled
20 The West
22 Place
23 Broom
24 Male
25 Testudos

Radial

1 Appeared
2 Poems
3 Incline one's head
4 Out of
5 Measure
6 Single object
7 Imitator
8 Shade
9 Entrance
10 Alright
11 Mind
12 Ratio
13 Unctuous liquids
14 Decapod crustacean
16 Frozen water
21 Carry out
22 Mathematical sign

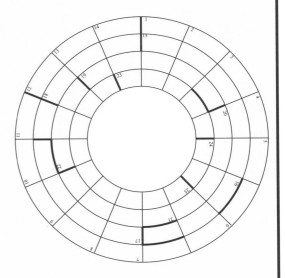

SOLUTION ON PAGE 310

807 THESPIAN SEARCH

Turn the dials on this diagram to give 8 forenames and 8 surnames of famous actresses. Then match them up to give their full names. Who are they? (A score above 5 is very good!)

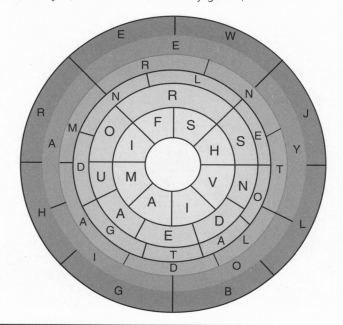

SOLUTION ON PAGE 310

808 PLANE PROBLEM

Can you work out what letter needs to be inserted in the middle to form four airlines by combining opposite segments?

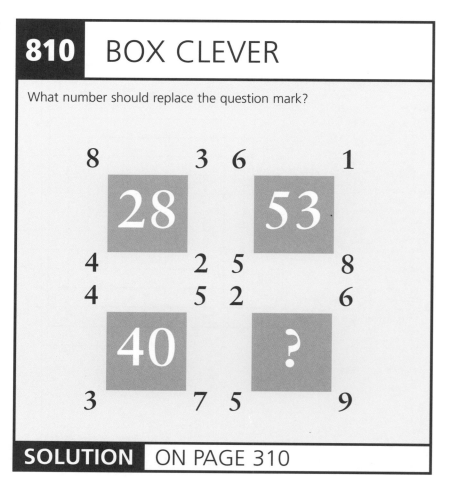

SOLUTION ON PAGE 310

809 STAR SOLUTION

The names of the following 10 film stars can be found in this grid on vertical, horizontal and diagonal lines. Can you find them?

John Cleese
Tom Cruise
Mel Gibson
Hugh Grant
Tom Hanks
Val Kilmer
Bruce Lee
Al Pacino
Sean Penn
Brad Pitt

W	Z	Q	E	P	R	V	H	E	F	M
T	O	U	S	Y	J	A	H	E	E	Z
T	N	S	I	G	K	L	U	L	S	W
I	I	E	U	F	H	K	G	E	E	P
P	C	A	R	H	X	I	H	C	E	H
D	A	N	C	H	B	L	G	U	L	J
A	P	P	M	S	Q	M	R	R	C	R
R	L	E	O	J	R	E	A	B	N	G
B	A	N	T	T	Z	R	N	P	H	Y
S	K	N	A	H	M	O	T	W	O	S
Y	R	B	X	F	Q	J	X	N	J	S

SOLUTION ON PAGE 310

810 BOX CLEVER

What number should replace the question mark?

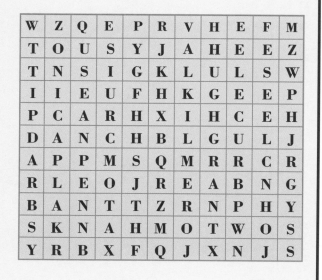

SOLUTION ON PAGE 310

811 MAD CAR

Why did the driver accelerate quickly to ram the car in front of him on the three-lane freeway?

1. He had not been drinking or taking drugs.
2. He did not know the driver in the car in front of him.
3. His foot had not had a muscle spasm; his action was deliberate.
4. He did not wish to harm anyone.
5. It was not a result of an act of nature such as an earthquake.
6. It was not to leap over a broken bridge or hole in the road.

SOLUTION ON PAGE 310

812 MAGIC SQUARES

Answers to 16 of the clues are four-letter words, which when placed correctly in the grids will form three Magic Squares where the same four words can be read horizontally and vertically. Three bonus clues are provided for three seven-letter words, which appear across and down at the connecting lines of the three squares.

Four-letter clues

(in no particular order)

Chatter
Conceal
Dress
Entice
Exploit
Hand over for a price
Image of worship
In close proximity
Itinerary
Monarch
Notion
Plant of the iris family
Room in prison
Sea-eagle
Shed blood
Stylish

Bonus clues

Jumbled account
Person who plays a particular string instrument
Speaking

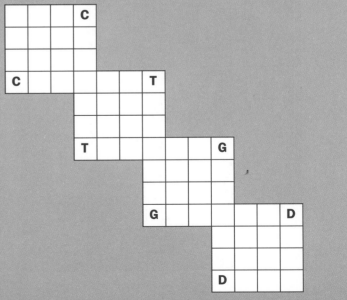

SOLUTION ON PAGE 310

813 TILE TROUBLE

Which number should replace the question mark?

3 4 6 13

32 **29**

10 5 12 2

4 6 9 3

22 **?**

8 14 7 10

SOLUTION ON PAGE 310

814 SQUARE SOLUTION

Which letter should replace the question mark?

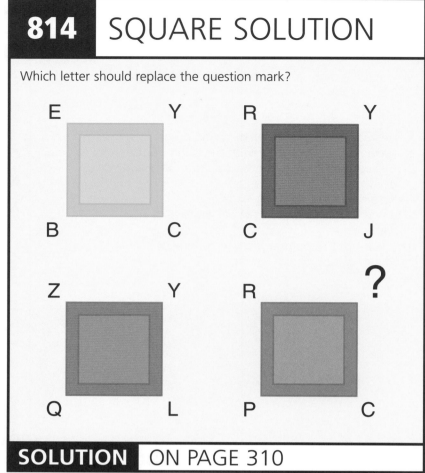

E Y R Y

B C C J

Z Y R **?**

Q L P C

SOLUTION ON PAGE 310

815 SQUARE ENIGMA

Which letter should replace the question mark?

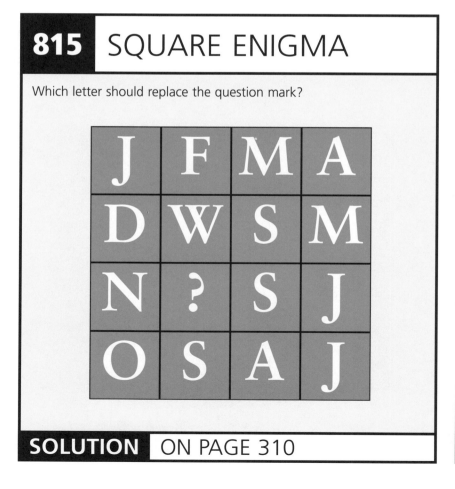

J	F	M	A
D	W	S	M
N	?	S	J
O	S	A	J

SOLUTION ON PAGE 310

816 DISC DILEMMA

Which letter should replace the question mark?

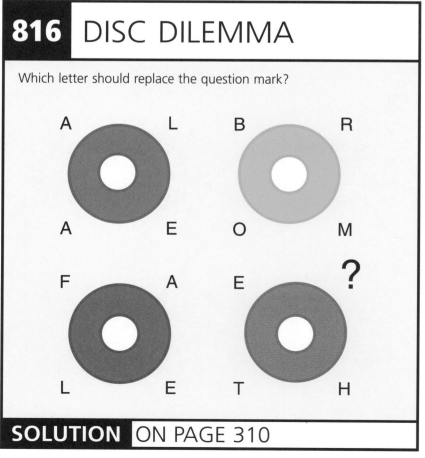

A L B R

A E O M

F A E **?**

L E T H

SOLUTION ON PAGE 310

817 BANK BUST

The child watched in total amazement as a man blew up a bank, killing three people. The child had a clear view of the whole event and was the only person to witness what went on. The police did not need to question him. Why?

1. The child was 12 years old.
2. The child told his parents what he had seen and they did not report it.
3. The family were not afraid of repercussions.
4. The man was not known to the child but he could describe the killer and all of the events clearly.
5. The child was not one to lie.
6. The killer did not own up to the killing.

SOLUTION ON PAGE 310

818 WORD PROBLEM

The blank squares have been removed from this crossword and spurious letters have been inserted in their place. Find and fill in the black squares to make a symmetrical crossword.

P	E	T	T	E	D	A	R	E	P	A	S	T
U	R	I	D	V	A	L	I	D	A	R	T	I
G	A	M	B	I	T	U	G	E	R	B	I	L
D	N	B	A	L	E	M	O	N	P	O	E	T
O	D	E	S	I	S	I	R	U	M	U	S	E
G	O	R	E	S	I	D	E	S	I	R	E	D
A	R	T	W	A	Y	O	T	O	N	O	T	O
F	I	N	E	D	A	T	A	B	I	G	O	T
I	C	E	R	S	S	O	B	C	M	E	N	U
N	R	E	B	O	P	E	R	A	H	A	I	R
I	O	D	I	N	E	W	E	C	A	R	T	E
A	P	E	R	C	E	D	A	R	E	E	V	E
L	I	D	D	E	D	A	D	E	A	D	E	N

SOLUTION ON PAGE 310

819 ON THE RIGHT TRACK

Find at least 32 words in the grid that can be prefixed with "on the" to form a phrase. Words run horizontally, vertically, diagonally, forward or back, but always in a straight line.

C	O	N	T	R	A	R	Y	T	B	R	T
W	W	F	P	A	E	H	C	I	O	O	W
B	A	L	L	B	T	F	L	L	I	P	X
H	G	R	O	O	L	E	V	E	L	E	T
T	O	U	P	E	M	I	I	S	S	S	U
G	N	S	H	A	M	R	N	U	R	O	R
D	X	S	G	O	T	M	O	K	Q	O	N
O	N	D	V	O	O	H	A	F	C	L	I
L	L	E	R	X	W	F	D	K	I	S	D
E	T	T	M	A	N	X	S	A	E	P	A
S	Y	E	I	E	P	Q	N	M	O	D	F
Q	K	Z	J	W	Y	Y	D	H	Z	R	W

SOLUTION ON PAGE 310

820 DIAL PROBLEM

Turn the dials on this diagram to reveal 13 musical terms. A score above 8 is very good.

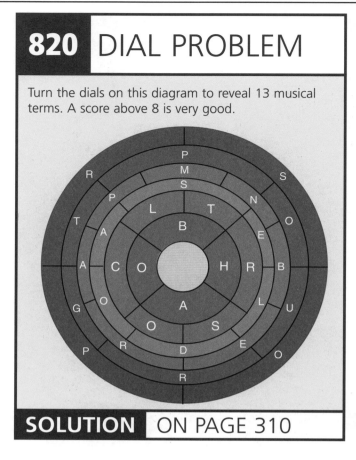

SOLUTION ON PAGE 310

821 CODE CORNER

If the name **ELIZABETH TAYLOR** is

Who are the other legendary film stars?

1.
2.
3.
4.
5.

SOLUTION ON PAGE 310

822 CAR CONUNDRUM

The names of the following 10 car manufacturers can be found in this grid on vertical, horizontal and diagonal lines. Can you find them?

Citroen
Jaguar
Peugeot
Renault
Rolls Royce
Rover
Skoda
Toyota
Volkswagen
Yugo

R	N	B	L	F	K	X	C	D	R
E	N	D	C	W	Q	H	S	O	E
N	E	G	A	W	S	K	L	O	V
A	O	H	J	K	O	L	B	P	O
U	R	G	V	D	S	F	Y	J	R
L	T	C	A	R	A	U	G	A	J
T	I	T	O	E	G	U	E	P	M
P	C	Y	T	O	Y	O	T	A	B
J	C	F	V	G	Z	C	W	D	K
E	K	D	P	M	H	Q	G	Y	F

SOLUTION ON PAGE 310

823 LOST LETTER

What letter should replace the question mark?

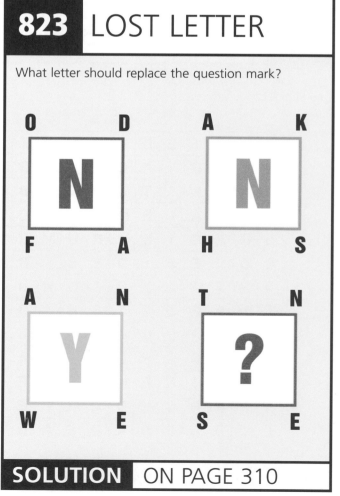

SOLUTION ON PAGE 310

824 SHAPE SHIFTING

Using two straight lines, split the grid, right, into four sub-groups so that the sum of the symbols in each one has a value of 22.

1 **2** **4** **8**

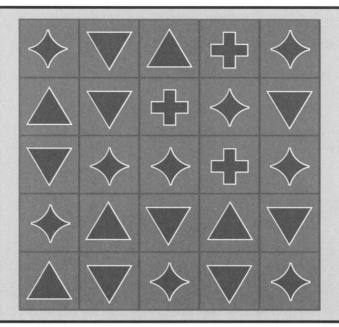

SOLUTION ON PAGE 310

825 CROSSWORD

Fit the words into the grid.

AGATE	MISER
BESOM	NASAL
BIGOT	OZONE
BISON	PAGAN
CANON	RELAY
CIDER	RIDES
DEFER	RIVAL
DETER	ROLES
DUCAT	RULER
ELUDE	SYNOD
ERODE	TANGY
EVADE	TOTAL
FETID	TUDOR
GENUS	UNITE
IRATE	USAGE
LEPER	VIGIL
LEVER	VIVID
LOVAT	
LYRIC	

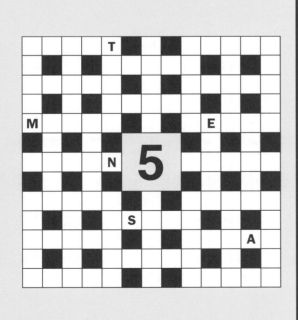

SOLUTION ON PAGE 310

826 HEXAGON HUDDLE

Fit the 12 six-letter words into the spaces encircling the numbers on the diagram. The words may go clockwise or anti- (counter) clockwise. Each word will correctly interlink with the two words on either side. Four clue letters have been given.

ASPIRE
DIVOTS
PIVOTS
READER
SCREAM
TREATS
DISMAY
MORTAL
POKERS
REALMS
STOOKS
VOTERS

SOLUTION ON PAGE 311

827 WORDFRAME

The wordframe below, when filled with the correct letters, will give the name of a film star. The letters are arranged in the coded square below. There are two possible alternatives to fill each square of the wordframe, one correct, the other incorrect. Who is the film star?

1E	2C	3D		3A	4E	2D	5D	3B	1C

4A 5B 1B 1C 5B 4E 2C 4C 3D

	A	**B**	**C**	**D**	**E**
1	A	L	R	F	M
2	Q	J	E	H	C
3	G	Y	P	N	W
4	D	Z	O	K	B
5	T	I	V	S	X

SOLUTION ON PAGE 311

828 KNIGHT MOVES

A knight, which moves either one square horizontally and two vertically or two horizontally and one vertically, starts at the shaded square of this chess board visiting each square without returning to the same square twice. Find the route which spells out six famous movie stars.

O	T	E	S	I	O	T	I
M	O	P	S	L	B	G	R
E	O	G	N	D	N	G	O
N	E	B	O	R	A	I	O
H	V	E	J	D	L	M	T
S	R	A	E	F	D	R	N
E	W	B	U	A	I	R	C
O	I	M	N	E	R	E	T

SOLUTION ON PAGE 311

829 SMELLY SOLUTION

The names of the following 10 perfumes can be found in this grid on vertical, horizontal and diagonal lines. Can you find them?

Amarige

Anais Anais

Coco

Dune

Miss Dior

Obsession

Paris

Safari

Samsara

Spellbound

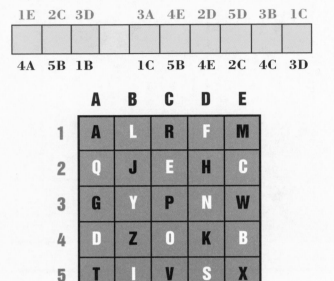

S	I	A	N	A	S	I	A	N	A
A	P	D	G	H	F	P	J	C	R
F	C	E	G	I	R	A	M	A	A
A	F	H	L	D	J	R	K	F	S
R	Y	Q	U	L	Z	I	Z	R	M
I	R	N	Z	X	B	S	F	X	A
Q	E	V	K	W	O	O	Y	J	S
B	H	K	V	D	W	C	U	G	I
O	B	S	E	S	S	I	O	N	G
R	O	I	D	S	S	I	M	C	D

SOLUTION ON PAGE 311

830 DOMINOES

If the term **ANCIENT GODS** is

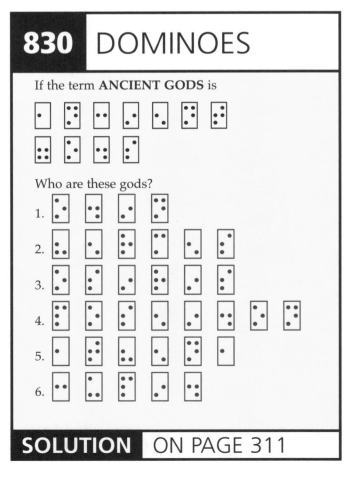

Who are these gods?

1.

2.

3.

4.

5.

6.

SOLUTION ON PAGE 311

831 THE CASINO

Five people sat on the edge of a large casino and played from 10.00 p.m. to 3.00 a.m. They were professionals and did not stop for a break and nobody joined or left them. They played together without the assistance of anyone from the casino. They kept their own scores and, at the end, all of them went home with more than they had to start with. How could this be?

1. They were not playing against machines such as slot machines or blackjack machines.
2. They were not playing bingo or against the house.
3. Each of them went home not losing and always gaining whenever they played together at the casino.

SOLUTION ON PAGE 311

832 CROSSWORD

All of the answers to this cryptic crossword can be found in the wordsearch grid on the right. Answers in the wordsearch go vertically, horizontally, diagonally, up, or down but always in a straight line.

Across

6 If you have an ache, get into bed and arrive on the seashore (7)
7 It is not Al that has got the claw (5)
9 Down the pit in the middle with malice (5)
10 Entraps your mother and father (7)
12 Something that the bookmaker's clerk is doing all of the time (11)
14 Could be the act of taking care of Nessie (11)
18 This soft-shoed person could be seen climbing walls (7)
19 Hangs around the flower, doesn't she? (5)
21 Raged at the result of the examination (5)
22 Five score sounds like a fear of Attila's men (7)

Down

1 Cause the plate to jump off the table (5)
2 I find a Scot fixing the molding (6)
3 The man with a degree goes east to rest (3)
4 With beer and explosive you may find a special gift (6)
5 Put on your jacket when you are giving the ceiling a thin layer of paint (7)
8 It wouldn't be successful if you had an A1 fling (7)
11 Does the cur mind being cleaned? (7)
13 Guaranteed to give you reflections (7)
15 All the sadder to cause fears (6)
16 Dye a little saint to enable him to be firmly in place (6)
17 The ice-cream may be this thin! (5)
20 It sounds as though there are no sisters in the convent (3)

SOLUTION ON PAGE 311

833 WORDFRAME

The wordframe below, when filled with the correct letters, will give the name of a female athlete. The letters are arranged in the coded square below. There are two possible alternatives to fill each square of the word frame, one is correct, but the other one is incorrect. Who is the athlete?

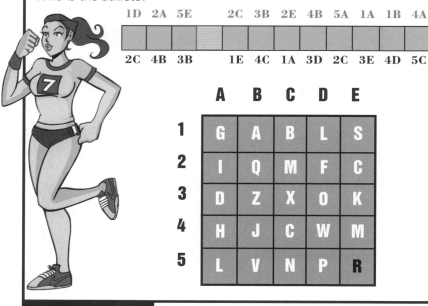

	1D	2A	5E		2C	3B	2E	4B	5A	1A	1B	4A
	2C	4B	3B		1E	4C	1A	3D	2C	3E	4D	5C

	A	**B**	**C**	**D**	**E**
1	G	A	B	L	S
2	I	Q	M	F	C
3	D	Z	X	O	K
4	H	J	C	W	M
5	L	V	N	P	R

SOLUTION ON PAGE 311

834 SQUARE SOLUTION

Rearrange these boxes in a 3 x 3 square in such a way that the adjoining letters are always the same. Then add the alphanumeric values of each line of three outer letters and convert back to letters to give the name of a Greek god.

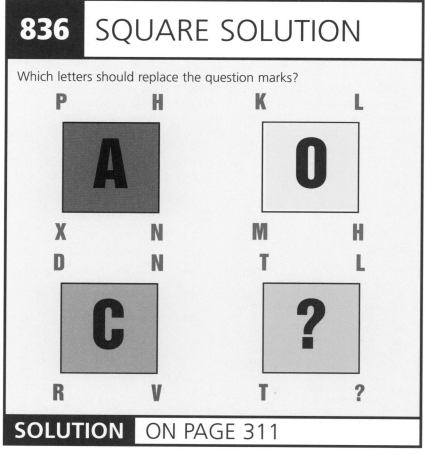

SOLUTION ON PAGE 311

835 DIAL DILEMMA

Turn the dials on this unusual safe to give 12 surnames of sports stars from the past and present. (More than 8 is a good score.)

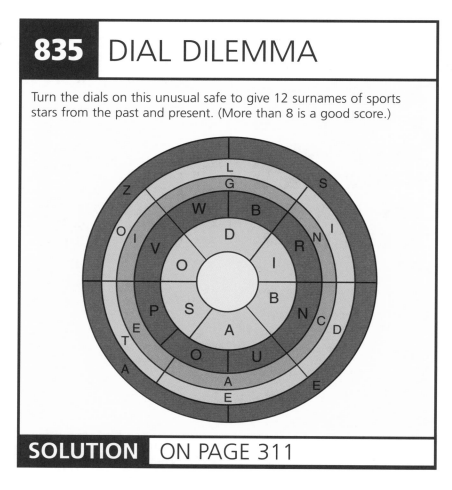

SOLUTION ON PAGE 311

836 SQUARE SOLUTION

Which letters should replace the question marks?

P		H		K		L
A					**O**	
X		N		M		H
D		N		T		L
C					**?**	
R		V		T		?

SOLUTION ON PAGE 311

837 CORPORAL NOURISHMENT

A man sat down in a restaurant and started to read the menu out loud, but to himself. "Steak and fries, $7; steak, egg, and fries, $8.50; salad, $4 ..." etc. The waiter went up to the man and said, "You must be a corporal in the Army". He was correct but how did he make this connection?

1. They had not met before and the man was alone.
2. They were not near an army base.
3. The man's voice was not disturbing anyone.
4. He did not speak like a drill-sergeant.

SOLUTION ON PAGE 311

838 CROSSWORD

A straightforward crossword puzzle.

Across

2 A woman who writes tickets for parking violations (5,4)
7 Bloodsucking insect (4)
8 Waggish persons (5)
9 Anthropoid (3)
10 Semi-aquatic carnivorous mammal (4)
11 Generosity (7)
14 The discharging tube of a gun (6)
15 Straight man (6)
16 Part of a horse's leg (7)
19 Impress clearly in the mind (4)
20 Tavern (3)
21 Strong fiber from various tropical American plants, genus Agave (5)
22 A movable barrier (4)
23 Woodchuck (6-3)

Down

1 The best of its kind (8)
2 North Atlantic food fish (8)
3 A sudden sharp excitement (6)
4 The upright member between two stair treads (5)
5 Astound (5)
6 Robe (5)
12 A zero on a scoreboard (5,3)
13 Discerning quality (8)
15 Rough drawing (6)
16 Hurl (5)
17 Latin-American dance (5)
18 Constellation represented by the figure of a hunter (5)

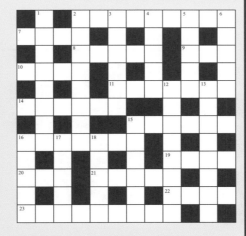

SOLUTION ON PAGE 311

839 QUOTE

Insert the answers to the clues and read down lines A and E to find a quotation.

1 Document giving authority
2 Reverence
3 Core of commerce
4 Indeterminate
5 Pertaining to the earth
6 Blow free of chaff
7 Half right-angled
8 Hypnotize
9 Take advantage of
10 Nut-bearing
11 Act of inferring from premises
12 Whinnies
13 Old
14 Crime of having two wives
15 Radioactive metallic element
16 Thinly scattered
17 Take legal possession of
18 Propose as candidate
19 Odd, whimsical
20 Bones of an animal
21 Wise
22 Rise in price
23 Make laws
24 Wooden lining
25 State of being held in suspension
26 Rare metallic element
27 Siberian breed of dog

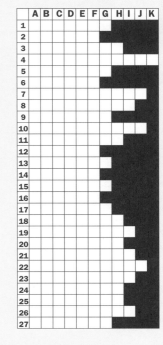

SOLUTION ON PAGE 311

840 COLOUR CONUNDRUM

Each of the colours has a numerical value. The shapes affect this value in some way. Discover the connection between shape and colour and you will be able to find the missing number.

603   220   436   ?

SOLUTION ON PAGE 311

841 SHAPE SHIFTER

Using three straight lines, split the grid into 6 sub-groups so that the sum of the symbols in each has a value of 16.

SOLUTION ON PAGE 311

842 CODE BREAKER

If the following says
THREE WHEELER FOLLOWS VEGAN

What do the characters below say?
The letters have been mixed up but all letters of the same colour belong together.

SOLUTION ON PAGE 311

843 BARD BRAIN BUSTER

The letters conceal a well-known phrase from a Shakespeare play. The letters of each word are the same colour, though they have been mixed up. Letters of other colours have been introduced to add confusion.

W		T		T		D		J
A		S		H		M		H
U		O		G		A		I
E		T		L		E		R
T		E		W		O		D
O		F		W		U		T
O		R		H		S		P
R		O		H		Y		O
E		D		A		A		M
R		P		I		J		H
				E				

SOLUTION ON PAGE 311

844 CHESS MATCH?

The 16 squares of a miniature chessboard are enclosed by 16 matches. You have to place an odd number of matches inside the square so as to enclose four groups of four squares each. There are four ways of doing this.

SOLUTION ON PAGE 311

845 SQUARE HOOTS

What number should replace the question mark?

4	3		6	2		8	6		2	5
	6			**14**			**9**			**?**
3	5		7	3		3	4		3	7

SOLUTION ON PAGE 311

846 CROSSWORD

To fill the grid you must choose the correct words from the following list and then try to make them fit.
To make the task more challenging we have given you more words than you actually need.

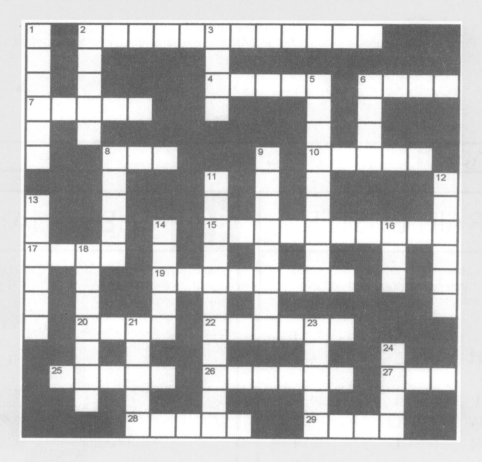

Violet	Cream	Cinnabar	Oatmeal	Lilac
Royal blue	Ruby	Magnolia	Poppy	Black
Cerise	Ultraviolet	Khaki	Silver	Jet
Puce	Green	Aquamarine	Gold	Tan
Earth	Russet	Purple	Red	Grey
Chocolate	Livid	Orange	Navy	Bronze
Midnight blue	Pink	Rose	Infrared	
Terracotta	Mauve	Scarlet	Sky	
Pea green	Beige	Leaden	Vermilion	
Brown	Indigo	Stone	Denim	

SOLUTION ON PAGE 311

847 MAGIC SYMBOLS

The colours all have a numerical value, though this time it is rather an unusual one. Just one of the shapes also has a numerical significance. When you have worked out what the colours and shapes mean you will be able to find the missing number.

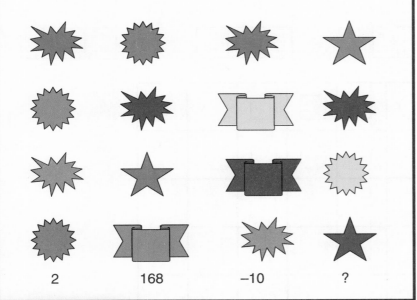

2   168   −10   ?

SOLUTION ON PAGE 311

848 COLOUR CODED

The grid contains a famous name (but not that famous, so you'll need help to find it). You need to move from square to touching square (including diagonals). The colours of the letters used in the name have something in common.

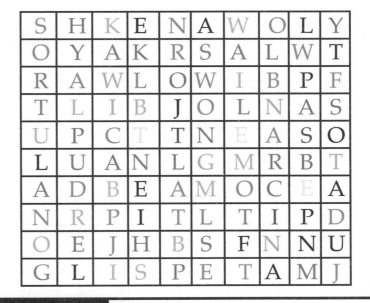

SOLUTION ON PAGE 311

849 HIDDEN MESSAGE

There is a message hidden in the table below. If you can work out which colours to use you will be able to read it.

A	M	P	N	O	S
T	Z	J	H	K	B
E	R	C	U	V	O
N	J	T	N	V	L
I	N	Q	G	C	R
D	O	G	L	D	X
E	P	F	X	S	Q

SOLUTION ON PAGE 312

850 PATTERN POSER

Which one of the five pieces shown correctly fits into the vacant section of the grid?

SOLUTION ON PAGE 312

851 MATCH MAYHEM

This simple calculation uses Roman numerals made from matches. Move two matches to make the sum work.

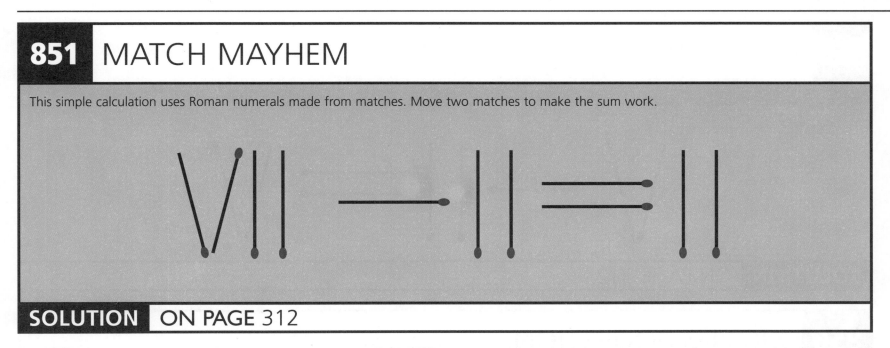

SOLUTION ON PAGE 312

852 SHAPE SHIFTER

Which of the figures A–E is the odd one out?

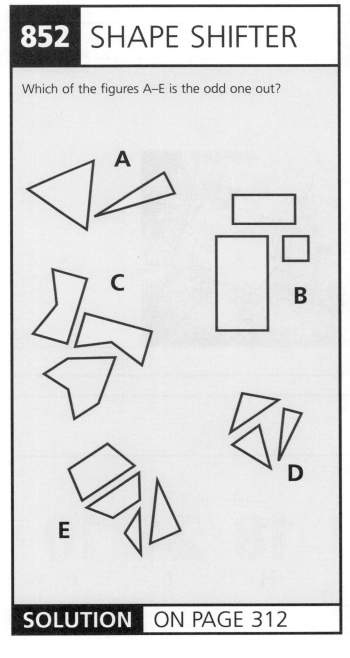

SOLUTION ON PAGE 312

853 INDIAN QUEEN

Once, in India, a queen owned two horses and used them to help destroy a neighbouring king. There was a hard fought battle in which all the king's men were killed. When the battle was over the victors and the vanquished all lay side by side in the same place. Explain.

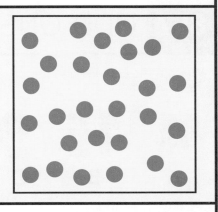

SOLUTION ON PAGE 312

854 DOTTY DILEMMA

Use five straight lines to divide this square into seven sections containing 1, 2, 3, 4, 5, 6, and 7 spots. The lines always touch one edge of the box, but not necessarily two.

SOLUTION ON PAGE 312

855 MATCH PLAY

This is a sum using Roman numerals made out of matches. Move one match to make the sum correct.

SOLUTION ON PAGE 312

856 MOVING QUESTION

Dave and Anne moved into their new home and then went to the DIY store to make an important purchase. "How much is one?" asked Dave. "$3," came the reply. "What about 20?" "That'll cost you $6." "OK, well we need 2042." What were Dave and Anne buying and how much did it cost them?

SOLUTION ON PAGE 312

857 ODD ONE OUT

Which is the odd one out?

4	15	9	12	5	8	30	18	24	10
A	B	C	D	E	F	G	H	I	J

SOLUTION ON PAGE 312

858 CUBE CONUNDRUM

Which of the following cubes below can be made using the flat one shown here?

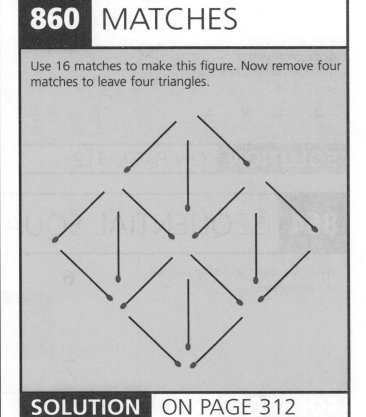

A   **B**   **C**   **D**   **E**

SOLUTION ON PAGE 312

859 GIRL TROUBLE

Eddie has a reputation for being, let's say, economical. There are two girls he's interested in and he has the chance to take them both to the movies. His problem is that he wants a good deal. Will it be cheaper for him to take them both together, or should he take them separately?

SOLUTION ON PAGE 312

860 MATCHES

Use 16 matches to make this figure. Now remove four matches to leave four triangles.

SOLUTION ON PAGE 312

861 SHARK PROBLEM

Dan and his best friend Dave were out fishing when they noticed a shark circling their dinghy. Whenever they tried to move the boat the shark would barge into it nearly causing it to capsize. "Never mind," said Dan, "if we wait long enough it'll get tired and while it's asleep we can sneak away." Was this good advice?

SOLUTION ON PAGE 312

862 DIAMOND SIGNS

Insert one of the four basic mathematical signs in each space to complete the sum, starting from the top. One sign is used twice, the rest once. Each letter represents its position in the alphabet, where A = 1 and Z = 26.

L
=
E   G
E
O   F
C

+   −   x   ÷

SOLUTION ON PAGE 312

863 LOST NUMBER

How much is the question mark worth?

4
23   92
117   8
13   15
9   ?

SOLUTION ON PAGE 312

864 SEQUENTIAL SQUARES

What number should replace the question mark?

6		3 6		5 8		4 6		3
51		**61**		**45**		**?**	
7		4 2		4 3		2 7		5

SOLUTION ON PAGE 312

865 | LOST IN LONDON

You have become lost in London. Use the grid to locate the following well-known places. Names may be spelt in any direction, not necessarily in a straight line.

CHARING CROSS
WHITEHALL
COVENT GARDEN
HYDE PARK
SOHO
KINGS CROSS

GOLDEN SQUARE
WESTMINSTER
TRAFALGAR SQUARE
CHELSEA
PICCADILLY CIRCUS
KNIGHTSBRIDGE

REGENT'S PARK ZOO
WATERLOO
TOWER OF LONDON
BUCKINGHAM PALACE

A	N	O	W	T	H	W	E	S	T	M	I	N	S	T	E	R	E	K	R
B	C	L	A	Q	P	O	D	Y	U	P	D	P	Z	Z	L	E	F	I	I
N	I	H	T	S	I	H	E	S	T	I	Y	U	U	A	R	E	D	N	W
H	A	E	E	C	N	A	R	E	T	L	H	C	E	O	S	E	P	G	E
O	P	R	R	L	C	E	G	O	L	I	N	G	I	T	S	O	C	S	O
U	I	G	L	O	O	A	H	I	U	W	P	S	R	O	M	R	E	C	C
A	S	N	H	T	H	A	D	T	S	H	W	H	C	U	S	A	A	R	T
I	G	C	W	A	S	O	H	O	N	I	T	T	O	K	O	H	G	O	E
R	E	I	R	S	I	M	L	J	G	T	I	N	G	N	W	L	M	S	Y
G	U	T	O	O	T	N	E	D	G	E	H	A	L	L	A	U	N	S	T
A	N	S	D	W	S	S	H	R	T	A	T	D	O	F	B	O	G	K	I
G	O	L	D	E	N	E	T	A	O	F	O	R	A	M	D	Y	N	T	R
O	L	E	B	S	O	U	K	G	W	E	Y	R	U	N	C	K	A	I	L
U	B	A	Q	S	L	R	T	T	E	L	T	F	O	A	P	L	G	H	T
E	I	U	F	Y	A	O	N	U	R	O	F	L	L	A	M	C	A	N	S
R	A	R	O	P	A	E	E	T	H	S	T	A	Y	A	U	E	A	B	Y
E	A	D	E	L	V	R	L	G	I	N	C	S	H	O	R	L	R	L	A
R	A	D	M	O	R	A	L	E	E	E	C	G	P	A	R	I	E	T	Y
E	Y	S	C	A	T	B	U	C	K	I	N	W	H	A	D	Y	N	O	U
H	N	O	T	C	H	E	L	S	E	A	J	O	E	G	R	K	Z	O	O

SOLUTION ON PAGE 312

866 DECOMPOSERS

Mario Peroni, the world-famous musician, left his studio window open only to find that the wind had destroyed his precious sheet music. Can you put together the names of 10 famous composers from the pieces shown here?

BAR PUC RACH MAN
IUS MAH EL ZART
RIM
SKY SCHU CELL SIB
KOR US MO
DE BERT OV CI
NI SAKOV IN
TOK LI LER PUR

SOLUTION ON PAGE 312

867 SERIES SOLUTIONS

1 What is the missing letter in this series?

B C D E I K O X

SOLUTION ON PAGE 312

868 LOST LETTER

What letter does the question mark represent?

5	KP	7
X ?		U B
6	O G	8

SOLUTION ON PAGE 312

869 LOST IN PARIS

You are lost in Paris, but if you search carefully you will find the following well-known places cunningly concealed. Names may be spelt in any direction, not necessarily in a straight line.

MADELEINE
MONTMARTRE
OPERA
GARE DE LYON
LOUVRE
JARDIN DES PLANTES

RUE DE RIVOLI
BOIS DE BOULOGNE
MOULIN ROUGE
CHAMPS ELYSEES
CLICHY
RUE LAFAYETTE

PERE LACHAISE
SACRE COEUR
ARC DE TRIOMPHE

SOLUTION ON PAGE 313

870 COLD COMFORT

"You're really going to fly around the Earth from North to South?" said the young man to the aviator. "I'll bet you'll need your thermal underwear when you pass over the Poles!" "Actually," the intrepid flyer replied, "the Poles are the least of my worries. I shall have to pass twice over a much colder area than that." What could it be?

SOLUTION ON PAGE 313

871 BARBAROUS!

In Dead Men's Gulch, Colorado, there was a barber who had a hold over the local mayor. The mayor was manipulated into passing a law that no man might shave himself and no man might grow a beard. This was all very well and the barber did well out of it but, nevertheless, even one so rich was not above the law. Who shaved the barber?

SOLUTION ON PAGE 313

872 TRIANGLE TROUBLE

What letter should replace the question mark?

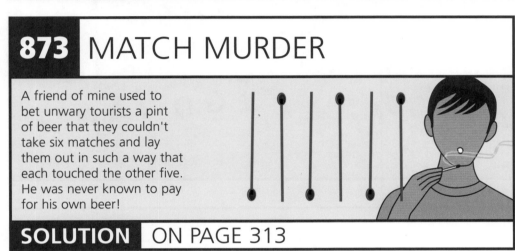

873 MATCH MURDER

A friend of mine used to bet unwary tourists a pint of beer that they couldn't take six matches and lay them out in such a way that each touched the other five. He was never known to pay for his own beer!

SOLUTION ON PAGE 313

874 TESTING TRIANGLE

What letter should replace the question mark?

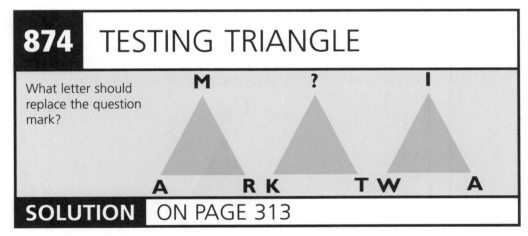

SOLUTION ON PAGE 313

875 ODD ONE OUT

Which is the odd one out?

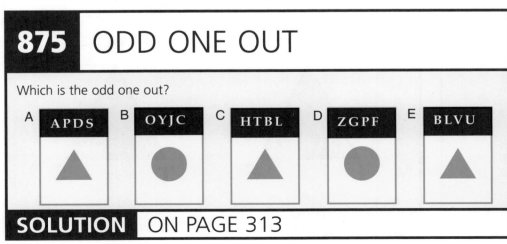

A APDS
B OYJC
C HTBL
D ZGPF
E BLVU

SOLUTION ON PAGE 313

876 TRIANGLES

Look at these triangles. Can you work out what the missing letter is?

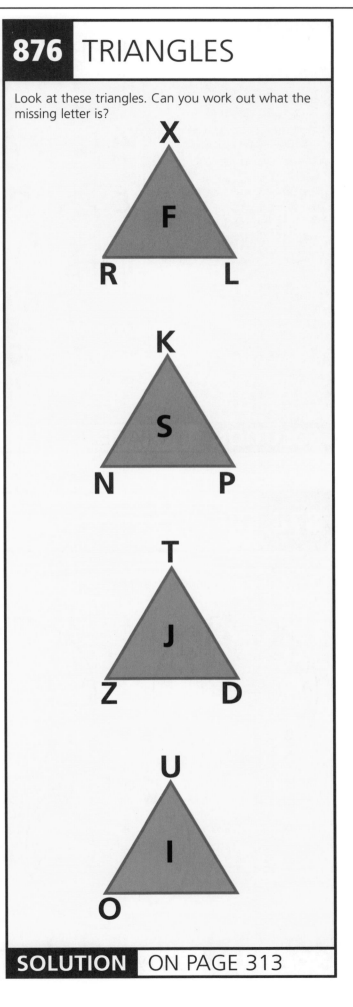

SOLUTION ON PAGE 313

877 POTTY PROBLEM

Professor Potts has had a disaster. A shelf in his museum gave way and ten priceless busts of Roman emperors have been smashed. Fortunately, each had a name plate on it. Can you put the fractured names back together?

AU PA TI VALE
NE TIAN
DIO AU GAL CA BER DI
TUS LA US TRA GUS SIAN
RO BA VES CL CLE
IUS RIAN LI GU JAN

SOLUTION ON PAGE 313

878 BOOK CIRCLE

The circles of letters below contain the names of three works of literature. Can you unravel them?

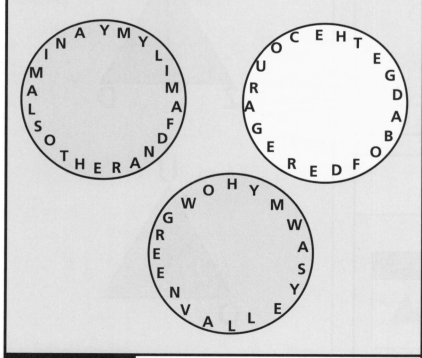

SOLUTION ON PAGE 313

879 CAKE CRISIS

A cake decorator baked these triangles to go on a cake celebrating a famous person. Unfortunately, a slight mistake was made, but can you discover what it was?

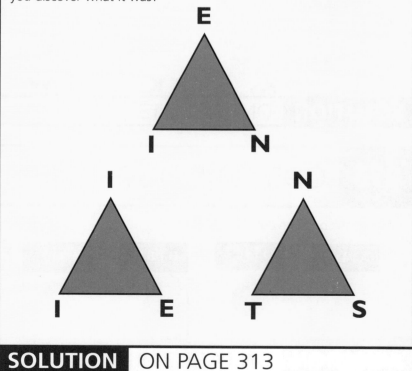

SOLUTION ON PAGE 313

880 VOWEL FAMINE

All these famous playwrights have had the vowels removed from their names and the first name joined to the surname. Can you sort them out? (The nationalities are given in brackets to help you.)

1. DWRDLB (American)
2. SMLBCKTT (Irish)
3. BRTHLTBRCHT (German)
4. NLCWRD (English)
5. NTNCHKV (Russian)
6. RTHRMLLR (American)
7. LGPRNDLL (Italian)
8. JNRCN (French)
9. SPHCLS (Greek – one word)
10. TNNSSWLLMS (American)

SOLUTION ON PAGE 313

881 CLOCK CONUNDRUM

Try to work out the fiendish logic behind this series of clocks and replace the question mark.

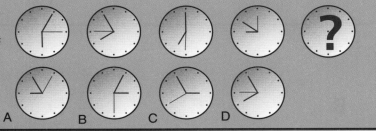

A   B   C   D

SOLUTION ON PAGE 313

884 SHAPE SHIFTER

Which is the odd one out?

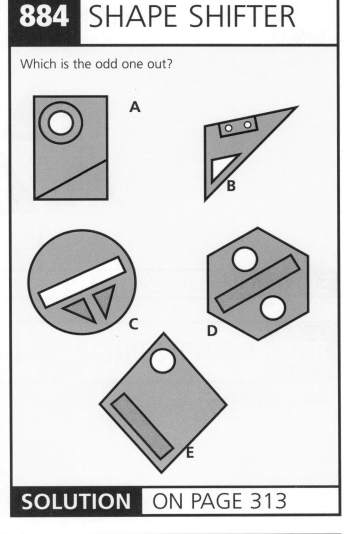

SOLUTION ON PAGE 313

882 EARTHQUAKES?

Are there earthquakes on the Moon?

SOLUTION ON PAGE 313

883 TORN TRIANGLES

Which of the following completes a diamond when fitted with the diagram below?

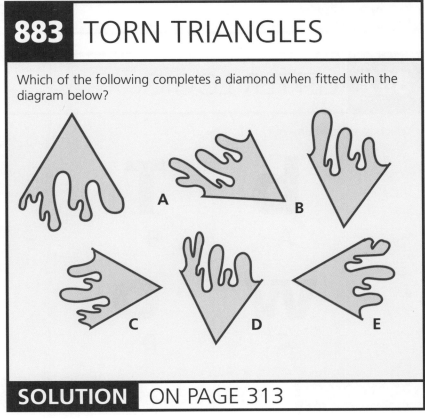

SOLUTION ON PAGE 313

885 TRICKY TRIANGLE TRIAL

What letter should replace the question mark in the last triangle?

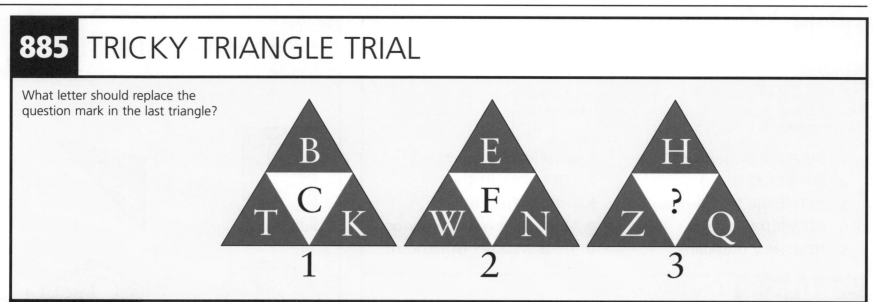

1   2   3

SOLUTION ON PAGE 313

886 PISTON PROBLEM

Which is the odd one out?

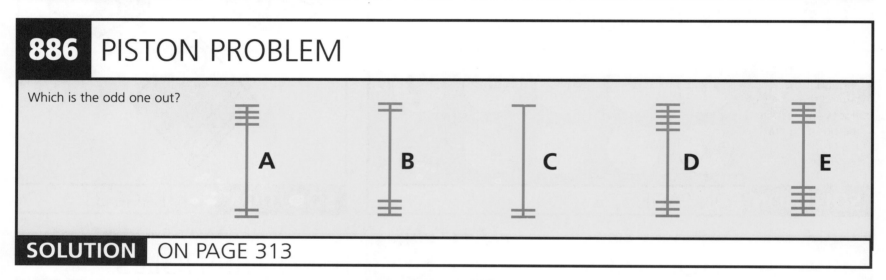

A   B   C   D   E

SOLUTION ON PAGE 313

887 LETTER LOGIC

Which is the odd one out?

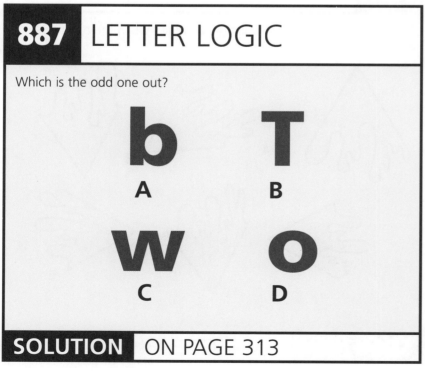

A

B

C

D

SOLUTION ON PAGE 313

888 TIME TEASER

Can you work out the logic behind this series of clocks and pick one to replace the question mark?

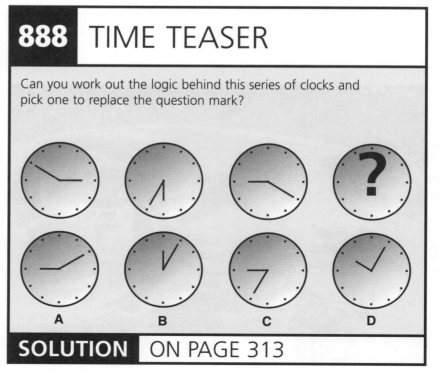

A   B   C   D

SOLUTION ON PAGE 313

889 PATTERN POSER

The words below are all hidden in the grid. Can you find them? The words may be spelled in any direction and may even bend once or twice. Good luck!

X	E	T	E	L	P	E	D	T	S	E	D	S	B	V
V	T	R	A	N	S	K	V	O	C	P	I	U	X	I
D	L	A	N	R	C	L	M	N	A	U	T	I	O	N
M	B	M	R	F	R	D	X	T	L	R	S	G	A	C
S	T	V	U	T	I	E	E	M	O	M	E	L	O	G
U	T	R	I	S	B	G	V	A	L	U	A	O	T	V
X	S	R	R	M	E	D	N	P	Q	U	V	E	X	A
J	E	S	A	B	R	I	R	B	C	F	G	I	P	T
E	T	G	Q	T	L	B	E	S	L	U	V	N	O	C
J	E	L	R	S	E	I	N	G	U	N	E	A	O	H
U	G	O	A	T	B	G	D	J	I	K	L	N	M	T
N	A	P	T	V	X	U	I	A	B	D	V	C	F	N
E	T	R	M	O	S	P	T	C	A	E	U	E	I	I
P	L	A	U	S	I	B	L	E	X	B	C	D	A	L
X	T	R	S	U	E	M	I	L	B	U	S	P	S	P

TRANSCRIBE   PLAUSIBLE   ABRIDGED   GOLEM
SEDITION   CONVEX   SUBLIME   DEPLETE
CONVULSE   VOCAL   GLOAT   TAGETES
STRATEGIC   JEJUNE   PLINTH

SOLUTION ON PAGE 313

890 TRIANGLE TROUBLE

Look at the triangles below. What geometrical shape should logically be placed in the fourth triangle?

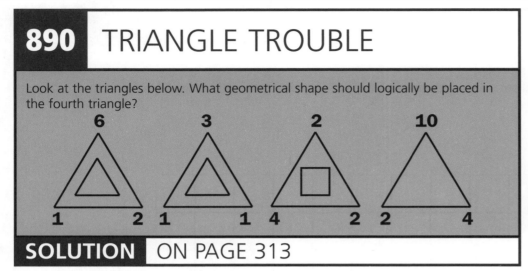

SOLUTION ON PAGE 313

891 MATCH MAYHEM

Here's a challenge! Make the sum below work without moving any matches at all.

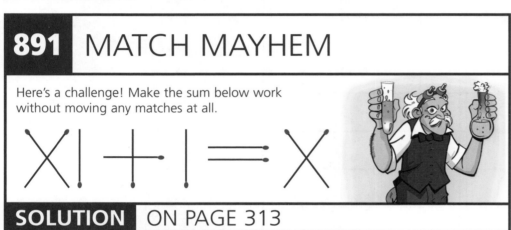

SOLUTION ON PAGE 313

892 ODD ONE OUT

Which is the odd one out ?

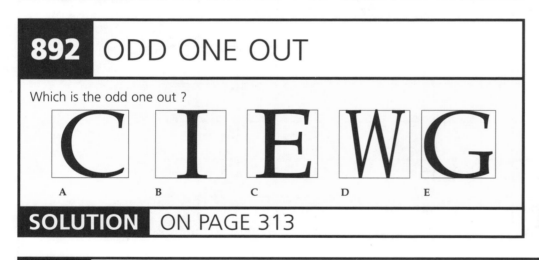

SOLUTION ON PAGE 313

893 RACING POSER

This is a true story. A racing cyclist came off his bike at speed, fell awkwardly and broke nearly all the bones in his right hand. After hospital treatment the hand was much improved and, one day, a consultant invited a group of students to consider the case.

"This man," he said, "is not a professional cyclist. He works as a graphic designer. How long after the accident do you think he was able to return to work?"

The students examined x-rays of the hand taken just after the accident and offered a variety of opinions. What would your answer have been?

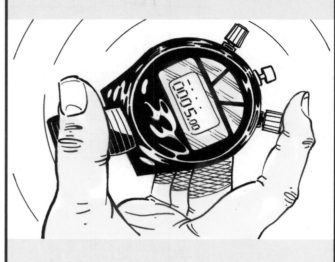

SOLUTION ON PAGE 313

894 FISH FURORE

Which is the odd one out ?

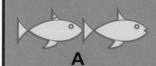
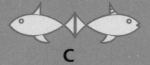
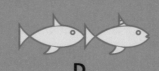
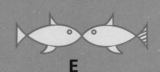

SOLUTION ON PAGE 313

895 MATCH PROBLEM

Take a matchbox and pull it apart. Then put the parts together as shown in the diagram. Now turn the whole thing upside down. You may hold the case by a finger and thumb only but you must not touch the tray at all.

SOLUTION ON PAGE 313

896 DODGY DIVISION

Here is a long division sum showing all the working and the result. What could be simpler? The sum works out exactly with no remainder. The slight complication is that all the numbers have been replaced with letters on a random basis. However, one letter always represents the same number. Can you reconstruct the original sum?

```
          CDEFG
      AB │ ADGAAHD
          AJ K
          AKA
          AAG
           FA
           J F
           AGH
           AEE
            FD
```

SOLUTION ON PAGE 314

897 SHAPE SHIFTER

Which is the odd one out?

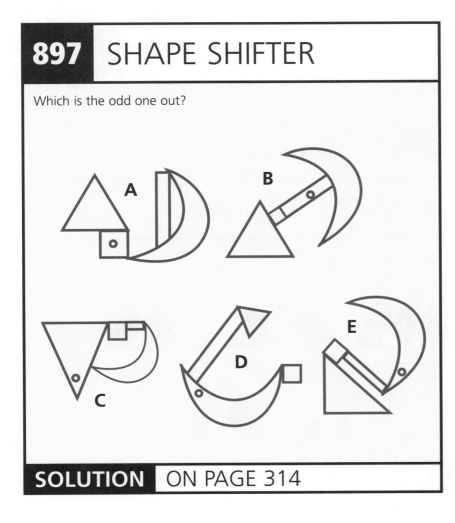

SOLUTION ON PAGE 314

898 WORDS AND MUSIC

Each letter in this word box is used once only to create three words with a musical theme. What are they?

S	V	E	Z
A	T	H	Y
R	E	M	S
A	E	N	R

SOLUTION ON PAGE 314

899 SYMBOL ORDER

These objects can be arranged in a logical order in which the black square is first and the yellow hexagon is last. What is the order?

SOLUTION | ON PAGE 314

900 CODE CORNER

The following is a coded message. The only clue you get is that the answer is related to the colours used.

T	J	S	H	I	V
K	S	D	J	M	E
S	S	R	T	A	Z
G	E	L	I	S	D
H	M	I	Q	D	A
M	E	X	T	W	L
N	V	L	C	G	K

SOLUTION | ON PAGE 314

901 TRIANGLE TEASE

What letter should replace the question mark?

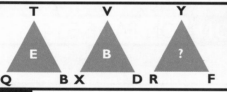

SOLUTION | ON PAGE 314

902 SYMBOL LOGIC

Which of these figures is the odd one out?

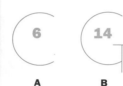

6   14   30   31   34

A   B   C   D   E

SOLUTION | ON PAGE 314

903 MISFIT

Which of the following is the odd one out?

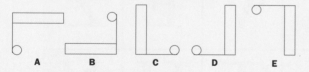

A   B   C   D   E

SOLUTION | ON PAGE 314

904 SYMBOL ENIGMA

Which of the following is the odd one out?

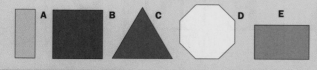

SOLUTION | ON PAGE 314

905 TRIANGLE TROUBLE

Which of the following is the odd one out?

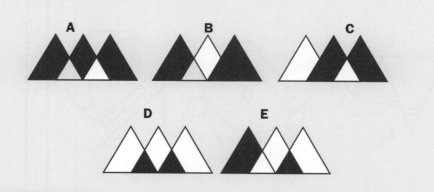

SOLUTION | ON PAGE 314

906 SQUARE SOLUTION

Which of the following is the odd one out?

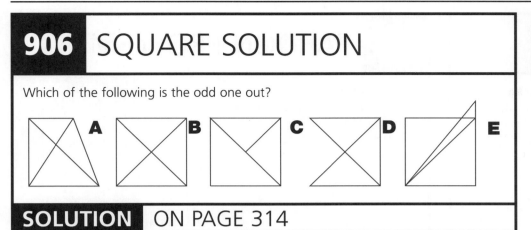

SOLUTION ON PAGE 314

908 ODD ONE OUT?

Which of the following is the odd one out?

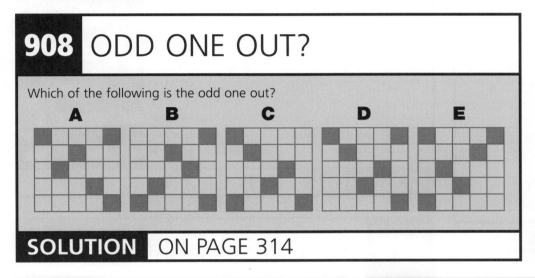

SOLUTION ON PAGE 314

907 MISSING NUMBER

To find the missing number you need to discover the significance of the coloured shapes.

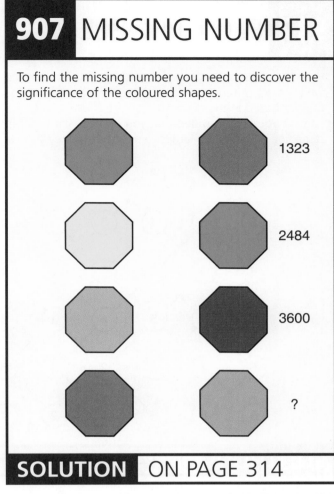

1323

2484

3600

?

SOLUTION ON PAGE 314

909 MISFIT

Which of the following is the odd one out?

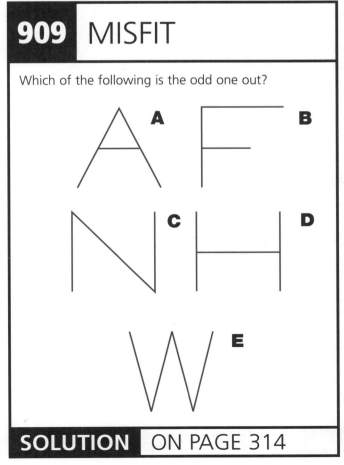

SOLUTION ON PAGE 314

910 FIGURE FRENZY

Which of the following is the odd one out?

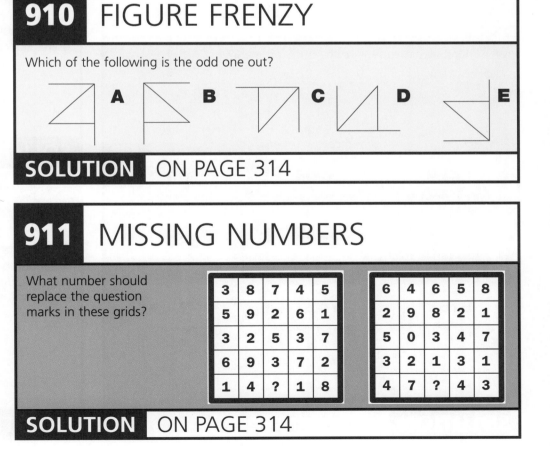

SOLUTION ON PAGE 314

911 MISSING NUMBERS

What number should replace the question marks in these grids?

3	8	7	4	5
5	9	2	6	1
3	2	5	3	7
6	9	3	7	2
1	4	?	1	8

6	4	6	5	8
2	9	8	2	1
5	0	3	4	7
3	2	1	3	1
4	7	?	4	3

SOLUTION ON PAGE 314

912 PLOT PROBLEM

Here is a piece of land marked off with 36 circular plots, on each of which is deposited a bag containing as many gold coins as the figures indicated in the diagram. You are allowed to pick up as many bags as you like, provided that you do not take two lying on the same line. What is the largest amount of money you can pick up?

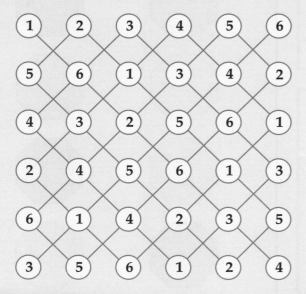

SOLUTION ON PAGE 314

913 PARDON PROBLEM

A life prisoner appealed to the king for pardon. Not being ready to grant the appeal the king proposed a pardon on condition that the prisoner should start from cell A and go in and out of each cell in the prison, coming back to cell A without going in any cell twice. How could it be done?

SOLUTION ON PAGE 314

914 NUMBER LOGIC

What number should replace the question mark?

6459	5204	200
7288	5166	360
9768	7422	?

SOLUTION ON PAGE 314

915 PENTAGON PROBLEM

Draw a pentagon, and connect each point with every other point by straight lines, as in the diagram. How many different triangles are contained in this figure?

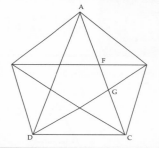

SOLUTION ON PAGE 314

916 SYMBOL VALUES

What number should replace the question mark and what are the values of the symbols?

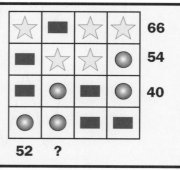

SOLUTION ON PAGE 314

917 SQUARE SOLUTION

Which of the four bottom grids should replace the question mark?

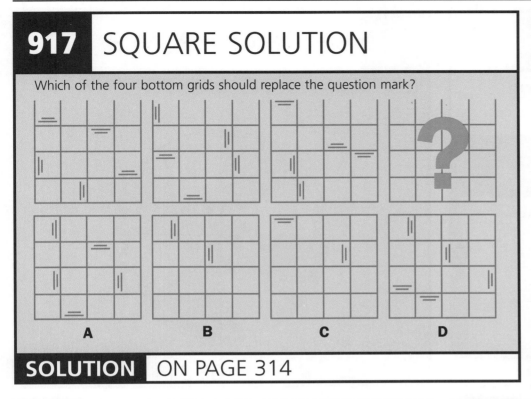

A   B   C   D

SOLUTION ON PAGE 314

918 ODD ONE OUT?

Which of the following is the odd one out?

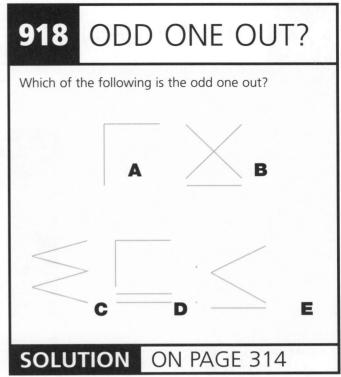

SOLUTION ON PAGE 314

919 NUMBER PROBLEM

What number should replace the question mark?

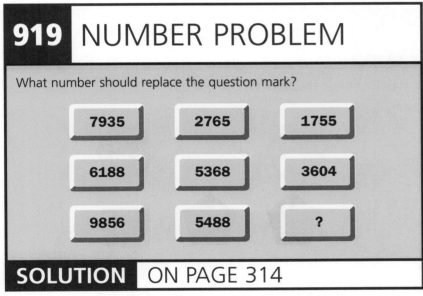

7935   2765   1755

6188   5368   3604

9856   5488   ?

SOLUTION ON PAGE 314

920 SHAPE SHIFTER

Which of the following shapes is the odd one out?

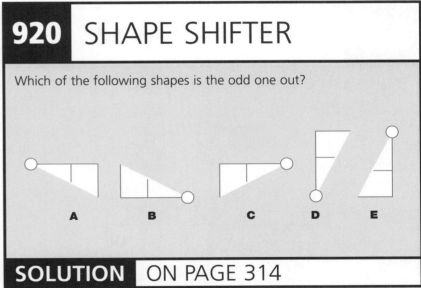

A   B   C   D   E

SOLUTION ON PAGE 314

921 SOMETHING LOST

Which of the four bottom boxes should replace the question mark?

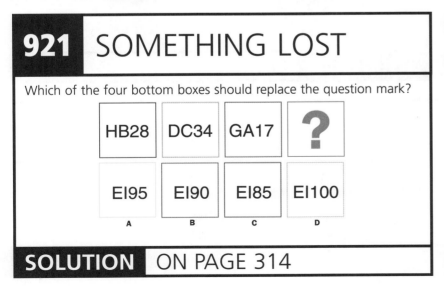

| HB28 | DC34 | GA17 | ? |

| EI95 | EI90 | EI85 | EI100 |
| A | B | C | D |

SOLUTION ON PAGE 314

922 LOST NUMBER

What number should replace the question mark?

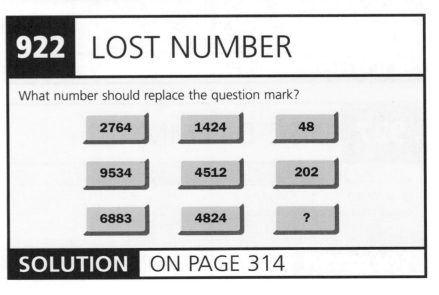

2764   1424   48

9534   4512   202

6883   4824   ?

SOLUTION ON PAGE 314

923 CODE CORNER

The numbers contain a hidden message. What is it?

7	12	19	2	18	14	5
8	9	18	26	4	18	21
15	17	12	15	9	25	22
19	7	26	24	19	8	14
9	23	13	19	6	7	12
23	5	22	3	21	15	24
12	23	10	14	11	15	22

SOLUTION ON PAGE 314

924 PIE CHART POSER

What number should replace the question mark?

8 4
2 7
6 3
15 9
3 10 ? 6
6 13 11 5
9
10
9
8 5
2 7 6

SOLUTION ON PAGE 314

925 HEART PROBLEM

What number should replace the question mark?

8 3
2 7
7 2
? 10
7 8 4 8
6 12 6 10
0 6
3 5
5 4
8 6

SOLUTION ON PAGE 314

926 ODD ONE OUT

Which of these shapes is the odd one out?

SOLUTION ON PAGE 314

927 DISC DILEMMA

The numbers under the coloured rings have a significance, but what is it? When you have worked it out you will be able to replace the question mark with a number.

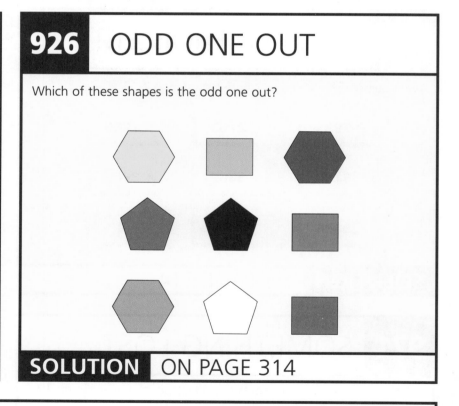

2 2 0 ?

SOLUTION ON PAGE 314

928 FIELD FRENZY

This is a field in which grow 16 trees. The eccentric farmer decided to erect five straight fences so that every tree should have a separate enclosure. How did he do it?

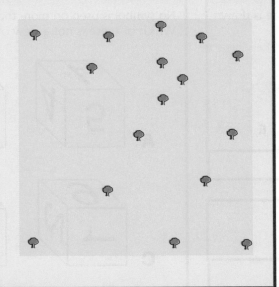

SOLUTION ON PAGE 315

929 MAGIC SQUARE

In this square, as every cell contains the same number – 1234 – the three columns, three rows, and two long diagonals naturally add up alike. The puzzle is to form and place nine different four-figure numbers (using the same figures) so that they shall form a perfect magic square. Remember that the numbers must contain nine of each figure 1, 2, 3, 4 and you cannot use fractions or any form of trickery.

1234	1234	1234
1234	1234	1234
1234	1234	1234

SOLUTION ON PAGE 315

930 NUMBER LOGIC

Some of the numbers in the grid have been put in the wrong place, and a couple have been duplicated. Your task is to use each number from 1 to 19 and find a way of ensuring that each line of three numbers has the sum of 23.

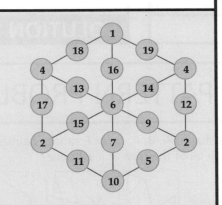

SOLUTION ON PAGE 315

931 PIE POSER

What number should replace the question mark?

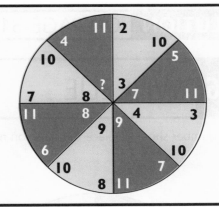

SOLUTION ON PAGE 315

932 TRAIN TROUBLES

The diagram represents a simplified railway system and you have to find how many different ways there are of getting from A to E if you never go along the same line in any journey

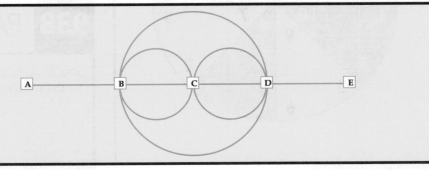

SOLUTION ON PAGE 315

933 SHAPE SHIFTING

Which of the shapes A, B, C, D, or E cannot be made from the dots if a line is drawn through all of the dots at least once?

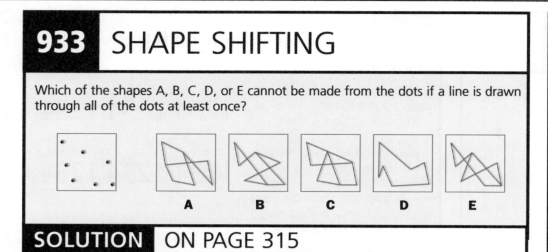

A   B   C   D   E

SOLUTION ON PAGE 315

934 CUBE PUZZLE

No symbol is used on more than one side of the box. Which of these is not a view of the same box?

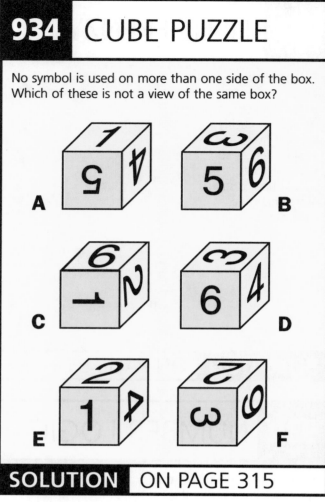

A   B   C   D   E   F

SOLUTION ON PAGE 315

935 PATTERN PROBLEM

Which of the shapes below should replace the question mark?

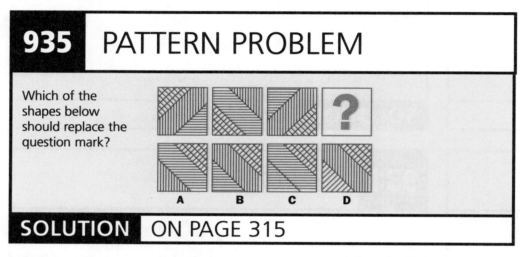

A   B   C   D

SOLUTION ON PAGE 315

936 WHEELIE

What number should replace the question mark?

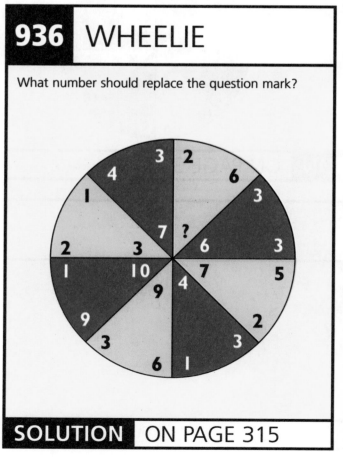

SOLUTION ON PAGE 315

937 PATTERN PROBLEM

Which of the shapes A, B, C, D, or E cannot be made from the dots if a line is drawn through all of the dots at least once?

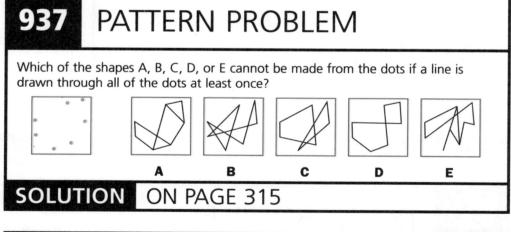

A   B   C   D   E

SOLUTION ON PAGE 315

938 PATTERN PROBLEM

Should A, B, C, or D fill the empty circle?

A   B   C   D

SOLUTION ON PAGE 315

939 SQUARE SOLUTION

Can you discover which of the four mirror images has an error in it?

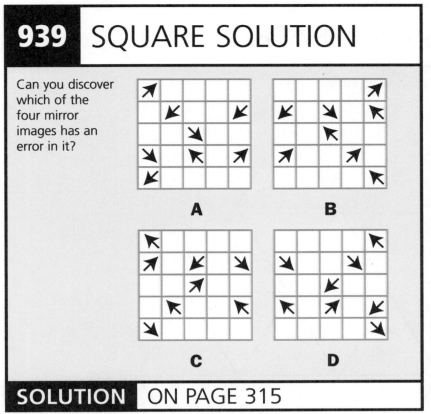

940 PATTERN POSER

Can you discover which of the four mirror images has an error in it?

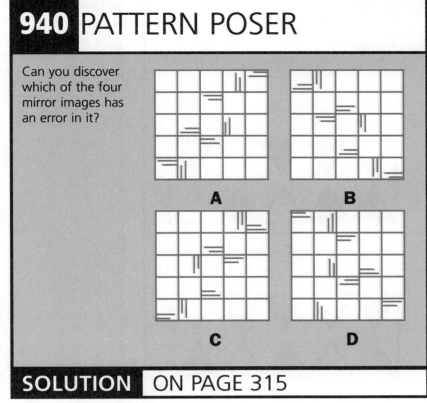

SOLUTION ON PAGE 315

941 MIRROR IMAGE

Can you discover which of the four mirror images has an error in it?

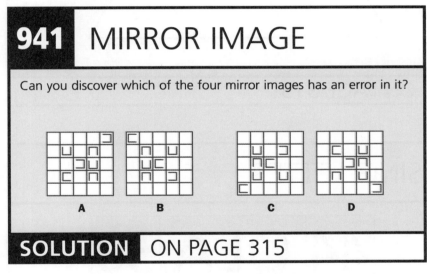

SOLUTION ON PAGE 315

942 REFLECTOR

Can you discover which of the four mirror images has an error in it?

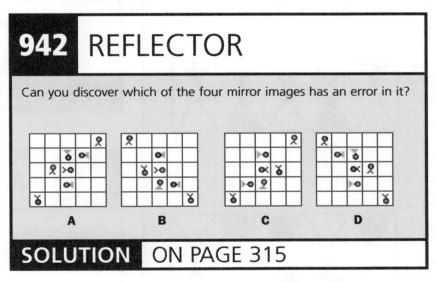

SOLUTION ON PAGE 315

943 BOX BOTHER

Which of these boxes can be made from the template?

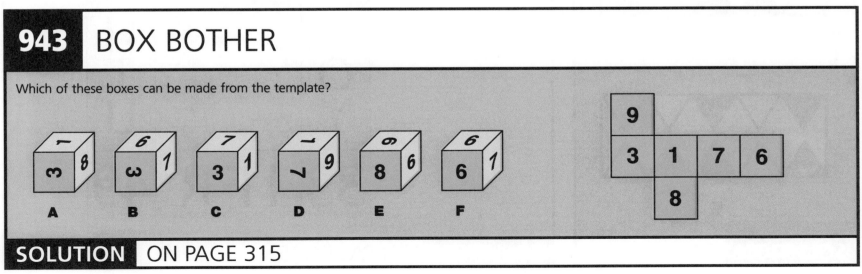

SOLUTION ON PAGE 315

944 MISFIT

Which is the odd one out?

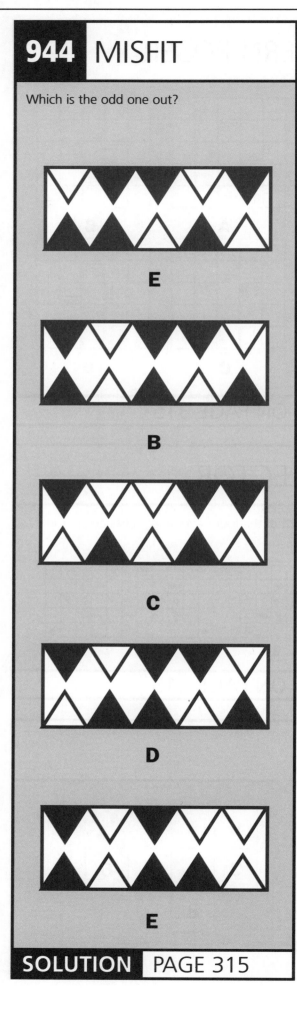

E

B

C

D

E

945 MISSING SHAPE

What shape is missing and where should it go?

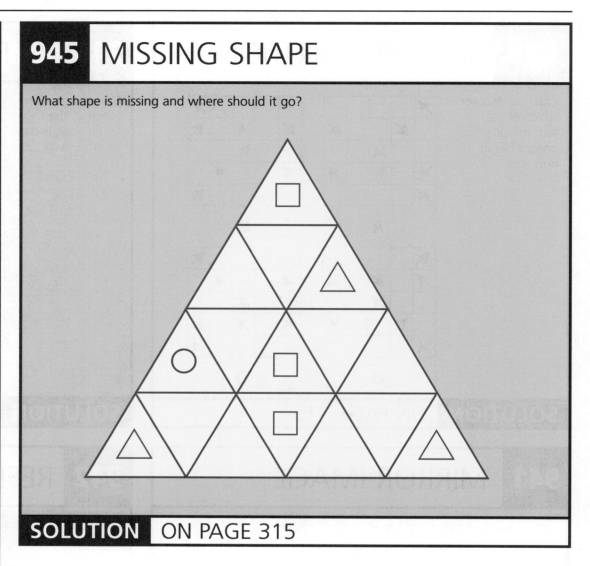

946 MISSING LETTER

What letter does the question mark represent ?

44	QLA	30
?OY		HTU
33	IFR	49

947 MISSING NUMBER

What number should replace the question mark?

A	B	C	D	E
5	3	7	23	33
12	2	2	12	16
8	9	10	56	114
6	4	8	35	45
5	7	6	40	?

SOLUTION ON PAGE 315

948 DOTTY DILEMMA

Each pattern is worth either 1, 3, 5 or 7 points. The total value is 34. What is each pattern worth?

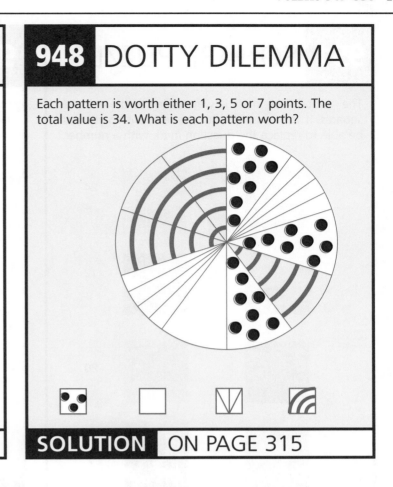

SOLUTION ON PAGE 315

949 LOST NUMBER

How much is the question mark worth?

SOLUTION ON PAGE 315

950 ANALOGY PROBLEM

W is to n as d is to:

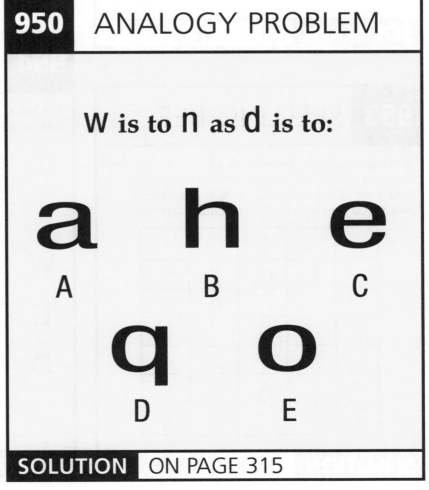

SOLUTION ON PAGE 315

951 SQUARE PUZZLE

The numbers are in some way related to the coloured squares. If you can work out the relationship you will be able to replace the question mark with a number.

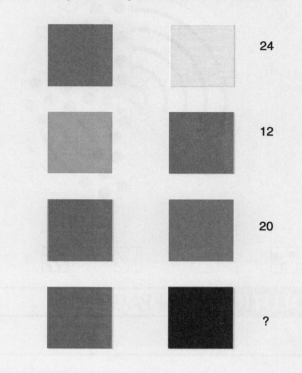

24

12

20

?

SOLUTION ON PAGE 315

952 CODE CORNER

This is a really simple code that depends on the colours of the letters for its solution.

R G E H D

Q I T S T

V H P E S

C T O L M

O X U T R

SOLUTION ON PAGE 315

953 SPELLING BEE

In the grid below is the name of a European country. To find it you must move from square to touching square (including diagonals). To help you, colours making up the name have something in common.

A	S	C	O	T
O	D	G	L	M
H	O	U	E	A
E	K	R	N	L
S	M	C	G	A
T	E	A	N	V
I	D	J	O	Y

SOLUTION ON PAGE 315

954 BARD BRAIN

The letters can be rearranged to make a well-known Shakespearean phrase. The colours will help you.

T I O D U

I T N O E E

W C H O F T

E R S N T R

O N W N S I

SOLUTION ON PAGE 315

955 NUMBER LOGIC

Place the numbers 1 to 19 in the 19 circles so that wherever there are three in a straight line they shall add up to 30.

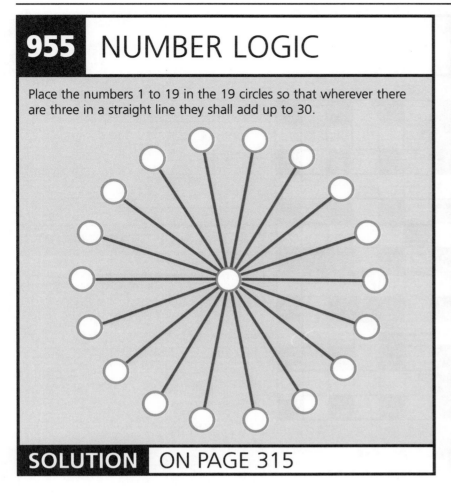

SOLUTION ON PAGE 315

956 SYMBOL SEARCH

What letters should go in the blank square?

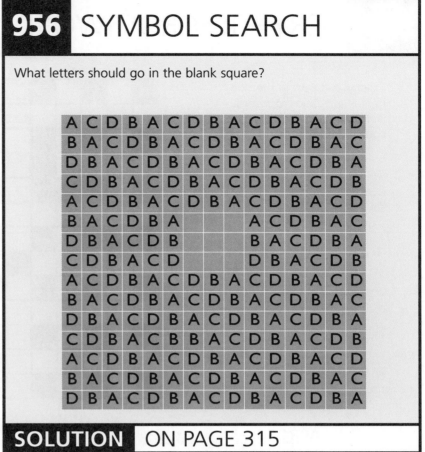

SOLUTION ON PAGE 315

957 TRIANGLE TRICK

What letter should replace the question mark in triangle 3?

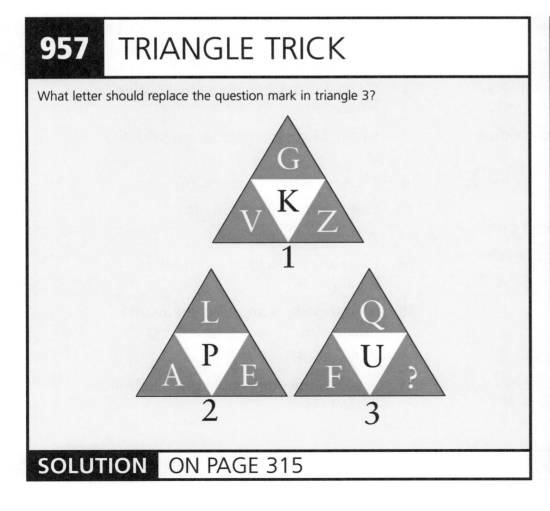

SOLUTION ON PAGE 315

958 DOT TO DOT

Where should the dot go in the square with the question mark?

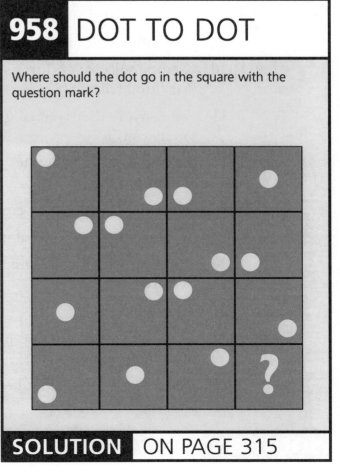

SOLUTION ON PAGE 315

959 | CRYPTIC CROSSWORD

Exactly as it says in the title, here is a cryptic crossword. Didn't we add that it is, of course, fiendish.

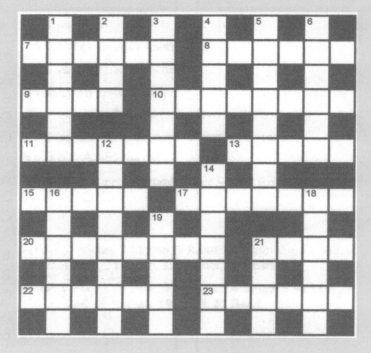

ACROSS

7   The colour! Love it! (6)

8   Robin deserts nonbeliever for football team? (6)

9   Ascended colourfully (4)

10 Campanologist endures small loss for floral tribute (8)

11 Gainsayers deprived of gin conduct analysis (7)

13 Erased from degenerates gives rise to small mammal (5)

15 Troubled heart laid in ground (5)

17 Custard pie ads conceal image (7)

20 Unharnessing gran leads to good weather (8)

21 Ill swelling (4)

22 Save Tory from mediocrity to dominate Florence! (6)

23 Ale leaves Den feeling heavy-headed? (6)

DOWN

1   Lila no longer villainous but rather boozy (6)

2   Car, no longer curable, feels sad (4)

3   Me sm, sm, sma, SMART! (7)

4   Unrepaired gaberdines are a boring colour (5)

5   I watch Eros fret over green project (8)

6   I, Ceres, provide cherry! (6)

12 I sit in cart aesthetically (8)

14 Airborne arsonist? (7)

16 Pasteurizers lacking esprit give us the blues (6)

18 Man deserts submarine, discovers fortune (6)

19 Ashen with rage (5)

21 A bed is uncomfortable place to find trinket (4)

SOLUTION | ON PAGE 315

960　MAZE MAYHEM

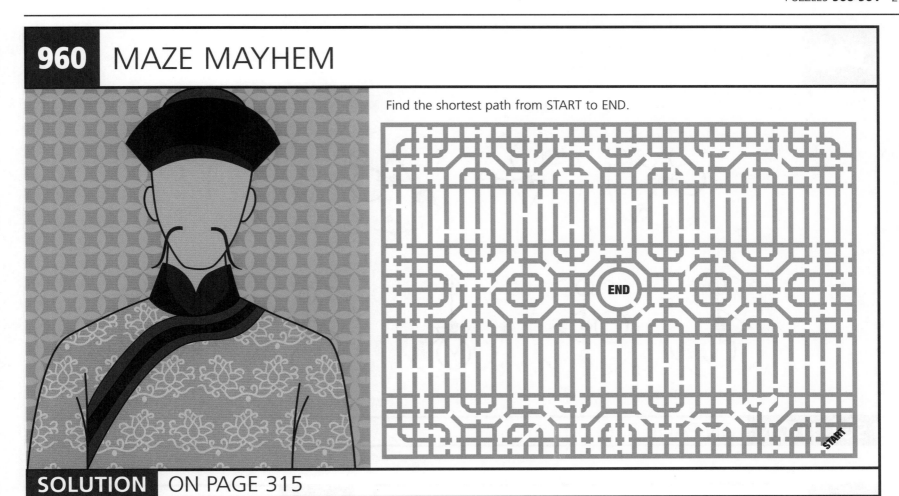

Find the shortest path from START to END.

SOLUTION　ON PAGE 315

961　NUMBER PUZZLE

These colours and shapes all have a numerical significance. Once you work out what it is you will be able to find the missing number.

SOLUTION　ON PAGE 316

962 PICTURE PUZZLE

Which of the circles at the bottom will continue the sequence above them?

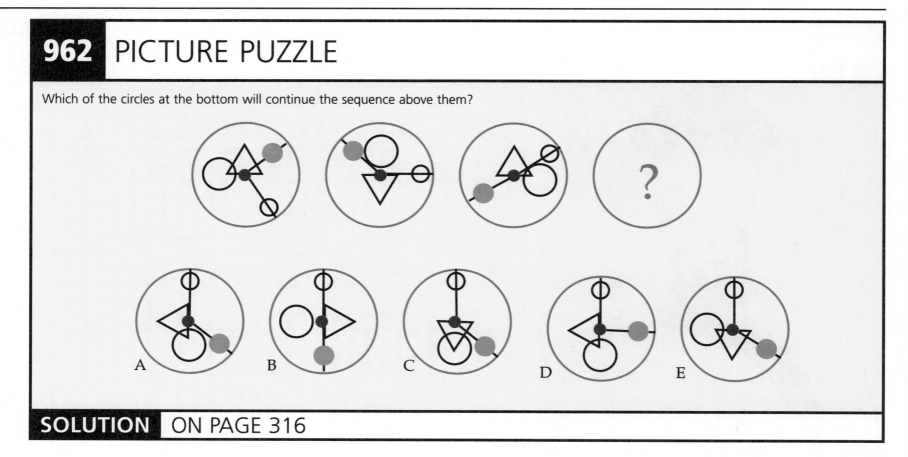

SOLUTION ON PAGE 316

963 LOST SPOT

Where should the dot go in the square with the question mark?

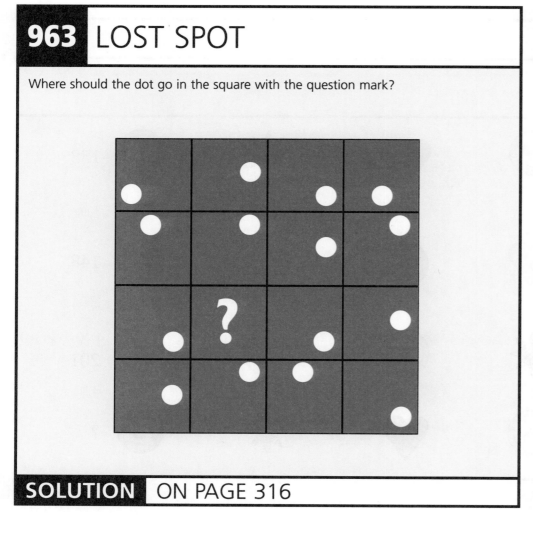

SOLUTION ON PAGE 316

964 NUMBER LOGIC

What number should replace the question mark?

SOLUTION ON PAGE 316

965 WICKED WORD SEARCH

This is anything but a straightforward word search puzzle. The 15 words at the bottom can all be found in the grid below, and all the letters are in their correct order. However, they do not necessarily go in a straight line, forward, backward, up, down or diagonal and some have more than one directional change. How quickly can you find the words and with the fewest of direction changes?

E	T	N	I	O	E	E	T	A	T	S	E	T	N	I
R	A	U	R	S	A	I	E	S	L	E	I	N	F	U
G	T	V	L	T	L	P	S	A	L	A	M	L	N	S
L	C	O	R	E	N	U	R	P	S	Z	D	L	O	I
A	C	I	A	L	M	O	F	U	A	E	B	A	D	M
B	L	V	Q	O	I	A	M	N	S	S	T	B	O	V
P	R	O	A	S	R	T	U	V	I	L	R	L	O	O
R	O	P	B	E	R	T	N	E	N	A	A	L	L	G
E	N	O	R	T	I	O	N	S	O	P	O	R	P	N
R	O	B	E	R	T	V	A	L	E	R	I	T	R	I
A	L	L	E	N	A	V	O	H	N	P	L	A	N	M
R	W	A	S	L	D	M	N	N	R	N	R	E	T	A
O	H	E	S	L	B	I	N	S	I	X	Y	O	R	L
U	R	E	A	D	O	R	O	T	V	C	A	B	L	F
G	N	A	L	S	T	U	I	T	A	N	O	T	N	I

ULEMA	PROPONENT	INTERGLACIAL	INFULAE
SLAVONIC	PROPORTIONAL	FLAMINGO	INHERIT
SLALOM	INTONATION	LANGUOR	INFUSION
SLEAZEBALL	INTESTATE	LANTERN	

SOLUTION ON PAGE 316

966 NUMBER LOGIC

Start at the top-left circle and move clockwise. Calculate the number that replaces the question marks in the following:

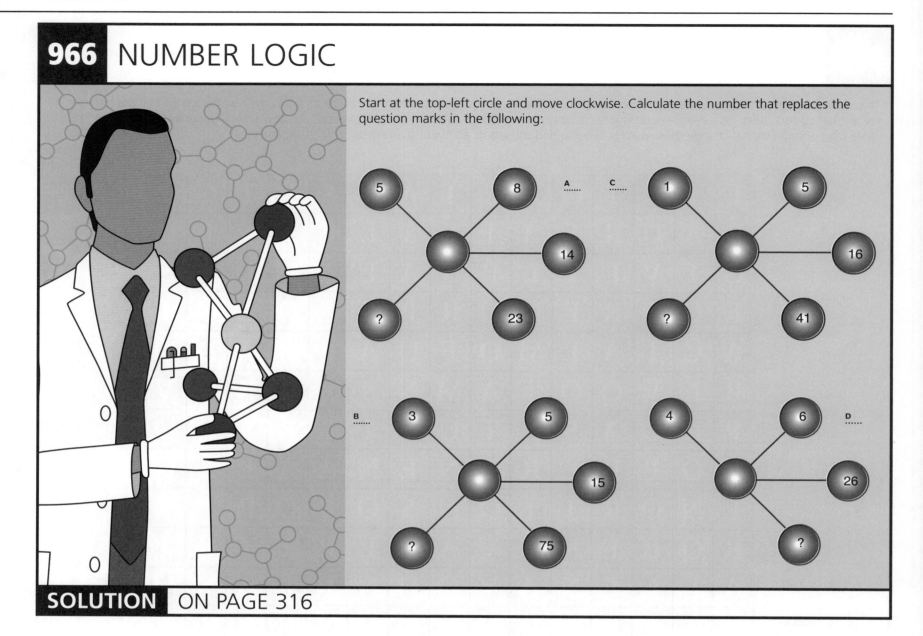

SOLUTION ON PAGE 316

967 SQUARE SOLUTION

Can you find out which numbers should replace the question marks?

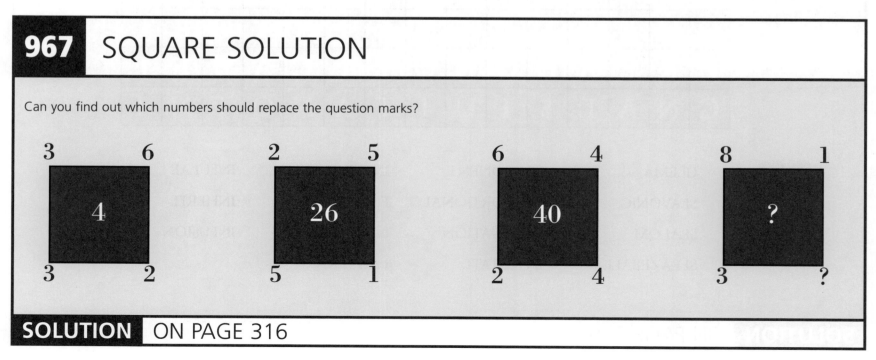

SOLUTION ON PAGE 316

968 STAR SOLUTION

What number should replace the question mark?

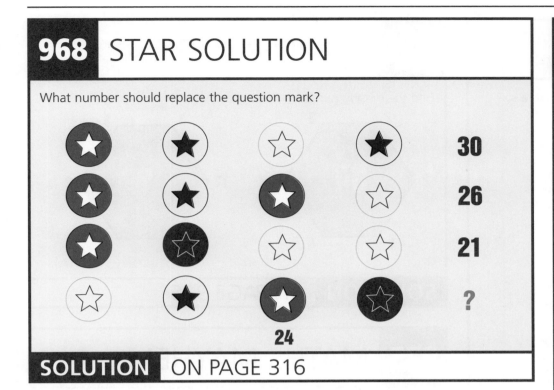

30

26

21

?

24

SOLUTION ON PAGE 316

969 SQUARE PROBLEM

What is the missing number?

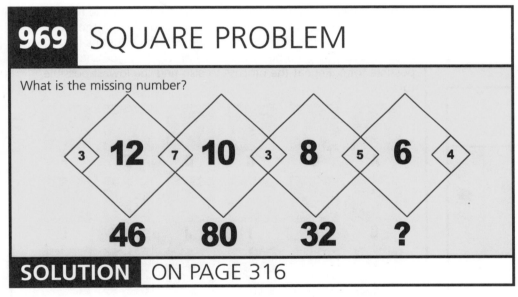

SOLUTION ON PAGE 316

970 SYMBOL ENIGMA

The symbols represent the numbers 1 to 9. Work out the value of the missing multiplier.

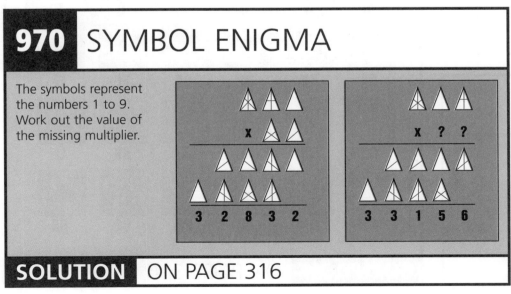

SOLUTION ON PAGE 316

971 CIRCLE ENIGMA

Which arrangement is missing from these sequences?

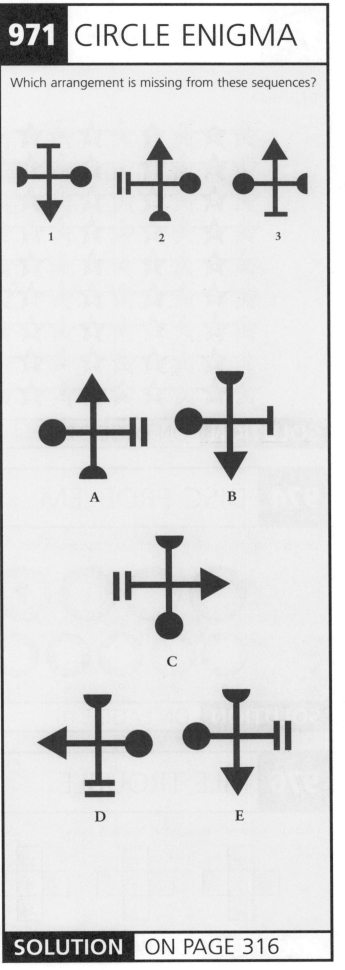

SOLUTION ON PAGE 316

972 STAR SHINE

Find hidden within the stars, a long multiplication sum with a six-figure result.

SOLUTION ON PAGE 316

974 DISC PROBLEM

Which arrangement is missing from these sequences?

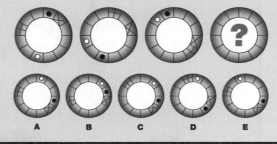

SOLUTION ON PAGE 316

976 TILE TROUBLE

What number will replace the question mark?

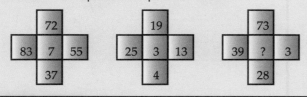

SOLUTION ON PAGE 316

973 NUMBER LOGIC

Find the missing number.

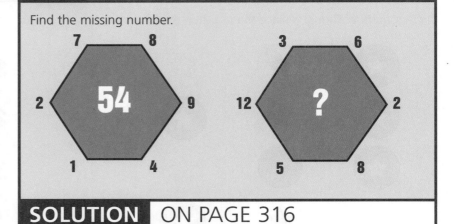

SOLUTION ON PAGE 316

975 MATHS MAYHEM

Find the block in each row which, when you multiply the highest two numbers together, and add the other two digits in the block to the product to arrive at a solution, then add the solutions from the chosen blocks in the other rows together, will give you the highest possible total. Repeat the process to also find the lowest possible total.

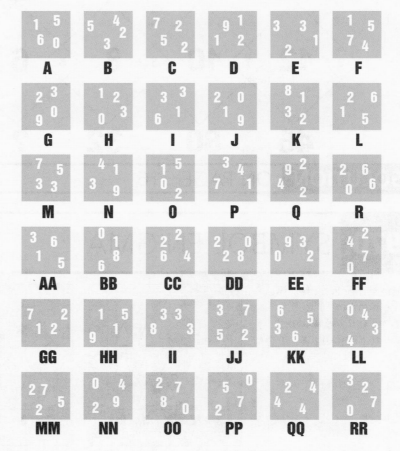

SOLUTION ON PAGE 316

977 A-MAZE-ING MAZE

Find the shortest path from START to END.

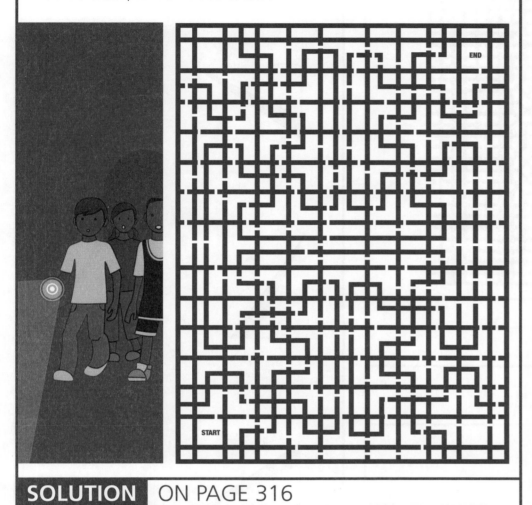

SOLUTION ON PAGE 316

979 WORDS

The letters in the box to the right can be used to create two words, one of which means tendencies and the other to destroy without trace. The letters are used once only and the two words are of differing lengths.

A	T	B	B
R	E	H	I
O	A	I	T
L	E	T	S

SOLUTION ON PAGE 316

978 DIAMOND STAR

Discover the vital relationship between all of these numbers to find the missing number.

41

2   23

11

43

3   29

13

47

5   31

17

53

7   37

?

SOLUTION ON PAGE 316

980 MAZE MURDER

Find the shortest path from START to END.

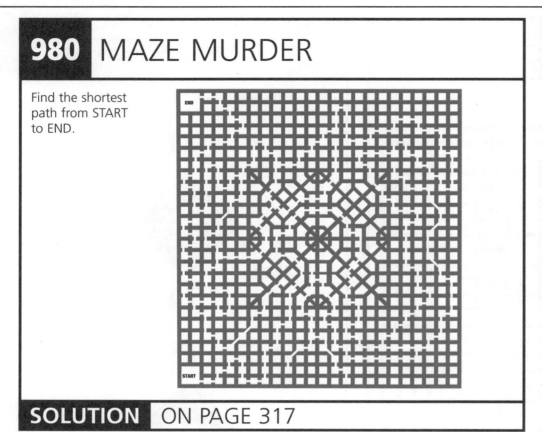

SOLUTION ON PAGE 317

982 TRIANGLE TROUBLE

What number should replace the question mark?

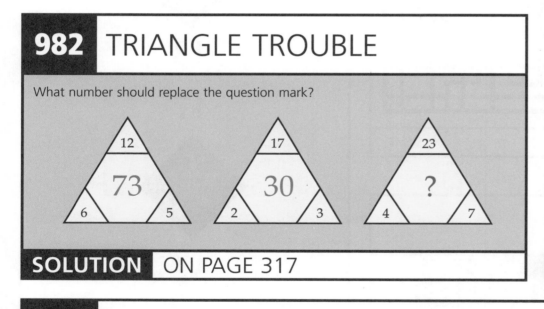

SOLUTION ON PAGE 317

981 ODD ONE OUT

Which of the following is the odd one out?

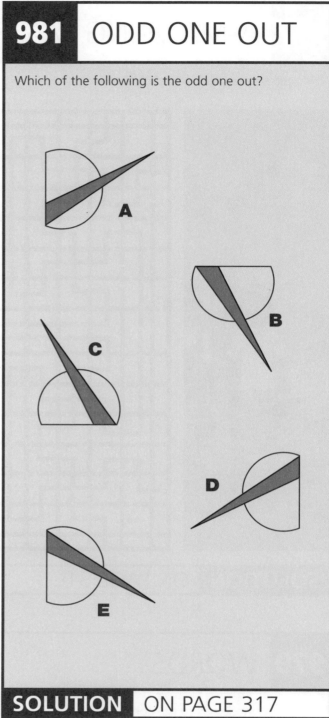

SOLUTION ON PAGE 317

983 SYMBOL SEQUENCE

Use logic to find which shape has the greatest perimeter.

SOLUTION ON PAGE 317

984 STAR PROBLEM

What number replaces the question mark?

985 LOST NUMBER

What number replaces the question mark?

SOLUTION ON PAGE 317

986 TILE TROUBLE

Can one of the four bottom squares complete the sequence?

SOLUTION ON PAGE 317

987 TILE SEQUENCE

Which square completes the sequence?

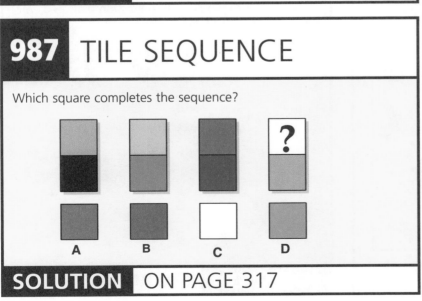

A   B   C   D

SOLUTION ON PAGE 317

988 SIGNPOST

Here is a strange signpost to the burial grounds in ancient Egypt. How far is it to the burial ground of Thoth?

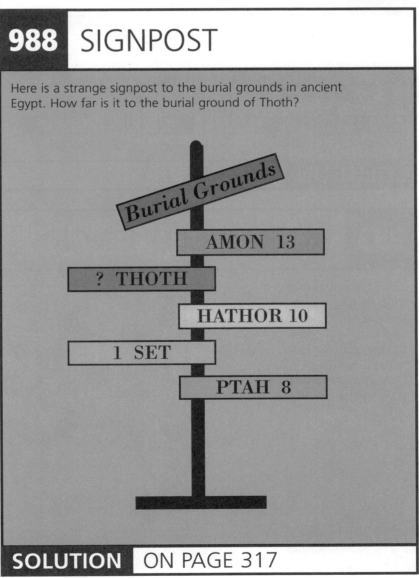

SOLUTION ON PAGE 317

989 BLOCKBUSTER

This figure is a collection of blocks rotated through four perspectives. How many blocks are there in total? There are no gaps between the invisible blocks

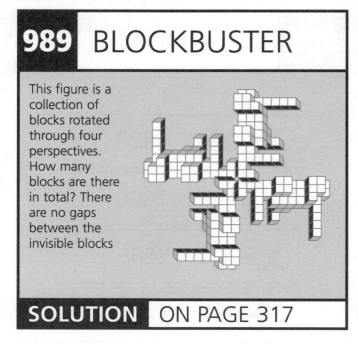

SOLUTION ON PAGE 317

990 PENGUIN POSER

Which of the following penguins is the odd one out?

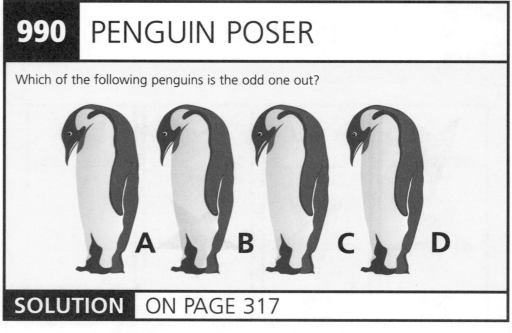

SOLUTION ON PAGE 317

991 ODD ONE OUT

Which of the following is the odd one out?

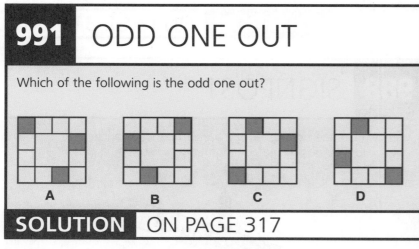

SOLUTION ON PAGE 317

992 SHAPE SHUFFLE

Which of the following is the odd one out?

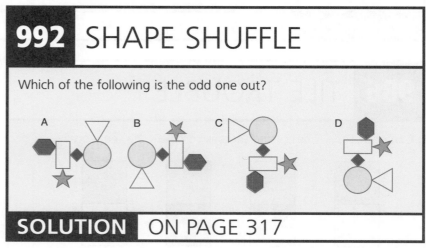

SOLUTION ON PAGE 317

993 SYMBOL SEQUENCE

Draw three straight lines that will give you six sections with one clock, two hares and three lightning bolts in each section. The lines do not have to go from one edge to another.

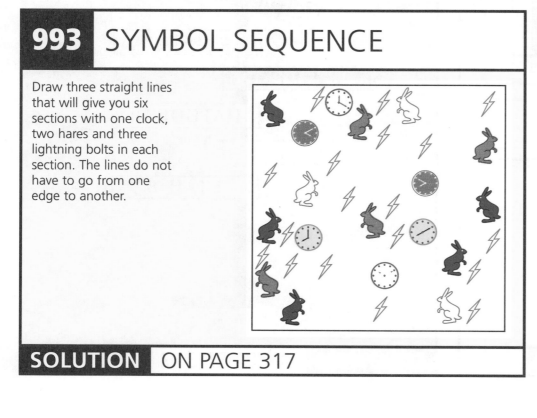

SOLUTION ON PAGE 317

994 COGITATION

If the black arrow pulls in the direction indicated, will the load rise or fall?

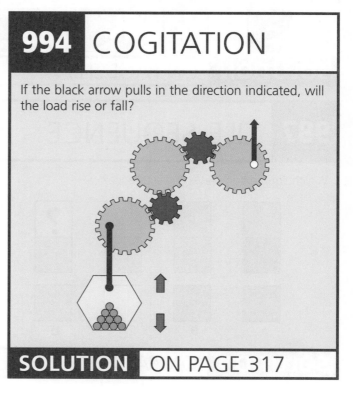

SOLUTION ON PAGE 317

995   BRAIN BUGS

Which two of these butterflies are identical?

A   B

C   D

E   F

SOLUTION   ON PAGE 317

996   ODD ONE OUT

Which of the following is the odd one out?

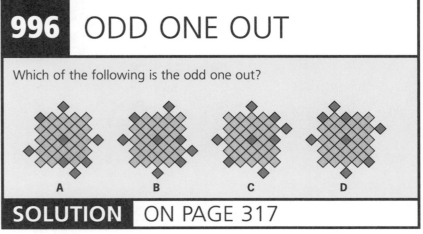

A   B   C   D

SOLUTION   ON PAGE 317

997   WEB WONDER

Which of these spiders and their webs make two identical pairs?

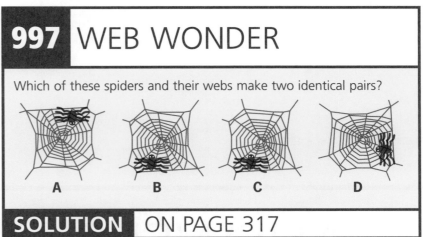

A   B   C   D

SOLUTION   ON PAGE 317

998   BIRD BRAINS

Which two birds are identical?

A   B   C   D

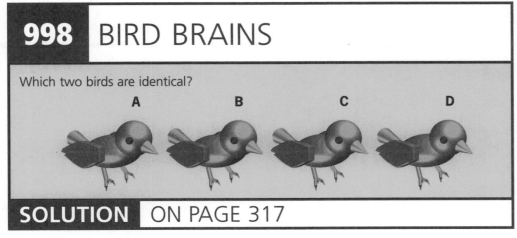

SOLUTION   ON PAGE 317

1000   MISSING YELLOW

How many blue spotted tiles are missing from the middle of this design?

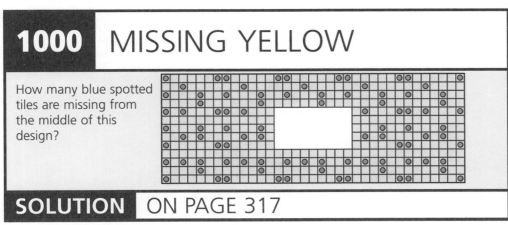

SOLUTION   ON PAGE 317

999   ANALOGY

Complete the analogy.

is to

as DIRT is to

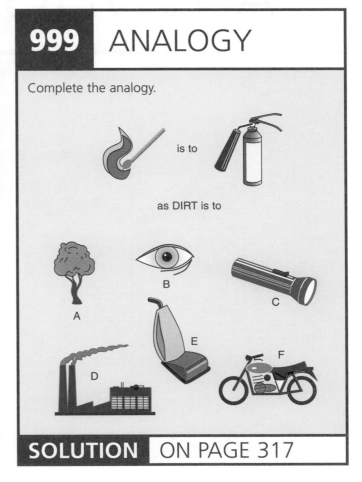

A   B   C   D   E   F

SOLUTION   ON PAGE 317

ANSWERS

1

E.

2

Rob Roy: Red Orange Blue, Red, Orange, Yellow.

3

4. Multiply the two numbers in the outer circle of each segment and place the product in the inner circle two segments on in a clockwise direction.

4

Brown. Letters in the names of opposite pairs of colours always add up to 10 (eg, Pink, four letters, and Yellow, six letters, make 10).

5

G. To give Angel (Glean), Anger (Range), Cigar and Logic.

6

Tide, Idea, Deer, and Ears.

7

Kindness.

8

E. In all the others the colours follow the same sequence: light blue, red, dark blue, green, yellow, pink.

9

Shell does not belong to the group. The linked words are Beast, Decor, Heron, Human, Pilaf, and Round. The first and last letter position in the alphabet totals 22.

10

Sleds, Slews, Slows, Glows, Grows, Gross.

11

Crimson.

12

7. Add the three numbers at the corner of each triangle, multiply by 2, and place that number in the middle.

13

They were traveling to their destination by cruise ship. The hull of the ship was rammed during the night, and their cabin was below the water line. The pressure of the water held the door shut, they could not escape, and the rescuers were too late to save them.

14

4. The number relates to the number of shapes in which the number is enclosed.

15

Argentina, Australia, and Indonesia.

16

8. Starting at H, and working clockwise, subtract the value of second letter, based on its value in the alphabet, from the value of the first letter, and put sum in following corner.

17

1.00. The minute hand moves forward 20 minutes, the hour hand moves back 1 hour.

18

House.

19

A. California
B. Texas
C. Nebraska
D. Alaska
E. Idaho
F. Oregon
G. Virginia
H. Florida
I. Colorado
J. Arizona

20

F. The symbols are reflected over a vertical line.

21

Abbreviation. The missing letters are, reading from top to bottom, V, B and N.

22

E. It contains no curved lines.

23

15. (Top x left) + right = middle. (7 x 8) [56] + 15 = 71. The others are (6 x 9) [54] + 19 = 73 and (9 x 6) [54] + 13 = 67.

24

B (946 : 42). Break down left number: (First digit x second digit) + third digit = right number. (9 x 4) [36] + 6 = 42. The example was (4 x 8) [32] + 2 = 34.

25

When you have to kill a man it costs nothing to be polite. Winston Churchill.

26

6.45. The minute hand moves back 15, 30 and 45 minutes. The hour hand moves forward 3, 6 and 9 hours.

27

10. Replace each letter by the value of its position in the alphabet. Start at E and add 1, then 2, then 3, then 4, then 5, then 1, then 2 etc. When you reach 26 (Z), go back to 1 (A).

28

The order is 2 +, 3 –, 2 ÷, 3 x. The puzzle goes in an inward clockwise spiral starting from the top left corner.

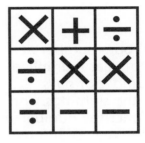

29

Orange and Pink. The other opposite pairs will make entirely new colours (not shades) when mixed.

30

D. The letters form five-letter words when you include the first letter of the colour in the square: baGel, peRIL, adObe, idYll.

31

Below, because it has only one syllable.

32

No, it has no "E" in it.

33

The judge ruled that the money be shared equally between the relatives, but that they should each give Bob a money order for the money taken. If these were not cashed within 1 year of Bob's cremation, then the money could be kept.

34

39. Tick = 6, star = 9, cross = 3, O = 24.

35
E and O. The letters are N, O, P and X.

36
Q. The letters are in the following alphabetical order: miss one, miss two, miss three, miss one etc.

37
Caffeine.

38
Take the room number at the time of year multiplied by the number of days between the sightings, and then subtract the number of days between sightings. The number of days between sightings increases by one for each period. The next sighting will be (9 x 4) – 4 = 32, thus Room 32 every fifth night.

39
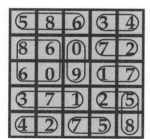

40
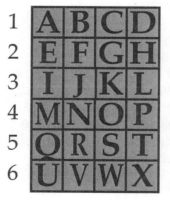

41
8. Add all the numbers together. In a yellow square you add 5 to the sum, in a green one you subtract 5.

42
R. Multiply the value of the three earliest letters, based on their value in the alphabet, by 2. The answer goes in the opposite tip. I (9) x 2 = 18 (R).

43
6.20. The minute hand advances 20 minutes each time, the hour hand goes back 2 hours each time.

44
B. The number of sides of the internal figures should increase by one each time. B is the odd one out because its internal figures should have 2 sides.

45
C. In all other cases the first letters of the colours form words: Gory, Ropy, Prop, Orgy.

46
Taking the first letters of the colours you will get the letters to form POPPY.

47
Thanksgiving Day.

48
None. The number of letters rises by one each time. There is no 7-letter colour in the spectrum.

49
P. To give CaPon, HiPpo, ImPly, and PaPer.

50
C & E.

51
72. Multiply all the numbers in the top sections to arrive at the number in the opposite bottom section. Multiply by 3 in the first circle, by 6 in the second one, and by 9 in the third circle.

52
Picasso, Rembrandt, Gaugin, Leonardo, Constable, Raphael, Van Gogh, Matisse. A= 1:4; B = 1:3; C = 1:2; D = 1:1; E = 2:4, etc.

	4	3	2	1
1	A	B	C	D
2	E	F	G	H
3	I	J	K	L
4	M	N	O	P
5	Q	R	S	T
6	U	V	W	X

53
Mary, Queen of Scots.

54
108. Each vowel in the name is worth 10 and each consonant is worth 22. These are all added

together to give the distance.

55
Aardvark.

56
21 ways.

57
C. The letters represent values based on their position in the alphabet. They represent the number of straight-sided figures in which they are enclosed. The circle is a red herring.

58
E and I.

59
Den.

60
A full circle. Go first along the top of the triangles, then along the bottoms. Each circle is filled one quarter at a time until the circle is complete, then reverts to one quarter filled.

61
8. The three points are added together and the sum is put in the middle of the triangle next to it

62
A. Add one new element to the face, then add one hair and an element to the face, then a hair, then a hair and an element to the face, repeat sequence.

63

(Word search grid)

```
P B A W N W O C H K T V E N T A C Y X O
A A D E F W O Y J U L I A R O B E R T S
C O U S T I N H O F F M A N B R M O N L
K A O L W O L N N Y G O R E S O T U V D
K M G E N E W I L D E R W O L O Z B R R
C A S K L E M U O T L B W J L K K E G O
P C M W V U W E A I J L G A H E T E B F
E L K E F O Z M A A T H E N A S E R O D
E S O A L L A M A A O E E O H I L L E
R T A S E G F A A N T O E F L I S T R R
T O M C R U I S E S R S E O T E E E P T
S A O E E B W B X M Q A N E L G N O R
L A A O H E R S T D A B D C D O A T E
Y A F G S V H T E O I B K A R S C E J B
R B P O A C F A J Z N A Y A A Y I X Q O
E N O Z E A L M A O C Y H F O G H E L R
M A E I N A Z E N I A C L E A H C I M B
C P L M A N N V W X E R S F L A Z O N
N U W M U F G Q S R A E L L A E S S O E
J O N Y F G I N O S P M O H T A M M D F
```

64
15. Start at the top left corner and add that number to each corner in a clockwise direction, e.g. 7 + 7 = 14 + 7 = 21 + 7 = 28 + 7 = 35.

65
23. Square = 9; Cross = 5; Z = 6; Heart = 7.

66
C and K.

67
Plant belongs to the group. The linked words are Burnt, Count, Event, Flint and Giant. All the words end in NT.

68
Magenta.

69
9 ways.

70
Hand.

71
D. Letters with only curves stay the same, letters with curves and straight lines turn by 90° and letters with only straight lines by 180.

72
B.The numerical value of each letter in the alphabet is two-thirds of the number in the opposite segment.

73
I and K. The figures are: matchstick man, triangle, half-moon, circle, stile.

74
Z. Take the value of the letters, based on their position in the alphabet. A back 3 is X; X forward 4 is B; B back 3 is Y; Y forward 4 is C, etc.

75
2. The faces represent numbers, based on the elements in or around the face (excluding the head). Multiply the top number with the bottom right number and divide by the bottom left number. Place the answer in the middle.

76
40. Star = 7; Tick = 8; Cross = 14; Circle = 11.

77
The McPhersons were given the numbers: 5, 6, 7, 8, 9, 12, 16, 18, 19, 22, 23, 24, 26, 27 and 30. If the count started at number 1 all of the McPhersons had to jump overboard.

78
Shop, Shoe, Sloe, Floe, Flee, Free.

79
O is missing. The letters spell Richard Nixon.

80
14 ways.

81
Step.

82
February.

83
Operator.

84
B and H.

85
16. All the other numbers can be divided by 3.

86
L and N.

87
Brides and Debris.

88
57. Each letter is given its positional value in the alphabet and these are added together.

89
Like.

90
H. To give Abhor, Ethic, Ochre and Usher.

91
Yard, Afar, Race and Drew.

92
Air-conditioning.

93
Taxpayer.

94
$330,000 ($15,000 increments)

95
3. The numbers refer to the number of shapes which surround each digit.

96
F + I + E – J + N – W + H = I.

97
M – E + B + D = N.

98
B. Start from top left corner and move in a vertical boustrophedon. Order is: 4 smiley face, 1 sad face, 3 straight mouth, 2 face with hair, etc.

99
Raver, Raves, Paves, Pares, Bares, Barks.

100
Take the letter before the one shown. They then spell Norah Jones.

101
Champagne, Chocolate, Orangeade.

102
O. Miss 2 each time.

103
The months above the line are those with no R.

104
The Spy Who Loved Me.

105
Band.

106
Imposter.

107
192. Each vowel is worth 6 and each consonant 8. The vowels are added together, as are the consonants. The totals are then multiplied.

108
Summer Vacations.

109
825. Multiply the value of the letters, based on their value in the alphabet, from each triangle and place the product in the triangle above or below.

110
D. Only the K has serifs.

111
Top half: + +; bottom half: + −.

112
E. Turn the diagram by 90° clockwise.

113
Well.

114
Characterization.

115
Back, Aeon, Cove and Knew.

116
J. To give EnJoy, MaJor, RaJah and DoJos.

117
Woodbine.

118
Start at top left corner and move in a vertical boustrophedon. The order is two hearts, one square root, two crossed circles, one cross, one heart, two square roots, one crossed circle, two crosses, etc.

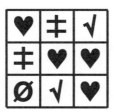

119
A and L. The numbers are 3, 4, 6 and 9.

120
5 x 4 ÷ 2 + 7 = 17.

121
4 x 7 ÷ 2 + 8 + 9 x 6 ÷ 3 = 62.

122
2. Relates to the number of shapes which enclose each figure.

123
D.

124
42. Take the number in the middle of the square, divide it by the number in the top left corner and place the new number in the bottom right corner. Again take the middle number, but now divide it by the number in the top right corner and place this new number in the bottom left corner.

125
C. The number in the middle is the sum of the squares of the numbers at the points of the triangles. C does not fit this pattern.

126
Misspend, squander. The missing letters are M and P (misspend), Q and D (squander).

127
A.

128
C (34). The sums are (top left x bottom right) − (bottom left − top right) = middle. The working is: (9 x 4) [36] − (5 − 3) [2] = 34. The others are (5 x 6) [30] − (7 − 4) [3] = 27; (6 x 7) [42] − (9 − 7) [2] = 40; (8 x 9) [72] − (5 − 4) [1] = 71.

129
E. Opposite segments are mirror images except that black and white shading is reversed.

130
D. The others all have identical pairs: A and H, B and G, C and F, and E and I.

131
9. Centre = (top + right) − (bottom + left).

132
D.

133
C (18). Reading from the left along each row, (first column x second column) − third column = fourth column. The working is: (7 x 4) [28] − 10 = 18. Others are: (6 x 2) [12] − 5 = 7; (8 x 3) [24] − 17 = 7; (9 x 2) [18] − 9 = 9.

134
3A.

135
2. The sums are (top x left) ÷ (right x bottom) = middle. (8 x 7) [56] ÷ (7 x 4) [28] = 2. The others are (8 x 9) [72] ÷ (4 x 6) [24] = 3; (10 x 4) [40] ÷ (5 x 8) [40] = 1; (7 x 6) [42] ÷ (3 x 7) [21] = 2.

136
D. The others all have identical pairs: A and E, B and F, and C and G.

137
A. The black and white dots change position; the full square becomes a half-square and vice versa; and the oval becomes a diamond and vice versa (remaining a half-shape where appropriate).

138
Adherent, believer. The missing letters are H and N (adherent) and B and E (believer).

139
D. The others all have identical pairs: A and E, B and F, and C and G, except that black and white shading is reversed.

140
C. The left part transfers across to lie touching the original, uppermost right side.

141
C. Reading across columns and down rows, unique elements in the first two are transferred to the third (bottom or right). Common elements disappear.

142
Piquet, lustrum, gnu.

143
Waxworks, effigies.
The missing letters are X and R (waxworks) and F and G (effigies).

144
4. The sum of diagonally opposite segments are the same. 6 + 4 = 8 + 2.

145
A. At each stage, the black circle rotates 90° clockwise and goes in and out of the parallelogram; the white circle rotates 90° anti-clockwise and also goes in and out of the parallelogram; the triangle rotates 180° and changes from black to white and vice versa.

146
Abatement.

147
9. Reading from left to right (first column – second column) x third column = fourth column. Working is:
(4 – 3) [1] x 9 = 9.
The others are:
(7 – 5) [2] x 9 = 18;
(6 – 3) [3] x 7 = 21;
(7 – 4) [3] x 8 = 24.

148
Profligate and chaste.

149
D. Different symbols in adjoining circles on the same row are carried into the circle between them in the row above. Similar symbols in the same place are dropped.

150
Hipflask. The missing letters are F and K.

151
58. Looking across each row and down each column, the third and fourth numbers are the differences of the numbers in the two previous squares.

152
8. The sum of each row of three digits is 20.

153
B. The two figures are mirror images of each other.

154
R. Add the alphanumeric values of the three letters around the triangle. The sum in each case is 23. The working is:
C [3] + B [2] + R [18] = 23.

155
A.

156

157
Copenhagen, Prague, London, Berlin, Tokyo, Amsterdam, Stockholm, Colombo, Madrid, Ankara.

158
E and M.

159
Emerald green, Sea blue, Code Red, Blood orange, Tobacco brown, Deep Purple (pop group)

160
L. Add the value of the two letters in each outer segment, based on their position in the alphabet, and place the answer letter in the opposite inner segment.

161
P. Each square gives a five-letter word if you include the first letter of the colour: anGel, acOrn, egYpt, apPle.

162
Indigo and Violet (colours of the rainbow).

163
26. The digits in each of the other balls add up to 10.

164

165
Top half: x ÷; bottom half: ÷ x.

166
Q. Reading clockwise from the top, numbers correspond to the alphabetic position of the following letter.

167
F. The numbers made up of odd numbers are reversed.

168
21. Find the value of each letter based on its position in the alphabet, then add the values of the top and left corner together. Subtract the bottom right corner from this number and place the new value in the middle of the triangle.

169
B, F and N.

170
8. Subtract the bottom left corner from the top left corner. Now subtract the bottom right corner from the top right corner, then subtract this answer from the first difference and put the number in the middle.

171
3. The numbers in each wheel add up to 30.

172
27. A number in the first circle is squared and the product is put in the corresponding segment of the second circle. The original number is then cubed and that product is put in the corresponding segment of the third circle.

173
C. In the others the small shapes added together result in the large shape.

174
The diamond. It is a closed shape.

175
A. Based on the alphabet, starting at B miss 2 letters, then 3, then 4, etc.

176
6 + 7 + 11 ÷ 3 x 2 + 5 – 12 = 9.

177
F – B + J – B = L.

178

179
35. Star = 6; Tick = 3; Cross = 17; Circle = 12.

180
6.50. The minute hand moves back 5, 10 and 15 minutes, while the hour hand moves forward 1, 2 and 3 hours.

181
A. Dallas

B. Seattle
C. Chicago
D. Milwaukee
E. Minneapolis
F. Portland
G. Detroit
H. Atlanta
I. Cincinnati
J. Indianapolis.

182
C. In all other cases, the biggest shape is also the smallest.

183
C. The minute hand moves forward 5 minutes and the hour hand moves forward 3 hours.

184
C. The smallest segment is rotated 90 degrees clockwise. The middle segment remains static and does not rotate. Largest segment rotated 90 degrees anti-clockwise.

185
D. Blue turns green, green turns blue. Pattern is reflected horizontally.

186
B.

187
B. There is no triangle intersection on the odd one.

188

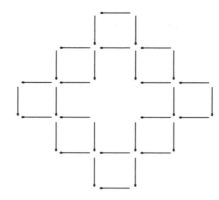

189
D (49). Alternate sectors increase by 1, 3, 5, 7, 9, 11 and 13. They are also squares of 1, 2, 3, 4, 5, 6 and 7.

190
B. In all other cases the smaller circle is within the larger circle.

191
His bet was for a race two weeks earlier when the horse trailed in last. The newspaper gave the previous day's results when the horse had won.

192
E. Largest shape is reflected horizontally and the size order is reversed.

193
16. The sum of inner and diagonally opposite outer segments totals 29.

194
Hijacker. The missing letters are J and K.

195
Ointment and liniment. The missing letters are: O and M (ointment) and L and M (liniment).

196
60. The sums are: (top x left) + (top x right) =

middle. The working is:
(4 x 6) [24] + (4 x 9) [36] = 60.
Others are:
(3 x 6) [18] + (3 x 8) [24] = 42;
(4 x 7) [28] + (4 x 3) [12] = 40;
(5 x 5) [25] + (5 x 4) [20] = 45.

197
B.

198
Impolite and insolent. The missing letters are: M and L (impolite) and S and T (insolent).

199
E. The circle becomes a square; a black circle on the top becomes white; and black and white swap left to right.

200
21. In each case (top – left) ÷ 5 = right. Working is:
(76 – 21) [55] ÷ 5 = 11. The others are:
(36 – 21) [15] ÷ 5 = 3;
(97 – 52) [45] ÷ 5 = 9.

201
Gangrene. The missing letter is G twice.

202
C. Credit is an anagram of direct as anger is of range, and tender is of rented.

203
D. The others all have identical pairs: A and B, and C and E.

204
Silent. Three letters of the left and right words transfer to the middle as follows:
T E N D O N
6 4 5
(S I L E N T)
1 2 3 4 5 6
L I L I E S
2 3 1

205
Trampolinist.
The missing letters are, reading from top to bottom: M and T.

206
30. The sums are: (top left – bottom right) x (bottom left + top right) = middle. The working is: (11 – 5) [6] x (1 + 4) [5] = 30. Others are: (13 – 7) [6] x (4 + 6) [10] = 60; (17 – 9) [8] x (3 + 2) [5] = 40; (9 – 8) [1] x (7 + 3) [10] = 10.

207
B. The number of sides of the inner figure should be half those of the outer ones. In the case of B, there is a square inside a seven-sided figure.

208
Z. Working through the alphabet there are 1, 2, 3 and 4 letter gaps.

209
B. Reading across columns and down rows of shields, common elements with the same shading in the first two are transferred to the third (bottom or right) and change shading. Unique elements disappear.

210
Follow this string:

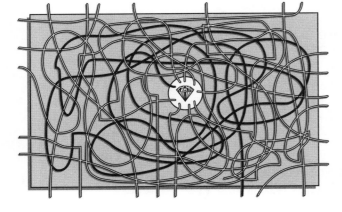

211
C. All the others have in the middle an enlarged version of the objects at top-left and bottom-right.

212
B. The pattern rotates two sunrays one step at a time.

213
D. One of the balls has been displaced relative to the other sets, which are all rotated versions of the same set.

214
D. The others are all rotated versions of the same figure on the top half, with the mirror images on the bottom half, but the mirror image of D is on top.

215
C. Any cross in the middle three vertical tiles is always in the middle column, and the blue spot is always in the same vertical column as in the tiles to the left and right of it.

216
B. It is the only one not enclosed by an outline of the same shape.

217
B. The others all have identical pairs: A and C, D and E, and F and G.

218
10. Find the square root of the numbers in the three angles, add them together. Put the answer in the middle of the triangle.

219
D. All three shapes move down one place at each stage and the star goes from black to white and vice versa.

220
C.

221
48. The sums are (bottom left – bottom right) x (sum of top three numbers) = middle. (11 – 7) [4] x (4 + 3 + 5) [12] = 48. Others are: (16 – 14) [2] x (7 + 3 + 2) [12] = 24; (17 – 14) [3] x (8 + 4 + 1) [13] = 39; (20 – 18) [2] x (9 + 7 + 2) [18] = 36.

222
Tribunal. The missing letters are T and B.

223
C (E). All the others are formed from 3 straight lines.

224
B. Reading across columns and down rows, unique elements in the first two are transferred to the third (bottom or right). Common elements disappear.

225
D. All the others are cities, Kansas is a state (Kansas City actually straddles the Missouri- Kansas border).

226
Jerrycan. The missing letters are J and R.

227
C. It is the only one with vertical, horizontal, and diagonal symmetry.

228
Imposter and Deceiver. The missing letters are P & T and C & V, respecitively.

229
A (0). The sum of the two left columns equals the sum of the two right columns. Also, the 1st and 3rd columns have the same values as the 2nd and 4th. The same applies to the rows.

230
F is wrong. In all the others the dot is in both the rectangle and the triangle.

231
F. A curve turns into a straight line and a straight line into a curve.

232
C. It is the only one which does not have half as many 'step' lines as triangles.

233
B. It is the only figure which, with an additional line, has a triangle adjoining the rectangle which overlaps the square.

234
– x + – ÷ +. 9 – 3 x 4 + 19 – 8 ÷ 5 + 4 = 11.

235
I. It is based on the number alphabet backwards. Add the top and bottom rows together and put the sum in the middle.

236
E, Vertical lines represent 1 integer, horizontal lines represent 5. The product of

the number of lines on each end equals the sum of lines in the middle.

237
Noughts and crosses move 2 spaces working from left to right, top to bottom.

238
8. The sum of hands on each clock is 13.

239
E. Based on the position of the letters in the alphabet, multiply column 1 by column 3 and place the product in the middle column.

240
It should have two dots. Add together the corner squares of each row or column and put the sum in the middle square of the opposite row or column.

241
29. Add together the corner squares of each row or column in a clockwise direction. Put the sum in the middle of the next row or column.

242
Idaho, Iowa, Maine, Texas, Utah. The dummy letters are K and L.

243
C.

244
B. It is the only one with the same number of vertical and horizontal lines.

245
The pattern sequence is: Z R T T U W W Z Z S. Start at the bottom right and work up in a horizontal boustrophedon.

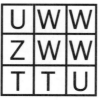

246
84. Multiply the hours of A by the minutes of B to get the tonnage of C, then B hours by C minutes to get D, C hours by D minutes to get E, D hours by E minutes to get A, and E hours by A minutes to get the tonnage of B.

247
23.

248
E. Divide each large triangle into 4 smaller ones. Apart from E each of these will consist of 2 small blue triangles and two small yellow triangles.

249
No. 201. Add together the values of the letters based on their reversed alphabetical position, A = 26, Z = 1).

250
73235226252257. The numbers are in code from the newspaper titles. A–C = 1, D–F = 2, G–I = 3, J–L = 4, M–O = 5, P–R = 6 S–U = 7, V–X = 8, Y–Z = 9.

251
D. All the others are symmetrical.

252
12. Add together the values in the same segments in wheels A and C and put the answer in the opposite segment in wheel B.

253
E. The shape has been folded along a horizontal line. A shaded piece covers an unshaded one.

254
B.

255
Spade = 2, Club = 4, Diamond = 6, Heart = 8.

256
D. M + R = 14 + 9 = 23 = D.

257
7. The colours are worth Green 4, Blue 5, Red 6, Orange 8. The formula is left side plus base, minus right side.

258
She was an astronaut, who on one occasion was in a stationary orbit over the Greenwich Date Line. As each date line revolved below her, she celebrated the New Year 24 times. The other times occurred while she flew from east to west, passing through three date lines when it was midnight on the ground.

259
H. Take the letter three before the given letter in alphabetical order (e.g., for D read A). If you also use the first letter of the given colour you will get four five-letter words: apRil, brOwn, eaGle, nePal.

260
6. The colours are worth Yellow 1, Green 3, Pink 4, Orange 5, Red 6, Purple 9. Add the outer numbers and put the result in the opposite segment.

261
10. The colours are worth Orange 2, Red 3, Green 5, Yellow 6. The formula is 'add all three sides together'.

262
21. Δ = 12, $*$ = 9, $\heartsuit$ = 3, % = 5, @ = 7.

263
8 x 8.

264
The colours are in the sequence Orange, Yellow, Pink, Red, Green and form an inward spiral starting at the top left.

265
Yellow. The colours are worth Pink 2, Yellow 3, Orange 4, Green 5, Purple 6, Red 7, Brown 8. In each segment subtract the smaller of the outer numbers from the larger and put the result in the centre of the next segment clockwise.

266
L. Take the letter after the one given. Use the first letters of the colours. You then get: biBle, rhYme, biRth, emPty.

267
Bartok, Boulez, Chopin, Delius, Mahler.

268
The pattern is +2 scales, +3 scales, −1 scale. A fish with an even number of scales faces right, odd faces left.

269
B. The digits of all the others add up to 6.

270
A. Each shape increases by one of the same until there are three and it then becomes one. The image is reflected for a shape with two elements.

271
D. The number of edges of the shapes in each square increases by 1 in each column, starting from the top.

272
D.

273
16.

274
4.

275
B.

276
3. The numbers rotate anti-clockwise from one square to the next and decrease by 2 each time.

277
9. Multiply the values in the same segments in wheels 2 and 3 and put the answer in the next segment in wheel 1, going clockwise.

278
576. Multiply the number by its speed and put the product as the distance for the next balloon.

279
M. These are the letters with straight sides only.

280
JOL 1714. Go 5 forward and 3 back in the alphabet. The numbers continue from the alphabetic position of the letter.

281
G. Add 3 to odd numbers, subtract 2 from even numbers.

282
Add the number of segments in column 1 to the number of segments in column 3. Draw this number of segments in to column 2.

283
Kebab, Pasta, Pizza, Tacos, Wurst.

284
G. It is a tempo; the others are dances.

285
A. Each ring contains one cross more than the previous example, and the first and last cross in each adjacent circle are level.

286
C.

287
F. The circles and squares become squares and circles respectively. The largest element loses all internal elements.

288

4	2	2
1	5	5
7	1	1

The pattern sequence is 7, 1, 1, 3, 2, 2, 5, 5, 4, 1. It starts at the top right and works in an anti-clockwise spiral.

289
21. Multiply each number by the number on the opposite side of the wheel on the same side of the spoke and put the product in that segment next to the centre.

290
V. The letters are based on the number alphabet backwards (Z = 1, A = 26, etc). The values on the bottom corners and the value in the middle added together result in the value on the apex.

291
The corresponding sections in each orange should contain a dark section in each compartment.

292
A. For all except A the total product of the diagonal lines on each corner equals the 'number' in the middle.

293
D. Add consecutive clockwise corners of the diamond and place the sum on the corresponding second corner. Add the four numbers together and place the sum in the middle.

294
C. Convert each letter to its value based on its position in the alphabet. The values on each corner of a triangle added together result in the new letter in the middle.

295
R. Starting on the top left hand corner, work through the alphabet, missing a letter each time, in a vertical boustrophedon.

296
A.

297
B. Each time the square becomes the circle, the triangle the square and the circle the triangle.

298
No. 2. Take the first digit of the weight from the second to arrive at new number.

299

3	3	2
2	3	4
3	2	1

The pattern sequence is 1, 2, 2, 3, 4, 4, 1, 2, 3, 3, 4. Start at the top left and work in a horizontal boustrophedon.

300
Camus, Defoe, Dumas, Verne, Wells.

301
1980. Vowels = 243, Consonants = 126.

302
Brunel, Darwin, Edison, Pascal, Planck.

303
92. Multiply diagonally opposite numbers on the corners of each box and add the products. Put the sum in the box to the left (sum of box 1 goes in box 4).

304
3.13. Start time A minus Finish A = Finish B. Start time B minus Finish B = Finish C, etc.

305
C. Starting at the top right hand corner, work through the alphabet, missing 1, 2, 3, 4, 5, 4, 3, 2, 1, 2, etc. letters each time, in a vertical boustrophedon.

306
D. It is the only one to which a circle can be added where the triangle overlaps the circle and a right-angled line runs parallel to the whole of one side of the triangle.

307
D. They are all in alphabetical order except for D.

308
3.

309
61. Letters are worth the value based on alphabetical position (A=1, etc.). However, alternate letters are worth the value based on the reversed alphabet (A=26, etc.).

310
2.

311
E. All elements consist of 3 straight lines except E which includes 4 straight lines.

312
E. From A to Z letter in first row moves forward 2 letters; in second row moves forward 3; in third row moves forward 4.

313
B.

314
9. The numbers rotate clockwise and increase by 1 each time.

315
Washington.

316
44. The numbers increase clockwise first missing one spoke, then two at the fourth step. Each circle increases by a different amount (2, 3, 4).

317
A. The other four shapes have a maximum of one blank segment.

318
Bacon, Bosch, Klimt, Manet, Monet.

319
F. The small and large elements become large and small respectively.

320
C. The number of small circles equals the number of edges of the shape, except for 'C' where there is one more circle than edges.

321
48. In each box of four numbers, multiply the top two numbers, put the product in the bottom right box, then subtract the top right number from the bottom right one and put the difference in the bottom left box.

322
C. Venus is closer to the Sun; Mars, Jupiter, Saturn and Uranus are more distant.

323
Alternating each move, go forward 1

segment, then back 3, always in a clockwise direction.

324
E. All the others consist of 3 consecutive letters in the alphabet.

325
His father was the Italian Ambassador and he moved from Rome to Washington. Daniel only spoke Italian.

326
18. Multiply the numbers in the outer section, reverse the product and put in the middle of the next section.

327
D. Each column of elements alternates and moves up two rows.

328
B. Working in an anti-clockwise spiral pattern, in the first square there are eight lines, one missing, seven lines, one missing, etc. The number of lines before the first break decreases by one with each square.

329
B. Each arch moves closer to its opposite end by an equal amount each time.

330

331
1956. The numbers represent the leap years clockwise around the triangles starting at the apex. Miss one leap year each time.

332
C. Add the digits to get the alphabetic number of the town's initial letter.

333
Blake, Byron, Dante, Donne, Plath.

334
20. Multiply hours by minutes and divide by 3 to get the number of the rider.

335
Forward, back, forward, back.

336

S	T	A	T	U	E	O	R	T	S	T	A	T	U	E	S
S	R	E	B	I	L	F	O	E	U	T	A	T	A	T	D
L	S	T	A	T	U	L	I	B	E	R	T	O	F	F	A
I	L	I	B	E	R	T	E	L	I	B	E	R	L	O	T
B	O	F	L	I	B	U	E	O	S	T	A	I	F	S	U
E	T	S	T	A	T	U	E	O	F	S	B	T	S	O	F
R	O	F	L	A	S	U	F	T	L	E	T	T	A	S	L
T	I	C	T	B	T	L	R	I	T	Y	A	S	T	T	I
Y	U	S	E	A	T	S	B	Y	T	T	A	T	U	A	B
E	L	I	T	B	E	E	S	T	A	T	U	E	T	E
R	T	S	L	Y	R	Y	T	R	E	B	L	F	O	U	R
S	T	R	A	T	U	S	O	F	L	I	B	E	R	T	Y
L	T	I	S	B	E	T	O	F	S	T	A	T	U	E	O
X	T	A	T	U	E	A	F	O	T	R	E	B	I	L	F
E	B	I	L	F	O	T	S	T	A	T	U	E	O	E	L
R	T	S	T	A	T	U	T	S	F	O	T	R	E	B	I

337
G. Starting at the bottom left corner, work through the alphabet in an anti-clockwise spiral. Miss 1 letter, then 2 letters, 1 letter, etc., going back to the start of the alphabet after reaching Z.

338
9.05. The minute hand goes forward 25 minutes, the hour hand back by 5 hours.

339
13.

340
B. It is the only figure that does not have three boxes in one row.

341
6. In each square, multiply the top and bottom left together, then multiply the top and bottom right. Subtract this second product from the first and put this number in the middle.

342
A.

343
987. The tractor number is divided into the weight to give the acreage. The weights have been mixed up.

344

Add one leaf. Add two petals. Deduct 1 petal and add 1 leaf. Repeat.

345

S	E	R	E	P	E	N	S	T	I	N	E	R	E	S	E
E	E	S	E	N	R	P	E	N	S	E	R	P	E	N	T
R	S	R	S	E	N	S	R	T	E	R	P	E	N	T	I
P	E	P	P	S	E	T	P	I	N	E	N	E	S	S	S
E	R	E	S	N	T	N	N	N	E	R	I	N	N	N	E
N	P	N	E	R	T	E	T	E	P	N	S	E	E	I	R
T	E	T	R	P	S	I	I	T	R	T	P	T	R	T	P
N	N	I	P	E	E	N	N	T	R	R	S	E	P	N	E
E	T	N	E	N	T	E	E	E	E	S	E	T	E	E	N
I	N	E	N	T	R	S	E	S	R	E	T	S	N	P	T
S	E	R	T	P	E	N	T	I	N	E	T	S	T	R	I
S	E	R	N	P	E	N	T	I	N	E	E	N	I	E	T
E	S	R	E	I	S	E	R	P	E	N	T	I	N	S	E
S	E	T	E	N	N	I	T	N	E	P	R	E	S	T	E
R	S	E	N	E	I	T	N	I	P	R	E	S	E	S	T
S	E	R	P	E	N	S	N	I	T	N	E	P	R	E	S

346
384. Starting at the top right hand corner work through the square in a vertical boustrophedon, multiplying by 4 and dividing by 2 alternately.

347
15. Take the minutes in the hours, add the minutes and divide by 10. Ignore the remainder.

348
C. Each row and file must contain two Orange and two Green squares.

349
14. Colours are worth Purple 2, Yellow 3, Orange 5, Green 6. Add sides together and put sum in centre of triangle.

350
10. The colours are worth Pink 1, Green 2, Orange 3, Yellow 4, Red 5, Purple 6. The numbers are added and placed in the centre of the opposite segement.

351
A and N. The series is B, D, F, H, J (2, 4, 6, 8, 10). Add 1, 2, 3, 4, 5 respectively to the values to get the letters in the second triangle.

352
19. Write the alphabet in a circle. The numbers represent values of letters based on the alphabet backwards (A = 26, Z = 1). Start at A, miss 2, D (= 23), miss 2, G, etc.

353
Rossini, Puccini, Debussy, Berlioz, Corelli. The extra one is Cezanne.

354

Start at the top right and move across the square in a horizontal boustrophedon. The pattern is: miss 1 square, turn by 180°, turn by 90° clockwise, miss 1, turn by 90° clockwise, turn by 180°.

355
As the value of each row is not given, no value can be given to any of the squares.

356
They were all female birds.

357
8. The two numbers added together give the number the minute hand points at on the next clock. The hour hand points at the number three spaces before.

358
K. K is the same number of spaces in the alphabet from H and N, O and G, and E and Q.

359
72. Halve the number on the top left, multiply the number on the top right by 3. Multiply the two resulting numbers with each other, and put the product in the bottom square.

360
7. Add the three numbers on the outside of each square (A). Add the digits of the sum (B). Divide A by B and place in the small square.

361
A = 5, B = 4, C = 15.

362
A la Recherche du Temps Perdu by Marcel Proust.

363
C. It is the only circle with an asymmetrical shape.

364
D. Take the values of the first two letters of each starting town, the irst based on the alphabet forward (A = 1, Z = 26) and the second on the alphabet backward (A = 26, Z = 1). Add the values together. The new letter of that value in the forward alphabet will be the first letter of the new town.

365
K. K is the same number of spaces in the alphabet from H and N, O and G, and E and Q.

366
E. If you look carefully you'll see the letters spell out W. Shakespeare.

367
S. D is the 4th letter from the start of the alphabet, W is the 4th from the end. F is the 6th from the start, U the 6th from the end, etc.

368
38. Regard the alphabet as a circle. The number is double the number of spaces between the letters.

369
43. Add the alphanumeric values together and put the sum in the middle.

370
11. Divide the number of sides of the letter by 2 and add the value of the letter,

based on its position in the alphabet.

371
Brezhnev, Disraeli, Thatcher, Adenauer, Pompidou.

372
N. The letters spell Wittgenstein.

373
M. Add 9 to the value of each letter in the first circle. C + 9 = L.

374
D. These are the first letters of Do, Re, Mi, Fa, So, La, Tee, etc.

375

376
I. All the others, when reflected on a vertical line, have an identical partner.

377
Hockney, Matisse, Gauguin, Hogarth, Vermeer. The extra one is Erasmus.

378
M. The value of the letter on the bottom left, based on its alphabetical position, minus the value of the letter on the bottom right, results in the letter in the middle. Incidentally the outer letters spell Mark Twain backwards but this is of no significance.

379
10. Multiply the two numbers on the outside of each segment, divide the product by 1,2,3 … 8 respectively and put the new number in the middle of the opposite segment.

380
C. The letters spell Henry Mancini backwards.

381
32. All the others have a partner, with the digits being reversed.

382
W. Starting from P go back 3 spaces in alphabet (M), forward 3 (S), back 5 (K), forward 5 (U), back 7 (I), forward 7.

383
9. The alphabet equivalents make up the name Nagasaki.

384
The extra word is Arrivederci.

D	R	I	V	E	R	I	D	V	E	R	D	D	R	I	V
R	D	R	I	V	E	R	D	R	I	V	E	R	V	E	R
I	V	E	R	D	V	E	R	D	D	R	I	V	E	R	V
V	D	R	I	V	E	R	D	E	R	C	I	E	V	V	E
E	D	R	I	V	E	E	D	E	R	C	I	E	V	V	E
D	R	I	V	E	R	V	D	E	R	I	V	E	R	D
V	D	E	R	I	D	I	V	E	R	D	R	I	V	E	R
D	R	I	R	V	E	R	D	R	I	D	R	D	V	D	E
D	R	R	V	T	D	R	E	V	E	R	D	R	I	V	E
D	A	D	R	I	V	E	D	R	I	V	D	R	I	V	E
I	R	D	R	E	V	I	R	D	R	E	V	I	R	D	R
V	E	R	D	D	R	I	V	E	R	D	R	I	V	E	D
V	I	V	I	V	E	V	R	D	E	V	D	E	V	I	R
E	R	E	R	E	D	E	D	R	R	I	R	V	E	R	I
R	D	R	D	R	R	R	R	I	D	R	I	I	R	D	V
I	I	D	I	D	I	D	E	V	I	D	V	R	D	R	E

385
O and V. The others spell Charlie Chaplin.

386
I. Reading from top to bottom, left to right, the letters are the second of the first five numbers. oNe, tWo, tHree, fOur and fIve.

387
Anouilh, Moliere, Ionesco, Osborne, Marlowe. The extra name is Connery.

388
S. Add the values of the letters on the top and right, and the values of the letters on the left and bottom. Subtract the second sum from the first, and put either the new number or alternatively the letter based on the value of that number into the middle.

389
C. Add together the values of the letters (Z = 1, A= 26) and subtract the individual digits from the sum.

390
5. Add both numbers in one segment, add the digits of that sum and place new number in the next segment going clockwise.

391
22. Regard the alphabet as a circle. The number is the spaces between letters reading clockwise.

392
Occasion and incident. The missing letters are C and N in both cases.

393
A (0). The sum of the two left columns is the same as the sum of the two right columns. Also, the 1st and 3rd columns have the same values as do the 2nd and 4th columns. The same applies to the rows.

394
A. The top two items separate; the larger one rotates 90° clockwise and moves to the bottom, and the smaller one becomes large and goes in the middle. The bottom item rotates 180° and moves to the top.

395
A. Reading across columns and down rows, unique elements in the first two are transferred to the third (bottom or right). Common elements disappear.

396
E. The right and left halves of the figure switch positions as illustrated below:

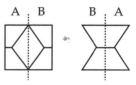

397
6. A + B = D. D − 3 = C. C + B = E.

398
156
339
400
461
644
949.

399
A. 24. Opposite numbers are divided or added to give 24. B. 3. Opposite numbers are multiplied or divided by 3.

400

6	2	9	3	7
3	7	6	2	9
2	9	3	7	6
7	6	2	9	3
9	3	7	6	2

401
16.

 = 4    = 5

 = 6   = 7

402

1	1	0	1	1	1	0	0	1	0	1
1	1	0	1	1	1	1	0	0	0	1
0	0	1	1	0	1	0	1	0	1	1
1	1	0	0	1	1	0	1	1	1	1
0	1	1	1	1	1	0	0	0	0	1
0	0	0	1	1	0	0	1	0	1	0
0	1	1	1	0	1	0	0	1	0	1
0	1	1	0	1	1	0	1	0	1	1
1	1	1	0	0	0	1	1	0	0	1

D. The the binary numbers start at the top and work left to right, line by line.

403
400. The numbers are the squares of 14 to 21 inclusive.

404

12	21	30	-17	-8	1	10
20	29	-11	-9	0	9	11
28	12				17	19

		-10	-1	8		
-13	-4	-2	7	16	18	27
		6	15	24		

-5	-3				26	-14
3	5	14	23	25	-15	-6
4	13	22	31	-16	-7	2

D. This is the only patch that works for all the lines.

405
25. Circle = 4; Triangle = 8;

Diamond = 5; Square = 2. The values are added when the shapes are combined.

406
E, G, G. These represent the numbers 577, which are added to the sum of the previous top and middle line, to get the bottom line.

407
Add 4 big balls on the right and remove one small ball from the left.

408
3. Convert number of rosettes into digits. Add the rosettes and take the middle line from the top line.

409
7 people.

410
Follow this route.

411

22	21	13	5	46	38	30
31	23	15	14	6	47	39
40	32	24	16	8	7	48
49	41	33	25	17	9	1
2	43	42	34	26	18	10
11	3	44	36	35	27	19
20	12	4	45	37	29	28

412
D. The least number of faces touching each other gives the greatest perimeter.

413
1. A + B = KL, C + D = MN, and so on.

414
18. Elephant = 2; Walrus = 3; Camel = 4; Pig = 5.

415
28. Each row is a sequence of A + D = C, D + C = B and B + C = E.

416
6. Add the value of the top two stars of each column to value of the middle two stars to get the value of the bottom two stars.

417
A. 40 (opposite pairs added make 40).
B. 10 (opposite pairs subtracted leave 10).

418
10. Snowflake = 5; Candle = 3; Sun = 2.

419
19. The top pair of numbers are multiplied together and added to the result of multiplying the bottom pair of numbers together. (2 x 8) + (3 x 1).

420
One of the family named BULL who owns the nearby farm charged them $20 to cross his land.

421
A. 42. B. 54, Opposite numbers are multiplied, divided, or added to get the numbers in the middle.

422
48. Multiply the top digits, then the bottom digits and subtract.

423

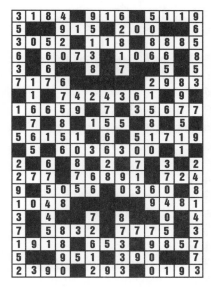

424
C.

425
30. The total of the top and bottom numbers is always the same as the difference between the left and right numbers.

426
2. Multiplying the top two digits together gives a number composed of the bottom digits.

427
78. Multiply opposite numbers and add the results to get the numbers in the middle. Thus 24 + 24 + 30 = 78.

428
25. Star = 9; Whorl = 5; Square = 3

429
248. Long lines = 2, short lines = 1. Add the values on the right to arrive at the answer.

430

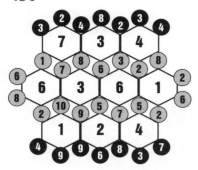

431
B. The shaded spots represent the hands of a clock. 3:00 – 9:00 = 6:00.

432
9 minutes and 9 seconds after 1.

433
27. The bottom two digits are expressed as a number, subtracted from the top two digits, also expressed as a number. The difference is halved and the result is put in the middle. 78 – 24 = 54. 54 ÷ 2 = 27.

434
D. The least number of faces touching each other gives the greatest perimeter.

435
32.
Diamond = 7; Circle = 4; Hexagon = 13; Square = 8.

436

3		5		4		4		3		3
	90		120		64		144		54	
2		3		2		2		6		1
	48		96		16		72		36	
1		8		2		2		3		2
	160		80		20		150		30	
4		5		1		5		5		1
	180		10		40		100		15	
9		1		2		4		1		3
	27		8		32		12		81	
3		1		4		1		3		9
	24		28		84		45		135	
8		1		7		3		5		1
	144		42		63		225		25	
3		6		1		3		5		1

437
7. Take the middle number from the top left number. Multiply that by 2 to get the top right number. Add 5 to the top right number to get the bottom number.

438
4. Start from the top left of the spiral and work in, successively subtracting and adding: 9 – 7 = 2, 2 + 5 = 7.

439
42. The bottom number goes next to the top one to make a two-digit number; the left and right do the same. Then subtract the second number from the first. 96 – 54 = 42.

440
20. Add top left, top right and bottom right, then subtract bottom left. Multiply difference by two.

441
7. There are 7 areas of intersection at this position.

442
12, 19, 26, 3, 10. The bottom line of a Magic Square, in which all rows, columns, and long diagonals equal 70.

443
22. Rectangle = 8 Triangle = 3 Hexagon = 2

444
0. In all the shapes the top two numbers are multiplied, then halved, 3 x 0 = 0.

445
2. C = A – B, with the result reversed 496324 – 235768 = 260556.

446
24 ways. There are six ways with each suit at the left.

447
96. 4^2 = 16; 16 x 6 = 96

448
15:03 (or 03.15 (pm) if the watch has the capacity to switch to 12-hour mode).

449
To put out the fire they used airplanes to scoop water out of the nearest lake. When they scooped the water out, they scooped him out as well. Water dropped on the fire and put it out but the fall killed the diver.

450
7162 and 3581.

451
2. The top four numbers, plus the number in the middle, equals the bottom four numbers. Hence 8765 + 567 = 9332.

452
D. For all except D a smaller circle is joined to a larger one on the edge directly opposite the previous join.

453
2. The weight is positioned 8 units along, so it needs a weight of 2 units (8 x 2 = 16) to keep the system in balance.

454
H. Large square rotates 90° anti-clockwise followed by reflection about the horizontal axis.

455
9 earth months. Zero has an orbit that takes $\sqrt{4^3}$ (8) times as long as Hot.

456
72. It is the only non-square number.

457

458
279. The numbers are added together and the sum + 1 is put in the next triangle. 106 + 172 = 278 + 1 + 279

459
16 people.

460

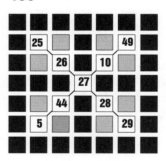

461
100. The numbers inside each triangle total 200.

462
456. The first symbols are worth 789; the middle symbols are worth 456; the right-hand symbols are worth 123.

463
+ 29, x 7, – 94, x 4 and – 435. The sum is: 29 x 7 (203) – 94 (109) x 4 (436) – 435 = 1.

464
27. The left number is one-third of the top. The right number is taken from the top to give the bottom.

465
19. Pink = 9, Black = 5, Lilac = 4, White = 3. Add 1st, 2nd, 3rd and 4th of each column to get total.

466
Z. An alternate letter puzzle. In left shapes go: top, left, middle, right, bottom; in right, go: left, top, middle, bottom, right.

467
C and F.

468

The shapes form a series in order of value:

469

Start at the top right and move in an anti-clockwise spiral. The dot moves clockwise around the square.

470
20. Left hand x right hand ÷ waist = head. Left foot x right foot ÷ waist = head.

471
A. The edges of all the symbols in one square, added together, increase by 2 with each square (i.e., 12, 14, 16, 18, 20).

472
M. Starting with the top triangle and letter A move round the diagram in a clockwise direction. Move then on to the diagram on the right and last to the diagram on the left. Miss three letters with each move.

473
The little girl was in her playhouse. She had to go through the front door of the playhouse first, and then the front door of the family house to get to the front garden.

474
D. The formula is: left + (middle x right) = top + (middle x bottom), but in D, the answers are 26 and 25 respectively.

475
R. These are the second letters of the days of the week.

476
A.

477

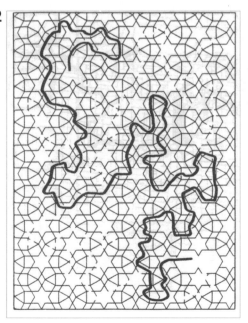

The formula is (right x left – top) x pink fraction of circle = bottom

478
P. Write the alphabet in a circle. NOP are the letters diametrically opposite ABC.

479
20. Take two numbers in adjacent circles. If both are odd, add them. If both are even, multiply them. If one number is odd and one is even take the difference. Put the new number in the overlapping section.

480

481

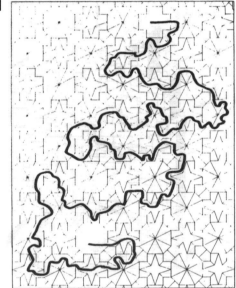

482

483

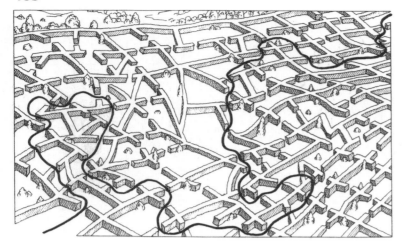

487

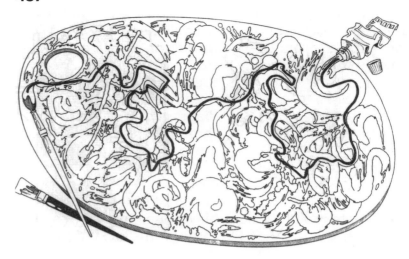

484

485

488
56. (Head x left foot) ÷ waist = right hand; (head x right foot) ÷ waist = left hand). (14 x 15) ÷ 5 = 42; (14 x 20) ÷ 5 (56).

489
9. Multiply the two outer numbers in each segment, and divide the product by 2 and 3 alternately. Place the new number in the middle of the opposite segment.

490

486

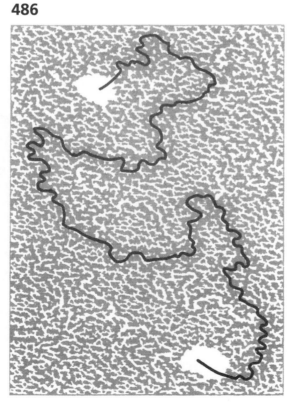

491
A Midsummer Night's Dream by William Shakespeare.

492
B. The balls on the diamond have switched places.

493
It will rise.

494
E. The squares with lines from the bottom left to the top right have arrows pointing up or right. Squares with lines from the bottom right to the top left have arrows pointing down or left.

495
G.

496
11. It is a series of prime numbers.

497
The letter contained a white feather, a symbol of cowardice. In order to rid his family name of this slur, he was forced to act with bravery.

498
T. It spells Marcel Proust.

499
D. The formula is: (right x shaded fraction of left) – (top x shaded fraction of bottom) = middle shape's number of sides. Therefore, in example D: (18 x 2/3 [12]) – (12 x 3/4) [9] = 3. The answer shape should be 3-sided, so it is the odd one out.

500
91. All the others are prime numbers.

501
5. Three numbers in a horizontal line add up to the fourth number.

502
E. The outer letters are displaced four places in the alphabet (e.g., E = A, I = E, etc). The answers have then been swapped in adjacent pairs of squares, aeGis, hiPpo, eiGht, maPle. The initial letters of the square colours are incorporated.

503
77. The colours are worth Purple 3, Green 4, Yellow 6, Orange 9. Add the left side to the right side and multiply by the base. This is Result 1. Now add the two upper internal colours

and subtract the lower. This is Result 2. Then subtract Result 2 from Result 1.

504
34. The colours are worth Green 3, Red 4, Yellow 5, Purple 7. Add colours in each square together.

505
19. Colours are worth Orange 3, Green 4, Red 5, Purple 7.

506
D. The whole figure is reflected on a horizontal line. Any shape with straight lines is then rotated by 90° clockwise and a dot in a round shape disappears.

507
Answer: 26. The colours are worth Red 3, Yellow 6, Purple 8, Green 9.

508

509
B and F.

510
27. The colours are worth Yellow 2, Red 3, Green 4, Purple 6. Multiply the sides of the triangle together to get Result 1. Add the inner numbers together to get Result 2. Subtract Result 2 from Result 1 to get the answer.

511
19. The colours are worth Orange 3, Red 5, Purple 7, Green 4. Add colours in the same row/column together.

512
A. In the other cases the addition of a vertical or horizontal straight line would form a capital letter.

513
A la Recherche du Temps Perdu, To Kill a Mockingbird, A Thousand and One Nights.

514
Answer: 105. The colours are worth Yellow 4, Pink 5, Green 6, Orange 7. Add the value of the colour to the number in each square.

515

516
28. Colours are worth Purple 5, Orange 2, Yellow 3, Green 6. Each colour represents a number under 10.

517
The hours move back 3, 4, 5 and 6 hours. The minutes move forward 4, 8, 16 and 32 minutes. The seconds move back 1, 2, 3 and 4 seconds. The time on the fifth watch should be 21.14.51.

518
C.

519

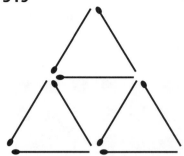

520
D. An unshaded ringed planet becomes a shaded ringed planet; a star containing a shaded planet becomes an unshaded planet; a shaded ringed planet becomes an unshaded ringed planet; an unshaded planet becomes a star containing a shaded planet. The symbols are then vertically reflected.

521
D. In all other cases the number of cross pieces on top of each vertical line is multiplied by the number of cross pieces on the bottom. All give even answers apart from D.

522
Blue = 8; Green = 9.

523
A.

524
Penultimate triangle on the bottom row. The sequence, starting from the top and working from left to right, is: dot, miss 1 triangle, dot, miss 2, dot, miss 3, dot, miss 4.

525
A square. If the three numbers around the triangle add to an even number the shape is a square; if it is odd, then it is another triangle.

526
Ben Gurion, Gatwick, Las Palmas.

527

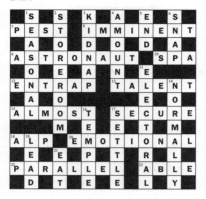

528
She fell into a storage bath containing mercury. She was taken to hospital to be decontaminated because mercury can cause health problems. At room temperature mercury does not leave the skin feeling wet.

529
Make all of the car park spaces at right angles to the wall.

530
B. A red spot changes into four blue; 2 blues can change into 1 red; string of spots moves 72 degrees clockwise.

531
D. Add a cross piece each time, alternating between adding them vertically and horizontally. A vertical cross piece changes the colour of the arrow head.

532
X. The value of letter given by position in the alphabet is added together. An even answer should give a triangle, an odd answer a circle. X gives a value of 60.

533
a) 3 x 4 - 5 + 6 = 13;
b) 7 + 8 x 9 - 10 = 125;
c) 11 + 12 - 13 x 14 = 140.

534
C. Curved lines gradually encroach on space within triangle.

535
D.

536
D. One tip of the star is missing.

537
1. Start at 63, and working clockwise, subtract 1, 2, 4, 8, 16 and 32, respectively, in alternate segments.

538
D. Circle and triangle alternate. After a circle the next figure moves anti-clockwise one space, staying on the same side of the line. After a triangle it moves on 2.

539
He was on a boat and had to wait for the next high tide to get into the unloading dock.

540
B is the only one that contains no triangle.

541
C. Small square becomes a big square and vice versa. A small square with a triangle goes to small square alone. A triangle on big square remains a triangle.

542
C.

543
Heathrow, McCoy, O'Hare, Dalaman, Dar Es Salaam, Ho Chi Minh City, Houston, El Paso, Charles De Gaulle, Benito Juarez, Kranebitten.

544
12 ways.

545
B.

546
Rainbow.

547
His house is built into a hill/ the house is built below ground level.

548
A. 65. The others are all multiples of 20. B. 400. The other numbers are multiples of 27.

549
A4 and D1.

550
Andrew is 1 year old. The ages relate to the alphabetical position of the first letter of each child's name.

551
7.10. The clock moves 15, 20 and 25 minutes forward.

552
Switzerland.

553
Elephant. All the others are meat-eating animals.

554
1. Should I sail 2. Did Ray smile 3. Sheila said yes 4. Museum has old dolls 5. She sells sea shells.

555

556
31. It is the only odd number.

557

558
A. 8 rows of three rabbits
B. 28 rows of two rabbits
C. 6 rabbits in three rows of three rabbits can be done like this:

 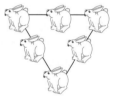

559
C.

560
15. ★ = 3, ● = 2, ■ = 5.

561
6. Subtract the two bottom numbers from the top to give the middle number.

562
B.

563
12.30. Each clock moves forward 1 hour and 10 minutes.

564
B1 and A3.

565
James is a teacher.

566
Blue cheese, Blackboard,

Purple prose, Orange juice, Pink gin, White House.

567

568
Style belongs to the group. The linked words are AbYss, BuYer, CoYpu, IdYll and MaYor. All the words have Y as the third letter.

569
E. Except for E only one dot appears in each vertical / horizontal strip.

570
H. Reflection horizontally.

571
The first casualty when war comes is truth. Hiram Johnson.

572
One method is: Pong, Pang, Rang, Rant, Cant.

573

ASTONISHING :	AMAZING
DOCILE :	LAPDOG
ORGAN :	LUNG
SUFFOCATING :	OPPRESSING
LOOKING :	PEEPING
INSECT :	EARWIG
ASKING :	REQUESTING
RASCAL :	SCALLYWAG

574
Cannelloni, Macaroni and Spaghetti.

575
Journals.

576
21. Sums of opposite pairs equal 55.

577
20. Each vowel is worth 4 and each consonant 2. The totals of the vowels and consonants are added.

578
Cast.

579
9 ways.

580
Circle. Triangle = 5, Square = 8, Circle = 9. Add the values in each row / column.

581
Mow, Jewel, Blanket and Down.

582
The fruits are made of wax; they are candles, and the woman lit them before leaving the room so that they had burned down.

583
Dances with Wolves.

584

The "red herring" words are SPOKESMAN and DEER.

585
A. To give KoAla, ShAde (or HeAds), PeAce and WhAle.

586
Word, Oboe, Rode and Deep.

587
Misunderstanding.

588
Bird.

589
Baseball.

590
17 ways.

591
Gesture.

592

593
The bag contained candyfloss. Rain got into the hole in the top of the bag, and the candy dissolved into a small amount of pink liquid.

594
Loon, Loop, Poop, Pomp, Pump.

595
Disqualification.

596
Flute does not belong to the group. The five associated words are Decoy, Steam, Tulip, Abbey and Hippo. The first two letters of each word are in alphabetical order.

597
26 ways.

598
Nineteen.

599
Low.

600
Satinwood, Jacaranda and Greengage.

601
A = 17, B = 18, C = 14. The sum of the numbers in all vertical and horizontal lines is 50.

602

603
3D in column 1 on row 2.

604
Snow white, Jet black, Blood red, Emerald green, Midnight blue.

605
Opera, books, music, paint, poems.

606
He had melted; he was a snowman.

607
Left to right: 24, 22, 25, 23.
★ = 7, ● = 6, ■ = 5.

608

609
10. The alphabetic position of the first letter multiplied by 10.

610
Nein. The others are "yes" in European languages. Nein is "no" in German.

611
Birmingham.

612
44. Add the three outer numbers together, double them and put the answer in the middle.

613
10.

614

615

6	8	1	2	4
8	0	9	5	2
1	9	9	6	7
2	5	6	5	1
4	2	7	1	3

616
1i in the outer circle, between 1i and 1c.

617
Basic, proud, scrap, price, clasp.

618
GARDEN. Odd ones out are: Group (others are singles),

Almond (others are plants), Rain (others are seasons), Dark (others are light), End (others are start), Nail (others are kitchen implements).

619
Grandmother.

620
A4 and D1.

621
1. Subtract the top row from the middle row to give the bottom row.

622
21. ★ = 5, ● = 4, ■ = 8.

623
A.

624
The odds of the deciding lot would be the same for each round, and over time that child (unless unlucky) would be required to wash dishes on a Sunday as many times as each of the other children.

625
C.

626
£24. Consonants are worth £5, vowels are worth £2.

627
20. Each vowel is worth 10.

628
Boris Becker and Andre Agassi.

629
4.

630
A and E. B, C and D are rotated images of each other.

631
Venezuela.

632
Maximum is 59, minimum is 50.

633
5.25. Hours advance 5; minutes advance 20.

634
2. The outer numbers, when multiplied, give the inner one.

635
Orange. If you take the initial letters of the colours you get words reading across: bow, boy, row, bog.

636
Plague, passed, create, fungus, growth.

637
Orange. It is the only one to start with a vowel.

638
No, the number of letters decreases but there is no colour with only two letters.

639
Mark. The note said "?$" and the cop worked it out as "Question Mark Price!"

640
Group B. All the colours in Group B have an E in them, none of the As do.

641
14. Just add the outer numbers and put the total in the middle.

642
20. ★ = 2, ● = 4, ■ = 7.

643
48. Add together the

bottom two numbers, multiply the total by the top and place the answer in the middle.

644
7. It is a run of consecutive prime numbers.

645
1 and 6. On each row, add the two outer numbers to give the middle one.

646
Beethoven.

647
18. ★ = 6, ● = 5, ■ = 4.

648
3. In each row, subtract the middle number from the left to give the right.

649
10.50. The time moves backwards 1 hour, 5 minutes on each clock.

650
It was a seaplane. The water that it was to use at the first landing site was too rough for a safe landing so the pilot diverted to an airfield on land.

651
4 (26 ways).

652

9	1	4	6	3
1	2	5	3	1
4	5	8	0	2
6	3	0	9	6
3	1	2	6	7

653
1. Monet
2. Dali
3. Rembrandt
4. Donatello

5. Ernst
6. van Gogh.

654
4A and 4D.

655
The clock he saw was a reflection. It was showing 12:45, but this appeared to be 11:15 since the clock only had dashes on it rather than actual numbers.

656
Glockenspiel.

657
104. Multiply the alphabetic position of the first and last letters of each place.

658
4 each of $1, 25c, 5c and 1c.

659
Hockey, Karate and Tennis.

660
0 and 5. Subtract the lower line from the one immediately above it and put the answer directly below.

661
A. Galileo
B. Archimedes
C. Oppenheimer
D. Einstein
E. Heisenberg
F. Bell
G. Fleming
H. Ampere
I. Celsius
J. Pascal.

662
The locksmith had been shut in with the manager after he had set the automatically activated system. He was inside the room just collecting the last items from the manager. The room had no light and the lock could not be tampered with from the inside.

663
East.

664
10. The numbers in each sector are added together and the diagonally opposite sectors have the same total.

665
3 diamonds.

666
E.

667

8   **12**

The numbers at the top, middle and left are consecutive. The top and left numbers are then added together to give the right number.

668

1	5	4	7	6
5	2	0	3	3
4	0	8	5	8
7	3	5	2	6
6	3	8	6	4

669
Mike Tyson.

670
P. The letters read RED, PURPLE, with one P missing.

671
The two parts were lined up using strings with weights to guide the head down. Several piles of sugar or other water-soluble materials were stacked at strategic locations on the plinth. The head was lowered and the ropes removed. The piles were then treated with a water spray starting from the central piles. (Dry ice could also be used.)

672
D. The names of the colours are written round the outside of the squares. D is the only letter missing.

673
2U on row 4 in column 4.

674
8.05. The clocks move 4 hours and 50 minutes forward each time.

675
8 ways.

676
8.

677
Your first shot should go behind you or deliberately in the air. You can't shoot at Count Nevermiss because if you did and were unlucky enough to hit him, Lord Bullseye would polish you off with the next shot or two. If you shoot at Lord Bullseye and hit, Count Nevermiss will certainly get you. If you miss Lord Bullseye, Count Nevermiss would not and his chances against you are 2 : 1 in his favour. If you hit Count Nevermiss, Lord Bullseye's probability of winning against you is 6/7, yours is 1/7. But if you deliberately miss, you will have another shot against either one of the other two. If Lord Bullseye hits the Count, you will have a 3 in 7 probability. With 1 in 2 probability, the Lord will miss the Count (in which case the Count will dispose of the Lord). Thus your chances are 1 in 3 against the Count. The odds are increased by shooting in the air: the first shot will be 25 in 63 (about 40%). Lord Bullseye's odds become 8 in 21 (38%); Count Nevermiss's odds are 2 in 9 (22%).

678
Below, all those above have an initial B, those below have P.

679
Above. Those above the line have only one syllable, those below have two.

680
Nine trips are required. Label the children A, B, C, D and E in ascending age, and the sides of the river "Near" and "Far" to create the table below:-

Trip No.	Near Side	Children in boat	Far Side
1.	A,C,E	B,D	None
2.	A,C,E	B	D
3.	B,E	A,C	D
4.	B,E	A,D	C
5.	B,D	A,E	C
6.	B,D	C,E	A
7.	B,D	C,E	A
8.	B,D	None	A,C,E
9.	None	B,D	A,C,E

Each child has had 3 one-way trips

681
1251. The values of the Roman numerals in each star's name are added together.

682
4 and 1. A 5-figure sum, subtract the top from the middle to get the bottom.

683
Babe Ruth and Joe Montana.

684
6.00 am.

685
4 stars.

686
West. The order is West, South, East, North, North, and it runs continuously down column 1, up column 2, down column 3, etc.

687
2.45. The hour hand moves forward 2 hours each time, the minute hand moves alternately forward 5 minutes and back 10.

688
2 squares.

689
10. The three numbers in each sector are added together and the totals in the bottom four segments are double those of their diagonally opposite ones.

690
F.

691
24 squares.

692
52. ★ = 17, ● = 13, ■ = 21.

693
9.15. In each case the hour hand moves forward 1 hour and the minute hand 15 minutes forward.

694

4	5	1	9	2
5	6	3	1	4
1	3	9	5	1
9	1	5	7	8
2	4	1	8	2

695
The cube has two diagonal dovetail slots. The top can be pushed off by pushing at 45° to the face.

696
1. On each row, subtract the two right numbers from the two left ones. The answer is put in the middle.

697
Lowest is 45, highest is 83.

698
2A and 3C.

699
16. ★ = 5, ● = 1, ■ = 2.

700
It will rise.

701
D. The small square moves clockwise with the circle gaining an extra line each time. The T moves anti-clockwise and rotates through 180°.

702
5a in the inner circle.

703
6. On each row, 1 is added to the first number to give the second number. Column three has 3 subtracted from column two and column four is double the value of column three.

704
The yellow P. All the other letters also represent their colour.

705
18500. Each line is deducted from the line above to give the line below.

706
The pipe to the basin has frozen so the plughole was also frozen. Therefore, as long as Sally did not run the hot tap, the water would stay in the basin.

707
Little Boy Blue.

708
Orange juice.

709
E.

710
Minimum is 97, maximum is 105.

711

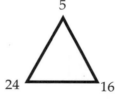

The right number doubles; the left number goes up by 6 and the top number goes down by 5.

712

713
1.00. In each case, the time is moving back 2 hours 10 minutes.

714
It was the earliest days of commercial jet aircraft flight and a few unexplained accidents involving the Comet needed to be investigated. The Comet was the first commercial transatlantic passenger jet. It flew higher and faster than all other commercial planes, and was therefore subjected to stresses that other planes had not endured. The main problems came when the pressures in the fuselage were greater than those outside. The design engineers found that this was best simulated by putting water in the fuselage under pressure. This identified a number of weaknesses in the design, especially around the windows. The findings have made all jet travel much safer.

715
Barbados.

716

717
4.20. The times move forward by 1 hour and 5

minutes, 2 hours and 10 minutes, 4 hours and 20 minutes and 8 hours and 40 minutes.

718
Bottom right = 256, middle = 64. The left and top numbers are multiplied and the answer is put in the middle. The top and middle numbers are then multiplied and this answer goes to the right.

719

M	A	D	A	M		S		M	U	T	E	D
U		U		A	P	P	L	E		R		E
L	I	N	E	N		R		D	R	I	L	L
E		C		O	K	A	P	I		B		T
S	M	E	A	R		T		A	R	E	N	A
	A		R							E		O
S	N	A	I	L		**5**		A	B	O	U	T
	I		S							E		N
R	A	T	E	S		K		P	L	U	S	H
E		I		P	A	N	E	L		N		I
M	A	N	G	O		O		A	D	D	E	R
I		G		R	O	W	A	N		E		E
T	H	E	R	E		N		E	A	R	E	D

720
370. Add the alphabetic position of the first and last letters, then multiply by 10.

721
E.

722
The sea had eroded the cliffs to within 30 yards of the garden. He found that it would be uneconomical to protect the house from further erosion. Experts had told him that it might only be 5 years before the mansion would be in the sea.

723
8 ways.

724

1–2:	DISSIPATE	10–11:	TURMOIL
2–3:	ESPIONAGE	11–12:	LAUNDRY
3–4:	EGOTISTIC	12–13:	YELL
4–5:	CLAYMORE	13–14:	LISLE
5–6:	EVIDENCE	14–15:	ERA
6–7:	ENTHRAL	15–16:	ALPS
7–8:	LINEAGE	16–17:	STEM
8–9:	ERECT	17–18:	MIX
9–10:	TRANSIT		

D	E	R	O	M	Y	A	L	C
T	I	V	L	L	E	Y	I	L
U	I	S	I	I	R	T	I	A
R	M	S	S	D	S	N	A	R
M	I	E	N	I	E	L	R	H
O	X	U	T	A	P	N	E	T
I	A	O	G	S	R	A	C	N
L	G	E	R	E	C	T	T	E
E	G	A	N	O	I	P	S	E

725
1U in row 3 on column 4.

726
1. Phil Collins
2. Michael Schumacher
3. Sean Connery
4. Mike Tyson
5. John Lennon.

727
3. Apples = 6;
Bananas = –1;
Cherries = 4.

728
7 pairs of cherries.

729

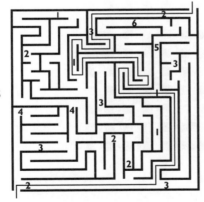

The lowest possible scoring route is 9.

730
The land was being reclaimed from the sea for industrial use. His company owned the reclamation contract. The land would soon be worth a fortune.

731
8.30 pm.

732
B.

733

G	X	R	V	F	S	H	P	L	A
D	A	N	U	B	E	Q	F	Z	K
R	P	N	E	N	I	H	R	W	Q
C	Y	F	A	J	N	M	F	J	D
Z	K	E	B	I	E	B	L	E	H
E	B	M	B	U	D	G	E	T	H
R	D	U	S	R	Y	N	Q	V	F
I	Z	E	Q	W	Q	J	A	P	X
O	N	P	J	H	T	A	G	U	S
L	Y	G	R	X	V	N	N	B	G

734
Half past midnight.

735

E	X	T	E	N	U	A	T	E		R
V		A		E		L		X	R	A	Y
E	N	N	U	I		P		T		M
A			T	R	A	V	E	R	S	E
C	R	A	S	H		C		N		H
C		E		A	S	T	R	A	L	
S	I	E	R	R	A		P		C	
S		U		B		A	L	I	K	E
A	S	S	E	S	S	O	R		L	
I		F		E		R	U	L	E	R
E	S	A	U		I		O		E	Y
M		L	I	L	Y	W	H	I	T	E

736

S	F	C	S	W	S	L	T	J	R	V	H	Y	G
T	A	D	Z	Z	H	A	R	E	N	T	R	A	P
A	L	N	I	Q	O	S	S	K	M	E	T	E	G
R	L	E	L	P	U	O	X	E	B	M	H	N	U
V	A	D	H	D	L	P	R	B	G	O	I	B	P
A	C	I	C	U	D	O	O	S	N	N	N	I	T
T	Y	V	T	A	E	R	M	H	I	E	K	S	E
I	F	I	I	H	R	P	S	A	H	Y	I	C	D
O	O	D	T	Q	E	R	R	R	C	T	N	U	A
N	R	C	S	T	D	T	I	P	N	Y	G	I	C
A	V	I	N	O	I	T	S	E	U	Q	F	T	R
W	E	I	G	H	T	F	I	N	R	R	E	Q	A
N	O	O	T	R	A	C	A	E	C	K	O	X	W
P	O	V	R	K	S	A	P	R	E	S	E	N	T

Aircraft	CARRIER	Number	CRUNCHING
Amusement	ARCADE	Pathetic	FALLACY
Animated	CARTOON	Pencil	SHARPENER
Binomial	THEOREM	Rocket	SCIENTIST
Birthday	PRESENT	Round	SHOULDERED
Burning	QUESTION	Saturation	POINT
Circuit	TRAINING	Ship's	BISCUIT
Conscience	MONEY	Shuttle	DIPLOMACY
Counter	PROPOSAL	Sleep	STARVATION
Daylight	ROBBERY	Sleeping	PARTNER
Honeycomb	STITCH		
Interim	DIVIDEND		
Joint	RESOLUTION		
Lateral	THINKING		
Molecular	WEIGHT		

737
Hamburg.

738
12. Top x right – left = middle.

739
8. Heart = –2; Diamond = 3; Club = 4.

740
119. The alphabetic positions of all the letters of the names are added together.

741
The removal man took the stolen stamps to the biggest stamp dealer in the city, who recognized that they were stolen from his shop some years before. He called the police, who arrested both the homeowner and the removal man.

742
He had replaced all of the bar codes on the products with labels taken off small packs of the same items. The products he bought were all large packs and the bill should have been at least 3 times more. The shop assistant at the till raised the alarm when she saw one of the bar code labels was loose.

743

744
A to give Rumba, Samba, Polka, Tango.

745
Daniel, Exodus, Isaiah and Joshua can be found by pairing alternate segments.

746

747
Maryland.

748
E. Elgar, Bizet, Grieg, Verdi.

749
Bob Marley.

750
13. The sum is (Top left^2 + bottom left) − (top right + bottom right) = middle.

751
Malaysia and Hong Kong.

752
Michael Chang.

753
O. Cairo, Hanoi, Seoul, Tokyo.

754
Agassi, Becker, Hingis, Muster.

755
Alkaline (chemistry term) and Composer (musical word).

756

J	U	S	T	■	A	B	L	E
U	■	H	■	■	■	L	■	X
D	O	O	R	■	S	U	C	H
G	■	W	I	N	C	E	■	A
E	■	■	G	■	O	■	■	U
M	■	S	H	A	P	E	S	■
E	X	I	T	■	E	M	I	T
N	■	Z	■	■	■	I	■	E
T	H	E	Y	■	G	R	I	D

757

B	G	J	B	F	H	C	L	G	B
D	E	U	T	Z	E	A	A	O	M
C	T	V	H	W	N	P	L	S	F
P	R	V	E	S	R	L	A	S	H
S	A	L	O	N	I	Q	Y	E	K
K	N	N	J	N	O	X	A	T	D
B	I	W	G	V	T	G	Q	B	W
D	U	E	Z	K	F	X	E	Y	G
F	R	E	G	O	R	L	O	P	Y
Q	G	X	V	C	H	X	Z	O	D

758

759
i) Bill Clinton ii) Abraham Lincoln iii) George Washington iv) Harry S. Truman v) John F. Kennedy vi) Ulysses Grant

760
In the pink.

761

C	O	O	P	E	R
M	U	R	P	H	Y
M	A	R	V	I	N
M	A	R	T	I	N
G	A	R	C	I	A
R	E	E	V	E	S

Tony Curtis.

762
16. Add the numbers and put the sum in the next triangle along.

763
A. The initial letters of the others make words (ROPY, GROW).

764
Joe beat him at a game of chess (or something similar).

765

766

Top crossword grid for 766.

Bottom crossword grid for 766.

767
The cartoon characters are: Bambi, Cinderella, Pluto and Yogi.

768
Winnipeg.

769
9. The numbers above the triangle go in the middle of the top triangle, and the same goes for right and left.

770

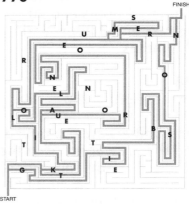

Turner, Kilmer, Taylor, Gibson. The first letter of two of the routes is the same, and the last letter of three of the routes is the same.

771

L 30	N 27	H 10	A 23	R 36	D 25
U 11	I 22	E 29	A 26	S 9	S 20
I 28	E 31	O 8	A 21	H 24	E 35
J 7	A 12	E 5	A 2	I 19	D 16
S 32	S 1	X 14	U 17	H 34	M 3
E 13	L 6	T 33	U 4	O 15	S 18

The books are: Samuel, Joshua, Exodus, Isaiah, Daniel and Esther.

772

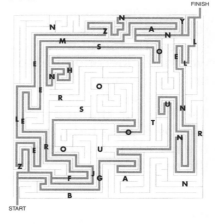

Gunnell, Freeman, Johnson, Zelezny. The last letter of two of the routes is the same.

773
A. The letters outside are consonants of famous tennis players. They are: (top) Borg and Graf, (bottom) Agassi and Cash. The letters inside the triangles are the initials of their nationality. They are Swedish, German, American and Australian respectively.

774
Portland.

775
Boston, Dallas, Denver and Newark can be found by pairing opposite segments.

776
Carter, Eisenhower, Johnson, Reagan, Roosevelt.

777

B	R	Y	A	N
A	N	B	R	Y
R	Y	A	N	B
N	B	R	Y	A
Y	A	N	B	R

778
Pizzicato, Crescendo, Larghetto.

779
N. Hymen, Venus, Diana, Woden.

780

Y	N	J	Z	B	W	K	X	B	T	N	F	G
G	I	O	R	G	I	O	A	R	M	A	N	I
T	E	S	S	O	B	O	G	U	H	R	G	A
X	L	V	E	S	V	R	Y	C	R	N	B	N
R	K	Q	S	H	F	X	B	E	V	O	K	N
Z	N	G	S	W	L	J	D	O	Q	C	M	I
J	I	T	E	M	P	O	F	L	W	R	Q	V
Y	V	K	L	K	R	S	B	D	Z	E	S	E
W	L	N	L	D	B	H	P	F	Q	P	D	R
F	A	T	E	G	U	C	C	I	X	S	Y	S
X	C	A	L	T	P	Q	M	E	H	A	W	A
V	D	G	J	V	Z	D	Y	L	G	J	Z	C
S	T	U	S	S	Y	F	K	D	B	J	B	E

781
The items stacked on the piano had fallen toward Joe, and he had said to Alf, "Give me a hand to move them off!" Alf rushed into the department store and removed a hand from a mannequin and put it in Joe's top pocket.

782

O	O		A	D	O	R	E
U	N	T	O		E		A
I		H		S	P	O	I
J	E	E	P		O		N
A		R	O	A	S	T		T
	W		W		E	A	C	H
R	E	A	D	Y		U		I
E		E		S	N	U	G
S	K	I	R	T		T		H

783
i) Minnesota; ii) Texas; iii) Alaska; iv) California; v) Florida; vi) Louisiana.

784
Gail Devers.

785
G should be orange (then the initials in each line would make a word – PROP, BROW, GYRO).

786
Red. The colours are in alpha order going clockwise.

787
10. The sum is (top left^2 + bottom right^2) – (top right^2 + bottom left^2) = middle.

788
T. The cities, without vowels and the initial of the states they are in. Orlando (Florida), Detroit (Michigan), Denver (Colorado) and Dallas (Texas).

789
16. Add all top lefts, then answer in top left. Repeat.

790.
7.

791
Brad Pitt.

792

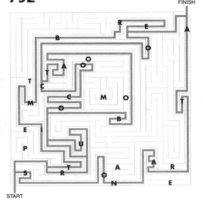

Rococo, Rubato, Sonata, Timbre. The first letter of two of the routes is the same and the last letter of two of the routes is the same.

793

T	R	Y	J	P	Q	X	G	D	H	K	X
M	A	D	N	V	R	K	F	Z	F	W	Z
J	R	N	O	D	D	E	S	Y	J	O	T
P	S	N	O	T	A	R	E	H	S	Z	F
C	H	E	P	P	L	E	W	H	I	T	E
H	C	H	I	P	P	E	N	D	A	L	E
D	M	B	Y	Z	H	I	S	C	P	G	J
F	T	A	G	W	F	T	L	Y	I	B	M
X	U	K	D	D	U	O	D	L	N	T	X
M	V	C	P	A	C	K	L	W	I	G	K
K	W	G	R	K	M	O	V	R	U	H	Y
Z	H	T	R	X	W	W	B	N	Y	K	P

794
They were playing darts in the clubhouse. The object of the challenge was to see who could score the most with just 3 darts.

795
It was the consultant physician supervising the student doctor who suffered the cardiac arrest.

The student's prompt action saved his life. The farm worker was checked out, given a temporary plaster casing on his ankle, and was later allowed to go home.

796
Osprey, plover, budgie, marten, petrel, toucan. Key anagram: Pelican.

797
Biodegradability.

798
The writers are: Stephen King, Oscar Wilde, William Shakespeare and Jane Austen.

799
Darwin, Newton and Pascal can be found by pairing adjacent segments.

800
13. Dove = 2; football = 3; earth = 5; spiral = 4.

801
i) Roberto Baggio ii) Dennis Bergkamp iii) Kevin Keegan iv) Eric Cantona v) Jürgen Klinsmann.

802
Chicago.

803

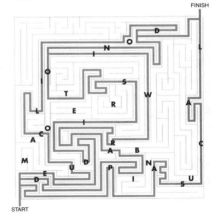

Edison, Darwin, Euclid, Pascal. The first letter of

two of the routes is the same and the last letter of two of the routes is the same.

804
He had put sugar in the first cup.

805

O	M	A	L	A	P	R	O	P	I	S	M	Q
R	A	F	F	L	E	D	G	L	I	N	Y	U
T	Y	D	O	D	E	C	A	G	O	G	S	A
S	E	N	D	U	L	C	I	N	N	U	T	D
R	R	E	E	B	R	A	S	E	D	I	A	R
E	P	U	E	M	D	E	S	A	O	S	G	O
K	S	N	W	A	N	R	I	R	L	T	O	P
N	O	N	E	H	E	R	E	B	I	E	G	H
O	L	I	L	L	A	E	R	O	E	M	U	O
Y	L	F	B	M	U	T	A	R	R	M	E	N
R	I	F	I	T	E	S	O	M	R	A	S	I
A	R	G	E	N	O	I	H	C	N	A	T	C
N	E	T	N	E	C	R	E	T	A	T	I	T

806

	Circular		Radial
1.	CONFIGURATION	1.	CAME
12.	ROC	2.	ODES
15.	ADORNING	3.	NOD
17.	PINK	4.	FROM
18.	AIR	5.	INCH
19.	LAMED	6.	UNIT
20.	OCCIDENT	7.	APER
22.	PUT	8.	TINT
23.	BESOM	9.	INTO
24.	HE	10.	OK
25.	TORTOISES	11.	NOUS
		12.	RATE
		13.	OILS
		14.	CRAB
		16.	ICE
		21.	DO
		22.	PI

807
Holly Hunter, Sally Field, Daryl Hannah, Meg Ryan, Demi Moore, Winona Ryder, Jane Fonda, Bette Davis.

808
A. India, China, Delta, Pan Am.

809

W	Z	Q	E	P	R	V	H	E	F	M
T	O	U	S	Y	J	A	H	E	E	Z
T	N	S	I	G	K	L	U	L	S	W
I	I	E	U	F	H	K	G	E	E	P
P	C	A	R	H	X	I	H	C	E	H
D	A	N	C	H	B	L	G	U	L	J
A	P	P	M	S	Q	M	R	R	C	R
R	L	E	O	J	R	E	A	B	N	G
B	A	N	T	T	Z	R	N	P	H	Y
S	K	N	A	H	M	O	T	W	O	S
Y	R	B	X	F	Q	J	X	N	J	S

810
34. The sum is (top left + bottom left + top right^2) – bottom right. Working is $(2 + 5 + 6^2)$ [43] – 9 = 34.

811
He saw someone cutting across from the opposite side of the road and they were spinning out of control and heading straight for him. He was boxed in, and rather than take a head-on impact, which might have killed both drivers, he took a minor bump on the car in front of him.

812

C	H	I	C						
H	I	D	E						
I	D	O	L						
C	E	L	L	I	S	T			
			I	X	E	A			
			S	E	L	L			
			T	A	L	K	I	N	G
					I	D	E	A	
					N	E	A	R	
					G	A	R	B	L	E	D
						L	U	R	E
						E	R	N	E
						D	E	E	D

813
33. A + B + C + D. Sq 1 goes to Sq 3, Sq 3 goes to Sq 1, Sqs 2 & 4 swap.

814
G. The letters are displaced by two and the initial of the colour is in the middle. GaPed, TaBle, TiGer, BaRns.

815
A. The initials of the 12 months and the 4 seasons of the year are in a spiral, clockwise, from the top left.

816
A. The middle letter is the initial of the colour: alGae, brOom, faBle, eaRth).

817
The child saw it on a TV movie.

818

P	E	T	T	E	D		R	E	P	A	S	T
U		I		V	A	L	I	D		R		I
G	A	M	B	I	T		G	E	R	B	I	L
D		B		L	E	M	O	N		O		T
O	D	E	S		S	I	R		M	U	S	E
G	O	R	E	S		D		S	I	R	E	D
R		W	A	Y		T	O	N		T		
F	I	N	E	D		T		B	I	G	O	T
I	C	E	R		S	O	B		M	E	N	U
N		E		O	P	E	R	A		A		R
I	O	D	I	N	E		E	C	A	R	T	E
A		E		C	E	D	A	R		E		E
L	I	D	D	E	D		D	E	A	D	E	N

819

C	O	N	T	R	A	R	Y	T	B	R	T
W	W	F	P	A	E	H	C	I	O	O	W
B	A	L	L	B	T	F	L	L	I	P	X
H	G	R	O	O	L	E	V	E	L	E	T
T	O	U	P	E	M	I	I	S	S	S	U
G	N	S	H	A	M	R	N	U	R	O	R
D	X	S	G	O	T	M	O	K	Q	O	N
O	N	D	V	O	O	H	A	F	C	L	I
L	L	E	R	X	W	F	D	K	I	S	D
E	T	T	M	A	N	X	S	A	E	P	A
S	Y	E	I	E	P	Q	N	M	O	D	F
Q	K	Z	J	W	Y	Y	D	H	Z	R	W

820
Alto, Bass, Chord, Largo, Lento, Opera, Opus, Presto, Rondo, Rubato, Sonato, Tempo, Tenor.

821
i) Yul Brynner
ii) Cary Grant
iii) Clark Gable
iv) Keanu Reaves
v) Tony Curtis.

822

R	N	B	L	F	K	X	C	D	R
E	N	D	C	W	Q	H	S	O	E
N	E	G	A	W	S	K	L	O	V
A	O	H	J	K	O	L	B	P	O
U	R	G	V	D	S	F	Y	J	R
L	T	C	A	R	A	U	G	A	J
T	I	T	O	E	G	U	E	P	M
P	C	Y	T	O	Y	O	T	A	B
J	C	F	V	G	Z	C	W	D	K
E	K	D	P	M	H	Q	G	Y	F

823
O. The middle letter of each name is in the middle of the box. Fonda, Hanks, Wayne and Stone.

824

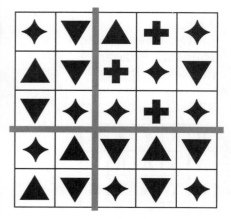

825

826

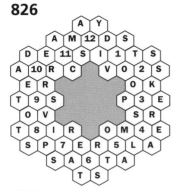

827

Mel Gibson.

828

The stars are: Tom Cruise, Mel Gibson, Robert De Niro, Steve Martin, Whoopi Goldberg, and Jane Fonda.

829

830

Odin, Hermes, Osiris, Poseidon, Athena, Cupid.

831

They were a band who played background music for the guests. They were paid by the casino and did not gamble.

832

Across		Down	
6.	BEACHED	1.	LEAPT
7.	TALON	2.	SCOTIA
9.	SPITE	3.	BED
10.	PARENTS	4.	TALENT
12.	CALCULATING	5.	COATING
14.	MINDFULNESS	8.	FAILING
18.	CREEPER	11.	SCOURED
19.	PETAL	13.	MIRRORS
21.	GRADE	15.	DREADS
22.	HUNDRED	16.	STEADY
		17.	WAFER
		20.	NUN

833

Liz McColgan.

834

Zeus.

835

Spitz, Borg, Bowe, Lewis, Ali, Pele, Zico, Senna, Lauda, Bats, David, Coe.

836

G

N

The letters read clockwise from the top left are the consonants in the state capitals and the state's initial is in the middle. Phoenix in Arizona, Oklahoma (City) in Oklahoma, Denver in Colorado and Atlanta in Georgia.

837

He was in uniform.

838

839

The quotation is: "When two men in a business always agree, one of them is unnecessary."

840

404. The colours have their alphanumeric value (yellow 92, purple 88, orange 60, pink 50, green 49, blue 40). The arrows work as follows: right (x 3), left (x 2), up (– 20), down (– 30)

841

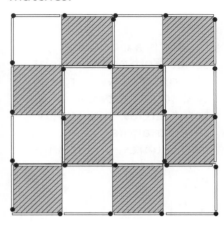

842

Where have all the flowers gone.

843

The red, black, green and orange letters spell out, "Wherefore art thou Romeo."

844

The diagram shows how to complete the task using 11 matches.

845

23. (tl x br) + (tr + bl) with answer in next box right.

846

Across: 2 Midnight blue, 4 Lilac, 6 Pink, 7 Livid, 8 Sky, 10 Cream, 15 Terracotta, 17 Rose, 19 Pea green, 20 Ruby, 22 Indigo, 25 Denim, 26 Leaden, 27 Red, 28 Earth, 29 Navy. Down: 1 Violet, 2 Mauve, 3 Gold, 5 Chocolate, 6 Puce, 8 Stone, 9 Infrared, 11 Ultraviolet, 12 Orange, 13 Cerise, 14 Poppy, 16 Tan, 18 Scarlet, 21 Beige, 23 Green, 24 Grey.

847

157. The colours have their alphanumeric values but the alphabet has been numbered backwards (Z = 1, A = 26). All the shapes are added except for the explosion which is always subtracted.

848

Answer: Wittgenstein. The letters are all made up of

colours with six-letter names (orange, yellow, purple).

849

"Another cunning code." Use only the letters made from colours with six letters in their name (purple, yellow, orange).

850

C. This is a clockwise spiral series from the top right. The order is two circles, two squares, two triangles, three circles, two squares, three triangles, one circle, two squares, one triangle.

851

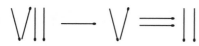

The sum also works as V11-11=V

852

D. If you add together the total number of sides of all the shapes, D is the only one with an odd total.

853

We are talking about a chess game.

854

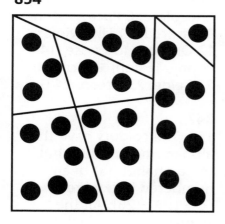

855

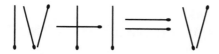

856

They were buying digits for their house number. Four at $3 each cost $12.

857

F. The number 8 is the only one which is symmetrical.

858

E.

859

Two girls at the same time would mean buying three tickets. One girl twice would require four tickets as he buys for himself on both occasions.

860

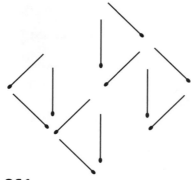

861

No, sharks don't sleep.

862

L – G x F ÷ C + O ÷ E = E.

863

120. Working clockwise starting from 9, each 2 adjacent small numbers (under 25) are multiplied to get the adjacent total.

864

42. Top left^2 – top right + bottom right^2 – bottom left. The answers go in different squares, as follows:
answer 1 in square 4
answer 2 in square 3
answer 3 in square 2
answer 4 in square 1

865

A	N	O	W	T	H	W	E	S	T	M	I	N	S	T	E	R	E	K	R
B	C	L	A	Q	P	O	D	Y	U	P	D	P	Z	Z	L	E	F	I	I
N	I	H	T	S	I	H	E	S	T	I	Y	U	U	A	R	E	D	N	W
H	A	E	E	C	N	A	R	E	T	L	H	C	E	Q	S	E	P	G	E
O	P	R	R	L	C	E	G	O	L	I	N	G	I	T	S	O	C	S	O
U	I	G	L	O	O	A	H	I	U	W	P	S	R	O	M	R	E	C	C
A	S	N	H	T	H	A	D	T	S	H	W	H	C	U	S	A	A	R	T
I	G	C	W	A	S	O	H	O	N	I	T	T	O	K	O	H	G	O	E
R	E	I	R	S	I	M	L	J	G	T	I	N	G	N	W	L	M	S	Y
G	U	T	O	O	T	N	E	D	G	E	H	A	L	L	A	U	N	S	T
A	N	S	D	W	S	S	H	R	T	A	T	D	O	F	B	O	G	K	I
G	O	L	D	E	N	E	T	A	O	F	O	R	A	M	D	Y	N	T	R
O	L	E	B	S	O	U	K	G	W	E	Y	R	U	N	C	K	A	I	L
U	B	A	Q	S	L	R	T	T	E	L	T	F	O	A	P	L	G	H	T
E	I	U	F	Y	A	O	N	U	R	O	F	L	L	A	M	C	A	N	S
R	A	R	O	P	A	E	E	T	H	S	T	A	Y	A	U	E	A	B	Y
E	A	D	E	L	V	R	L	G	I	N	C	S	H	O	R	L	R	L	A
R	A	D	M	O	R	A	L	E	E	E	C	G	P	A	R	I	E	T	Y
E	Y	S	C	A	T	B	U	C	K	I	N	W	H	A	D	Y	N	O	U
H	N	O	T	C	H	E	L	S	E	A	J	O	E	G	R	K	Z	O	O

866

Bartok, Delius, Mahler, Mozart, Puccini, Purcell Rachmaninov, Rimsky-Korsakov, Sibelius, Schubert.

867

H. All the letters can be reversed vertically and remain the same.

868

R. Number preceding each pair of letters shows how many letters the second letter is after the first, e.g. P is 5 letters after K in alphabetical order.

869

870
The air above the Equator is much colder than the air over the Poles (because at the point there is a greater height of air and therefore the temperature can fall lower).

871
No one. The barber was the mayor's wife.

872
V. Each letter takes its alphanumeric position. The sum is (top x 2) + left + right = middle.

873

874
N. The letters spell Mark Twain.

875
E. The value of letter given by position in the alphabet is added together. An even answer should give a triangle, an odd answer a circle.

876
O. The letters represent a number based on their position in the alphabet. The total for each triangle equals 60.

877
Augustus, Caligula, Claudius, Diocletian, Galba, Nero, Tiberius, Trajan, Valerian, Vespasian.

878
My Family and Other Animals, The Red Badge of Courage, How Green Was My Valley.

879
Einstein was the name but there was an extra "I".

880
Edward Albee, Samuel Beckett, Bertholt Brecht, Noel Coward, Anton Chekov, Arthur Miller, Luigi Pirandello, Jean Racine, Sophocles, Tennessee Williams.

881
D. The second hand moves forward 30 and back 15 seconds alternately, the minute hand moves back 10 and forward 5 minutes alternately, and the hour hand moves forward 2 and back 1 hour alternately.

882
No, they have moonquakes.

883
C.

884
D. All except D have odd number of edges.

885
I. Each series of letters moves on three places.

886
D. In all other cases the number of cross pieces on top of each vertical line is multiplied by the number of cross pieces on the bottom. All give even answers apart from D.

887
B. In all other cases the letters, if reflected along an imaginary vertical line, still form a letter.

888
B. The minute hand moves back 15 minutes and the hour hand moves forward 3 hours.

889
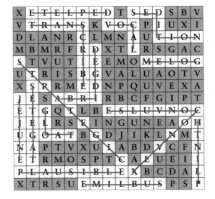

890
A square. If the three numbers around the triangle add to an even number the shape is a square; if it is odd, then it is another triangle.

891
Move yourself! If viewed upside down the equation is correct.

892
D. All the others touch the sides in two separate places, but this one touches the sides in four places.

893
The graphic designer was left-handed. He was injured on a Saturday and was able to return to work on the next Monday morning.

894
C. When fish face outwards mouth should be open.

895
Pick up the matchbox by forefinger and thumb and bring the case up to your mouth. Suck gently to make the tray stick to the case and then very carefully

turn the whole thing over.

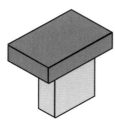

896
Problem is 1641106 ÷ 19. The answer is 86374. Values 0–9 are H A K E G J D C B.

897
C. It is the only instance where a square is not touching a triangle.

898
The three words are:
Rhythm,
Stanza,
Verse.

899
Taking the colours in alphabetical order: black square, blue heart, brown cube, green crossed circle, orange square, pink sun, purple smiley, red cross, yellow hexagon.

900
"This message is hidden." Take only the letters that have no 'e' in name of the colour.

901
M. This a straightforward alphanumeric puzzle. The actual sum is top – (left – right) = middle and in the last triangle, it is expressed as (Y (25) – (R (18) – F (6) [12]) = M (13).

902
D. The number is twice the alphanumeric value. P should be 32, not 31.

903
D. A & B and C & E form diagonal mirror images.

904
C. Others are symmetrical around their horizontal axis.

905
C. The others all have a large blue triangle at rear.

906
D. Others have six lines.

907
2940. Add the alphanumeric values of each letter of the colour and multiply the pairs.

908
D. Others rotate into the same shape.

909
E. It contains four lines; the others have only three.

910
A. Others rotate into each other.

911
Right. 4.The two-digit number on the left minus the two-digit number on the right gives the middle number.
Left. 4.The two-digit number on the right minus the two-digit number on the left gives the middle number.

912
47 coins contained in 10 bags all deposited on outside plots, thus 4, 5 and 6 in the first row, 5 in the second, 4 in the third, 3 in the fourth, 5 in the fifth, and 5, 6, 4 in the bottom row.

913
Follow the diagram as shown until you reach point B. Then place one foot in C and say, "As one foot has been in cell C it has undoubtedly been entered. However, when that foot is withdrawn into B I do not enter B for a second time because I never left it."

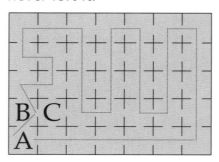

914
184. In each row the two outer digits of the first number are multiplied to give the two outer digits of the second number. The two middle of the first number are multiplied to give the middle digits of the second number. Sum is: 7 x 2 =14; 4 x 2 = 8; 184.

915
35.

916
☆ = 17   ● = 5   ■ = 15
Answer is 42.

917
D. Short and long lines swap places and rotate clockwise.

918
C. Others are Roman numerals rotated 90° clockwise.

919
4752. In each number the first two digits are multiplied by the last two digits to give the next number along the row. 54 x 88 = 4752.

920
C. Others rotate into the same shape.

921
A. The alphanumeric values of the two letters are reversed.

922
328. Along each row multiply first two digits of first number to get first two digits of second number. Multiply last two digits of first number to get last two of second number and join them. Working is: 4 x 8 = 32, 2 x 4 = 8; 328.

923
Take only the red numbers. They represent letters of the alphabet numbered backwards (Z = 26, A = 1). The message is: "This will be hard to decode."

924
10. Add the outer numbers in a segment and put the answer in the next same-coloured clockwise segment.

925
10. Subtract the outer numbers in a segment and put the answer in the next same-coloured anti-clockwise segment.

926
The red rectangle. In all the others the number of sides of the shape is the same as the number of letters in the colour.

927
1. Take the number of letters in the names of the colours. In each column subtract the bottom number from the top.

928

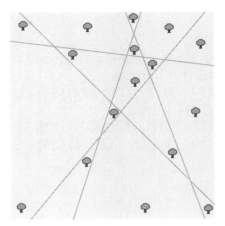

929

2243	1341	3142
3141	2242	1343
1342	3143	2241

930

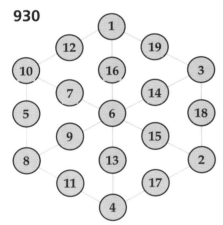

931
6. Add the outer segment numbers and put the sum of the answer in the middle.

932
There are 2501 possible routes.

933
D.

934
D.

935
A. Box rotates 90° anti-clockwise.

936
8. Add the outer numbers in each segment and put the answer in the inside of that segment.

937
8. In each segment add the two outer numbers and put the answer in the middle.

938
C. Horizontal object moves down, small shape moves down then up again.

939
B.

940
D.

941
C.

942
D.

943
A.

944
B. In all other cases there are two white and two blue triangles at the corners.

945
A circle in the second triangle on the bottom row. Starting from the top, working from left to right, sequence of square, miss 2 , triangle, circle, miss 1, square, miss 2, and so on.

946
D. Letters take their value from their order in the alphabet, where A = 1, Z = 26. Each 3 letters are added together to give the value at the end of each set, so Q + L + A = 30, moving in a clockwise direction.

947
32. Working along each row from left to right, (A + B) x C – D = E.

948
Dots = 1; Curved lines = 3; Blank = 5; Straight lines = 7.

949
10. The numbers in each row of triangles equal 12, 24, 36, 48, when added together, starting from the top.

950
D. The vertical mirror image of w is m, the letter before n. The vertical mirror image of d is p, the letter before q.

951
15. Take the number of letters in the name of each colour and multiply pairs together.

952
If you use only the red letters you get the message "Red is the colour."

953
Germany. The colours all have five-letter names.

954
"Now is the winter of our discontent." Letters of the same colour go together.

955
All you have to do is place 10 in the centre

and write in their proper order round the circle 1, 2, 3, 4, 5, 6, 7, 8, 9, 19, 18, 17, 16, 15, 14, 13, 12, 11.

956

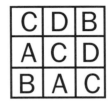

957
J. Imagine the letters in a circle. Each letter is five places after the previous one in same segment of the triangle.

958
E. Top left. The sequence here is top left, bottom right, bottom left, middle, top right, reading along each row from top to bottom.

959
Across: 7 Violet, 8 Eleven, 9 Rose, 10 Magnolia, 11 Assayer, 13 Genet, 15 Earth, 17 Picture, 20 Sunshine, 21 Bubo, 22 Medici, 23 Leaden. Down: 1 Vinous, 2 Blue, 3 Stammer, 4 Beige, 5 Reforest, 6 Cerise, 12 Artistic, 14 Firefly, 16 Azures, 18 Rubies, 19 Livid, 21 Bead.

960

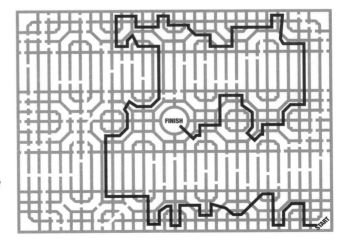

961
158. All colours have their alphanumeric value. A smiley face means subtract 20, a heart means subtract 15, a crossed circle means subtract 10, a star means subtract 5. The value of each row is added and the total placed at the end.

962
C. At each stage, the triangle rotates 180 degrees, the large circle rotates 90 degrees clockwise, the small outline circle rotates 45 degrees anti-clockwise, and the orange circle rotates 90 degrees anti-clockwise.

963
Top. Reading from top left, clockwise, dots remain opposite as they rotate 45°.

964
12. In each case (top left x top right) – (bottom left x bottom right) = middle. (8 x 5) [40] – (7 x 4) [28] = 12. The others are: (7 x 4) [28] – (2 x 3) [6] = 22; (6 x 8) [48] – (3 x 5) [15] = 33; (7 x 6) [42] – (4 x 7) [28] = 14.

965

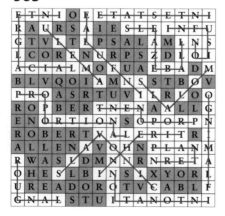

966
(n = previous number)
A. 35. (n + 3), (n + 6), (n + 9), etc.

B. 1125. Multiply the previous two numbers.
C. 94. (2n + 3), (2n + 6), (2n + 9), etc.
D. 666. (n^2 – 10).

967

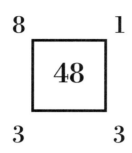

In each box, multiply the two bottom numbers and square the product to get the two top numbers. Read the top and bottom numbers as 2-digit figures and subtract the smaller from the larger. $\sqrt{81}$ = 9; 9 ÷ 3 = 3; 81 – 33 = 48.

968
23. The shapes have the following values:

7   9   5   2

969
39. Each diamond contains three numbers. To get the bottom number, multiply the left by the middle, and add the product to the sum of the right and the left. (5 x 6) + 5 + 4 = 39.

970
36.

971
D. Small circles move left to right and bottom to top.

972

973
78. Multiply opposite numbers and add the results to get the numbers in the middle. Thus 24 + 24 + 30 = 78.

974
A. Each shape rotates in a set sequence.

975
The highest possible total is 268, using boxes F, L, M, BB, HH, OO. The sums are:
(7 x 5) [35] + 4 + 1 = 40.
(6 x 5) [30] + 2 + 1 = 33.
(7 x 5) [35] + 3 + 3 = 41.
(8 x 6) [48] + 1 + 0 = 49.
(9 x 5) [45] + 1 + 1 = 47.
(8 x 7) [56] + 2 + 0 = 58.
40+33+41+49+47+58=268.

The lowest possible total is 87, using boxes E, H, O, DD, GG, QQ. The sums are:
(3 x 3) [9] + 2 + 1 = 12.
(3 x 2) [6] + 1 + 0 + 7.
(5 x 2) [10] + 1 + 0 = 11.
(8 x 2) [16] + 2 + 0 = 18.
(7 x 2) [14] + 2 + 1 = 17.

(4 x 4) [16] + 4 + 2 = 22.
12+7+11+18+17+22 =87.

976
9. (Top + right) – (bottom + left) = middle.
(73 + 3) [76] – (39 + 28) [69] = 9.
Others are:
(72 + 55) [127] – (83+37) [120] = 7
(19+13) [32] – (25+4) [29] = 3

977

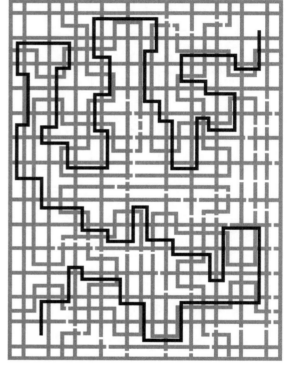

978
19. Reading from top to bottom (and anti-clockwise) it is a sequence of prime numbers.

979
The words are Habits and Obliterates.

980

981
E. Others rotate into the same shape.

982
88. The sum is: left^2 + right^2 + top = middle. 4^2 [16] + 7^2 [49] + 23 = 88. Others are: 6^2 [36] + 5^2 [25] + 12 = 73; 2^2 [4] + 3^2 [9] + 17 = 30.

983
A. The thinnest shape to cover an area always has the greatest perimeter.

984
10. (the colours are turned into numbers by taking the alphanumeric values of the letters, then subtracting the lower from the upper).

985
2668 (alphanumeric values multiplied).

986
No. Totals for the pairs (using the number of letters in each colour) are 7, 9, 11. It is not possible to make 13.

987
C. Pairs add up to 11 letters.

988
12. The difference between the first and last letters quoted alphanumerically.

989
212 blocks, 53 in each set.

990
C. The penguin's bill is more open.

991
B. This is a mirror image of the other shapes rotated.

992
D. This is a mirror-image of the other shapes rotated.

993

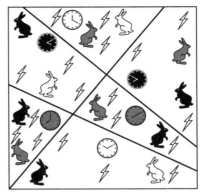

994
It will fall.

995
A and F.

996
B. It is a mirror image of the others rotated.

997
A and B, C and D.

998
B and C.

999
E. Fire is extinguished by a fire extinguisher as dirt is removed by a vacuum cleaner.

1000

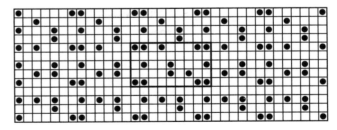

14 spotted tiles.

The publishers would like to thank the following source for their kind permission to reproduce the pictures in this book:

Corbis: 33, 140, 195, 197, 239; /Alan Schein Photography, Inc.:162; /Archivo Iconografico, S.A: 28 ; /ATC Productions: 161; /Craig Aurness: 211; /Brendan Beirne: 213; /Bettmann: 60, 126, 199 ; /Johnny Buzzerio: 185; /Charles Gupton Photography:171 ; /Steve Jay Crise: 189; /James D'Addido: 229; /Dex Images, Inc.: 233; /Duomo: 219; /George Hall: 166; /John & Dallas Heaton: 203; /Eric & David Hosking: 108; /Hulton-Deutsch Collection: 154, 191 ; /Martin Jones: 180; /Ed Kashi: 193; /Wolfgang Kaehler: 99; /Kelly-Mooney Photography: 80; /Karen Huntt H. Mason: 200; /Becky Luigart-Stayner: 175; /Bill Miles: 205; /Museum of Flight: 207; /The Purcell Team: 17 ; /Galen Rowell: 10; /Benjamin Rondel: 231; /Chuck Savage: 214; /Kevin Schafer: 209; /Richard Hamilton Smith: 164, 227; /Stock Photos: 133; /Nick Wheeler: 237